Royal Air Force Aircraft XA100 - XZ999

Compiled by James J Halley

CW00394982

Published by : Air-Britain (Historians) Ltd

Registered Office : 12, Lonsdale Gardens, Tunbridge Wells, Kent TN1 1PA

Sales Department : 41 Penshurst Road, Leigh, Tonbridge, Kent TN11 8HL

Membership Enquiries : 1 Rose Cottages, 179 Penn Road, Hazlemere, Bucks HP15 7NE

Further information is available on our website: http://www.air-britain.com

ISBN O-85130-311-0

Printed by Bell and Bain Ltd, Glasgow

Published in Great Britain by

Air-Britain (Historians) Ltd
12 Lonsdale Gardens, Tunbridge Wells, Kent

Correspondence to:

J.J.Halley, 5 Walnut Tree Road,
Shepperton, Middlesex, TW17 0RW
and not to the Tunbridge Wells address

ISBN 0 85130 311 0

Front cover: To celebrate the 60th Anniversary of the first non-stop
                 crossing of the Atlantic by Alcock and Browne,
                 Phantom XV424 made a repeat crossing piloted by another
                 Alcock and Browne.

Back cover: Jet Provost T.3 XM466 in the display markings of No.1
                 Flying Training School

Printed by:
Bell & Bain Ltd
303 Burnfield Road
Glasgow, G46 7UG

Lightning F.2 XN787 of No.19 Squadron

Introduction

This volume in the Royal Air Force Aircraft series continues on from where the WA100 to WZ999 volume left off. It follows the same lay-out as the twenty-two original volumes, plus the five revised publications, in that it shows the type of aircraft, serial number, flying units to which each is allocated and its final fate.

The XA-XZ batch of aircraft does, however, differ from those batches previous published in that many remain in service. The longevity of airframes manufactured in the past thirty years has meant that many stay in service over a long period of time. Earlier registers have waited until all aircraft had left service, apart from a handful in the WA-WZ series.

During an aircraft's service, there were often modifications of Mark number; in at least one case, a written-off aircraft was completely rebuilt from parts of various other aircraft.

Another result of aircraft leaving service within the last decade is the lack of exact dates for being struck off charge. Changes of unit are also dependent on information in the public domain as original documents are restricted by the provisions of the Public Records Act. The conversion of aircraft movement records from manuscript to computer format will also cause problems for future historians.

The Tables

As in all previous volumes of this series, the format is basically an index of which units used each aircraft so that persons compiling histories of types and units can extract lists for further investigation. The 'fate' column contains information on the final disposal of an aircraft, either as scrap, sale or accidental destruction.

In the case of some long-lived types, the units column has grown far longer than in earlier volumes. In some cases, aircraft were pooled between two or more squadrons and these are shown as e.g. 24-36. In other cases they were allotted to bases for the use of all units on that base and are shown as 'wings' e.g. 'Scampton Wg', or 'LTW' for all the transport squadrons based at Lyneham.

It became evident that aircraft had in later years become interchangeable between units. Two squadrons might exchange aircraft very frequently, for example Nos.19 and 92 Squadrons in Germany. To cut down on space, these have been shown as '19&92'. There were also periods when aircraft were loaned to another squadron; these have not been included since such loans were often frequent and for short periods.

During specific operations, as in the Gulf War, aircraft were detached from their parent units to equip a task group although remaining on charge of the original squadron, even when flown by crews from a different squadron. No attempt has been made to log these frequently-changing detachments except for that in Belize, before the unit there received a separate designation.

Details of terminal accidents are similar to those to be found in the chronological record of RAF accidents, *Broken Wings*, published in 1999 by Air-Britain. Details of aircraft sold normally do not go beyond the initial sale as they subsequently often changed hands. In the case of ground instructional airframes, the destination shown is the first allocation. These airframes often changed locations and roles and some were later to be rebuilt privately to flying condition after disposal by the Ministry of Defence.

Dates of sale are not available for recent years. Where an aircraft was sold and civil-registered, the date of registration has been shown as a guide to the date of disposal. However, there could be a time gap between disposal and registration.

Similarly, aircraft sold to Commonwealth and foreign air forces are shown with their first serial, where known. In some cases, the serial systems altered later in their subsequent service.

The absence of any note in the fate column should not be taken to mean that the aircraft is still in service; it often only means that no exact details of disposal are known. Many aircraft go out of service and are then removed to a storage unit where they remain until sold or scrapped.

Acknowledgements

Since the draft of the XA-XZ register was published in *Aeromilitaria* in the 1980s, many readers have contributed to the tables by pointing out errors and omissions or providing additional information. We are grateful to all those who have contributed.

As always, the Air Historical Branch of the Ministry of Defence have provided facilities for extracting information on these aircraft. For over forty years, they have patiently put up with our digging into their records. Other branches have help us to piece together some of the missing links.

Unfortunately, the workings of the Thirty-Year Rule has meant that checking the Form 540s held at the Public Record Office is possible only for a small part of the series.

Special thanks are due to Michael Austen who worked through the manuscript and added many details on more recent events, while at the same time picking up typing errors and mis-transcribed items.

Buccaneer S.2s of No.12 Squadron and Phantom FG.1s of No.43 Squadron at Luqa, XV347 in foreground

Beverley C.1s XB269 and XB290 of No.47 Squadron

TABLES

XA100 - XA131	Sea Vampire T.22s for Royal	
XA152 - XA172	Navy to Contract 6/Acft/7704	
XA177	Auster B.4 G-AMKL for evaluation at A&AEE to Contract 6/Acft/7708	
XA181, XA186	Supermarine 545 prototypes to Contract 6/Acft/7711; XA181 not completed; XA186 cancelled	
XA191, XA192	Serials allotted to Yorks G-AMGK and G-AGNM for trooping purposes	
XA197 - XA202	Vickers Wild Goose research models to Contract 6/Acft/2171	
XA203, XA204	Cancelled Wild Goose models	
XA209, XA213	Seamew AS.1s for Ministry of Supply to Contract 6/Acft/7762	
XA216	Seamew airframe for structural tests	
XA219 - XA221	Sycamore HR.50s for Royal Australian Navy to Contract 6/Acft/7865	

XA225 - XA244	Grasshopper TX.1 gliders to Contract 6/Acft/7585 for ATC	

* * * * * * * * * *

28 Miles Marathon T.1s delivered between April 1952 and April 1954 by Handley Page, Reading, to Contract 6/Acft/2613

XA249	-	Ex G-ALUB; SS 15.1.59
XA250	AAEE/2 ANS/ 1 ANS	Ex G-ALVW. Undercarriage leg jammed and collapsed on landing, Topcliffe, 10.12.57; DBR
XA251	1 ANS	Ex G-ALVX; SOC 16.11.57
XA252	1 ANS	Ex G-ALVY; sold 31.12.58 to Miles
XA253	2 ANS/1 ANS	Ex G-ALXR. Undercarriage retracted in error for flaps after landing, Topcliffe, 5.5.58; DBR
XA254	2 ANS	Ex G-AMAX. Overshot landing and undercarriage raised to stop; hit sea wall, Thorney Island, 9.1.56; DBR
XA255	2 ANS/1 ANS	Ex G-AMAY. Damaged in heavy landing, Topcliffe, 27.3.57; to 7465M 8.8.57 at Topcliffe
XA256	1 ANS/2 ANS/ 1 ANS	Ex G-AMDH. Undercarriage collapsed in hangar, Thorney Island; SOC 7.11.57
XA257	1 ANS	Ex G-AMEK; SS 24.4.59
XA258	2 ANS/1 ANS	Ex G-AMEL; SS 15.1.59
XA259	1 ANS/2 ANS/ 1 ANS	Ex G-AMEM; SS 24.4.59
XA260	AAEE	Ex G-AMEP; SS 24.4.59

XA261	1 ANS	Ex G-AMER; Sold 11.5.59; reverted to G-AMER
XA262	-	Ex G-AMET; sold 11.5.59 for spares
XA263	-	Ex G-AMEU; SS 24.4.59
XA264	-	Ex G-AMEV; SS 24.4.59
XA265	C(A)	Ex G-AMEW; Sold 28.8.57; reverted to G-AMEW
XA266	1 ANS/2 ANS/ 1 ANS	Ex G-AMGN; SS 15.1.59
XA267	1 ANS	Ex G-AMGU; SS 8.1.59
XA268	1 ANS/2 ANS/ 1 ANS	Ex G-AMGP. Nosewheel detached on landing, Topcliffe, 11.2.58; not repaired
XA269	1 ANS	Ex G-AMGR; SS 26.5.59; reverted to G-AMGR
XA270	1 ANS/2 ANS/ 1 ANS	Ex G-AMGS; SS 15.1.59
XA271	2 ANS	Ex G-AMGT. Outer wings broke up; dived into ground 1½m SSE of Calne, Wilts., 30.9.54
XA272	1 ANS/2 ANS/ 8 FTS/2 ANS 1 ANS	Ex G-AMGU; SS 24.4.59
XA273	2 ANS/1 ANS	Ex G-AMGV. Undercarriage collapsed on landing, Thorney Island, 30.11.57
XA274	Hdlg Sqn/1 ANS	Ex G-AMHT; Sold 29.12.58; reverted to G-AMHT
XA275	2 ANS/1 ANS	Ex G-AMHU; SS 24.4.59
XA276	C(A)/1 ANS	Ex G-AMHX; SS 24.4.59
XA277	-	Ex G-AMHY; not delivered and sold to HP 25.2.54; became JA-6009
XA278	-	Ex G-AMHZ; not delivered and sold to HP 25.2.54; became JA6010

* * * * * * * * * *

XA282 - XA313		Slingsby Cadet TX.3 gliders to Contract 6/Acft/6023 for ATC
XA319 - XA364; XA387 - XA411		Gannet AS.1s for Royal Navy to Contract 6/Acft/8203
XA412 - XA436; XA454 - XA474		Gannet AS.4s for Royal Navy Contract 6/Acft/8203
XA508 - XA530		Gannet T.2s for Royal Navy
XA531		Cancelled Gannet T.2

* * * * * * * * * *

One English Electric Canberra B.2 delivered by English Electric, Preston, in May 1953 to Contract 6/Acft/3520

XA536	50/15/Cv T.11/ 228 OCU/TFS West Raynham/MoA/ 228 OCU/85/ Cv T.19/85/7/100	To 8605M 30.8.78

* * * * * * * * * *

XA539		Sea Venom FAW.21 for MoS to Contract 6/Acft/7062

* * * * * * * * * *

40 Gloster Javelin FAW.1s delivered between October 1954 and March 1956 by Glosters, Moreton Valence, to Contract 6/Acft/8336

XA544	Mkrs & RAE/AAEE	To 7558M 19.12.57 at Cosford

XA545	Mkrs	SOC 28.7.60
XA546	Mkrs	Spun into Bristol Channel on test flight, 21.10.54
XA547	Mkrs/AAEE/Hdlg Sq/AWDS/MoA/ AFDS	SS 30.7.62
XA548	Mkrs & AAEE	MoS aircraft
XA549	Mkrs/AAEE/CSE/ I Avn Med/87	To 7717M 23.2.62; to Swanton Morley for display
XA550	Mkrs	To 7484M 14.11.57 at Weeton
XA551	Mkrs/RAE/AAEE	To 7586M 26.11.58 at Halton
XA552	-	Retained by MoS for Gyron Junior testbed
XA553	Mkrs	To 7470M 13.8.57; preserved
XA554	Mkrs/AAEE/Mkrs/ RAE/AAEE/Mkrs/87	To 7662M 19.7.61 at Halton
XA555	Mkrs/CFE/MoS/ AFDS	SS 30.7.62
XA556	Mkrs/RAE/Mkrs/ MoS/CFE/MoS/ AFDS	SS 30.7.62
XA557	Mkrs	Sapphire 100 testbed; SOC 29.12.60
XA558	Mkrs/AAEE/Mkrs/ 87	Abandoned after both engines flamed out on approach 1½m SE of Bruggen, 5.6.58
XA559	Mkrs/AAEE/Mkrs/ 87	Engine caught fire starting up, Bruggen, 22.7.58; DBR
XA560	Mkrs & A-S	Sapphire 7 testbed; to 7619M 26.10.59 at Henlow
XA561	Mkrs/AAEE	Abandoned in spin, Ashley, Isle of Wight, 8.12.55
XA562	Mkrs	To Rolls-Royce 22.12.55
XA563	Hdlg Sqn/AAEE/ RAE	To 7627M 2.2.60 at Newton
XA564	Bristols	To 7464M 12.7.57 at Locking
XA565	CFE/46/87	SS 19.3.62
XA566	CFE/46/87	SS 30.7.62
XA567	Mkrs & BP	To 7551M 16.3.58 at Melksham
XA568	CFE/46/Coll of Aeronautics/AAEE	SOC 31.12.64
XA569	46/87	Crashed after accidental ejection of pilot, Katwyck-an-Zee, Netherlands, 18.2.59
XA570	46	Flew into ground on approach at night 1½m ESE of Odiham, 12.6.56
XA571	46/87	To 7663M 23.6.61 at Halton
XA572	46/87	SS 30.7.62
XA618	46/87	SS 19.3.62
XA619	46/87	SS 30.7.62
XA620	46/87	To 7723M 18.7.61 at Cosford
XA621	46/87	SS 30.7.62
XA622	46/RAE	To MoS 24.8.59
XA623	AAEE/46/87/MoS/ AWDS/MoA/AFDS	SS 19.3.62
XA624	46/87	SS 30.7.62
XA625	46/87	Caught fire starting up at Bruggen, 12.5.58; DBF
XA626	46/87	To 7666M 8.7.60 at Yatesbury
XA627	46/87	To 7661M 14.10.60 at St.Athan
XA628	46/87	To 7720M 26.7.61 at Melksham

* * * * * * * * * *

12 Gloster Javelin FAW.4s delivered between September 1955 and July 1957 by Glosters, Moreton Valence, to Contract 6/Acft/8336

XA629	Mkrs/3	SOC 13.6.63; to Ternhill for fire practice
XA630	Mkrs/Hdlg Sqn/3	SS 20.3.61
XA631	AAEE/23/72/87/11	SS 16.8.63
XA632	AW/11	SS 11.3.65
XA633	Mkrs/3/11	SS 31.7.63

XA634	Mkrs	To 7641M 2.6.60; preserved
XA635	Mkrs/3/11	SS 11/3/65
XA636	141/41/87	SS 20.3.63
XA637	141/41/11	SS 31.7.63
XA638	141/41/3	SS 17.10.62
XA639	141/41/87/3	SS 17.10.62
XA640	141/3	Nosewheel jammed up; overshot landing into wood, Geilenkirchen, 8.4.60; DBR

* * * * * * * * * *

59 Gloster Javelin FAW.5s delivered between September 1956 and October 1957 to Contract 6/Acft/8336
XA644 was FAW.4; XA662 to XA667, XA688 to XA719 built by Armstrong Whitworth, remainder by Gloster

XA641	Mkrs & AAEE/87/5	SS 21.9.64
XA642	AWDS	Both engines cut; crashed in sea 10m E of Skegness, Lincs., 6.12.57
XA643	CFE/228 OCU/11	SS 11.3.65
XA644	Glosters	FAW.4. Collided with Hunter XF980 over Wotton-under-Edge, Glos., 24.8.56
XA645	87/5	Rear fuselage caught fire; abandoned 4m NW of Wesel, W.Germany, 7.6.62
XA646	72/228 OCU/ AWFCS	Caught fire starting up, West Raynham, 25.7.62; SOC 17.9.62 for fire practice
XA647	151/11	SS 25.9.63
XA648	AWDS	Stalled recovering from dive and abandoned 3m WSW of Fakenham, Norfolk, 20.9.58
XA649	Hdlg Sqn/5	SS 21.9.64
XA650	151/11	SS 21.9.64
XA651	151	SS 25.9.63
XA652	151/228 OCU/ AWFCS	SS 21.9.64
XA653	151/228 OCU/ AWFCS/CFCS	SOC 31.7.64 for fire practice
XA654	23/72/AWFCS/ CFCS	SS 25.9.63
XA655	151	SS 25.9.63
XA656	228 OCU/AWFCS/ CFCS	SS 21.9.64
XA657	AWDS/5	SS 25.9.63
XA658	41/5	SS 21.9.64
XA659	AWDS/5	SS 21.9.64
XA660	AWDS/228 OCU/11	SS 25.9.63
XA661	151/11	Engine caught fire starting up, Geilenkirchen, 29.10.62; not repaired
XA662	228 OCU	Engine caught fire and second shut down after fire warning; abandoned, Leyburn, Yorks., 29.9.59
XA663	228 OCU/AWFCS/ 11/5	SS 21.9.64
XA664	228 OCU/AWFCS/5	SS 25.9.63
XA665	NFLS/AWFCS/ 228 OCU/11	SS 11.3.65
XA666	228 OCU/41/5	SS 11.3.65
XA667	228 OCU/41/72/ 228 OCU/11	SS 25.9.63
XA688	AWFCS/228 OCU/ 151/AWFCS/CFCS	SOC 18.11.62 for fire practice
XA689	228 OCU/AWFCS/ 151/5	SS 11.3.65
XA690	228 OCU/11	SS 25.9.63
XA691	228 OCU/AWFCS/ 11	SS 25.9.63
XA692	I Avn Med	Sold to Glosters 1.10.59

XA693	228 OCU	SS 25.9.63
XA694	228 OCU/151/11	SS 21.9.63
XA695	228 OCU/11	SS 25.9.63
XA696	AWFCS/11	SS 21.9.64
XA697	AWFCS/5	SS 25.9.63
XA698	228 OCU	SS 21.9.64
XA699	151/5	To 7809M 14.2.64 at Locking
XA700	228 OCU/AWFCS/ CFCS	SOC 17.3.64 for fire practice
XA701	228 OCU/AWFCS/ CFCS	Engine caught fire starting up, West Raynham, 4.10.62; to 7765M
XA702	228 OCU/AWFCS/ CFCS	SS 21.9.64
XA703	228 OCU/41/72/ 228 OCU/AWFCS/ CFCS	SS 21.9.64
XA704	AWFCS/5	SS 11.3.63
XA705	AWFCS/5	SS 25.9.63
XA706	228 OCU	Jet pipe broke and electrics failed; forcelanded at Leeming, 29.6.60; to 7649M
XA707	41/5	SS 25.9.63
XA708	151	SS 25.9.63
XA709	Mkrs & AAEE/5	SS 21.9.64
XA710	151	SS 25.9.63
XA711	Mkrs & AAEE	To MoA 31.12.61
XA712	151	SS 25.9.63
XA713	151	SS 25.9.63
XA714	228 OCU/151/11	SS 25.9.63
XA715	151	SS 21.9.64
XA716	228 OCU/11	SS 25.9.63
XA717	151/11	SS 25.9.63
XA718	228 OCU/AWFCS/5	SS 25.9.63
XA719	228 OCU	SS 21.9.64

* * * * * * * * * *

37 Gloster Javelin FAW.4s delivered between March 1956 and April 1957 by Armstrong Whitworth (to XA762) and Glosters, Moreton Valence to Contract 6/Acft/8336

XA720	Mkrs & AAEE/11	SS 16.8.63
XA721	Mkrs & AAEE/3	SS 31.5.62
XA722	23/72	Engine blew up after take-off; force-landed, Leconfield, 7.7.59; not repaired and SOC 27.10.60
XA723	CEPE Namao/11	SS 11.3.65
XA724	AWA & Glosters/11	SS 16.8.63
XA725	AWA/AAEE/3/11	SS 11.3.65
XA726	23/72	SS 20.3.63
XA727	141/23/72	SS 20.3.63
XA728	23/72	SS 20.3.63
XA729	23/72	SS 20.3.63
XA730	23/72/AWFCS	SS 16.8.63
XA731	23/72	SS 20.3.63
XA732	23	Ventral tank detached and aircraft caught fire taxying at Horsham St.Faith, 25.5.57; DBR
XA733	23/72/87	SS 20.3.63
XA734	23	Engine caught fire in turbulence; abandoned near Wymondham, Norfolk, 11.2.58
XA735	AWDS/96/3	SS 20.3.63
XA736	23/72	SS 20.3.63
XA737	23/72	SS 20.3.63
XA749	AWDS/3	SS 20.3.63
XA750	141/41/96/3	Rolled after take-off, stalled and spun into ground 1½m NW of Norvenich, 20.6.59
XA751	141	Abandoned in spin during aerobatics 1½m NW of Wattisham, 11.7.58

XA752	23/72	Hit barrier on approach at night and undercarriage leg collapsed on landing, Leeming, 2.3.61; not repaired
XA753	23/72/AWFCS	SS 16.8.63
XA754	23/72	Jet pipe split; aircraft overheated during run-up, Leconfield, 27.10.60; DBR
XA755	23/72	To 7725M 16.8.61 at St Athan
XA756	141/41/11	SS 11.3.65
XA757	141/41/87	SS 31.5.62
XA758	141/41/11	SS 11.3.65
XA759	141/41/11	SS 16.8.63
XA760	141/41/11/AAEE	SS 10.5.62
XA761	141/41/87	SS 17.10.62
XA762	141/41/3	SS 17.10.62
XA763	AWDS/96/3	SS 17.10.62
XA764	AWDS/3/11	SS 16.8.63
XA765	Glosters/11	SS 16.8.63
XA766	141/41/11	SS 16.8.63
XA767	141/41/11	SS 11.3.65

*   *   *   *   *   *   *   *   *   *

30 Gloster Javelin FAW.2s delivered between April 1956 and November 1957 by Gloster, Moreton Valence, to Contract 6/Acft/8336

XA768	Glosters/46	To MoA 13.3.62
XA769	C(A) at AAEE	SS 31.5.62
XA770	C(A)	SS 31.5.62
XA771	C(A)/AAEE	To MoS 30.3.60
XA772	46	SS 20.3.63
XA773	46	SS 17.10.62
XA774	89/85	SS 22.3.62
XA775	89/85	SS 22.3.62
XA776	46	SS 17.10.62
XA777	46	SS 17.10.62
XA778	C(A)/Mkrs & AAEE	MoS aircraft
XA779	89	Stalled off turn on to approach and spun into ground, Stradishall, 19.9.58
XA780	46	To MoA 29.1.62
XA781	89/85	SS 20.3.63
XA799	89/85	SS 20.3.63
XA800	89	SS 31.5.62
XA801	46	To 7739M 26.1.62; preserved
XA802	46	Starter exploded starting up; caught fire, Sylt, 9.3.59; DBR
XA803	46	SOC 2.5.61
XA804	89/85	SS 20.3.63
XA805	46	SS 17.10.62
XA806	AFDS/89/85	SS 20.3.63
XA807	46	To MoA 29.1.62
XA808	AWDS/46	SS 17.10.62
XA809	AWDS/46	SS 17.10.62
XA810	46	SS 20.3.63
XA811	46	To MoA 29.1.62
XA812	46	To MoA 29.1.62
XA813	46	Jet pipe fractured and airframe damaged by heat build-up in flight, 12.4.61; not repaired
XA814	46	To MoA 13.3.62

*   *   *   *   *   *   *   *   *   *

22 Gloster Javelin FAW.6s delivered between August 1957 and March 1958 by Gloster, Moreton Valence to Contract 6/Acft/8336

XA815	89/85	SS 24.6.63
XA816	89/85	SS 13.7.62; to Catterick for fire practice
XA817	29	SS 17.12.62
XA818	29	SS 17.12.62

XA819	29	SS 24.6.63
XA820	89/85	To 7752M 10.5.62
XA821	Mkrs & AAEE/29	To 7749M 12.4.62
XA822	29	SS 17.12.62
XA823	29	Collided with XA835 and abandoned NE of Scarborough, Yorks., 21.5.60
XA824	29	SS 17.12.62
XA825	29	Flew into hill descending in cloud, Bowbeet Hill, 4m NE of Peebles, 21.11.60
XA826	29	SS 24.6.63
XA827	29	SS 24.6.63
XA828	29	SS 24.6.63
XA829	-	SOC 5.4.62
XA830	46/89/85	SOC 30.7.63; to Catterick for fire practice
XA831	FTU/I Avn Med	To 7808M 21.10.63
XA832	89/85/AFDS	SS 29.3.63
XA833	-	SS 29.3.63
XA834	Hdlg Sqn	SS 29.3.63
XA835	29	Collided with XA823 and abandoned 4m NW of West Hartlepool, Co.Durham, 21.5.60
XA836	89/85/29	SS 24.6.63

*   *   *   *   *   *   *   *   *   *

XA842		Sikorsky S-55 ex WW339 and G-AMHK for evaluation by RAE
XA847, XA853 XA856		English Electric P.1B prototypes for MoS Contract 6/Acft/5175
XA862-XA871		Whirlwind HAR.1s for Royal Navy to Contract 6/Acft/8379
XA876		Slingsby T.34A Sky glider to Contract 6/Acft/8146 for ETPS

*   *   *   *   *   *   *   *   *   *

Two de Havilland Devon C.1s delivered in October 1952 and September 1953 by de Havilland, Chester, to Contract 6/Acft/7383

XA879	ETPS	SOC 7.68
XA880	TRE/RRE/RAE/ Cv C.2/RAE/ TEE Llanbedr	

*   *   *   *   *   *   *   *   *   *

XA885		Cancelled Swift FR prototype to Contract 6/Acft/8309

*   *   *   *   *   *   *   *   *   *

25 Avro Vulcan B.1s delivered between June 1955 and December 1957 to Contract 6/Acft/8442 by Avro, Woodford

XA889	Avro/AAEE/Avro/ BSE/Avro/AAEE	SOC 22.8.67
XA890	Avro/AAEE/RAE/ AAEE/BLEU	To MoA 31.8.55; SOC 5.5.69
XA891	Mkrs	MoA aircraft. Crashed on test near Walkington, Yorks, 24.7.59
XA892	Mkrs/AAEE/ BSE/RAE	To 7746M 21.6.62 at Halton
XA893	Mkrs/AAEE	MoA aircraft 24.1.56; 5591M allotted 6.63 at Cosford; preserved
XA894	Mkrs/BSE	MoS aircraft; Olympus testbed; DBF on ground, Filton, 3.12.62

XA895	230 OCU/Hdlg Sqn/	
	Cv B.1A/230 OCU/	
	AAEE/BCDU	SS 19.9.68
XA896	230 OCU/44/	To MoA 25.6.64
	230 OCU/BSE	Olympus 100 testbed
XA897	230 OCU	Hit ground on GCA approach in bad weather and crashed on runway, Heathrow, 1.10.56
XA898	230 OCU/101/	
	230 OCU	To 7856M 26.8.64 at Halton
XA899	Mkrs/AAEE	To 7812M 26.6.63 at Cosford
XA900	230 OCU/101/	
	230 OCU/101/	
	Cv B.1A/230 OCU	To 7896M 24.2.66 at Cosford
XA901	230 OCU/617/	
	230 OCU/44/	
	Cv B.1A/230 OCU	To 7897M 26.11.65
XA902	230 OCU/AAEE/R-R	Spey testbed
XA903	Mkrs/BSE	MoA aircraft; Blue Steel trials and Olympus testbed
XA904	83/Cv B.1A/44	Ran out of fuel on landing; lost power on controls and undercarriage collapsed while landing beside runway, Waddington, 1.3.61; nose to 7738M at Finningley
XA905	83/44/230 OCU/	
	Waddington Wg	to 7857M 14.9.64 at Newton
XA906	83/44/Cv B.1A/	
	44/Waddington Wg	SS 8.11.68
XA907	83/44/Cv B.1A/	
	44/Waddington Wg/	
	BCDU	SS 20.5.68
XA908	83	Dived into ground after electrical failure of power controls, Detroit, Mich., USA, 24.10.58
XA909	101/Cv B.1A/50/	Abandoned after explosion in engine
	Waddington Wg	3m E of Valley, 16.7.64
XA910	101/230 OCU/101/	
	Cv B.1A/50/Wadd-	
	ington Wg	To 7995M 10.11.67 at Cottesmore
XA911	83/230 OCU/	
	Cv B.1A/	
	Waddington Wg	SS 8.11.68
XA912	101/Cv B.1A/101/	
	Waddington Wg	SS 20.5.68
XA913	101/Cv B.1A/101/	
	Waddington Wg	SS 20.5.68

* * * * * * * * * *

25 Handley Page Victor B.1s delivered between January and September 1958 to Contract 6/Acft/8441 by Handley Page, Radlett
Conversions to BK.1 redesignated K.1 in June 1967
(not shown in table)

XA917	HP/AAEE/RAE/	
	101/15/232 OCU	To 7827M 18.1.64
XA918	HP/Cv BK.1A/	
	AAEE&HP	SS 20.7.70
XA919	HP/AAEE/HP	To 7724M 16.5.61 at Locking
XA920	HP&AAEE	SOC 13.8.63
XA921	10/AAEE/HP	SOC 17.10.62
XA922	Hdlg Sqn/AAEE/	
	RAE/HP/HSA	SS 27.4.73
XA923	232 OCU/RRF/	
	232 OCU	To 7850M 27.5.64 at Cosford
XA924	232 OCU/RRF/	
	232 OCU/10	To 7844M 20.4.64 at St Athan
XA925	232 OCU/RRF/	
	232 OCU/15	To MoA 28.4.64; SOC 14.7.66
XA926	232 OCU/Cv BK.1A/	
	57/55/57	SOC 22.11.76
XA927	10/15/Cv BK.1A/214	SOC 1.2.77

XA928	10/Cv BK.1A/57/214	SOC 16.12.76
XA929	10/232 OCU/10	Overshot abandoned take-off and broke-up, Akrotiri, 16.6.62; DBF
XA930	AAEE&HP/10/232	
	OCU/55/57/Cv	
	BK.1A/55/214	SOC 17.4.75
XA931	232 OCU/10/	
	232 OCU	SOC 30.4.74
XA932	232 OCU/10/HP/	
	AAEE/Cv BK.1A/	
	214/AAEE/55/57	To 8517M 2.2.77 at Marham
XA933	232 OCU/HP/	
	55-57/57/TTF	SOC 1.10.71
XA934	232 OCU/RRF/	Engine failed on night take-off;
	232 OCU	abandoned after two more cut on approach 3m SW of Gaydon, 2.10.62
XA935	10/Cv B(PR).1/	
	RRF/15/232 OCU/	
	10/232 OCU	SOC 30.4.74
XA936	10/233 OCU/	
	Cv BK.1A/214	SOC 20.9.76
XA937	10/15/Cv BK.1A/	
	AAEE/57/214	SOC 7.2.77
XA938	10/15/Cv BK.1A/	
	214/RAE	To MoD(PE) 30.9.76 for RAE
XA939	10/15/Cv BK.1A/214	SOC 29.3.76; to Catterick for fire practice
XA940	10/232 OCU/10/15/	
	232 OCU/55/57/TTF	SOC 31.8.73
XA941	15/10/55/232 OCU/	
	10/15/55/57/HP/	
	Cv K.1A/214	SOC 22.11.74

* * * * * * * * * *

XA947-XA952	Vickers Swallow variable sweep aerodynamic models to Contract 6/Acft/2171
XA957 - XA993;	
XB102 - XB151;	Cancelled Short & Harland-built
XB169 - XB185;	Swift F.2s to Contract 6/Acft/8509
XB206 - XB241	
XB246	Allotted to DC-3 G-AMBW for trooping

* * * * * * * * * *

Six Westland Dragonfly HR.4s delivered in December 1952 and January 1953 by Westland Helicopters, Yeovil to Contract 6/Acft/8552

XB251	Casevac Flt/194/	
	CFS/SF Gutersloh/	
	Hdlg Sqn	SOC 11.5.62
XB252	Casevac Flt/194/	
	Hdlg Sqn/CFS/	
	SF Gutersloh	SS 11.9.63
XB253	194	Lost power on take-off from jungle clearing and crashed near Bentong, Malaya, 7.11.53
XB254	194	Tail cone fractured after take-off; dived into ground, Grik, Malaya, 16.10.54
XB255	194	Sank back into trees on take-off and overturned, Paddy's Ladang, Malaya, 3.3.56
XB256	194	Gear box failed; lost power and crashlanded near Kuala Lumpur and overturned, 14.9.54

* * * * * * * * * *

20 Blackburn Beverley C.1s delivered between March 1955 and October 1956 by Blackburn Aircraft, Brough, to Contract 6/Acft/8631

XB259	Mkrs/RAE	MoS aircraft; temporarily registered G-AOAI
XB260	Mkrs/47-53/ 48-FETS/34	Temporarily registered G-AEOK; SOC 14.2.68
XB261	AAEE	Sold to MoA 20.3.59; to Southend Museum, 6.10.71
XB262	AAEE/48/34	SOC 23.10.67
XB263	AAEE/47-53/ 30/47-53/47	SS 5.9.67
XB264	47/47-53/34	SOC 1.10.67
XB265	47/47-53/242 OCU	SS 6.7.67
XB266	AAEE/84/47-53/ 84/30/84	SS 27.11.67
XB267	47/47-53/47	SS 25.9.69
XB268	47/47-53/53	Flew into ground on approach at night and in cloud, El Adem, 13.4.63
XB269	47/47-53/MoA/47	SS 25.9.69
XB283	47/47-53/34	SS 14.2.68
XB284	47/47-53/MoA/ 47-53/47/84	SS 7.1.69
XB285	47/47-53/MoA/ 47/MoA/47	SS 8.1.69
XB286	47/53/47-53/ 242 OCU/47	SS 25.9.69
XB287	53/47-53/MoA/47	SS 25.9.69
XB288	53/47-53/47	SS 8.1.69
XB289	53/47-53/34	SOC 14.2.68
XB290	53/47-53/ 242 OCU/47	SS 25.3.70
XB291	53/47-53/34	SOC 14.2.68

*   *   *   *   *   *   *   *   *   *

XB296 - XB332;	
XB355 - XB404;	Grumman Avenger AS.4s for Royal
XB437 - XB449	Navy
XB474 - XB481;	
XB513 - XB524	Hiller HT.1s for Royal Navy

*   *   *   *   *   *   *   *   *   *

371 North American Sabre F.2s (first three) and F.4s delivered between December 1952 and December 1953 by Canadair, Montreal, under MDAP

	RCAF		
XB530	19378	1 OFU/FTU	To RCAF 30.7.54
XB531	19384	1 OFU/FTU/ 229 OCU	SOC 26.12.57
XB532	19404	1 OFU/FTU/ 229 OCU/CFE	To USAF 19.9.56 for Italian Air Force as MM19404
XB533	19464	-	To USAF 25.4.56 for Italian Air Force as MM19464
XB534	19465	1 OFU	Dived into ground out of cloud on delivery flight 3m SE of Prestwick, 19.12.52
XB535	19466	FTU/26	To USAF 14.1.57
XB536	19467	3/234	To USAF 21.8.56
XB537	19468	1 OFU/FTU	To USAF 6.7.56 for Yug AF
XB538	19469	1 OFU/FTU/ 67	SOC 18.12.58
XB539	19470	-	To USAF 14.9.56 for Italian Air Force as MM19470
XB540	19471	CGS/FWS	To USAF 9.2.56
XB541	19472	3	SOC 18.12.58
XB542	19473	SCF/66	To USAF 7.6.57 for Yugoslav AF as 11.046
XB543	19474	1 OFU/FTU	To USAF 7.7.57 for Italian Air Force as MM19474
XB544	19475	1 OFU/FTU	To USAF 5.6.57 for Yug AF
XB545	19476	1 OFU/FTU	To USAF 11.12.56 for Italian Air Force as MM19476
XB546	19477	FTU/CGS/ FWS	To USAF 11.7.56 for Italian Air Force as MM19477
XB547	19478	FTU/3	SOC 18.12.58
XB548	19479	1 OFU/FTU/ 93	Flew into ground recovering from dive, Meppen ranges, W.Germany 3.8.55
XB549	19480	147	Ailerons seized on ferry flight; under-carriage collapsed on landing, Stornoway, 10.3.53
XB550	19481	3/71/67/71	To USAF 30.6.56 for Italian Air Force as MM19481
XB551	19663	Hawkers	To USAF 17.5.56
XB575	19482	20/234	SOC 18.12.58
XB576	19483	112/93	To USAF 10.4.56 for Italian Air Force as MM19483
XB577	19484	26	To USAF 10.4.56 for Italian Air Force as MM19484
XB578	19485	234	To USAF 12.9.57
XB579	19486	-	SOC 18.12.58
XB580	19487	26	To USAF 28.9.56 for Italian Air Force
XB581	19488	3	To USAF 21.2.57 for Italian Air Force as MM19488
XB582	19489	3/234	To USAF 8.11.57 for Yugoslav AF as 11-047
XB583	19490	FTU/93	To USAF 9.10.56 for Italian Air Force
XB584	19491	414/413	Loaned to RCAF; to USAF 9.11.56 for Italian Air Force
XB585	19492	FTU/3	SOC 18.12.58
XB586	19493	67	To USAF 18.3.57 for Italian Air Force as MM19493
XB587	19494	SCF	To USAF 28.6.57 for Yug AF as 11-048
XB588	19495	26/20	SOC 18.12.58
XB589	19496	FTU/20/ 234/3	SOC 18.12.58
XB590	19497	3	SOC 18.12.58
XB591	19498	SCF	To USAF 5.12.56 for Italian Air Force
XB592	19499	SCF	To USAF 6.11.56 for Italian Air Force as MM19499
XB593	19500	SCF/26	To USAF 13.6.56 for Italian Air Force
XB594	19501	20	To USAF 15.3.57
XB595	19502	26	To USAF 10.4.56
XB596	19503	67	To USAF 5.10.56 for Italian Air Force as MM19503
XB597	19504	20	To USAF 9.3.56
XB598	19505	67	To USAF 18.3.57 for Italian Air Force as MM19505
XB599	19506	71	To USAF 30.5.56 for Italian Air Force as MM19506
XB600	19507	67	Bellylanded after electrical failure, Wildenrath, 22.3.54; not repaired
XB601	19508	FTU/147/ CGS/FWS	To USAF 12.10.56 for Italian Air Force as MM 19508
XB602	19509	SCF	To USAF 15.2.57 for Italian Air Force as MM19509
XB603	19510	SCF	Lost power on overshoot and crash--landed; broke up, Wildenrath, 15.6.53
XB608	19511	71	To USAF 6.11.56 for Italian Air Force as MM19511
XB609	19512	3/26	To USAF 27.6.56 for Italian Air Force as MM19512
XB610	19513	147	Dived into ground after instrument failure 7m NE of Grantown-on-Spey, Moray, 5.4.53
XB611	19514	SCF/71	To USAF 17.12.57 for Yugoslav AF as 11-049
XB612	19515	3	SOC 9.57
XB613	19516	26	To USAF 12.11.56 for Italian Air Force
XB614	19517	3/234	SOC 18.12.58
XB615	19518	234/WL Geil-enkirchen	Engine cut; forcelanded 1m E of Puffendorf, W.Germany, 3.5.55
XB616	19519	SCF/229 OCU	To USAF 5.12.56 for Yugoslav AF as 11-050

Serial	No.	Unit	Fate
XB617	19520	3	To USAF 12.7.57 for Italian AF as MM19520
XB618	19521	SCF	To USAF 12.9.56 for Italian AF as MM19521
XB619	19522	WL Wilden-rath/3	SOC 18.12.58
XB620	19523	RAE	To USAF 27.11.56 for Italian AF as as MM 19523
XB621	19524	3	To USAF 16.4.57 for Yugoslav AF as 11-051
XB622	19525	AFDS	To USAF 24.4.56 for Italian AF
XB623	19526	26	Yawed on take-off and hit snow-bank, Oldenburg, 24.2.55; not repaired
XB624	19527	67/71	To USAF 16.7.57 for Yugoslav AF as 11-052
XB625	19528	67	To USAF 19.2.57 for Italian AF
XB626	19529	67	SOC 18.12.58
XB627	19530	67	Ran out of fuel and crashed in forced landing 3m S of Peer, Belgium, 7.9.54
XB628	19531	71	Collided with XB729 during dummy attack and abandoned 10m NW of Krefeld, W Germany, 26.10.54
XB629	19532	112/93/3	SOC 18.12.58
XB630	19533	71	SOC 18.12.58
XB631	19534	71	To USAF 5.6.56 for Italian Air Force as MM19534
XB632	19535	67/71	To USAF 23.10.57 for Yugoslav AF as 06-071, later 11-053
XB633	19536	3	Sank back on take-off and overshot into bomb dump and blew up, Eindhoven, 26.6.55
XB634	19537	67	Collided with Anson TX238 on approach 1m E of Wildenrath, 5.4.55
XB635	19538	71/SCF	To USAF 27.3.57
XB636	19539	26	To USAF 31.5.57 for Yugoslav AF as 06-027, later 11-054
XB637	19540	71	SOC 18.12.58
XB638	19541	20	Hit tree on approach and dived into ground, Oldenburg, 5.8.54; DBF
XB639	19542	67	To USAF 20.4.56 for Italian Air Force as MM19542
XB640	19543	3	To USAF 13.3.57
XB641	19544	147/229 OCU	To USAF 12.1.56 for Italian Air Force as MM19544
XB642	19545	234	SOC 18.12.58
XB643	19546	3	Flew into high ground in formation during GCA training, Henri-Chapelle, Belgium, 24.2.54
XB644	19547	3/229 OCU	To USAAF 25.6.56 for Yug AF
XB645	19548	20	To USAF 1.3.57 for Italian Air Force as MM19548
XB646	19549	20/3	SOC 18.12.58
XB647	19854	4	Ex XD102. Stalled on overshoot, rolled and dived into ground 3m SSW of Jever, 8.7.54
XB648	19855	130	Ex XD103. Tyre burst on take-off; swung and nosewheel retracted, Bruggen, 3.6.54; not repaired and SOC 28.4.55
XB649	19856	112	Ex XD104; to USAF 27.7.57 for Yug AF as 11-025
XB650	19857	112	Ex XD105; to USAF 16.7.57 for Yug AF as 06-045, later 11-113
XB664	19550	67	To USAF 5.12.56 for Italian Air Force as MM19550
XB665	19551	SCF/71/67	To USAF 14.11.56 for Italian Air Force as MM19551
XB666	19552	AFDS/ 229 OCU	To USAF 26.2.57
XB667	19553	3	Flew into ground on GCA training, Henri-Chapelle, Belgium, 24.2.54
XB668	19554	67	To USAF 7.9.56 for Italy
XB669	19555	71	To USAF 30.6.56 for Italian Air Force as MM19555
XB670	19556	3	To USAF 23.5.57 for Yugoslav AF as 06-018 later 11-055
XB671	19557	67	SOC 18.12.57
XB672	19558	3	To USAF 6.5.57 for Yugoslavia
XB673	19559	SCF/3	SOC 18.12.58
XB674	19560	67	To USAF 4.3.57 for Italian Air Force as MM19560
XB675	19561	SCF/Hawkers	To USAF 23.5.56
XB676	19562	SCF	Damaged on ground, 17.6.53; not repaired
XB677	19563	AFDS/92	Failed to take-off and overshot runway, Linton-on-Ouse, 24.6.55; DBF
XB678	19564	67	To USAF 28.2.57
XB679	19565	67	To USAF 15.2.57 for Italian Air Force as MM19565
XB680	19566	234	To USAF 14.5.57 for Yugoslav AF as 06-013, later 11-056
XB681	19567	3	Overshot landing and undercarriage raised to stop, Geilenkirchen, 10.2.54; DBR
XB682	19568	SCF/67	To USAF 3.6.57 for Yugoslav AF as 06-029, later 11-057
XB683	19569	67	Abandoned in spin after controls jammed by pilot's helmet 6m S of Liège, Belgium, 17.9.53
XB684	19570	3	To USAF 27.1.56 for Italian Air Force as MM19570
XB685	19571	FTU/147/3	To USAF 30.11.56 for Italian Air Force as MM19571
XB686	19572	SCF/71	To USAF 4.2.57 for Italian Air Force as MM19572
XB687	19573	71	To USAF 21.9.56 for Italian Air Force as MM19573
XB688	19574	SCF	To USAF 19.1.57 for Italian Air Force as MM19574
XB689	19457	-	To USAF 13.8.57 for Yug AF
XB690	19576	67	Collided with XB730 during formation change and abandoned near M-Gladbach, 6.11.53
XB691	19577	71	To USAF 14.1.57
XB692	19578	67	To USAF 9.10.57 for Italy
XB693	19579	67	To USAF 12.1.57 for Italy as 2-53
XB694	19580	SCF/92	To USAF 3.6.57 for Yugoslav AF as 06-030, later 11-058
XB695	19581	67/93	To USAF 22.3.57 for Italian Air Force as MM19581
XB696	19582	229 OCU	To USAF 11.7.56 for Italian Air Force as MM19582
XB697	19583	93	To USAF 13.6.57 for Yugoslav AF as 11-059
XB698	19584	229 OCU	To USAF 20.3.56 for Italian Air Force as MM19584
XB699	19585	3	Dived into ground near Lontzen, Netherlands, 16.5.55
XB700	19586	SCF/71/26	Collided with Sea Hawk WM964 3m E of Yeovilton, 17.8.55
XB701	19587	67/93	To USAF 22.5.57 for Yugoslav AF as 11-060
XB702	19588	WL Wilden-rath/WL Bruggen/67	To USAF 4.3.57 for Italian Air Force as MM195887
XB703	19589	3	To USAF 9.5.56
XB704	19590	3	SOC 18.12.58
XB705	19591	67	To USAF 15.2.57

XB706	19592	67	To USAF 24.6.57 for Yugoslav AF as 11-061
XB707	19593	26/20/3	To USAF 29.5.57 for Yugoslav AF as 11-062
XB708	19594	26	To USAF 14.9.56
XB709	19595	20	To USAF 31.5.56 for Italian Air Force as MM19595
XB710	19596	71	To USAF 21.4.56 for Italian Air Force as MM19596
XB711	19597	229 OCU	Missing from formation, presumed crashed in sea, 23.10.54
XB712	19598	93	To USAF 13.3.57 for Italian Air Force as MM19598
XB713	19599	229 OCU	To USAF 1.3.57 for Italian Air Force as MM19599
XB726	19600	SCF/93	To USAF 20.3.57 for Italian Air Force as MM19600
XB727	19601	234	To USAF 6.11.56 for Italian Air Force as MM19601
XB728	19602	SCF/71	To USAF 27.7.57 for Italy
XB729	19603	71	Collided with XB628 during combat practice and abandoned 10m NW of Krefeld, 26.10.54
XB730	19604	67	Collided with XB690 during formation change near M-Gladbach and blew up, 6.11.53
XB731	19605	20/3	SOC 18.12.58
XB732	19606	130	To USAF 21.8.57 for Yugoslav AF as 06-055
XB733	19607	AAEE	To USAF 25.8.56 for Italian Air Force as MM19607
XB734	19608	26	Undercarriage jammed up; crash-landed at Oldenburg, 2.9.54; DBR
XB735	19609	234	Engine cut on approach; hit pylon and broke up, Brindisi, 2.9.55
XB736	19610	3	To USAF 3.10.57 for Yugoslav AF as 06-069/11-064
XB737	19611	67	To USAF 13.3.57
XB738	19612	SCF/3	To USAF 30.6.56 for Yugoslav AF
XB739	19613	71	To USAF 16.5.57
XB740	19614	3	To USAF 26.7.57
XB741	19615		To USAF 6.5.57 for Yugoslav AF as 06-005/11-065
XB742	19616	93	To USAF 10.8.56 for Italian Air Force as MM19616
XB743	19617	-	To USAF 28.3.57 for Italian Air Force as MM19617
XB744	19618	3	To USAF 29.3.57 for Italian Air Force as MM19618
XB745	19635	130/3	To USAF 17.6.57 for Yugoslav AF as 06-035 later 11-066
XB746	19620	112/93	To USAF 5.10.56 for Italian Air Force as MM19620
XB747	19621	3	To USAF 5.9.57
XB748	19622	234	To USAF 29.5.57 for Yugoslav AF as 06-036 later 11-067
XB749	19623	20/3	To USAF 20.6.57 for Yugoslav AF as 06-036 later 11-068
XB750	19624	234	SOC 18.12.58
XB751	19625	26	To USAF 4.3.57 for Italian Air Force as MM19625
XB752	19626	20/234	SOC 18.12.58
XB753	19627	-	To USAF 24.9.56 for Italian Air Force as MM19627
XB754	19628	67	To USAF 22.3.57 for Italian Air Force as MM19628
XB755	19458	93/20	To USAF 14.1.57
XB756	19630	FTU/147/229 OCU	To USAF 4.5.56 for Italian Air Force as MM19630
XB757	19631	92	To USAF 24.6.57 for Yugoslav AF as 06-041 later 11-069
XB758	19632	FTU	To USAF 14.12.56 for Italy
XB759	19633	26	To USAF 28.2.56 for Italian Air Force as MM19633
XB760	19634	71	Control lost in cloud; dived into ground 2m W of Julich, W.Germany, 4.2.55
XB761	19459	-	To USAF 22.6.56 for Yugoslavia
XB762	19636	229 OCU	To USAF 6.11.56 for Italy
XB763	19629	229 OCU	To USAF 21.3.57
XB764	19638	26	To USAF 29.5.56 for Italian Air Force as MM19638
XB765	19639	229 OCU	To USAF 10.1.57
XB766	19640	234	SOC 18.12.58
XB767	19641	26	To USAF 31.10.56 for Yugoslav AF as 11-070
XB768	19642	93	SOC 18.12.58
XB769	19460	-	To USAF 12.9.56 for Italian Air Force as MM19460
XB770	19858	4	To USAF 16.5.56 for Italy
XB771	19859	112	To USAF 4.4.57
XB772	19860	112	To USAF 6.5.57 for Yugoslav AF as 11-113
XB773	19861	4	To USAF 6.5.57 for Yugoslav AF as 11-114
XB774	19862	112	To USAF 5.10.57 for Yugoslav AF as 11-115
XB775	19863	4	To USAF 19.1.57
XB790	19644	130/20/3	To USAF 20.11.56
XB791	19645	20	To USAF 29.8.56 for Italian Air Force as MM19645
XB792	19646	234/3	To USAF 20.6.57 for Yugoslav AF as 11-071
XB793	19647	229 OCU	To USAF 4.3.57 for Italian Air Force as MM19647
XB794	10648	234	To USAF 29.4.57 for Yugoslav AF as 06-001, later 11-072
XB795	19649	229 OCU/66	To USAF 8.3.57 for Italian Air Force as MM19649
XB796	19650	71	To USAF 18.9.56
XB797	19651	130/20	To USAF 6.5.57 for Yugoslav AF as 11-073
XB798	19652	-	To USAF 23.7.56 for Italian Air Force as MM19652
XB799	19653	229 OCU	To USAF 31.5.57 for Yugoslav AF as 11-074
XB800	19654	130/26	To USAF 6.2.57 for Italian Air Force as MM19654
XB801	19655	229 OCU	To USAF 21.3.57
XB802	19656	112/93	SOC 18.12.58
XB803	19657	20/93/234	SOC 18.12.58
XB804	19658	112/93	To USAF 4.4.57 for Italian Air Force as MM19658
XB805	19659	-	To USAF 30.6.56 for Italian Air Force as MM19659
XB806	19461	-	To USAF 6.5.57 for Yugoslav AF as 06-011 later 11-045
XB807	19661	234	To USAF 14.3.57
XB808	19662	112/20	Flew into ground recovering from dive, Meppen ranges, W.Germany, 16.8.55
XB809	19543	-	To USAF 25.10.56
XB810	19664	CGS/FWS	To USAF 27.3.56 for Italian Air Force as MM19664
XB811	19665	229 OCU	To USAF 6.5.57 for Yugoslav AF as 11-075
XB812	19666	112/93	To USAF 26.7.56 for Italian Air Force as MM 19664; now in RAF Museum; allotted 9227M 14.2.94
XB813	19667	229 OCU	To USAF 9.10.57
XB814	19668	-	To USAF 29.9.56 for Italian Air Force as MM19668
XB815	19669	20	To USAF 30.8.57 for Yugoslav AF as 11-076
XB816	19454	93	To USAF 26.2.57

XB817	19671	234	SOC 18.12.58
XB818	19672	112/26	To USAF 29.8.56 for Italian Air Force as MM19672
XB819	19673	234	Engine flamed out due to fuel starvation; crashlanded 4m ESE of Julich, West Germany, 29.6.54
XB820	19674	67	To USAF 20.9.57 for Yugoslav AF as 11-077
XB821	19675	414/413/ 229 OCU	To USAF 15.3.57 for Italy
XB822	19676	112/93	Engine cut; undershot landing, Jever, 1.10.55
XB823	19677	444/229 OCU	To USAF 19.9.57 for Yugoslavia
XB824	19678	130/93	To USAF 21.6.57 for Yugoslav AF as 11-078
XB825	19575	229 OCU	To USAF 9.10.56
XB826	19680	444/414	To USAF 14.1.57 for Italian Air Force as MM19680
XB827	19681	WL Geilen-kirchen/234	To USAF 25.5.57 for Yugoslav AF as 11-079
XB828	19682	414	To USAF 29.3.57 for Italian Air Force as MM19682
XB829	19683	147/112/93	To USAF 11.7.56 for Italian Air Force as MM19683
XB830	19684	444	To USAF 15.6.56 for Italian Air Force as MM19684
XB831	19685	-	To USAF 17.5.56 for Italian Air Force as MM19685
XB832	19686	26	To USAF 21.9.56
XB833	19687	130/93	To USAF 18.9.56 for Italian Air Force as MM19687
XB834	19688	130/26	To USAF 13.5.57 for Yugoslav AF as 06-012
XB835	19455	229 OCU	To USAF 18.7.56
XB836	19690	130/234	To USAF 27.7.57 for Italy
XB837	19691	92	To USAF 27.6.57 for Italy
XB838	19692	130/234	To USAF 27.1.58 for Yugoslav AF as 11-080
XB839	19693	130/26	Dived into ground 8m SSW of Oldenburg, 10.2.55; cause not known
XB851	19864	130	To USAF 8.5.56
XB852	19865	130	SOC 15.11.56
XB853	19866	-	To USAF 14.6.58 for Italy
XB854	19867	20/4	To USAF 6.5.57 for Yugoslav AF as 11-116
XB855	19868	112/66	To USAF 10.4.57 for Italy
XB856	19694	93	To USAF 14.9.56 for Italian Air Force as MM19694
XB857	19695	-	To USAF 12.6.56 for Italian Air Force as MM19695
XB858	19696	130/3	To USAF 11.5.56
XB859	19697	130/3	To USAF 23.11.57
XB860	19698	234	Broke up in air and pilot thrown out, Wintraal, Netherlands, 29.10.54
XB861	19699	130/20/234	SOC 18.12.58
XB862	19700	130/26/20	To USAF 5.11.57 for Yugoslav AF as 11-081
XB863	19701	147	Lost radio aids in cloud and crashed 6m NE of St.Felix de Valois, Canada, 5.6.53
XB864	19702	-	To USAF 3.10.57 for Yugoslav AF as 11-082
XB865	19703	112/26	Overstressed, caught fire and abandoned 4m WSW of Hede, W.Germany, 23.7.54
XB866	19704	26	Missing after reporting compass trouble in cloud; presumed ditched in Heligoland Bight, 24.2.54
XB867	19705	234	SOC 18.12.58
XB868	19706	26	To USAF 13.6.57 for Yugoslav AF as 11-083
XB869	19732	67/71	SOC 18.12.58
XB870	19733	71	To USAF 12.4.57 for Italian Air Force as MM19733
XB871	19734	130/93/3	SOC 18.12.58
XB872	19735	34	To USAF 30.9.57
XB873	19736	234	To USAF 1.5.57 for Yugoslav AF as 11-087
XB874	19737	SCF/93	To USAF 4.2.57
XB875	19738	71	To USAF 5.11.57 for Yugoslav AF as 11-088
XB876	19739	71	To USAF 10.1.57
XB877	19740	26	To USAF 27.5.56
XB878	19741	71	To USAF 28.8.7 for Yugoslav AF as 11-089
XB879	19742	71	To USAF 31.5.57 for Yugoslav AF as 11-090
XB880	19743	71	Lost height on approach and hit ground; blew up, Bruggen, 15.7.55
XB881	19744	-	To USAF 7.11.56
XB882	19745	147	Explosion in fuselage; ejector seat fired as hood opened 4½m N of Broughty Ferry, Angus, 18.7.53
XB883	19746	26	To USAF 5.12.56
XB884	19747	112	Controls failed after electrical failure on approach; abandoned, Bruggen, 16.6.54
XB885	19748	234	To USAF 5.10.56
XB886	19774	20/26/WL Oldenburg/ 20/93	To USAF 3.7.57 for Yugoslav AF as 11-097
XB887	19775	-	To USAF 3.9.56 for Italian Air Force as MM19775
XB888	19776	20	To USAF 4.6.57
XB889	19777	20	SOC 18.12.58
XB890	19778	234	To USAF 29.6.56 for Italian Air Force as MM19778
XB891	19779	130/93/234	SOC 18.12.58
XB892	19780	20	To USAF 23.10.56 for Italian Air Force as MM19780
XB893	19781	112/WL Bruggen/93	To USAF 21.5.57 for Yugoslav AF as 11-098
XB894	19782	130	To USAF 12.12.56 for Italian Air Force as MM19782
XB895	19783	20	To USAF 3.7.57 for Yugoslav AF as 06-046 later 11-099
XB896	19784	71	To USAF 12.12.56 for Italian Air Force as MM19784
XB897	19785	234	To USAF 22.11.57 for Yugoslav AF as 11-100
XB898	19786	234	SOC 18.12.58
XB899	19787	20	Bellylanded in error, Schleswigland, 22.9.54; DBR
XB900	19788	20	To Bristol Engine Co, 28.4.59
XB912	19789	112	Ex XB901. Lost power on overshoot and crashlanded, Bruggen, 3.3.54
XB913	19790	112/93/3	Ex XB902; SOC 18.12.58
XB914	19791	112/20	Ex XB903; to USAF 12.9.57
XB915	19792	112/20	Ex XB904; to USAF 15.10.56 for Italian Air Force as MM19792
XB916	19803	130	Ex XB905; to USAF 25.9.56
XB917	19804	112	Ex XB941; to USAF 12.7.56
XB918	19805	130	Ex XB942; SOC 18.12.58
XB919	19806	112	Ex XB943; to USAF 7.9.57 for Yugoslav AF as 11-101
XB920	19807	112	Ex XB944; to USAF 14.6.57 for Yugoslav AF as 11-102
XB921	19808	4/130/71	Ex XB945; to USAF 30.9.57
XB922	19809	130	Ex XB946; to USAF 22.10.57 for Yugoslav AF as 11-103
XB923	19810	4	Ex XB947; to USAF 20.11.56
XB924	19811	130	Ex XB948; to USAF 31.5.56
XB925	19812	147	Ex XB949. Lost power on approach on ferry flight and crashlanded, Kinloss, 28.9.53

XB926	19813	SCF/112	Ex XB950; to USAF 7.1.58; for Yugoslav Air Force as 06-178 later 11-104
XB927	19814	130	Ex XB951. Engine cut on approach; bellylanded, Bruggen, 29.10.54
XB928	19815	130	Ex XB952; to USAF 25.7.57
XB929	19816	130	Ex XB953; to USAF 22.5.57 for Yugoslav AF as 06-015 later 11-105
XB930	19817	130	Ex XB954; to USAF 8.11.56
XB931	19818	26/4	Ex XB955; SOC 5.9.55
XB932	19819	130	Ex XB956. Engine failed to pick up; on approach; undershot and wing hit ground, Bruggen, 12.7.55
XB933	19820	130	Ex XB957; to USAF 29.3.57 for Italy
XB934	19821	112	Ex XB958; to USAF 17.7.57 for Yugoslav AF as 06-147 later 11-106
XB935	19822	SCF/4	Ex XB959; to USAF 24.5.56 for Italian Air Force as MM19822
XB936	19823	Hdlg Sqn/67	Ex XB960. Failed to become airborne and crashed, Wildenrath, 4.3.54
XB937	19824	4	Ex XB961. Dived into sea 9m SE of Sylt, 8.10.54; believed pilot blacked out
XB938	19825	4/3	Ex XB962; to USAF 7.11.57
XB939	19826	67/112	Ex XB963; to USAF 29.8.57 for Yugoslav AF as 11-107
XB940	19827	14	Ex XB964. Forcelanded short of fuel on autobahn E of Hamburg, 22.6.54
XB941	19828	4/66	Ex XB965; to USAF 27.6.57 for Italy
XB942	19829	130	Ex XB966; to USAF 12.6.56 for Italian Air Force as MM19829
XB943	19830	71/130	Ex XB967; to USAF 6.7.56 for Italian Air Force as MM19830
XB944	19831	112	Ex XB968; SOC 18.12.58
XB945	19832	WL Bruggen/ 130	Ex XB969; to USAF 21.6.56
XB946	19833	112	Ex XB970; to USAF 17.7.57 for Yugoslav AF as 11-108
XB947	19834	112	Ex XB971; SOC 18.12.58
XB948	19835	WL Jever/ WL G'kirchen	Ex XB972; to USAF 30.10.56 for Italy
XB949	19836	3/234/130	Ex XB973; to USAF 12.6.57 for Italy
XB950	19837	112	Ex XB974. Engine blew up; caught fire and dived into ground 1m E of Heerlen, Neth., 5.7.55
XB951	19838	130	Ex XB975; to USAF 22.6.56 for Italy
XB952	19839	71/SCF/130	Ex XB976; to USAF 15.10.56 for Italian Air Force as MM19839
XB953	19840	3/130	Ex XB977; to USAF 26.9.57 for Yugoslav AF as 11-109
XB954	19841	130	Ex XB978; to USAF 7.9.56 for Italian Air Force as MM19841
XB955	19842	4	Ex XB979; to USAF 28.9.56
XB956	19843	112	Ex XB980; to USAF 15.11.57 for Italy
XB957	19844	3/112	Ex XB981; to USAF 13.6.57 for Italy
XB958	19845	112	Ex XB982; to USAF 28.2.57
XB959	19846	130	Ex XB983; to USAF 19.9.57
XB960	19847	112	Ex XB984; to USAF 24.5.57 for Yugoslav AF as 11-110
XB961	19848	26/4/130	Ex XB984; to USAF 28.2.57 for Italian Air Force as MM19848
XB973	19849	4/3	Ex XB986; to USAF 19.8.57 for Yugoslav AF as 11-111
XB974	19850	4/71	Ex XB984; to USAF 24.6.57 for Yugoslav AF as 11-112
XB975	19851	234/130	Ex XB988; to USAF 1.6.5.57 for Italian Air Force as MM19851
XB976	19852	112	Ex XB989; to USAF 2.12.57 for Italy
XB977	19853	20/4	Ex XB990; to USAF 24.8.56 for Italian Air Force as MM19853
XB978	19869	112	Ex XD117; to USAF 29.5.57 for Yugoslav AF as 06-023 later 11-118
XB979	19870	112	Ex XD118; to USAF 26.11.57 for Italy
XB980	19871	4	Ex XD119; to USAF 9.10.56
XB981	19872	4/130/71	Ex XD120; SOC 18.12.58
XB982	19873	92	Ex XD121; to USAF 6.3.57
XB983	19874	4	Ex XD122; to USAF 30.10.56 for Italy
XB984	19875	3	Ex XD123; to USAF 8.11.57 for Yugoslav AF as 11-117
XB985	19876	130	Ex XD124; to USAF 5.9.57 for Italy
XB986	19877	130	Ex XD125; to USAF 6.12.56 for Italian Air Force as MM19877
XB987	19878	130/WL Bruggen/71	Ex XD126; to USAF 27.5.57 for-120 for Yugoslav AF as 11-120
XB988	19879	130	Ex XD127. Caught fire on night navex and dived into ground 7m NE of Kassel, 19.10.54
XB989	19880	147/4/71	Ex XD128; SOC 18.12.58
XB990	19881	4	Ex XD129; to USAF 6.12.56 for Italy
XB991	19882	130	To USAF 10.2.56
XB992	19883	AAEE	SOC 18.12.58
XB993	19884	4	To USAF 25.4.46 for Italy
XB994	19885	4	To USAF 9.5.56
XB995	19886	4/71/112	SOC 18.12.58
XB996	19887	4	To USAF 14.11.56 for Italian Air Force as MM19887
XB997	19888	Hawkers	To USAF 27.6.56 for Italian Air Force as MM19888
XB998	19889	92	To USAF 4.1.57
XB999	19890	71	To USAF 20.8.57 for Yugoslav AF as 11-119

* * * * * * * * * *

XD143		Allotted to incomplete Swift PR.6 to Contract 6/Acft/8700; to 7289M
XD145, XD151		SR.53 prototypes to Contract6/Acft/8703
XD153		Cancelled SR.53
XD158		Javelin FAW.2 prototype for MoS to Contract 6/Acft/1485; became 7592M at Halton

* * * * * * * * * *

10 Westland Whirlwind HAR.2s and HAR.4s delivered in July and October 1954 to Contract 6/Acft/8593

XD163	RN/155/275/228/ Cv HAR.4/228/ Cv HAR.10/AAEE/ SAR Flt Akrotiri/ CFS	8645M NTU; to Rotorcraft Museum 20.3.80 and preserved
XD164	AAEE/22/1360 Flt/ 22/1300 Flt/217/ Cv HAR.10/CFS	Engine cut; ditched in Holyhead Bay, Anglesey, 25.11.63; to 7853M
XD165	RN/155/225/22/ Cv HAR.10/228/ 202/SAR Wg	To 8673M 2.2.81 at Halton
XD182	RN/155/Cv HAR.10/ 228/202/22/202	To 8612M 8.1.79; to Catterick for fire practice
XD183	155/275/228/Cv HAR.10/110	Engine lost power; forcelanded in plantation 8m S of Dungun, Malaysia, 22.6.70
XD184	155/228/Cv HAR.10/ 1563 Flt/84	To 8787M 2.9.83 for display
XD185	155	Engine lost power; forcelanded in river bed near Fort Selim, Malaya, 31.1.58

XD186	155/CFS/Cv HAR. 10/228/202/SAR Wg	To 8730M 10.5.82; to Chivenor for display
XD187	155	Ran short of fuel during crop spraying and crashed in jungle, Johore, Malaya, 2.4.57
XD188	155	Sank into ground on landing, rolled over and caught fire 8m E of Tanah Rata, Malaya, 14.12.56

*   *   *   *   *   *   *   *   *   *

Two Bristol Sycamore HR.13s delivered in April 1953 to Contract 6/Acft/8736 for evaluation

XD196	275	Engine cut; crashlanded in trees ½m SSE of Linton-on-Ouse, 13.1.54
XD197	275	Hit ground during practice auto-rotation and rolled over, Thornaby, 17.11.55; DBR

*   *   *   *   *   *   *   *   *   *

XD203, XD207		Cancelled Westland Whirlwinds to Contract 6/Acft/8724
XD212 - XD250; XD264 - XD282; XD316 - XD333		Scimitar F.1s for Royal Navy to Contract 6/Acft/8812
XD334 - XD357		Cancelled Scimitars
XD361		Swift F.1 ordered to replace WK198 to Contract 6/Acft/5969 but cancelled

*   *   *   *   *   *   *   *   *   *

Vickers Varsity T.1 delivered in April 1953 as replacement for WJ900 to Contract 6/Acft/5946

XD366	2 ANS/CFS	SOC 30.6.69

*   *   *   *   *   *   *   *   *   *

XD371		München Mü.13A glider for Royal Navy

*   *   *   *   *   *   *   *   *   *

160 de Havilland Vampire T.11s delivered between September 1953 and July 1954 by D.H., Christchurch, Chester and Hatfield to Contract 6/Acft/8981

XD375	73/2 CAACU/ 1 FTS/4 FTS	To 7887M 28.5.65 at Winterbourne Gunner
XD376	92/CFS/8 FTS	SOC 27.4.64 for fire practice
XD377	66	To 8203M 28.7.72 at 487 Sqn ATC Cosford;
XD378	28	Lost aileron control; bounced on landing and swung into river, Kai Tak, 5.9.55
XD379	7 FTS/CFS/5 FTS	Engine cut; abandoned after fire warning and crashed on Graveley airfield, 1.3.62; DBF
XD380	14 RNZAF	Crashed on landing, Tengah, 7.6.55
XD381	CFS/8 FTS	SS 5.3.64
XD382	208 AFS/206 AFS/ 5 FTS/RAFC/CNCS/ CATCS	To 8033M 13.6.68
XD383	SF W.Malling/229 OCU/CFS/1 FTS	SOC 1.7.65; to Leeming for fire practice

XD384	208 AFS/206 AFS/ 5 FTS/1 FTS	SS 5.3.64
XD385	208 AFS/206 AFS/ 5 FTS/8 FTS	SOC 9.3.65; to Valley for fire practice
XD386	208 AFS/206 AFS/ 5 FTS	To 7629M 29.2.60 at Swinderby
XD387	208 AFS/206 AFS/ 5 FTS	SS 5.10.60
XD388	4 FTS/5 FTS/1 FTS	SOC 26.3.65; to Manston for fire practice
XD389	CFS/229 OCU	SS 5.10.60
XD390	5 FTS	Dived into ground, presumably after loss of control in turbulence, 1½m NW of Lavendon, Bucks., 21.1.57
XD391	228 OCU/SF Leuchars	SS 13.5.63
XD392	206 AFS/5 FTS	SS 5.10.60
XD393	CFS/5 FTS	To 7732M 1.11.61 at Church Fenton
XD394	5 FTS/RAFC/4 FTS/ RAFC/8 FTS	Sold 9.12.68 to BEA
XD395	208 AFS/10 FTS/ 7 FTS/5 FTS	Sold 7.12.67 to HSA
XD396	206 AFS/5 FTS	SS 5.3.64
XD397	208 AFS/10 FTS/ 9 FTS/7 FTS	SS 5.10.60
XD398	206 AFS/45/ SF Butterworth	SOC 29.9.59
XD399	206 AFS/5 FTS/ 7 FTS/5 FTS	SOC 14.6.60; to Catterick for fire practice
XD400	233 OCU	SS 29.7.60
XD401	206 AFS/5 FTS	SS 5.3.64
XD402	206 AFS/5 FTS/ RAFC	SS 5.3.64
XD403	4 FTS/5 FTS/7 FTS/ 1 FTS/4 FTS/8 FTS	Sold 2.12.68 to HSA
XD404	7 FTS/5 FTS	SS 27.2.61
XD405	CFS/5 FTS/4 FTS	Sold 30.10.67 to HSA
XD424	205 AFS/5 FTS	Abandoned in inverted spin ½m N of Whipsnade Church, Beds., 21.6.55
XD425	7 FTS/2 ANS/ 5 FTS/8 FTS	Sold 30.11.67 to HSA
XD426	206 AFS/5 FTS/ 7 FTS/5 FTS/ RAFC/8 FTS	SOC 13.3.64; to Syerston for fire practice
XD427	202 AFS/7 FTS/ 5 FTS/3-4 CAACU/ 1 FTS/7 FTS	SOC 26.7.66; to Cambridge for fire practice
XD428	206 AFS/5 FTS/ 263/1/3-4 CAACU	SS 30.6.64
XD429	7 FTS/CNCS/RAFC	SOC 10.2.64
XD430	7 FTS/5 FTS	To 7450M 8.8.57
XD431	202 AFS/7 FTS/ 5 FTS	Caught fire in air and abandoned 8m N of Sculthorpe, 9.1.61
XD432	206 AFS/5 FTS/ 41/APS Sylt	SOC 5.4.60
XD433	CGS/FWS	SS 19.8.59
XD434	7 FTS/5 FTS	Sold 1.12.67 to HSA
XD435	41/5 FTS/8 FTS	Sold 13.11.67; preserved
XD436	CFS/CNCS	SS 5.3.64
XD437	202 AFS/7 FTS/ 2 ANS/5 FTS	SS 5.3.63
XD438	5 FTS/8 FTS	SS 30.6.64
XD439	CNCS	SOC 10.1.62
XD440	7 FTS/5 FTS	Sold 31.12.64 to HAS; to Swiss AF as U-1238
XD441	130/112/130	Undercarriage retracted in error for flaps after landing, Bruggen, 16.7.56; DBR
XD442	206 AFS/5 FTS/ RAFC	SS 23.7.63
XD443	7 FTS/RAFC/ CFS/8 FTS	SS 31.3.65

Serial	Units	Fate
XD444	23/141/23/5 FTS/ 4 FTS/1 FTS/7 FTS	To 7918M 28.7.66 at ATC Broxburn
XD445	5 FTS/4 FTS	Sold 1.12.67 to HSA
XD446	FWS/CFS	SS 18.3.63
XD447	5 FTS/RAFC/8 FTS	Sold 1.12.67 to HSA
XD448	CFS/8 FTS	Hit birds; abandoned take-off and hit barrier, Swinderby, 4.9.62
XD449	Vamp TF Wunstorf/ 11/266/5/CNCS/ 4 FTS/1 FTS	SS 21.4.64
XD450	206 AFS/5 FTS/ CNCS/8 FTS	SOC 14.6.60; to Catterick for fire practice
XD451	206 AFS/5 FTS	Engine cut after night roller landing; hit trees on overshoot and caught fire, Oakington, 14.11.55
XD452	5 FTS/8 FTS/1 FTS/ 7 FTS/3 FTS	To 7990M 19.2.68; to Salisbury Hall
XD453	26/Oldenburg/ 1 FTS/Linton/ 1 FTS	To 7890M 13.8.65; to 1010 Sqn ATC at Salisbury
XD454	CFS/7 FTS	Undercarriage leg jammed; belly-landed at Valley, 22.5.57; not repaired
XD455	7 FTS/2 ANS/CFS	SS 30.6.64
XD456	9 FTS/7 FTS/ 5 FTS/CFS	SS 19.3.62
XD457	7 FTS/CFS	To 7423M 12.4.57 at Little Rissington
XD458	4/7 FTS/1 FTS/ 7 FTS/1 FTS/CNCS	SS 5.3.64
XD459	56/253/151/ 233 OCU/229 OCU/ 3-4 CAACU	Sold 6.1.72 to Exeter Airport
XD460	206 AFS/5 FTS/ CNCS	SS 27.2.61
XD461	7 FTS/5 FTS/RAFC	SS 5.3.64
XD462	206 AFS/5 FTS	SOC 5.5.55
XD463	7 FTS/5 FTS/ 3-4 CAACU/ CATCS	To 8023M 10.7.68 at St Athan
XD506	206 AFS/5 FTS/ CNCS/CATCS	To 7983M 7.9.67 at Finningley
XD507	222/Hdlg Sqn/ 3-4 CAACU	Hit slipstream and lost drop tank in dive, 19.4.61; overstressed and SOC
XD508	CGS/FWS	SS 19.8.59
XD509	130	SS 27.2.61
XD510	206 AFS/5 FTS/253	SS 29.7.60
XD511	206 AFS/5 FTS/ RAFC	To 7814M 4.10.63 at 221 Sqn ATC Gorleston
XD512	206 AFS/5 FTS/ 33/CFS	SS 30.6.60
XD513	206 AFS/5 FTS	SS 5.10.60
XD514	206 AFS/5 FTS	Spun into sea off Great Yarmouth, Norfolk, 27.7.54; cause not known
XD515	206 AFS/5 FTS/ 1 FTS/7 FTS/3 FTS	To 7998M 5.1.68; to Linton-on-Ouse for display
XD516	206 AFS/5 FTS/ CNCS	SS 21.4.64
XD517	206 AFS/5 FTS	Abandoned after fire warning 1½m NW of Winfarthing, Suffolk, 26.11.54
XD518	206 AFS/5 FTS	Throttle jammed; undershot emergency landing, Marham, 9.4.55
XD519	7 FTS/5 FTS/7 FTS	To 7651M 17.7.60 at Valley
XD520	206 AFS/5 AFS/ 8 FTS	Mushed into ground descending in cloud, 2.2.60; not repaired
XD521	206 AFS/5 FTS	Engine failed to respond on overshoot; undershot and hit hedges, Graveley, 21.8.56
XD522	206 AFS/5 FTS/ CNCS	SS 30.6.64
XD523	CFS	SS 5.3.64
XD524	7 FTS/3-4 CAACU/ 8 FTS	Sold 9.12.68 to BEA
XD525	7 FTS/5 FTS/ 4 FTS/1 FTS	To 7882M 8.4.65 at Cranfield
XD526	10 FTS/CFS/7 FTS	SOC 27.5.63
XD527	9 FTS/CFS/RAFC/ 8 FTS	Sold 24.11.67 at HSA
XD528	10 FTS/9 FTS/ RAFC/FECS	To 8159M 5.5.72 at 395 Sqn ATC Stafford
XD529	CGS/FWS	SS 19.8.59
XD530	10 FTS/9 FTS	Flew into ground in low cloud 4½m E of Merryfield, 20.8.54
XD531	CFS	SS 6.3.64
XD532	CFS/3-4 CAACU	Sold 4.7.63 to DH Hatfield for Indian Air Force
XD533	7 FTS/5 FTS	Lost hood, 1.6.57; airframe distorted and SOC
XD534	10 FTS/9 FTS/ CFS/7 FTS	Sold 30.10.67 to HSA
XD535	93/1 ANS/5 FTS/ 4 FTS	Sold 28.11.67 to HSA
XD536	234/SF G'kirchen/ 5 FTS	To 7734M 7.9.61 at 2287 Sqn ATC at Southall
XD537	CGS/FWS	SS 19.8.59
XD538	9 FTS/CFS/ CNCS/CATCS	To 7951M 24.4.67 at Aldergrove
XD539	54/SF Odiham	Ran out of fuel and abandoned, Frensham, Surrey, 3.11.55
XD540	33/1 FTS/8 FTS	Sold 12.12.68 to HSA
XD541	CFS/CNCS	SS 31.3.65
XD542	CGS/FWS	To 7604M 22.6.59 at Melksham
XD543	9 FTS/CFS/5 FTS	SS 5.3.63
XD544	5 FTS/RAFC	Sold 17.12.64 to HSA for Swiss AF
XD545	4 FTS/5 FTS	SS 5.3.64
XD546	257/8 FTS/CNCS/ CATCS	SOC 28.6.68; to Syerston for fire practice
XD547	263/IRS Tangmere/ DH/8 FTS/CATCS	Sold 22.3.71 to Glasgow University
XD548	SF Nicosia	To RJAF 1.7.55 as T-209
XD549	3/5 FTS	Collided with Varsity WJ914 and dived into ground 7m SSW of Oakington, 7.7.60
XD550	111/608/602/1/ SF Odiham/CFS/ 3 FTS	SOC 1.7.69; to Swinderby for fire practice
XD551	CNCS/8 FTS	SOC 9.11.62; to Shawbury for fire practice
XD552	SF Nicosia	To RJAF 1.7.55 as T-210
XD553	CFS/CNCS	Undercarriage leg jammed; belly-landed on grass, Shawbury, 13.9.57; not repaired
XD554	9 FTS/5 FTS/1 FTS	SS 5.3.64
XD588	23/141/FWS/FCS/ 3-4 CAACU	SS 5.3.64
XD589	93/SF Celle/7 FTS/ 1 FTS/7 FTS/ 8 FTS/1 FTS/ 7 FTS	SOC 25.6.66
XD590	CFS/FWS	SS 11.7.60
XD591	4 FTS/7 FTS/ MCCS/Wroughton	SS 11.7.60
XD592	2 TAF Vamp Flt/ 20/SF Oldenburg/ CNCS/1 FTS	Lost radio aids; abandoned out of fuel 7m NNW of Acklington, 4.9.61
XD593	4 FTS/5 FTS/FWS/ RAFC/CFS/8 FTS	Sold 12.12.68 to HSA
XD594	2 TAF CSU/ 2 TAF CS/5 FTS	Sold 22.12.64 to HAS for Swiss AF
XD595	4 FTS/7 FTS/ 5 FTS/1 FTS	Sold 6.11.67 to HSA
XD596	4 FTS/7 FTS/5 FTS/ CNCS/CATCS	To 7939M 14.2.67 at St Athan
XD597	4 FTS/7 FTS	SS 29.7.60
XD598	4 FTS/5 FTS/ APS Sylt	Sold 17.12.64 to HAS for Austrian AF as 5C-VA

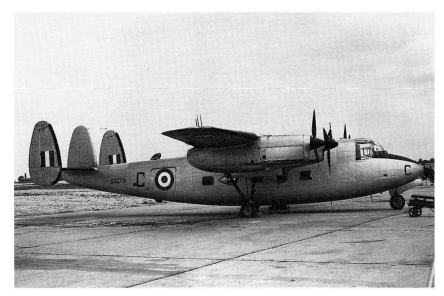

Marathon I XA273 was a navigation trainer that served with both Nos. 1 and 2 Air Navigation Schools.

It was based on the four-engined Miles Marathon civilian light airliner and fitted out with banks of navigation tables and equipment for training pupils before they went on to the operational conversion units.
(Peter Corbell)

Javelin FAW.1 was one of the original batch of Javelins which went to No.46 Squadron, before being passed on to No.87 Squadron whose unit markings are seen on the nose.
(Peter Corbell)

Sabre F.4 XB944 carries the traditional 'Sharksmouth' markings first used by No.112 Squadron in the Middle East when it received Tomahawks.

The paint scheme was the inspiration of the later American Volunteer Group in Burma which also flew P-40s and became famed as the 'Flying Tigers'.

18

Jet Provost T.1 XD674 was the first of a batch of ten aircraft produced to verify the viability of a jet-powered basic trainer.

When developed into the T.3, the undercarriage was shortened but the T.1 became well-known in its time through the flight of four which performed formation aerobatics in the hands of the Central Flying School.

The T.3 and its successors went on to provide 'all-through' jet training from elementary training to posting to an operational conversion unit.

XD816, Valiant BK.1 of No.214 Squadron in a line of Valiants at Marham.

Just visible is the flight refuelling logo on the fin.

Sycamore HR.14 XF269 of the Central Flying School at Ternhill with its two-letter code fore and aft of the roundel.

On 8 February 1966, XF269 rolled over while lifting-off, a not uncommon hazard with early unstable helicopters.

The Central Flying School's badge is carried on the nose.

Vampire

XD599	1/RAFC/CATCS	Sold 15.12.70 to Gloucester Tech College
XD600	CFS/CNCS/CATCS	SOC 13.7.64
XD601	4 FTS/7 FTS/ 2 ANS/RAFC/8 FTS	To 7878M 6.4.65 at Watson College
XD602	125/RAFC	Overstressed 29.9.61; to 7737M 6.10.61 at 495 Sqn ATC Sutton Coldfield
XD603	4 FTS/CFS/CNCS	SS 27.4.61
XD604	228 OCU/219/ 33/FWS	SS 19.8.59
XD605	CFS	SS 10.10.60
XD606	CNCS/1 FTS/ 7 FTS/8 FTS	SS 23.7.63
XD607	43/SF Oldenburg/ SF Ahlhorn/20	SS 29.7.60
XD608	5 FTS	Sold 8.12.64 to HAS for Swiss AF
XD609	FWS	Engine cut; abandoned 5m SE of Leconfield, 19.1.56
XD610	130/5 FTS	Sold 15.12.56 to DH Christchurch
XD611	CFE/8 FTS/ 3 CAACU	SS 23.7.63
XD612	11 FTS/CFS/ CNCS/8 FTS	SS 21.4.64
XD613	SF Odiham/CNCS/ CATCS	To 8122M 22.12.70 at Cosford
XD614	RAFC/CFS/1 FTS/ 7 FTS/3 FTS/CATCS	8124M NTU; to Chilean AF 10.11.72
XD615	FECS/60/FECS	SS 13.5.63
XD616	65/8 FTS/1 FTS/ 8 FTS	Sold 6.11.57 to HSA
XD617	SF Swinderby/ CFS/8 FTS	To 7815M 6.11.63 at 150 Sqn ATC Oxford
XD618	94/SF Laarbruch/ SF Ahlhorn/2 TAF CS/APS Sylt	SS 21.4.64
XD619	7 FTS/1 FTS	SS 21.4.64
XD620	7 FTS/1 FTS/ 7 FTS/4 FTS	Stalled on approach and dived into ground 4½m SE of Mona, 8.8.62
XD621	8 FTS/CFS/CNCS	SS 31.3.65
XD622	RAFC/118	To 8160M 2.7.71 at Church Fenton
XD623	3-4 CAACU	Damaged in heavy landing, Exeter, 29.9.65 and not repaired; SOC 3.5.66; to Exeter for fire practice
XD624	19/SF Church Fenton/CNCS/ CATCS	Sold 15.12.70 to Macclesfield College
XD625	DH/7 FTS/5 FTS/ 8 FTS	Sold 9.12.68 to BEA
XD626	CFS/RAFC/5 FTS/ CNCS/CATCS	Sold 19.7.67 to Coventry Tech College
XD627	RAE/DH/AAEE/ RRE/RAFC	Hit trees recovering from dummy RP attack in Lincolnshire; returned to base but not repaired, 20.7.59

*   *   *   *   *   *   *   *   *   *

Temporary serials allotted to civil aircraft:

XD632	Hermes IVA G-AKFP	
XD635	Viking G-AHOT	
XD636	Viking G-AHOW	
XD637	Viking G-AHOR	
XD649		Westland-Sikorsky WS-51 Mk.1A for trials at A&AEE ex G-AKTW; restored as G-AKTW and later became Widgeon G-APPR
XD653 - XD656		Sycamore HR.51s for RAN to Contract 6/Acft/9091/4

XD662	Cancelled Vickers1000 prototype to Contract 6/Acft/8630

Temporary serials allotted to civil Yorks:

XD667	G-AMUN
XD668	G-AMUU
XD669	G-AMUV
XD670	G-AGNU

*   *   *   *   *   *   *   *   *   *

Ten Percival Jet Provost T.1s delivered between May and December 1955 by Hunting-Percival, Luton, to Contract 6/Acft/9265

XD674	H-P/A-S/H-P/A-S/ AAEE	To 7570M 23.4.58 at Bicester;
XD675	AAEE/2 FTS/ CFS	SS 9.5.60
XD676	AAEE/CFS/ 2 FTS/CFS	SS 9.5.60
XD677	Hdlg Sqn/CFS/ 2 FTS/CFS	SS 9.5.60
XD678	H-P/2 FTS/CFS	Ex G-42-1; SS 9.5.60
XD679	CFS/2 FTS/CFS	SS 9.5.60
XD680	2 FTS/CFS/Mkrs	SS 9.5.60
XD692	2 FTS	Engine flamed out; bellylanded in field and hit wall 8m WNW of Hullavington, 30.8.56;7369M NTU
XD693	2 FTS/CFS	SS 9.5.60
XD694	Cv T.2/AAEE/ Hdlg Sq/2 FTS	SS 13.10.60

*   *   *   *   *   *   *   *   *   *

XD696, XD701	Avro 720s to Contract 6/Acft/9354 not completed

*   *   *   *   *   *   *   *   *   *

60 North American Sabre F.4s delivered between July and September 1953 by Canadair under MDAP

	RCAF		
XD706	19707	66	SOC 18.12.58;
XD707	19708	66	Flew into high ground in cloud, Kinder Scout, Derby, 22.7.54
XD708	19709	66	To USAF 6.11.56; to Italian Air Force as MM19709
XD709	19710	92	To USAF 26.8.57 for Yugoslav AF as 11-084
XD710	19711	66/92	Abandoned take-off and swung on to grass; nosewheel collapsed, Acklington, 5.4.55
XD711	19712	66	Collided with XD716 and abandoned 4m WNW of Hornsea, Yorks., 16.6.54
XD712	19713	66	Broke up recovering from dive out of cloud and spun into sea 9m E of Scunthorpe, Lincs., 16.6.55
XD713	19714	92	Tyre burst on take-off and undercarriage raised to stop, Linton-on-Ouse, 29.1.55
XD714	19715	92	To USAF 29.12.56
XD715	19716	66	To USAF 27.7.57 for Italy
XD716	19717	66	Collided with XD711 and abandoned 4m WNW of Hornsea, Yorks., 16.6.54
XD717	19718	92	To USAF 3.7.57
XD718	19719	66	SOC 12.7.56
XD719	19720	66/92	To USAF 10.1.57 for Italian Air Force as MM19720
XD720	19721	66	To USAF 23.5.57; to 11-085

XD721	19722	66	To USAF 10.8.56 for Italian Air Force as MM19722
XD722	19723	66	Engine flamed out; undershot emergency landing at Langham, 6.5.54
XD723	19724	92	To USAF 8.11.56 for Italian Air Force as MM19724
XD724	19725	66/92	To USAF 19.12.57; to Yug AF as 11-086
XD725	19726	66	To USAF 3.7.57
XD726	19727	92	To USAF 9.10.57
XD727	19728	92	SOC 18.12.58
XD728	19729	92	To USAF 22.6.56
XD729	19730	66	Lost power on attempted overshoot; bellylanded, Linton-on-Ouse, 25.1.56
XD730	19731	66	Flew into high ground in cloud, Kinder Scout, Derbyshire, 22.7.54
XD731	19749	66	To USAF 13.9.56 for Italian Air Force as MM19749
XD732	19750	92	SOC 18.12.58
XD733	19751	92	Flew into high ground on night navex, Hood Hill, Hambledon Hills, Yorks., 21.9.54
XD734	19752	92	To USAF 3.1.57 for Italian Air Force as MM19752
XD735	19753	66	To USAF 20.3.57 for Italian Air Force as MM19753
XD736	19754	92	To USAF 19.2.57 for Italian Air Force as MM19754
XD753	19755	66	To USAF 21.8.57; to Yug AF as 11-091
XD754	19756	92	To USAF 31.5.57
XD755	19757	66	Stalled on approach and dived into ground ½m SW of Driffield, 16.3.55
XD756	19758	92	To USAF 21.8.57; to Yug AF as 11-092
XD757	19759	66	To USAF 19.8.57; to Yug AF as 11-093
XD758	19760	66	Abandoned after fire warning 2½m NE of Helmsley, Yorks., 22.7.54
XD759	19761	92	SOC 18.12.58
XD760	19762	92	To USAF 28.6.57; to Yug AF as 11-094
XD761	19763	66	To USAF 13.9.57; to Yug AF as 11-095
XD762	19764	66	SOC 18.12.58
XD763	19765	66/Linton-on-Ouse	SOC 18.12.58
XD764	19766	92	To USAF 19.9.56 for Italian Air Force as MM19766
XD765	19767	66	To USAF 22.8.57; to Yug AF as 11-096
XD766	19768	92	SOC 18.12.58
XD767	19769	92	To USAF 28.5.57
XD768	19770	66	Engine lost power; swung in forced landing at Full Sutton airfield and nosewheel collapsed, 10.8.54
XD769	19771	92	SOC 18.12.58
XD770	19772	66	SOC 18.12.58
XD771	19773	92	Engine cut on approach; bellylanded in field 2m ENE of Linton-on-Ouse, 29.9.54
XD772	19793	66	Engine lost power; abandoned after fire warning ½m E of Kelston, Lincs., 29.11.54
XD773	19794	66	Engine lost power; undershot landing, Linton-on-Ouse,13.5.54
XD774	19795	66	To USAF 8.1.58 for Yugoslav AF
XD775	19796	147	Tail controls failed on delivery flight; crashed, St Hubert, PQ, 18.8.53
XD776	19797	66	Caught fire and abandoned 12m SW of North Luffenham, 27.8.54
XD777	19798	66	To USAF 7.1.57 for Italian Air Force as MM19798
XD778	19799	66	To USAF 28.3.57
XD779	19800	92	To USAF 4.11.57
XD780	19801	AFDS/229 OCU/92	Stalled on to runway and under-carriage collapsed, Linton-on-Ouse, 14.5.55
XD781	19802	AFDS	To USAF 23.10.56

*   *   *   *   *   *   *   *   *   *

XD759		Fairey Jet Gyrodyne to Contract 6/Acft/7270 for trials; ex-G-AJJP; duplicated serial; renumbered XJ389
XD763 - XD772		Whirlwind HAR.3s to Contract 6/Acft/9410; renumbered XJ393-XJ402
XD777 - XD784 XD795 - XD806		Whirlwind HAR.4s for Royal Navy; to Contract 6/Acft/9409; renumbered XJ407 - XJ414 and XJ426 - XJ437

*   *   *   *   *   *   *   *   *   *

38 Vickers Valiant BK.1s delivered between July 1956 and September 1957 by Vickers, Weybridge, to Contract 6/Acft/9446

XD812	207/214/207/214	SOC 5.3.65
XD813	207/90	SOC 1.3.65
XD814	Marshalls/AAEE/148/138/90	SOC 15.12.64
XD815	148/207/138/90	SOC 1.3.65
XD816	Marshalls/VA/148/214	To BAC 21.9.64; nose to RAF Museum
XD817	148/90/138/90	SOC 1.3.65
XD818	49	To 7894M 18.10.65; preserved
XD819	148/SAC Bbg Sqn/148	SOC 14.12.64
XD820	148/90/214/90	SOC 1.3.65
XD821	VA/148/214/148/138/232 OCU	SOC 30.10.67
XD822	49	SOC 5.6.65
XD823	49	SOC 1.3.65
XD824	49/138/49	SOC 5.3.65
XD825	49/543/49	SOC 10.6.65
XD826	VA/7/90/138/232 OCU/543	To 7872M 5.3.65; nose preserved at Cosford
XD827	49	SOC 14.12.64
XD828	7/207	SOC 5.3.65
XD829	49/Marham	SOC 5.3.65
XD830	7/90	SOC 15.12.64
XD857	49	SOC 6.3.65
XD858	AAEE/214/138/207/214/SAC Bbg Sqn/214	SOC 4.3.65
XD859	214/138/148/214/SAC Bbg Sqn/214	SOC 10.6.65
XD860	214/138/214/SAC Bbg Sqn/214	SOC 1.1.67
XD861	214/138/214/SAC Bbg Sqn/214	SOC 5.3.65
XD862	90/148	SOC 5.3.65
XD863	90/7/90/Marshalls/90	SOC 10.6.65
XD864	7	Stalled, flew into ground and blew up, Spanhoe airfield, 12.8.60
XD865	90/207	SOC 5.3.65
XD866	138/232 OCU	SOC 4.3.65
XD867	90	SOC 1.3.65
XD868	138/BCDU/Finn-ingley/232 OCU	SOC 4.3.65
XD869	214	Flew into ground after night take-off 2½m NE of Marham, 11.9.59
XD870	214/148/214	SOC 4.3.65
XD871	90/7/138/214	SOC 4.3.65

XD872	VA/AAEE/VA/138/ VA&AAEE/138/ BCDU/7/90	SOC 10.6.65
XD873	207/49/207/SAC Bbg Sqn/207/138/ 7/232 OCU	SOC 4.3.65
XD874	214/49/214/148/ SAC Bbg Sqn/148/ Marham Wg	SOC 5.3.65
XD875	207/49/207/SAC Bbg Sqn/207/138/7	SOC 9.11.62
XD876 to XD893	-	Cancelled

* * * * * * * * * *

XD898		Gannet AS.1 for RAN to Contract 6/Acft.8203

* * * * * * * * * *

58 Supermarine Swift FR.5s delivered between October 1955 and April 1957 by Vickers-Armstrongs, South Marston, to Contract 6/Acft/9463

XD903	VA/AAEE/VA/ AAEE	MoS aircraft
XD904	VA/AAEE/VA	MoS aircraft; SS 6.1.59
XD905	Hdlg Sqn/79/ Ferry Sqn	Abandoned take-off and over-shot across road, Benson, 22.10.58; not repaired
XD906	VA & AAEE	SS 27.6.60
XD907	Hdlg Sqn	SS 27.6.60
XD908	2	SS 27.6.60
XD909	VA	Damaged 19.10.56; SOC 23.4.57
XD910	2	Hood came loose and presumably hit pilot; rolled and dived into ground 4m W of Aachen, 22.8.57
XD911	CFE	SS 27.6.60
XD912	2/VA	SOC 13.1.59
XD913	WL Gutersloh/79	Nosewheel jammed; landed on main-wheels, Gutersloh, 23.6.60; not repaired
XD914	2	SOC 30.5.60
XD915	2	SS 27.6.60
XD916	2	SS 27.6.60
XD917	AAEE	SS 27.6.60
XD918	CFE	SS 27.6.60
XD919	FTU	Engine lost power on take-off; hit trees and roof and crashed, Benson, 21.1.56
XD920	2	SOC 22.3.60
XD921	79	SOC 16.10.61; to Finningley for fire practice
XD922	2	SS 27.6.60
XD923	79	SS 27.6.60
XD924	2	SOC 4.8.60
XD925	79	SS 27.6.60
XD926	2	Nosewheel jammed; landed on mainwheels, Jever, 24.11.58; not repaired
XD927	2	SS 27.6.60
XD928	2	Engine flamed out; abandoned off Sylt, 9.4.59
XD929	2	SS 27.6.60
XD930	2	SS 27.6.60
XD948	79	Nosewheel jammed up; landed on mainwheels, Gutersloh, 1.8.57; not repaired
XD949	2	SS 27.6.60
XD950	2	SS 22.6.60
XD951	2	Taxied into XD914, 7.2.57; not repaired and to 7447M 21.6.57 at Kirkham
XD952	79	SS 27.6.60
XD953	79	SOC 16.9.60
XD954	79	SOC 5.9.60
XD955	79	Hydraulic fire in rear fuselage in air, 13.7.59; SOC 14.8.59
XD956	79	SS 27.6.60
XD957	79	SS 27.6.60
XD958	79/2	Wing root fillet tore away and airframe distorted, 30.4.58; SOC 9.9.58
XD959	2	SS 27.6.60
XD960	Benson	SS 27.6.60
XD961	79	Engine lost power; abandoned 2m E of Gutersloh, 17.7.59
XD962	2	SOC 4.10.61; to Bovingdon for fire practice
XD963	-	SS 27.6.60
XD964	2	SOC 10.7.61; to Manston for fire practice
XD965	-	SS 27.6.60
XD966	-	SS 27.6.60
XD967	2	Undercarriage jammed; bellylanded at Jever, 28.2.59; DBR
XD968	-	SS 2.5.61
XD969	79	Abandoned after engine flamed out on approach, Gutersloh, 7.3.60
XD970	-	SS 2.5.61
XD971	-	SS 27.6.60
XD972	2	SOC 8.9.60
XD973	2	SOC 6.4.61; to Oakington for fire practice
XD974	79	SOC 5.9.60
XD975	Mkrs/Hdlg Sqn	Rolled on approach and hit ground inverted, Wisley, 15.8.58; DBF
XD976	79/4	SOC 8.5.61; to Cottesmore for fire practice
XD977	VA	Sold to VA 11.9.58
XD978 to XD988	-	Cancelled
XE105 to XE116	-	Cancelled FR.5s
XE133 to XE164	-	Cancelled PR.6s

* * * * * * * * * *

25 Short Seamew AS.1s (for Royal Navy) and MR.2s delivered between January 1956 and May 1957 by Short Bros. & Harland to Contract 6/Acft/9478

XE169 to XE172	-	AS.1s for Royal Navy
XE173	-	To Royal Navy for storage
XE174	-	To Royal Navy for storage
XE175	-	Returned to Short & Harland
XE176	-	To Royal Navy for storage
XE177 to XE179	-	AS.1s for Royal Navy
XE180	-	Static test airframe
XE181 to XE186	-	AS.1s for Royal Navy
XE205 to XE211	-	AS.1s for Royal Navy
XE212 to XE231	-	Cancelled
XE263 to XE277	-	Cancelled

* * * * * * * * * *

Temporary serials allotted to DC-3s:

XE280: G-AMRA; XE281: G-AMZD

Serials allotted to Bristol 173s for trials to Contract 6/Acft/7425:

XE286: G-AMYF; XE287: G-AMYG; XE288 G-AMYH
Only XE286 flown

XE294 - XE299		Cancelled Valiant BK.1s to Contract 6/Acft/9446
XE304		Allotted to York G-AMUN but cancelled (see XD667)

* * * * * * * * *

17 Bristol Sycamore HR.14s delivered between November 1953 and November 1954 by Bristol Aircraft to Contract 6/Acft/9584

XE306	AAEE/275	Lost power in hover and hit ground; overturned, Linton-on-Ouse, 28.7.54
XE307	AAEE/103	Engine cut in hover and rotor blades hit ground; rolled, Tymbou, Cyprus, 17.9.59; DBR
XE308	Bristols & AAEE	Rolled on take-off and rotor blades hit ground, Boscombe Down, 3.11.65; SOC 27.7.66
XE309	SF Eastleigh/Aden PCSS/Khormaksar/ Khormaksar SAR Flt/CFS	Control lost at low level; hit ground 4½m S of Ternhill, 29.3.63
XE310	194/110	SOC 6.8.68; to Manston for fire practice
XE311	194/110	Caught fire after landing, Butterworth, 4.4.64; DBR
XE312	194	Rotor blades hit tree on landing, Tanah Rata Padang, Malaya, 5.2.57
XE313	194	Ex G-AMWK. Lost height on take-off from clearing and crashed in jungle 20m NE of Ipoh, 4.1.58
XE314	194	Ex G-AMWL. Lost speed on take-off and crashlanded, Fort Selim, 7.12.54
XE315	194	Ex G-AMWM. Tail rotor failed on approach; dropped into river and sank, Kuala Karu, Malaya, 4.5.55
XE316	194	Ex G-AMWN. Swung in gust, sank into ground and overturned, Fort Selim, 30.1.55
XE317	275/118/225/118/ CFS	Ex G-AMWO; to Royal Navy 6.5.72 as GI airframe
XE318	194	Rolled on take-off and overturned, Sungei Besi, Malaya, 13.9.55; DBR
XE319	194	Lost rotor blade and spun into ground 6m S of Kuala Lumpur, 21.2.59; DBF
XE320	CFS/APS Sylt/ 225/CFS	Became uncontrollable; damaged in heavy landing 1m S of Peplow, 13.10.65
XE321	194	Tail rotor drive failed; crashlanded in field, Ipoh, 6.9.56
XE322	194/110	Sank back on take-off from jungle; forcelanded in river, Cameron Highlands, Malaya, 20.3.61

* * * * * * * * *

XE327 - XE338	Sea Hawk FGA.4 s for Royal Navy to Contract 6/Acft/9601
XE339 - XE344; XE362 - XE411; XE435 - XE463; XE489 - XE490	Sea Hawk FGA.6s for Royal Navy to Contract 6/Acft/9601
XE491 - XE498	Cancelled Sea Hawks

* * * * * * * * *

Percival Provost T.1 delivered in September 1953 by Hunting-Percival to Contract 6/Acft/6848

XE506	CFS/6 FTS/RAFC	To RMAF as FM1035 31.10.69

* * * * * * * * * *

Four Scottish Aviation Pioneer CC.1s delivered between August 1953 and February 1954 by Scottish Aviation, Prestwick, to Contract 6/Acft/9613

XE512	1311 Flt/267/209	Ex G-AKBF. Ground-looped into ditch after heavy landing, Kuala Lumpur, 4.11.58
XE513	1311 Flt/267	Wingtip hit ground on landing and undercarriage leg torn off; rolled over on runway, Kuala Lumpur, 8.4.58
XE514	Hdlg Sqn/267	Ex G-ANAZ. Hit downdraught on approach and flew into ground; bounced and overturned, Fort Shean, 8.8.54
XE515	267/209	SOC 26.8.66

* * * * * * * * *

XE521		Fairey Rotodyne prototype for trials to Contract 6/Acft/5831

* * * * * * * * *

100 Hawker Hunter F.6s delivered between February 1956 and February 1957 by Hawkers, Kingston, to Contract 6/Acft/9629

XE526	-	Sold 19.2.58; to Swiss AF as J-4008
XE527	-	Sold 6.2.58; to Swiss AF as J-4006
XE528	-	Sold 19.2.58; to Swiss AF as J-4009
XE529	-	Sold 29.2.58; to Swiss AF as J-4005
XE530	RR/14/26/Cv FGA.9/ 208/8 & 43	To HSA 31.10.67; to Kuwait as T.67 No.220 22.5.69
XE531	RR/RAE/AAEE	Cv Mk.12; not delivered to RAF. Engine blew up on take-off; abandoned, Farnborough,17.3.82
XE532	RR/92/Cv FGA.9/ 208/8	Hit mast on range; abandoned after engine lost power 3m WSW of Dubai, 6.5.68
XE533	-	Sold 20.1.58; to Swiss AF as J-4002
XE534	-	Sold 31.10.58; to Lebanese AF as L-172
XE535	20/Cv FGA.9/ Kai Tak/20/28	Flew into Lion Rock Ridge, 2m NNW of Kai Tak, 28.12.62; cause not found
XE536	-	Sold 20.1.58; to Swiss AF as J-4001
XE537	-	Sold 5.9.57; to Indian AF as BA233
XE538	-	Sold 5.9.57; to Indian AF as BA234
XE539	-	Sold 5.9.57; to Indian AF as BA235
XE540	-	Sold 5.9.57; to Indian AF as BA236
XE541	-	Sold 20.1.58; to Swiss AF as J-4003
XE542	-	Sold 29.1.58; to Swiss AF as J-4004
XE543	AAEE & Hdlg Sqn	Sold 10.11.58; to RJAF as 707
XE544	66/208/Cv FGA.9/ 208	Abandoned take-off after fire warning; undercarriage raised to stop, Nairobi, 17.9.62
XE545	-	Sold 27.1.58; to Swiss AF as J-4007
XE546	93/26/Cv FGA.9/ 43/8-43/43/208/ 8/229 OCU/TWU/ 2 TWU/1 TWU	Sold 5.82; to Chilean AF as No.744
XE547	-	Sold 26.8.57; to Indian AF as BA237
XE548	4	To RRAF 2.3.63 as No.120
XE549	-	Sold 26.8.57; to Indian AF as BA238
XE550	93/Cv FGA.9/43/ 8-43/43	To Kuwait AF 28.12.67 as 216

XE551	Mkrs	To RJAF 7.11.58 as 700
XE552	263/65/Cv FGA.9/54/208/8-43/208/8/208/229 OCU/TWU/2 TWU	Dived into sea during combat practice 20m N of Lossiemouth. 23.2.81; cause not known
XE553	-	Sold 10.4.58; to Swiss AF as J-4012
XE554	-	Sold 2.4.58; to Swiss AF as J-4010
XE555	-	Sold 1.4.58; to Swiss AF as J-4011
XE556	208/Cv FR.10/2	Sold 3.3.71; to Indian AF as S1391
XE557	19/229 OCU	Sold 17.3.70; to Chilean AF as J-727
XE558	Mkrs	To RRAF 3.11.58 as No.701
XE559	74	To RRAF 15.12.62 as No.116
XE560	Mkrs/43/65/66	To RRAF 15.5.63 as No.126
XE561	54/247/43/19/54/1/229 OCU	Sold 17.3.70; to Chilean AF as J-726
XE579	208/Cv FR.10/8	Flew into ground approaching range and blew up 6m E of Zinjigar, Aden, 8.8.61
XE580	34-208/19/Cv FR.10/4	Sold 4.6.70; to Chilean AF as J-730
XE581	247/43/Cv FGA.9/8	Abandoned during tail chase 28m SW of Doha, Qatar, 22.11.61; reason unknown
XE582	247/66/Cv FGA.9/20/45/MoD(PE)/45/Hunter Wg/2 TWU/1 TWU	Sold 5.82; to Chilean AF as No.745
XE583	19	Control lost; rolled and dived into ground, Logumkloster, 16m SW of Skydstrup, Denmark,12.9.61
XE584	1/Cv FGA.9/1/8/208	Sold 12.2.76 to HAS as G-9-450
XE585	SF Church Fenton/DFLS/Cv FR.10/4/2	Sold 3.3.71; to Indian AF as S1392
XE586	263	Abandoned in inverted spin; crashed in Tuddenham Ave., Ipswich, Suffolk, 2.8.57
XE587	Mkrs	Sold to MoA 24.3.58 for RAE; to USA as N587XE 5.3.92
XE588	AAEE	Abandoned in spin during spinning trials 3m N of Ringwood, Hants., 9.11.57
XE589	74/Cv FR.10/8/1417 Flt	Sold 24.1.68; to Abu Dhabi AF as No.701
XE590	19/SF Jever/93/4	Hit bird in low flight near Jever, 9.11.60; not repaired
XE591	74/65/229 OCU/54/1/229 OCU	Sold 5.4.66; to R.Saudi AF as No.602
XE592	43/111/14/Cv FGA.9/54/8/8-43	Dived into sea 3m E of Masirah, 16.10.64
XE593	63/65	Engine blew up on starting, Duxford, 23.1.61; not repaired
XE594	66/63/56/229 OCU	Collided with XF433 during formation aerobatics and abandoned off Hartland Point, N.Devon, 7.3.63
XE595	66/65	Aircraft failed to lift off; abandoned take-off and undercarriage raised to stop; hit lights, Jever, 26.7.57
XE596	66/63/56/Cv FR.10/229 OCU	Dived into ground in bad weather 7m S of Paderborn, 19.3.70
XE597	66/63/56/Cv FGA.9/208/MoA/54/1/SF W.Raynham/229 OCU/TWU/2 TWU/1 TWU	To 8874M 4.10.85 at Bentley Priory
XE598	-	To Lebanese AF 31.10.58 as L-170
XE599	Hdlg Sqn/34-208/74/Cv FR.10/8/1417 Flt/8	Sold 4.11.71; to Singapore as No.535
XE600	Mkrs/Cv FGA.9/8	Stalled during run over range and crashed, Khormaksar ranges, 25.6.62
XE601	Mkrs	Sold to MoA 24.3.59 for ETPS
XE602	66/92/63/56/229 OCU	Throttle jammed open; overshot landing into barrier, Chivenor, 8.3.61; DBR
XE603	AFDS/19	Sold 9.6.66; to RJAF as 832
XE604	263/1/Cv FGA.9/1	Stalled during recovery from firing pass and dived into sea, Cowden ranges, 2.3.61
XE605	AAEE/Cv FR.10/Hdlg Sqn/2	Sold 17.5.71; to Singapore as No.523
XE606	CFE/54/65/74/92/229 OCU/Cv F.6A/TWU/1 TWU	8737M NTU / To 8841M 29.11.84 at Laarbruch
XE607	1/Cv FGA.9/208/8	Dived into ground during aerobatic display, Khormaksar, 30.3.62
XE608	CFE/AFDS/CFCS/229 OCU/TWU/Cv F.6A/1 TWU	To 8717M 25.9.81 at Bruggen
XE609	54/Cv FGA.9/208/8/8-43	Engine caught fire; overshot landing, Khormaksar, 5.4.66; not repaired
XE610	74/Cv FGA.9/20	Engine flamed out; abandoned off coast 40m S of Kuantan, Malaya, 26.6.68
XE611	FCS/43/Cv FGA.9/43/8-43/208/8-43/8/208	Overshot landing into gully, Lyneham, 6.12.68; sold to HSA, repaired and sold to Swiss AF as J-4103
XE612	74	Lost power on take-off; hit barrier and caught fire, Horsham St.Faith, 17.5.60
XE613	74/65	To RRAF 2.3.63 as No.118
XE614	1/Cv FR.10/8/1417 Flt/7	Sold 19.7.71; to Singapore as No.533
XE615	263/1/Cv FGA.9/1/54	Sold 31.10.69; to Singapore as No.508
XE616	263/1/Mkrs/Cv FGA.9/54/1	Dived into sea during combat practice 1m off Holkham, Norfolk, 21.5.69
XE617	66/92/65/Cv FGA.9/Mkrs/8-43/208	Ran out of fuel and undershot approach, undercarriage raised to avoid Heron on runway, Bahrein, 7.5.66
XE618	19/SF Church Fenton/SF Acklington/66/Cv FGA.9/208/8/8-43/43	To Kuwait AF 28.12.67 as No.217
XE619	263/1	Hit tree on approach, Stradishall, and crashlanded at Honington, 17.2.59
XE620	1/Cv FGA.9/8/8-43/208/8-43/43	Sold 1.5.68; to Indian AF as A967
XE621	66/92/63/65/Cv FR.10/AAEE/2	Stalled and dived into ground near Papenburg, W.Germany, 30.1.62
XE622	1/66/1/Cv FGA.9/28	Engine blew up on starting, Kai Tak, 12.7.66; not repaired
XE623	263/1/Cv FGA.9/208/43	Engine flamed out; abandoned 1½m NE of Khormaksar, 11.8.64
XE624	1/Cv FGA.9/1/SF West Raynham/229 OCU/TWU/2 TWU/1 TWU	To 8875M 4.10.85 at Brawdy for display
XE625	263/1/Cv FR.10/2/4	Sold 4.6.70; to Chilean AF as J-729
XE626	263/1/Cv FR.10/4/229 OCU	Sold 23.8.72; to Kenya AF as No.803 24.6.74
XE627	92/65/229 OCU/54/SF Horsham St Faith/54/1/54/229 OCU/1/229 OCU/TWU/Cv F.6A/TWU/1 TWU	To Duxford 14.11.86 for display

XE628	263/AFDS/1/66/	Dived into sea during combat
_____	1/Cv FGA.9/1	practice off Set Tehami, 24m E
		of Tobruk, 24.4.63
XE643	92/66/63/56/	Abandoned take-off; overshot and
	Cv FGA.9/208	undercarriage raised to stop,
		Mombasa, 9.12.61; nose to 8586M
XE644	66/92/63/65/	Sold 26.3.70; to Chilean AF
	229 OCU	as J-728
XE645	66/63/56/Cv FGA.9/	
	54/208/8-43	To RJAF 7.9.67 as No.827
XE646	263/FWS/1/	Abandoned after engine cut
	Cv FGA.9/1˙	in circuit, Leconfield, 30.12.66
XE647	92/63/56/	Collided with XK139 during
	Cv FGA.9/208	practice low level attack and
		abandoned off Dasa Island,
		Persian Gulf, 30.6.64
XE648	66/63/56	Overshot landing and hit
		fence, Nicosia, 9.9.59; DBR
XE649	66/92/65/Cv FGA.9/	Engine caught fire at low level;
	8/8-43/208/229	abandoned and crashed on
	OCU/TWU/1 TWU/	moors, Cwm Ystwyth, 15m SE
	2 TWU/1 TWU	of Aberystwyth, 13.5.82
XE650	263/1/Cv FGA.9/	
	1/208/8	Sold 12.2.76 to HAS as G-9-449
XE651	66/63/56/Cv	
	FGA.9/8/1/ 229	Abandoned after engine fire
	OCU/45/58/TWU	40m S of Brawdy, 13.5.77
XE652	66/DFLS/Cv FGA.9/	Sold 28.1.70; to Singapore
	20	as No.519
XE653	43/111/229 OCU/	
	TWU/Cv F.6A/TWU/	
	237 OCU/BAe	To 8829M 2.9.84 at Scampton
XE654	92/63/65/Cv FGA.9/	Flew into ground during practice
	8/208/8-43/8	attack near Sohat, Oman, 20.11.67
XE655	92/63/56/Cv FGA.9/	
	8/43/8-43/8	To RJAF 26.1.68 as No.817
XE656	DFLS/65/229 OCU/	
	92/229 OCU/4 FTS/	
	229 OCU/TWU	To 8678M 2.4.81 at Halton

* * * * * * * * * *

50 Hawker Hunter F.4s delivered between May and November 1955 by Hawkers, Blackpool, to Contract 6/Acft/9817

XE657	14/229 OCU	Sold 27.1.61 to HSA
XE658	54/74/FWS	SS 24.5.61
XE659	54/92/SF Odiham/	To 7785M 8.8.63 at Halton;
	229 OCU	later to Swiss AF as J-4149
XE660	247	Dived into ground out of cloud 2½m
		W of Alton, Hants., 5.12.56
XE661	DFLS/54/SF	Overshot abandoned take-off when
	Odiham/54/74	controls reverted to manual,
		Horsham St.Faith, 25.5.57; not
		repaired and SS 1.1.59.
XE662	247/74	Forcelanded on approach, Horsham
		St.Faith, 25.5.57; pilot mistook
		message to Javelin that aircraft was
		on fire as relating to his aircraft
XE663	4/43	Sold 16.8.61 to HSA
XE664	26	To Royal Navy 14.4.59 as T.8B
XE665	118	Cv to T.8 for Royal Navy;
	237 OCU/208/	Retd to RAF 5.80
	237 OCU	To Royal Navy 6.4.84
XE666	4/245/229 OCU	Sold 16.8.61 to HSA
XE667	4/98	Sold 23.3.61 to HSA
XE668	26	To Royal Navy 16.4.62 as GA.11
XE669	Mkrs & RAE/98	Jet pipe came loose; abandoned in
		in dive 1m SE of Jever, 4.12.56
XE670	26/93	To 7762M 28.3.63; later cockpit to
		8585M for display
XE671	54	Engine flamed out; abandoned
		2m E of Odiham, 1.5.56

XE672	112	SS 10.3.61
XE673	112/234	To Royal Navy 12.7.61 as GA.11
XE674	112	To Royal Navy 12.7.61 as GA.11
XE675	26/98/93/229 OCU	Sold 15.5.61 to HSA
XE676	222/FWS	Sold 30.8.61 to HSA
XE677	4/118/93/229 OCU	Sold to HSA 7.4.61; became
		GI airframe at Loughborough
XE678	222/FWS	To 7786M 18.6.63 at Halton;
		later to Swiss AF as J-4145
XE679	111/222	To 7787M 30.5.63 at Halton; later to
		Singapore as 541
XE680	130/234	To Royal Navy 16.4.62 as GA.11
XE681	66/FWS	SS 10.3.61
XE682	118	To Royal Navy 2.11.60 as GA.11
XE683	54/74	Sold 28.4.61 to HSA
XE684	98/4/118/93/	
	229 OCU	SS 10.3.61
XE685	98/93	To Royal Navy 4.4.62 as GA.11
XE686	AFDS/247/245/	
	229 OCU	Sold 30.8.61 to HSA
XE687	118/93/98	Sold 23.3.61 to HSA
XE688	222/74	SS 10.3.61
XE689	67/130/234	To Royal Navy 2.11.60 as GA.11
XE702	Hdlg Sqn/92/43	To 7794M 19.2.63 at Sealand; later
		to Swiss AF as J-4204
XE703	4/93/118	Sold 12.9.61 to HSA
XE704	112/CFS	To 7788M 12.7.63; later to
		Chilean AF as J-736
XE705	111/92/43	Ingested bird on take-off; overshot
		into mudflats, Leuchars, 3.10.56
XE706	66/92/43	Sold 14.3.61
XE707	118/93/98	To Royal Navy 17.1.61 as GA.11
XE708	14/229 OCU	SOC 23.4.63
XE709	222/43	Sold 14.3.61 to HSA
XE710	14	Sold 23.3.61 to HSA
XE711	RAFFC	Sold 16.8.61 to HSA
XE712	222/43	To Royal Navy 31.5.61 as GA.11
XE713	66	Sold 29.3.61 to HSA
XE714	67/WL Bruggen/	
	67/112/234	Sold 21.7.61 to HSA
XE715	3/130/112	To 7807M 30.5.63; SS 9.9.63
XE716	65/112	To Royal Navy 28.8.61 as GA.11
XE717	67/112/234	To Royal Navy 16.4.62 as GA.11
XE718	93/98	Sold 12.7.61 to HSA

* * * * * * * * * *

XE722 - XE735;		ML-120D targets to Contract
XE749 - XE754		6/Acft/5535
XE758 - XE762;		Slingsby Cadet gliders for ATC
XE784 - XE812		to Contract 6/Acft/9708

* * * * * * * * * *

135 de Havilland Vampire T.11s delivered between June 1954 and July 1955 by D.H., Christchurch, Hatfield and Hawarden to Contract 6/Acft/9751

XE816	-	To SRAF 2.3.55 as SR116
XE817	-	To SRAF 2.3.55 as SR117
XE818	-	To SRAF 2.3.55 as SR118
XE819	-	To SRAF 28.1.55 as SR122
XE820	4 FTS/CNCS	SS 5.10.60
XE821	4 FTS/1 FTS/	
	5 FTS/4 FTS	SS 31.3.65
XE822	4 FTS	To 7585M 27.8.58 at Swinderby
XE823	-	To SRAF 28.3.55 as SR119
XE824	-	To SRAF 28.3.55 as SR120
XE825	-	To SRAF 28.3.55 as SR121
XE826	-	To SRAF 28.1.55 as SR123

Serial	Units	Fate
XE827	4 FTS/7 FTS/8 FTS	Engine blew up in air and controls jammed; forcelanded, Weston-super-Mare, 14.7.60; not repaired
XE828	4 FTS/7 FTS/4 FTS	Undercarriage jammed; bellylanded, Worksop, 25.4.57; to 7461M
XE829	4 FTS/7 FTS	SS 5.10.60
XE830	4 FTS/1 FTS	Flew into ground after night take-off 1½m SW of Linton-on-Ouse, 30.12.59
XE831	CFS	SS 3.6.65
XE832	4 FTS	Abandoned after false fire warning and crashed, Stocksfield, Northumberland, 24.5.55
XE833	229 OCU	SS 5.3.64
XE848	4 FTS/3 CAACU	Abandoned take-off and over-shot runway, Exeter, 29.6.61; not repaired
XE849	4 FTS/1 FTS/7 FTS/ CNCS/CATCS/ 3 CAACU	To 7928M 13.10.66 at St Athan
XE850	4 FTS/7 FTS/4 FTS	SOC 31.7.58
XE851	4 FTS/7 FTS/4 FTS/ 7 FTS/8 FTS/5 FTS/ CNCS/CATCS	SOC 21.1.66; to Catterick for fire practice
XE852	4 FTS/1 FTS	Sold 30.10.67 as GI airframe to HSA
XE853	4 FTS/7 FTS/8 FTS	SS 30.6.64
XE854	4 FTS/1 FTS	Dived into ground out of cloud, Parkgate, near Rotherham, Yorks., 9.3.59
XE855	AWOCU	Sold 30.10.67 to HSA
XE856	226 OCU/SF North Weald/219	Sold 30.10.67 to HSA
XE857	4 FTS/7 FTS/5 FTS/ 4 FTS/1 FTS/7 FTS/ 3 FTS/CATCS	8125M NTU; to Chilean AF 10.11.72
XE858	SF Middleton St. George/4 FTS/ 1 FTS	SS 5.3.63
XE859	APS Acklington/ SF Stradishall/ CFS	SS 21.4.64
XE860	228 OCU/ 3-4 CAACU	Sold 6.1.72 to Exeter Airport
XE861	228 OCU	SS 13.5.63
XE862	4 FTS/7 FTS/8 FTS	SS 5.3.64
XE863	4 FTS/7 FTS/ 5 FTS/DH	SS 5.10.60
XE864	4 FTS/CFS/1 ANS/ 7 FTS/8 FTS	Sold 12.12.69 to HSA
XE865	4 FTS	Engine cut on take-off; bellylanded 3½m WSW of Middleton St.George, 14.10.55
XE866	4 FTS	Flew into ground descending in cloud, Stanage Edge, 6m N of Hathersage, Derbyshire, 8.8.57
XE867	233 OCU	SS 27.2.61
XE868	111/ITS West Raynham/54	SS 23.7.63
XE869	APS Acklington/ 2 CAACU	SS 15.10.60
XE870	226 OCU/North Weald/502	SS 30.6.66
XE871	APS Acklington	SS 30.6.60
XE872	CFS/7 FTS/8 FTS/ 3-4 CAACU/5 FTS	Sold 17.11.67 to HSA
XE873	4 FTS/7 FTS/ 4 FTS/RAFC	SS 31.3.65
XE874	7 FTS/4 FTS/7 FTS/ 8 FTS/4 FTS/1 FTS	Sold 30.10.67 to HSA; later to 8582M at Valley
XE875	4 FTS/RAFC/ 7 FTS/8 FTS	SS 3.6.65
XE876	247/SF Odiham/ CFS	SS 5.3.64
XE877	229 OCU/RAFC	SS 5.10.60
XE878	4 FTS	SS 21.4.64
XE879	ITS W.Raynham/ 229 OCU/ITS W. Raynham	SS 5.3.64
XE880	4 FTS	Undercarriage leg collapsed on landing, Worksop, 6.9.57; not repaired
XE881	11 FTS/8 FTS/ 5 FTS/8 FTS	SS 3.6.65
XE882	DH/7 FTS/1 FTS	Abandoned in spin 3m S of Aysgarth, Yorks., 23.1.61
XE883	AWOCU/8 FTS	Lost power on take-off and flew into rising ground, Swinderby, 10.6.60
XE884	7 FTS/25 Gp CF/ 7 FTS/5 FTS/4 FTS	SS 2.2.67
XE885	4 FTS/7 FTS	SS 23.7.63
XE886	34/ITS W.Raynham/ 2 CAACU	SS 5.10.60
XE887	4 FTS/7 FTS/4 FTS/ RAFC/3 CAACU	To 7824M 7.11.63 at 115 Sqn ATC at Orton, Peterborough
XE888	AWOCU/238 OCU/ 43/3-4 CAACU	SS 13.5.63
XE889	SF Nicosia/ Levant CF/208	SS 5.10.60
XE890	233 OCU/8 FTS/ 1 FTS	To 7871M 28.1.65 at Sealand
XE891	CFS/2 TAF CS	SS 7.3.64
XE892	253	Abandoned after engine explosion, Mount Pleasant Farm, Stowuplands, Suffolk, 28.4.57
XE893	Hdlg Sqn/CFS/ 8 FTS	Sold 9.12.68 to BEA
XE894	AWOCU/ITS West Raynham/IRS	SS 30.6.64
XE895	608/603/222/19/ SF Church Fenton	SS 10.10.60
XE896	23/141/FWS/ FLS/IRS	SS 30.6.60
XE897	43/5 FTS	Collided with WZ495 during formation aerobatics 4½m W of Oakington, 15.10.59; not repaired
———		
XE919	AAFCE/CNCS/ CATCS	Sold 3.2.71 to Brooklands College
XE920	AAFCE/5 FTS/ 8 FTS/CATCS	To 8196M 15.3.72; to RAF Museum 27.6.72
XE921	CFS/1 FTS/ 3-4 CAACU	Sold 16.12.71 to Exeter Airport
XE922	11 FTS/4 FTS	Overstressed in spin, 1.5.57; SOC
XE923	226 OCU/229 OCU	To 7446M 20.6.57 at 248 Sqn ATC Letchworth
XE924	257/SF Wattisham/ SF Stradishall/ RAFC/4 FTS/RAFC/ 1 FTS	SOC 16.7.63
XE925	151	SS 5.10.60
XE926	7 FTS	SOC 13.7.57
XE927	11 FTS/4 FTS/ 1 FTS/8 FTS	SOC 28.4.64
XE928	DH/74/3-4 CAACU	Sold 16.12.71 to Exeter Airport
XE929	SF West Malling/ 233 OCU	SS 27.2.61
XE930	RAFC	SS 18.2.63
XE931	11 FTS/8 FTS	SOC 5.7.57
XE932	11 FTS/8 FTS/ 1 FTS/7 FTS/ 3 FTS	To 7934M 10.2.67 at St Athan
XE933	RAFC	SS 13.5.63
XE934	APS Acklington/ 92/SF Middleton St.George	SS 30.6.60
XE935	8 FTS	Sold 8.11.67 to HSA

Vampire

XE936	RAFC	Collided with WR194 on overshoot ½m E of Cranwell, 31.1.59
XE937	RAFC	SS 23.7.63
XE938	-	To SRAF 8.6.55 as SR124
XE939	-	To SRAF 8.6.55 as SR125
XE940	-	To SRAF 8.6.55 as SR126
XE941	-	To SRAF 8.6.55 as SR127
XE942	16SF Celle//79/SF Wunstorf/SF Gutersloh	SS 6.3.64
XE943	APS Sylt	SS 6.3.64
XE944	11 FTS/8 FTS	Collided with WZ513 during formation loop and spun into ground 4m S of Binbrook, 24.3.61
XE945	2 TAF CS	Sold 9.7.63 for Indian AF
XE946	SF Nicosia/ SF Habbaniya	To 7473M 25.9.57 at 71 MU
XE947	APS Sylt	SOC 21.6.60
XE948	8 FTS	SOC 26.6.57
XE949	RAFC	SS 23.7.63
XE950	8/73	To 8175M 29.6.72 at Ottershaw School
XE951	8 FTS	SS 5.3.64
XE952	73	Engine lost power; abandoned after fire warning 2m NE of Xeros, Cyprus, 13.7.56
XE953	8 FTS	Engine shut down after fire warning; overshot landing and undercarriage raised to stop, Swinderby, 24.10.60
XE954	RAFC/1 FTS/5 FTS	SOC 16.9.63
XE955	54/SF Odiham	SS 11.7.60
XE956	67/APS Sylt/ 3 CAACU/8 FTS/ 1 FTS/CATCS	Sold 2.2.71 to St Albans College
XE957	14 RNZAF/28	To Indian AF 1.7.63
XE958	8 FTS	SS 21.4.64
XE959	8 FTS/5 FTS/ 8 FTS	SOC 28.6.56; to Little Rissington for fire practice
XE960	8	SOC 21.12.60;
XE961	8 FTS	Abandoned in inverted spin 4m N of Holbeach, Lincs., 1.11.55
XE975	8 FTS	SOC 3.6.65; to Woodvale for fire practice
XE976	8/73	SOC 12.8.57
XE977	8 FTS	To Irish Air Corps 29.7.63 as GI airframe 198
XE978	RAFC	Abandoned after controls failed; crashed ½m NNE of Bardney, Lincs., 25.3.57
XE979	RAFC/8 FTS/1 FTS	Sold 12.12.68 to HSA
XE980	SF Bruggen	SS 27.2.61
XE981	8 FTS	SS 2.2.67
XE982	RAFC	Hit by WL505 at dispersal, Cranwell, 21.9.56; to 7564M 15.5.58 at St Athan
XE983	6	Sold 26.6.63 to DH for Indian AF
XE984	SF Celle/145/SF Celle	SS 27.2.61
XE985	32/5 FTS	Sold 17.11.67 to HSA
XE986	8 FTS	Overstressed in dive, 13.5.57; SOC
XE987	8 FTS	SOC 8.6.64
XE988	8 FTS	SS 5.3.64
XE989	8 FTS	Engine caught fire; bellylanded at Swinderby, 12.12.55; to 7296M
XE990	8 FTS	Collided with XH321 4m S of Nottingham, 16.1.58
XE991	249/SF Eastleigh/142	SOC 21.12.60
XE992	6	SS 27.2.61
XE993	73/8	To 8161M 2.7.71 at Church Fenton
XE994	CFS	SS 30.6.64
XE995	32/5 FTS/8 FTS	Sold 9.12.68 at HSA
XE996	249/SF Eastleigh/142	SS 13.5.63
XE997	8 FTS/DH	SS 30.6.60
XE998	8 FTS/4 FTS/8 FTS	Sold 11.12.67 at HSA

* * * * * * * * * *

XF104 - XF109		Cancelled Swift F.4s to Contract 6/Acft/8509

* * * * * * * * * *

12 Supermarine Swift F.7s delivered in April and May 1957 to Contract No. 6/Acft/9757

XF113	VA/AAEE/ETPS	SOC 31.10.61 for spares
XF114	AAEE/VA/AAEE/ VA/C of Aeronautics	Sold to Flint Tech College Kelsterton, 14.4.67
XF115	GWDS	SOC 2.2.60
XF116	GWDS	SOC 2.2.60
XF117	GWDS	SOC 2.2.60
XF118	GWDS	SOC 2.2.60
XF119	GWDS	SOC 2.2.60
XF120	GWDS	SOC 2.2.60
XF121	GWDS	SOC 2.2.60
XF122	GWDS	SOC 2.2.60
XF123	GWDS	SOC 2.2.60
XF124	GWDS	SOC 2.2.60
XF125 to XF129	-	Cancelled
XF155 to XF180	-	Cancelled
XF196 to XF217	-	Cancelled
XF244 to XF253	-	Cancelled

* * * * * * * * * *

Three Westland Dragonfly HC.4s delivered in March and April 1954 to Contract No.6/Acft/9739

XF259	CFS	Engine cut; hit tree in forced landing 1m N of Calmsden, Glos., 15.5.58; SS 29.6.59
XF260	CFS	SS 11.9.63
XF261	CFS	SS 11.9.63

* * * * * * * * * *

Five Bristol Sycamore HR.14s delivered between December 1954 and February 1955 to Contract No.6/Acft/9584

XF265	275	Engine cut; ditched off Bell Rock, 15m ENE of Leuchars, 10.7.56
XF266	194/110	SOC 30.6.67
XF267	194	Lost rotor blade and spun into ground 3½m N of Kuala Lumpur, Malaya, 27.4.59
XF268	SF Nicosia	Sank into ground on practice approach; heeled over and slid down slope, Mount Olympus, Cyprus, 8.7.55; DBR
XF269	SF Nicosia/ Levant CF/103/ CFS	Rolled over on take-off, Ternhill, 8.2.66; DBR

* * * * * * * * * *

Seven Gloster Meteor T.7s delivered between November 1953 and July 1954 to Contract No.6/Acft/6411

XF273	-	To Belgian AF 25.1.54 as ED-37
XF274	Mkrs & AAEE	To MoS 7.54. Control lost during single-engined overshoot; dived into ground, Farnborough, 14.2.75
XF275	-	To R.Neth.AF 6.1.55 as I-310 or I-317
XF276	-	To R.Neth.AF 3.11.54 as I-311 or I-312

XF277	-	To R.Neth.AF 3.11.54 as I-311 or I-312
XF278	-	To R.Neth.AF 9.12.54 as I-314
XF279	-	To R.Neth.AF 9.12.54 as I-313

* * * * * * * * * *

Two Avro Yorks allotted temporary serials:

XF284 G-AMUL   XF285 : G-AMUM

* * * * * * * * * *

50 Hawker Hunter F.4s delivered between November 1955 and March 1956 by Hawker, Blackpool to Contract No.6/Acft/9817

XF289	67	To Royal Navy 23.4.59 as T.8
XF290	67	Engine cut after take-off; abandoned and dived into ground, Bruggen, 14.8.56
XF291	67/112	To Royal Navy 16.4.62 as GA.11
XF292	130/112	Sold 10.5.61 to HSA
XF293	112/234	Sold 12.9.61 to HSA
XF294	130/112	SS 10.3.61
XF295	130/112	Sold 16.8.61 to HSA
XF296	112/67/130/234	Sold 16.8.61 to HSA
XF297	130/234	To Royal Navy 25.9.61 as GA.11
XF298	130/112	Sold 8.9.61 to HSA
XF299	43	Sold 16.8.61 to HSA
XF300	71/234/130	To Royal Navy 19.12.61 as GA.11
XF301	43/229 OCU	To Royal Navy 19.10.61 as GA.11
XF302	43	To 7774M 19.12.62 at Halton; later to Chilean AF as J-733
XF303	66	To Royal Navy 27.3.63 as GI airframe A2565; later to Swiss AF as J-4105
XF304	66/Caledonian Sector	SS 13.9.63
XF305	67	Caught fire starting up, Sylt, 28.11.56; not repaired
XF306	112/229 OCU	To 7776M 12.12.62 at Halton; later to Swiss AF as J-4133
XF307	112	To 8002M 14.3.68 at Cosford
XF308	130/229 OCU	To 7777M 27.12.62 at Halton; later to Swiss AF as J-4135
XF309	112/229 OCU	To 7771M 28.11.62 at St Athan; later to Kenyan AF as No.805 8.12.74
XF310	Mkrs/Cv.T.7/20/ MinTech/1-54/RN/ 45/58/45-58/TWU/ 2 TWU/Laarbruch	To Royal Navy 5.8.81
XF311	130/Cv T.7/ 3-4 CAACU/ 56/1417 Flt/8	To Royal Navy as GI airframe A2566
XF312	71/112/26	To 7848M 17.11.64 at Halton; later to Swiss AF as J-4150
XF313	71/112/CFS	SS 11.9.63
XF314	43/229 OCU	SS 9.9.63
XF315	118/WL Jever	SS 13.9.63
XF316	71/112/229 OCU	To 7778M 23.11.62 at Halton; later to Swiss AF as J-4134
XF317	67/229 OCU	To 7773M 1.12.62 at Halton; later to Chilean AF as J-734
XF318	130/229 OCU	To Royal Navy 17.3.63 as GI airframe A2567; later to Swiss AF as J-4110
XF319	66/112/229 OCU	To 7849M 11.11.64 at Halton
XF320	247/245/229 OCU	SS 13.9.63
XF321	130/Cv T.7/ 3-4 CAACU/ 56/1417 Flt/8	To Royal Navy 28.1.70 as T.7

XF322	112	To Royal Navy 15.4.59 as T.8
XF323	RAFFC	To 8003M 26.7.68 at Halton; later to Chilean AF as J-732
XF324	92/SF North Weald/ 222/SF North Weald	SS 9.9.63
XF357	130	To Royal Navy 29.5.59 as T.8C
XF358	112	To Royal Navy 21.7.59 as T.8C
XF359	130/3	SS 11.9.63
XF360	130/234/3/ 229 OCU	To 7942M 12.6.67 at Halton; later to Singapore as No.542
XF361	130/229 OCU	Sold 29.5.68; to Swiss AF as J-4117
XF362	112/71/3-4 CAACU	Sold 18.9.68; to Abu Dhabi as No.705
XF363	92/66/3/229 OCU	To Royal Navy 26.11.62 as GI airframe A2560
XF364	130/234/3/229 OCU/ 3-4 CAACU	Sold 5.6.68; to Jordanian AF as No.843
XF365	71/229 OCU	To Royal Navy 12.11.62 as GI airframe A2561; later to Swiss AF as J-4109
XF366	112/71/229 OCU	To 8004M 5.7.68 at Halton; later to Singapore as No.537
XF367	71/RAFFC	Sold 19.8.68; to Abu Dhabi as No.706
XF368	4/3/229 OCU	To Royal Navy 26.10.61 as GA.11
XF369	71/234/RAFFC	To 7941M 16.5.67 at Halton; later to Singapore as No.538
XF370	4/118/APS Sylt	To 7772M 26.11.62 at St Athan; later to Swiss AF as J-4136

* * * * * * * * * *

100 Hawker Hunter F.6s delivered between June 1955 and October 1956 by Armstrong Whitworth, Coventry, to Contract No.6/Acft/9818

XF373	-	To R.Jordanian AF 7.11.58 as 703
XF374	Mkrs	To R.Rhodesian AF 15.5.63 as No.127
XF375	-	MoS aircraft; to 8736M 1.82 at Cranwell
XF376	Hdlg Sqn/Cv FGA.9/ 208/8/208/8/208/ 229 OCU/TWU/ 2 TWU/1 TWU	Sold 5.82; to Chilean AF as No.741
XF377	AAEE	To Lebanese AF 3.11.58 as L-173
XF378	Mkrs	To MoS 30.4.56 for cv to P.1109B
XF379	Mkrs	To R.Jordanian AF 10.11.58 as L-705
XF380	Mkrs/AAEE	To R.Jordanian AF 10.11.58 as No.710
XF381	AAEE	To R.Jordanian AF 3.11.58 as No.702
XF382	92/63/65/FCS/ 229 OCU/TWU/ Cv F.6A/TWU/ 1 TWU	WFU 10.7.84; to Midland Air Museum, Coventry, 1.12.86
XF383	263/111/65/ 229 OCU/4 FTS/ 237 OCU/216/12	To 8706M 19.1.82 at Wittering
XF384	66/92/63/65/ DFLS/FCS/ 229 OCU/4 FTS	Collided with XF387 on approach and crashed 1m W of Valley, 10.8.72
XF385	66/92/63/65/ 229 OCU	Engine lost power; undershot landing and nosewheel collapsed, Chivenor, 20.2.63; to 7803M at Halton
XF386	66/92/63/65/ 229 OCU/4 FTS/ SF Laarbruch	To 8707M 15.12.81 at Coltishall

XF387	66/63/56/229 OCU/ 4 FTS	Collided with XF384 on approach to Valley and broke up Rhoscolyn, 1m W of Valley, 10.8.72
XF388	Mkrs/65/Cv FGA.9/ 54/208/8	Abandoned after engine failure 50m SE of Dubai, 26.6.68
XF389	92/63/65/DFLS/ 63/56/229 OCU/ 54/229 OCU	Sold 23.5.68; to R.Jordanian AF as No.829
XF414	63/56/Cv FGA.9/ 20	Engine lost power; abandoned near Layang, Malaya, 20.2.67
XF415	26	Sold 9.8.62; to R.Jordanian AF as 802
XF416	43/111/Cv FGA.9/ 20/TWU/2 TWU/ 1 TWU	To Zimbabwe AF 11.4.84 as 1098
XF417	14/26	Sold 3.10.62; to R.Jordanian AF as 810
XF418	FCS/229 OCU/ TWU/Cv F.6A/ TWU/1 TWU	To 8842M 6.12.84 at Wildenrath
XF419	74/Cv FGA.9/1/ 229 OCU/45/58/ TWU/1 TWU/ 2 TWU/1 TWU	To Zimbabwe AF 5.10.87 as 8112
XF420	DFLS/54/SF West Raynham/1/ 229 OCU	Abandoned after engine lost power near Exbourne, Devon, 27.7.73
XF421	247/54/Cv FGA.9/ 208/8/8&43/8	Lost power and overshot runway into sea, Khormaksar, 23.2.67
XF422	208/19/Cv FR.10/ 2	Sold 17.5.71; to Singapore as No.524
XF423	93	Sold 5.7.62; to R.Jordanian AF as 803
XF424	247/43/Cv FGA.9/ 8	Hit bird near Sharjah, 29.3.60; SOC 10.12.60 as DBR
XF425	74	Collided with XF502 and abandoned, Langley Street, Norfolk, 25.8.59
XF426	208/Cv FR.10/MoA/ 2/229 OCU	To R.Jordanian AF 22.3.72 as 853
XF427	54	Dived into ground 2m E of Yarmouth, Isle of Wight, 13.3.57; cause not known
XF428	34 & 208/Cv FR.10/ 4/2/4/2	Sold 21.5.71; to Singapore as No.525
XF429	Mkrs/Cv FR.10/ 1417 Flt/8	Sold 30.9.71; to Swiss AF as J-4131
XF430	43/111/Cv FGA.9/ 54/229 OCU/1/HCT	Sold 17.1.75; to Lebanese AF as L-283
XF431	54/66/Cv FGA.9/ 43/ 208/8-43/8/229 OCU/ 208/45/TWU/2 TWU/ 1 TWU	To BAe 21.4.87 for Zimbabwe AF 30.9.87 as 1180
XF432	34 & 208/Cv FR.10/ 2/4	Sold 17.5.71; to Singapore as No.526
XF433	263/SF Wattisham/ 19/65/229 OCU	Collided with XE594 during formation aerobatics and abandoned 2m N of Hartland, Point, Devon, 7.3.63
XF434	247/43	Engine flamed out; abandoned 15m SSE of Nicosia, 9.4.60
XF435	247/43/Cv FGA.9/ 43/8/8-43/8/208/ 229 OCU/TWU/ 1 TWU	To 8880M at St Athan
XF436	34 & 208/Cv FR.10/ 8/1417 Flt/8	Sold 28.2.70; to Swiss AF as J-4115
XF437	247/43/111/ Cv FGA.9/20	Sold 22.12.69; to Singapore as No.503
XF438	34 & 208/208/ Cv FR.10/4	Sold 4.6.70; to Swiss AF as J-4102
XF439	247/43/19/54/ 229 OCU/TWU/ Cv F.6A/TWU/ 1 TWU	To 8712M 21.1.82 at Abingdon
XF440	247/43/Cv FGA.9/ 8/8 & 43/43	Caught fire in air and abandoned, Al Ittihad, Qatar, 20.2.67
XF441	34 & 208/208/1/ Cv FR.10/2/1417 Flt/2/8	Sold 25.9.71; to Singapore as No.545
XF442	54/43/Cv FGA.9/1/ Mkrs/1/8/58/TWU/ 2 TWU/1 TWU	Sold 23.4.82; to Chilean AF as No.743
XF443	66/92/65/229 OCU	Engine flamed out; abandoned on approach and crashed on railway 3m SE of Chivenor, 3.8.67
XF444	AAEE	Sold 12.11.58; to R.Jordanian AF as No.709
XF445	263/1/Cv FGA.9/ 43/208/8/8-43/ 208/229 OCU/TWU/ 2 TWU/1 TWU	Sold 6.1.83 to Chilean AF as No.751
XF446	43/111/Cv FGA.9/ 54	Sold 5.6.68; to Indian AF as A1010
XF447	66/92/65/229 OCU	Sold 18.9.69; to Chilean AF as J-723
XF448	74	Dived into sea recovering from loop off Winterton, Norfolk, 21.8.58
XF449	19/AFDS	Caught fire taxying at Binbrook, 6.6.63; not repaired
XF450	FCS/74/CFCS/ 229 OCU	Sold 1.4.66; to Saudi AF as 60-603
XF451	247/43/65/92/ 229 OCU	Engine lost power; crashed into barrier during emergency landing, Chivenor, 12.7.62; not repaired
XF452	Mkrs	Sold 11.11.58; to Jordanian AF as No.708
XF453	247/54/AFDS/ FCS/DFCS	Sold 14.7.67; to Chilean AF as J-716
XF454	247/43/Cv FGA.9/ 1/208/8 & 43/8	Sold 26.1.68; to R.Jordanian AF as No.816
XF455	247/43/Cv FGA.9/ 8/28/20	Crashed into estuary in bad visibility 15m NE of Changi, 19.9.64
XF456	247/43/Cv FGA.9/ 8 & 43/43/229 OCU	Sold 10.10.69; to Singapore as No.509
XF457	34 & 208/66/ Cv FR.10/2/4	Sold 1.8.74; to Lebanese AF as L-281
XF458	34 & 208/Cv FR.10/ 2/4/2/4/2/4/2	Sold 15.5.71; to Singapore as No.527
XF459	34 & 208/ Cv FR.10/4/2	Sold 3.3.71; to Indian AF as S1393
XF460	Cv FR.10/8/ 1417 Flt/8	Sold 25.9.71; to Singapore as No.546
XF461	-	Sold 3.11.58; to Lebanese AF as L-171
XF462	66/Cv FGA.9/ 1/208/8	Sold 10.3.70; to Swiss AF as J-4107
XF463	-	Sold 24.10.57; to Indian AF as BA241
XF495	-	Sold to Lebanese AF 12.11.58 as L-175
XF496	-	Sold 12.11.58; to R.Jordanian AF as No.706
XF497	-	Sold 6.11.57; to Indian AF as BA242
XF498	-	Sold 12.11.58; to R.Jordanian AF as No.704
XF499	-	Sold 2.1.10.57; to Indian AF as BA243
XF500	-	Sold 27.9.57; to Indian AF as BA240
XF501	-	Sold 21.10.57; to Indian AF as BA244

Hunter

XF502	74	Collided with XF425 and dived into ground, Cantley, Norfolk, 25.8.59
XF503	-	Sold 21.10.57; to Indian AF as BA245
XF504	19/74	Sold 19.4.63; to R.Rhodesian AF as No.125
XF505	-	Sold 21.10.57; to Indian AF as BA246
XF506	263/111	Sold 12.3.63; to R.Rhodesian AF as No.119
XF507	66/65	Dived into ground, Thrapston, Northants., 30.5.60; cause obscure
XF508	19/AFDS/ Cv FGA.9/20	Abandoned after false fire warning 3½m E of Pontian, Johore, Malaya, 3.2.69
XF509	54/AFDS/MoA/ 4 FTS	To 8708M 21.12.81 at Chivenor
XF510	DFLS/SF North Weald/Metropolitan Sector/SF North Weald	Engine flamed out in circuit; flew into ground on approach and abandoned unsuccessfully, North Weald, 30.7.57
XF511	74/111/Cv FGA.9/ 208/43/8/208/ 229 OCU/TWU/ 1 TWU/2 TWU/ 1 TWU	To Zimbabwe AF 11.4.84 as 1805
XF512	DFLS/FWS/FCS/ 63/FCS/CFCS/ 229 OCU	Sold 2.12.69; to Chilean AF as No.725
XF513	54	Overshot landing and under-carriage raised to stop, Nicosia, 27.8.58; DBF
XF514	247/43/DFLS/ 229 OCU	Sold 18.9.67; to R.Jordanian AF as No.718
XF515	247/43/SF Khor-maksar/229 OCU/ TWU/Cv F.6A/ TWU/237 OCU	To 8830M 2.9.84 at Scampton
XF516	66/92/56/229 OCU/ TWU/Cv F.6A/TWU/ 1 TWU/2 TWU	To 8685M 14.4.81 at Cranwell
XF517	92/Cv FGA.9/54/ 1/54	Dived into sea during combat practice off Blakeney, Norfolk, 15.1.69; cause not known
XF518	66/92/56	Sold 7.9.62; to R.Jordanian AF as No.809
XF519	92166/Cv FGA.9/ 1/208/45/58/TWU/ 2 TWU/1 TWU	To Zimbabwe AF 11.4.84 as 8106
XF520	19/92	Sold 3.6.66; to R.Jordanian AF as No.814
XF521	92/66/92/229 OCU	Sold 7.9.67; to Indian AF as A938
XF522	92/66/92	SOC 8.1.63
XF523	54/Cv FGA.9/54	Dived into ground during roll, Benina, 24.6.63
XF524	54	Dived into ground 14m SE of Nicosia, 5.11.57; possibly due to turbulence in cloud
XF525	19	Collided with XE621 during formation aerobatics and hit ground, North Weald, 7.6.57
XF526	66/63/56/43/ 56/229 OCU/ 4 FTS/Laarbruch	To 8679M 9.11.81 at Halton
XF527	SF Linton/SF Church Fenton/19/CFE/ 4 FTS/Laarbruch	To 8680M 2.4.81 at Halton

* * * * * * * * * *

XF532	Serial temporarily allocated to Viking G-AJBU	
XF537	Serial temporarily allotted to Tudor G-AGRY	

* * * * * * * * * *

50 Percival Provost T.1s delivered between December 1954 and June 1955 to Contract No.6/Acft/9850

XF540	-	SOC 28.11.63
XF541	RAFC/6 FTS	SS 12.3.62
XF542	RAFC/CFS	Hit tree during tailchase, Bruern Abbey, 1½m S of Kingham, Oxon., 4.12.58
XF543	2 FTS/6 FTS/5 AEF	SS 28.11.63
XF544	22 FTS/1 FTS/ 6 FTS	Sold 15.7.63
XF545	2 FTS/6 FTS	To 7957M 16.6.67 at Finningley
XF546	RAFC/6 FTS	SS 12.3.62
XF547	Hdlg Sqn	Sold 15.7.63; to R.Malayan AF as FM1037
XF548	2 FTS/6 FTS	Sold 13.7.64
XF549	3 FTS/6 FTS	SS 13.7.64
XF550	3 FTS/7 FTS/ RAFFC/6 FTS/ CNCS/5 AEF	SS 13.7.64
XF551	-	SS 28.11.63
XF552	3 FTS	Ran into ditch in forced landing short of fuel 2½m SSE of Feltwell, 25.1.56
XF553	-	SS 28.11.63
XF554	RAFC/CNCS/ CATCS	Sold 14.11.68; to G-AWTD 6.11.68
XF555	1 FTS	To 8037M 28.11.68
XF556	3 FTS /CNCS	Sold 28.11.63
XF557	-	SS 28.11.63
XF558	GUAS/CFS/2 FTS/ RAFFC/CAW	To RMAF 12.6.68
XF559	3 FTS/1 FTS	SS 30.3.62
XF560	CFS/22 FTS/1 FTS	SS 12.3.62
XF561	3 FTS/6 FTS	SS 12.3.62
XF562	3 FTS /CNCS	SS 1.11.61
XF563	CFS/2 FTS	SS 13.10.60
XF564	-	SS 28.11.63
XF565	CFS	SS 12.3.62
XF591	-	Sold 9.2.65
XF592	3 FTS/1 FTS/ 3 FTS/1 FTS	SS 12.3.62
XF593	3 FTS/1 FTS/ 3 FTS/CNCS	SS 24.8.60
XF594	3 FTS/1 FTS	SS 24.8.60
XF595	3 FTS/1 FTS/ 3 FTS/1 FTS	SS 30.3.62
XF596	3 FTS/6 FTS	SOC 21.7.59
XF597	RAFC/RAFFC/ CAW	Sold 22.11.67 to Flint Tech College
XF598	3 FTS/6 FTS	Engine cut in circuit; overshot down-wind landing and stalled into ground, Ternhill, 17.6.57; 7466M NTU
XF599	3 FTS/1 FTS/3 FTS/ 2 FTS/1 FTS	SS 12.3.62
XF600	CFS/2 FTS	SS 2.5.60
XF601	2 FTS/1 FTS	To RMAF 12.6.68
XF602	2 FTS/6 FTS/Ouston	Sold 28.11.63
XF603	RAFC/RAFFC/CAW	Sold 12.9.67
XF604	CFS	SS 12.3.62
XF605	CFS	SS 13.10.60
XF606	CFS	Sold to Hunting 28.11.63
XF607	CFS/6 FTS	SS 12.3.62
XF608	6 FTS/CNCS/CAW	To 7954M 28.6.67
XF609	CFS	SS 12.3.62

Provost

XF610	QUAS/HC Exam Unit/3 FTS/7 FTS/ RAFFC	Sold to Hunting 28.11.63
XF611	22 FTS/1 FTS	Stalled on approach and dived into ground, Spitalgate, 24.8.56; 7381M NTU
XF612	RAFC/CNCS/6 FTS	SS 13.7.64
XF613	3 FTS/1 FTS	Sold to Hunting 15.7.63
XF614	Glasgow UAS/CFS	Overshot and nosed over on landing, Little Rissington, 15.8.60

* * * * * * * * * *

Temporary serials allotted to civil aircraft

XF619	DC-3 G-AMYX	XF623	DC-3 G-AMYV
XF629	Viking G-AJBO	XF630	Viking G-AIVO
XF631	Viking G-AHPO	XF632	Viking G-AHPM
XF633	Viking G-AJCD	XF638	Viking G-AHPB
XF639	Viking G-AGRP	XF640	Viking G-AGRW
XF645	DC-3 G-AMVC	XF646	DC-3 G-AMSF
XF647	DC-3 G-AMVB	XF648	DC-3 G-AMSH (in error)
XF650	Freighter G-AMWA	XF651	Freighter G-AMWB
XF652	Freighter G-AMWC	XF653	Freighter G-AMWD
XF654	Freighter G-AMWE	XF655	Freighter G-AMWF
XF656	Freighter G-AGVB	XF657	Freighter G-AGVC
XF658	Freighter G-AHJP	XF659	Freighter G-AICS
XF660	Freighter G-AIFM	XF661	Freighter G-AIFV
XF662	Freighter G-AIME	XF663	Freighter G-AIMH
XF667	DC-3 G-AMSH		

Freighter: XF650 and XF661 not used

* * * * * * * * * *

Two Boulton Paul Balliol T.2s delivered in October 1953 by Boulton Paul, Wolverhampton, to Contract 6/Acft/4869

XF672	238 OCU	SS 3.9.57
XF673	238 OCU	SS 3.9.57

* * * * * * * * * *

16 Percival Provost T.1s delivered between March and May 1955 to Contract 6/Acft/9850

XF678	CFS	SS 12.3.62
XF679	HCCS/1 FTS/CFS	To RMAF 12.6.68
XF680	CFS	SS 28.11.63
XF681	Glasgow UAS/CFS	SS 12.3.62
XF682	-	To Muscat & Oman 2.3.59
XF683	-	To Muscat & Oman 27.3.59
XF684	Manchester UAS/ RAFC/CNCS/ 6 FTS	Collided with XF903 while overshooting at night and crashed 1½m W of Ouston, 14.8.62
XF685	ETPS	To MoA 20.1.60; became G-AWPI 6.9.68
XF686	-	SS 28.11.63
XF687	RAFC	Control lost during practice forced landing; hit ground and caught fire, Ingoldsby, Lincs., 21.7.58
XF688	-	To Muscat & Oman 2.3.59
XF689	RAE	To 8038M 26.11.68
XF690	QUAS/64 Gp CF/ CNCS/CATCS	8041M NTU To RAF Museum 25.11.68
XF691	RAFC/CNCS/ CATCS	Sold 14.11.68; regd G-AWTE 8.11.68
XF692	6 FTS	SS 12.3.62
XF693	2 FTS/CNCS/ CATCS	Sold 14.11.68; regd G-AWTC 8.11.68

* * * * * * * * * *

13 Avro Shackleton MR.3s delivered between August 1958 and May 1959 to Contract 6/Acft/6408

XF700	120/Avro/AAEE/206/ 201/206/201/Kinloss/ 203	SOC 26.10.71; to Nicosia for fire practice
XF701	120/AAEE/206/201/ 206/Kinloss/42	SOC 13.8.71; to Manston for fire practice
XF702	203/120/206/ AAEE/206/120	Dived into ground out of cloud, Creag Bhan, Lochailort, Inverness, 21.12.67; presumed iced up
XF703	203/120/203/206/ 201/MoA/120/ Kinloss/42	8168M NTU To RAF Museum 23.9.71
XF704	203/120/201	Flew into sea at night 8m N of Kinloss, 8.12.65
XF705	203/120/203/201/ 206/HSA&AAEE/ Kinloss/42	SOC 20.8.71; to Manston for fire practice
XF706	203/120/203/201/ 42/206/42	To 8089M 6.3.70; to St Mawgan for fire practice
XF707	201/206/42	SOC 28.4.71; to Benson for fire practice
XF708	201/120/HSA/203	To IWM Duxford, 23.8.72
XF709	201/120/203/HSA/ 201/Kinloss	SS 1.10.71
XF710	201/120	Engine caught fire at night; lost height and crashlanded, Smithton, Cullodin Moor, Inverness, 10.1.64; DBF
XF711 _____	201/Avro/AAEE/ HSA/AAEE/HSA/ 42/120/Kinloss/42	SOC 7.6.71; to Abingdon for fire practice
XF730	206/201/120/42	SOC 24.6.71; to Abingdon for fire practice
XF731 to XF734	-	Cancelled

* * * * * * * * * *

Temporary serials allotted to civil aircraft

Tudor I	XF739 : G-AGRI	
DC-3	XF746 : G-AMVL	XF747 : G-AMYJ
	XF748 : G-AMZG	XF749 : G-AMZF
	XF756 : G-AMPP	XF757 : G-AMJU
Viking	XF763 : G-AHPJ	XF764 : G-AHPC
	XF765 : G-AHOY	
DC-3	XF766 : G-AMSL	XF767 : G-AMNL
	XF768 : G-AMSJ	XF769 : G-AMSK

* * * * * * * * * *

Two Supermarine Swifts delivered in August 1956 to Contract 6/Acft/9929 for trials

XF774	AAEE/VA/AAEE/ ETPS	F.7; To structural test specimen at RAE 10.6.58; SOC 19.8.58
XF778	-	PR.6; cancelled 25.4.55
XF780	AAEE	PR.7; MoA aircraft; SOC 13.11.58

* * * * * * * * * *

XF785		Bristol Type 173 for trials; ex G-ALBN, became 7648M 7.60
XF791, XF792		Allotted to Dakotas G-ANAE, G-AMWX

* * * * * * * * * *

Swift FR.5 XD913 of No.79 Squadron formates with Hunter F.6s of Nos.14 and 26 Squadrons with the Mohne Dam in the background

Provost T.1s of the Central Flying School in formation, led by XF837. The CFS badge is carried on the cowling.

Shackleton MR.3 XF707 of No.206 Squadron over the Cornish coast. The squadron's octopus badge is on the fin while the Union Flag on the nose was used when aircraft were engaged on a 'flag-showing' tour.

Hunter FGA.9 XG254 of No.54 Squadron on the flight-line at West Raynham in 1960. With No.1 Squadron, No.54 was at this time part of No.38 Wing, Transport Command, tasked to provide ground-attack capability with bombs and rockets and to give fighter cover to transport aircraft and helicopters when deployed overseas.

Belvedere HC.1 XG453 of No.66 Squadron on a supply flight to Tepo, Borneo, in 1965, while supporting Malaysian forces during the Indonesian attempt to seize territory from Malaysia.

The Far East Air Force provided air support and transport aircraft and flew fighter cover over Malaysia until the Indonesians finally gave up their attempts.

Javelin FAW.9 XH793 of No.23 Squadron armed with Firestreak missiles.

Many Javelin FAW.9s had flight refuelling probes carried on the port side below the cockpit but XH793 was not fitted with one when this photograph was taken.

**Four Percival Pembroke C(PR).1s delivered in July and August 1956
to Contract 6/Acft/10009**

XF796	81/NCS/RAFG CS/ NCS/WCS/AAFCE CS/60	To 8461M 24.11.75; later to G-BFKK
XF797	81/18 Gp CF/NCS	SOC 16.12.71
XF798	267/209/18 Gp CF/ SF St.Mawgan/ WCS/SCS/207	SOC 21.6.72
XF799	2 TAF CS/RAFG CS/60	To 9043M 5.90; NTU and sold 4.91 to USA as N4273C

*　*　*　*　*　*　*　*　*　*

XF804 – XF823		Kenya Police Air Wing civil aircraft
XF828		Third prototype DH.110 Sea Vixen 20X to Contract 6/Acft/10224 for trials
XF833		Prototype Hunter F.6 to Contract 6/Acft/10032 for Ministry of Aviation trials

*　*　*　*　*　*　*　*　*　*

**66 Percival Provost T.1s delivered between June 1955 and March 1956
to Contract 6/Acft/10088**

XF836	Mcr UAS/RAFC/ CNCS/CATCS	To 8043M 6.1.69; Shuttleworth Trust 18.4.69; became G-AWRY 29.10.81
XF837	CFS	Sold to RMAF 12.6.68
XF838	Mcr UAS/RAFC/ CNCS/CATCS	Sold 14.11.68; regd G-AWTB 8.11.68
XF839	6 FTS/RAFFC/CAW	To RMAF 12.6.68
XF840	RAFC/CNCS	SOC 29.5.61
XF841	RAFC/CNCS/CFS	To 8039M 26.11.68
XF842	1 FTS	SS 13.7.64
XF843	3 FTS/7 FTS/ RAFFC/CAW	Sold to BAC 18.1.68
XF844	6 FTS	To MoA 3.2.63
XF845	-	To Hunting 15.7.63 for RMAF as FM1038
XF846	-	To Hunting 8.8.63
XF847	-	To Hunting 15.7.63 for RMAF as FM1039
XF848	-	To Hunting 15.7.63 for RMAF as FM1040
XF849	-	Direct to RRAF as No.140
XF850	-	Direct to RRAF as No.141
XF851	-	Direct to RRAF as No.142
XF852	-	Direct to RRAF as No.143
XF853	-	To Hunting 15.7.63 for RMAF as FM1043
XF854	-	To Hunting 15.7.63 for RMAF as FM1044
XF868	-	To Muscat & Oman 4.10.60
XF869	1 FTS	Swung on landing and under-carriage collapsed, Rufforth, 4.6.58
XF870	-	Direct to RRAF as No.144
XF871	-	Direct to RRAF as No.145
XF872	-	Direct to RRAF as No.146
XF873	-	Direct to RRAF as No.147
XF874	3 FTS/7 FTS/ RAFFC/CAW	To RMAF 24.5.67
XF875	1 FTS/Ouston	SS 13.7.64
XF876	2 FTS	SS 10.8.62
XF877	RAFC/CNCS	Sold 13.11.68; regd G-AWVF 28.11.68
XF878	-	Direct to RRAF as No.148
XF879	-	Direct to RRAF as No.148
XF880	-	Direct to RRAF as No.150
XF881	-	Direct to RRAF as No.151

XF882	RAFC	Abandoned in inverted spin and crashed 1½m E of London-thorpe, Lincs., 4.5.59
XF883	1 FTS	Sold to BAC 31.10.66
XF884	RAFC	Swung on landing and undercarriage collapsed, Barkston Heath, 24.9.59
XF885	3 FTS/2 FTS/1 FTS	Sold to BAC 31.10.66
XF886	RAFC/CNCS/ CATCS	Sold to Airwork 24.1.69 to R Saudi AF as GI airframe
XF887	Mcr UAS/6 FTS/ RAFFC/CAW	To Kenya 2.11.64 as 969
XF888	Mcr UAS/6 FTS/ 23 Gp CF/5 AEF	SS 13.7.64
XF889	Mcr UAS/1 FTS	SS 12.3.62
XF890	Mcr UAS/2 FTS/ CNCS	SS 28.11.63
XF891	Glasgow UAS/CFS	SS 10.8.62
XF892	CFS/5 AEF	SS 13.7.64
XF893	RAFC/6 FTS	Control lost at night; dived into ground out of cloud, Great Witley, Worcs., 7.2.61
XF894	1 FTS/Ouston/ RAFFC/CAW	Sold to BAC 18.1.68
XF895	CFS	Hit snow bank during night landing and undercarriage collapsed, Little Rissington, 21.2.63
XF896	1 FTS/6 FTS/CFS	To RMAF 12.6.68
XF897	Glasgow UAS/CFS/ 2 FTS	SS 12.3.62
XF898	RAFC/CFS	Sold 1.11.67 to Southall Tech Coll
XF899	RAFC	Engine cut; lost speed avoiding wires, hit ground and under-carriage collapsed 3m SE of Barkston Heath, 25.11.57
XF900	RAFC/CFS	SOC 22.11.63
XF901	RAFC	Engine overspeeded; stalled during forced landing, Welby, 2m NE of Spitalgate, 31.5.60
XF902	6 FTS	Engine failed to pick up; hit railway signal, bounded and undercarriage collapsed 1m N of Ternhill, 11.4.57; 7425M NTU
XF903	1 FTS/6 FTS	Collided with XF684 after night take-off, Ouston, 14.8.62
XF904	3 FTS/7 FTS/ RAFFC/CNCS	SS 12.3.62
XF905	6 FTS	SS 28.11.63
XF906	RAFC/6 FTS	Sold to Hunting 13.7.64
XF907	RAFC/RAFFC/ RAFC/6 FTS/ 11 AEF	To Muscat & Oman 17.5.65
XF908	-	Sold to Alvis 14.9.56; became G-ASMC
XF909	ULAS/HC Exam Unit/ULAS/ Glasgow UAS/ CFS/2 FTS	SS 12.3.62
XF910	3 FTS/7 FTS/ RAFFC/CNCS	SS 12.3.62
XF911	3 FTS/CFS	SS 12.3.62
XF912	3 FTS/7 FTS/ RAFFC/CNCS/Mkrs	SS 10.5.62
XF913	ULAS/Glasgow UAS/CFS	SS 12.3.62
XF914	ULAS/GUAS/ CFS/FTC CS	Sold 28.3.61; to Connah's Quay

*　*　*　*　*　*　*　*　*　*

XF919		Temporary serial for York G-AMUS

XF923, XF926   Bristol Type 188 research
aircraft for Ministry of Aviation to
Contract 6/Acft/10144.
XF926 preserved as 8368M

*   *   *   *   *   *   *   *   *   *

Three Boulton Paul Balliol T.2s delivered in May and June 1954 to Contract 6/Acft/6251

XF929	238 OCU	SS 26.6.57
XF930	238 OCU/Colerne/ 238 OCU	SS 3.9.57
XF931	238 OCU/Colerne/ 238 OCU/288	To 7654M 28.7.60 at St Athan

*   *   *   *   *   *   *   *   *   *

55 Hawker Hunter F.4s delivered between March and July 1956 by Hawker, Blackpool, to Contract 6/Acft/10344

XF932	234	Engine lost power; undershot forced landing and under-carriage torn off, Kleine Broghel, 22.9.56
XF933	71/CFS	To 7904M 17.3.66 at Cranwell; later to Swiss AF as J-4132
XF934	234/CFS	SS 9.9.63
XF935	234/CFS	Sold 4.9.68; to Abu Dhabi AF as No.707
XF936	234	Sold 16.11.67; to RJAF as No.844
XF937	112/71/130/ 234/RAFFC	Sold 7.10.68; to Swiss AF as J-4116
XF938	71/229 OCU	To RN as T.8C 13.2.63
XF939	71/229 OCU/ 3-4 CAACU	To RN as T.8C 16.5.63
XF940	71/74/ETPS	Ran out of fuel and crashed on approach, Farnborough, 13.10.61
XF941	71/229 OCU	To 8006M 14.3.68 at 2030 Sqn ATC Elmdon; later to Swiss AF as J-4139
XF942	71/229 OCU	To RN as T.8C 30.1.63
XF943	234/CFS	Lost hydraulic power; overshot landing into wall, Kemble, 27.6.62
XF944	234/CFS	To 7907M 25.3.66 at Cranwell; later to Swiss AF as J-4142
XF945	234	Engine flamed out; abandoned 15m SE of Aachen, 20.11.56
XF946	234/3	To 7804M 20.5.63 at Bicester for exhibition purposes
XF947	3/229 OCU	To RN 21.2.65 as GI airframe A2568; later to Swiss AF as J-4104
XF948	3/229 OCU	Engine caught fire during air-to-air firing; abandoned 10m N of Lundy Island, 7.11.57
XF949	3	Caught fire starting up, Geilen-kirchen, 11.1.57; not repaired
XF950	234/WL Geilen-kirchen/ 3	To 7956M 28.6.67 at Halton; later to Singapore ADC as No.536
XF951	3/229 OCU	To 7947M 1.6.67 at St Athan; later to Swiss AF as J-4202
XF952	234/229 OCU/ 3-4 CAACU	Sold 17.7.68; to RJAF as No.848
XF953	RAFFC	Damaged by bird strike, 10.11.59; not repaired
XF967	3/229 OCU/Cv T.8C 12/237 OCU/SF Honington/237 OCU/ 12/237 OCU/208/ 237 OCU	To RN but returned to RAF 9182M NTU To 9186M at Cranwell

XF968	3/229 OCU	Sold 24.7.68; to RJAF as No.847
XF969	3/ETPS	To 7935M 19.5.67 at Halton; later to Singapore ADC as No.529
XF970	130/234/26/ 229 OCU	To 7936M 19.5.67 at Halton; later to Singapore ADC as No.528
XF971	3/3-4 CAACU	Sold 1.10.68; to Abu Dhabi as No.709
XF972	3/26/229 OCU	To 7948M 1.6.67 at St Athan; later to Kenya AF as No.804
XF973	92/66/71/CFS	To 7908M 21.4.66 at Cranwell; later to Swiss AF as J-4143
XF974	3/26/229 OCU	To 7949M 1.6.67 at St Athan
XF975	3/229 OCU	To 7945M 1.6.67 at St Athan; later to Kenya as 806
XF976	3/229 OCU	To RN 3.12.62 as GI airframe A2569; later to Swiss AF as J-4112
XF977	118/APS Sylt	To RN as GA.11, 26.10.61
XF978	20/26/229 OCU	To RN as T.8B, 17.1.63
XF979	RAFFC	To RN as A2587; later sold 28.10.68; to RJAF as No.850
XF980	CFS	Abandoned after collision with Javelin XA644, Wotton-under-Edge, Glos. 24.8.56
XF981	71/RAFFC	Sold 16.11.67; to Swiss AF as J-4114
XF982	43/229 OCU/ 3-4 CAACU	To 7946M 1.6.67 at St Athan; later to Chilean AF as J-738
XF983	26/WL Oldenburg/ 26/229 OCU	To RN as T.8C 16.5.63
XF984	4/71/229 OCU	To RN 3.12.62 as GI airframe A2570; later to Swiss AF as J-4113
XF985	71/26/229 OCU	To RN as T.8C 24.1.63
XF986	112/234/229 OCU	Abandoned in spin and crashed Sutcombe, Devon, 7.8.59
XF987	93/118/229 OCU/ 3-4 CAACU	Sold 10.7.68; to RJAF as No.842
XF988	RAFFC	SS 13.9.63
XF989	26/229 OCU	SS 9.9.63
XF990	3/WL Geilenkirchen/ 3/229 OCU	To 8007M 21.3.68 at Catterick; later to Swiss AF as J-4141
XF991	234/229 OCU	To RN as T.8C 13.3.63
XF992	43/229 OCU	To RN as T.8C 19.4.63
XF993	SF Leuchars/43/ 229 OCU/74	SOC 15.7.60; to Horsham St Faith for fire practice
XF994	66/AFDS/R-R/ AFDS/229 OCU	To RN as T.8C 23.5.63
XF995	247/245/229 OCU/ 237 OCU/SF Honington/237 OCU/ SF Laarbruch/12	To 9237M 28.3.94 at Cranwell
XF996	98/229 OCU	Ailerons jammed on approach; abandoned, Chivenor, 6.5.59
XF997	43	Hit birds and lost power; forcelanded in mudflats 1m S of Leuchars, 28.6.57
XF998	54/247/245/ 229 OCU	To 7950M 1.6.67 at St Athan; later to Swiss AF as J-4140
XF999	CFS	Undercarriage jammed; rolled on approach and abandoned 3m E of Kemble, 24.10.56

*   *   *   *   *   *   *   *   *   *

110 Hawker Hunter F.6s delivered between August 1956 and February 1957 by Hawker, Kingston, and Armstrong Whitworth (XG150 to XG168), Bitteswell, to Contract 6/Acft/10345

XG127	66/63/Cv FR.10/2	Sold 14.1.69; to Swiss AF as J-4101

XG128	DFLS/65/ Cv FGA.9/8	Flew into rising ground, Wadi Yahar, Aden, 13.1.61
XG129	43/111/229 OCU	Sold 7.9.67; to Indian AF as A936
XG130	66/63/56/Cv FGA.9/ 54/1/SF West Raynham/ 208/45	Abandoned in cloud, Melton Mowbray, Leics., 17.6.74
XG131	14/229 OCU	Flew into high ground in cloud, Hill Farm, Davebrook Valley, Hawkridge, Devon, 19.3.71
XG132	AFDS	To RJAF 9.8.62 as 804
XG133	19	Stalled into ground after take-off and blew up, Duxford, 7.9.58
XG134	63/56/Cv FGA.9/208	Flew into ground recovering from dive in haze, Mutla Ridge, Kuwait, 11.7.61
XG135	19/Cv FGA.9/8/ 8-43/208/HCT/8/45	Abandoned after fire warning and crashed, Southey Wood, 2m E of Wittering, 6.4.73
XG136	AFDS/19/Cv FGA.9/ 8/43	Drop tank broke away during recovery from dive; rolled into ground, Haref, Aden, 17.4.64
XG137	DFLS/FWS/FCS/54/ 92/229 OCU	To RJAF 19.1.68 as No.813
XG150	-	Sold 6.11.57; to Indian AF as BA247
XG151	54/Cv FGA.9/ 54/ SF West Raynham/ 229 OCU/TWU/ 2 TWU	Engine flamed out on approach, abandoned, Lossiemouth, 3.4.81; to 8798M
XG152	DFLS/FWS/FCS/19/ 229 OCU/TWU/ Cv F.6A/TWU/ 1 TWU/237 OCU/ 1 TWU	To 8843M 23.1.85 at Gutersloh
XG153	19/92/66/Cv FGA.9/ 20	Sold 5.5.71; to Singapore ADC as No.520
XG154	66/Cv FGA.9/43/ 208/8/8-43/208/ 8-43/43/8/208/ 229 OCU	To 8863M 30.5.85 at RAF Museum
XG155	54/Cv FGA.9/54/ SF West Raynham/ SF Wittering/229 OCU/TWU/1 TWU/ 2 TWU/1 TWU	To Zimbabwe AF 11.4.84 as 1807
XG156	54/43/Cv FGA.9/54 229 OCU	Undercarriage jammed up; hit seawall on landing, Gibraltar, 9.10.71; DBR
XG157	56/1/229 OCU	Dived into ground out of cloud, Challacombe, 4m SSW of Lynton, N Devon, 16.6.66
XG158	DFLS/65/229 OCU/ 4 FTS/229 OCU/ TWU/4 FTS	To 8686M 14.4.81 at Farnborough
XG159	19/56/229 OCU	Sold 17.4.67; to RJAF as No.717
XG160	43/92/111/229 OCU/ TWU/Cv F.6A/TWU/ 1 TWU	To 8831M 2.9.84 at Scampton
XG161	DFLS/FCS/MinTech/ 229 OCU	Dived into sea during formation practice near Boscastle, Devon, 14.2.74
XG162	DFLS	Engine flamed out; abandoned on approach 1m S of West Raynham, 7.11.57
XG163	-	Sold 21.10.57; to Indian AF as BA248
XG164	111/74/1/SF West Raynham/Hdlg Sqn/ 229 OCU/4 FTS/ 229 OCU/TWU	To 8681M 2.4.81 at Halton
XG165	SF Middleton St. George	Engine flamed out; abandoned, Bowley, 2m N of Middlesbrough, Yorks., 18.4.58
XG166	14/229 OCU	Dived into sea out of cloud 4m N of Hartland Point, Devon, 17.2.64
XG167	19	To Lebanese AF as L-174, 31.10.58
XG168	208/66/Cv FR.10/ MoA/2/229 OCU	To RJAF 22.3.72 as 852
XG169	19/Cv FGA.9/8/208/ 8-43/208/8/229 OCU	Abandoned after engine cut, Holsworthy, Devon, 5.6.73
XG170	43/111/229 OCU	Sold 7.9.67; to Indian AF as A940
XG171	43/111/54/111	To R Jordanian AF 5.10.62 as 808
XG172	19/229 OCU/TWU/ Cv F.6A/TWU/ 1 TWU	To 8832M 2.9.84 at Scampton
XG185	19/CFE/4 FTS	Abandoned after fire in wing, Maltraeth Sands, Anglesey, 21.4.76
XG186	66/DFLS/FWS/ FCS/92	Sold 11.10.67; to Indian AF as A941
XG187	66/63/56	To R Jordanian AF 5.10.62 as No.811
XG188	19	Abandoned in spin, Thixendale, Yorks., 15.5.61
XG189	43/111/92	Sold 2.10.67; to Indian AF as A942
XG190	43/111/54/1/111/ 92/4 FTS	Sold 13.9.67; to Indian AF as A939
XG191	19/SF Leconfield/ 229 OCU/TWU/ Cv F.6A/TWU	Dived in sea after control lost 30m SW of Brawdy, 16.8.76
XG192	DFLS	Overshot abandoned take-off over embankment, Nicosia, 16.1.62
XG193	43/111	Collided with XG200 during aerobatic display and dived into ground near Wattisham, 10.6.60
XG194	43/111/92/Cv FGA.9/ 1/229 OCU/TWU/ 1 TWU	To 8839M 25.10.84 at Cosford
XG195	19/1/Cv FGA.9/ 1/208	Sold 12.2.76 to HAS as G-9-453
XG196	19/229 OCU/TWU/ Cv F.6A/TWU/ 1 TWU	To display airframe To 8702M 24.11.81 at Bracknell
XG197	DFLS/1/54/CFCS/ 229 OCU/Cv F.6A/ TWU/1 TWU	Abandoned after engine failure; crashed, Barras Nose, Tintagel, Cornwall, 6.7.79
XG198	263/111/63/74/ 92/229 OCU	Dived into ground 1m W of Kidwelly, Carmarthen, during practice on Pembrey ranges, 4.9.67
XG199	19/229 OCU	Sold 2.12.69; to Chilean AF as J-724
XG200	111/229 OCU	Collided with XG235 and dived into sea 3m WNW of Tintagel, Cornwall, 15.5.67
XG201	43/111/54/1/111/92/ MoA/54/229 OCU	Sold 7.9.67; to Indian AF as A937
XG202	66	Engine flamed out; abandoned 1¼m NNE of Morpeth, Northumberland, 13.12.57
XG203	111	Nosewheel collapsed on landing, overshot and broke up, North Weald, 30.4.57
XG204	FCS/DFCS/4 FTS	Flew into ground after take-off from Valley near Rhosneigr, Anglesey, 15.8.69

XG205	247/43/54/Cv FGA.9/8-43/208	Sold 1.4.70; to Singapore ADC as No.506
XG206	DFCS	Dived into sea out of cloud off St. Abbs Head, Berwickshire, 1.6.65
XG207	263/FWS/1/Cv FGA.9/1/MoA/54/ 229 OCU/45-58/ TWU/1 TWU/ 2 TWU/1 TWU	To Zimbabwe AF 11.4.84 as 1088
XG208	93/26	Engine lost power and radio failed; abandoned 3m W of Gutersloh, 24.3.59
XG209	DFLS/FCS/4 FTS/ 237 OCU/12	To 8709M 17.11.81 at Halton
XG210	14/19/CFE	To MoA 30.9.66; became GI airframe at RAE Apprentices School, Bedford 9.86
XG211	92/229 OCU	Sold 11.10.67; to Indian AF as A943
XG225	92/229 OCU/TWU/ Cv F.6A/TWU/ 237 OCU	To 8713M 15.2.82 at Cosford
XG226	92/66/92/229 OCU/ TWU/Cv F.6A/ TWU/1 TWU	To 8800M 15.2.83 at Catterick
XG227	92	Crashed in sea 5m E of Middlesbrough Bay, Yorks., 22.12.58; cause not known
XG228	92/Cv FGA.9/1/8/ 229 OCU/TWU/ 1 TWU	Sold to BAe 21.4.87; to Zimbabwe AF 30.9.87 as 1180
XG229	92/56/229 OCU/54/ 1/229 OCU	Abandoned after controls jammed, Moor Hill Farm, Merton, Devon, 27.8.71
XG230	92	Controls failed; abandoned and dived into ground, Easingwold, Yorks., 15.11.56
XG231	66/92	Sold 19.4.66; to RJAF as No.715
XG232	92/MoA	Sold 12.7.66; to Chilean AF as J-714
XG233	92/66	Flew into sea 6m SE of Famagusta, Cyprus, 20.8.58; cause not known
XG234	92	Sold 7.5.68; to RJAF as No.830
XG235	66/92/56/229 OCU	Collided with XG200 and abandoned in spin 3m WSW of Tintagel, Cornwall, 15.5.67
XG236	66	Control lost in cloud; dived into ground near Kielder Reservoir, Northumberland, 14.2.58
XG237	66/43/Cv FGA.9/8/ 8-43/208	Sold 25.10.67; to RJAF as No.828
XG238	66/92	Abandoned after fire warning over sea 2m off Pomos Point, Cyprus, 4.5.61
XG239	92	Abandoned take-off and under-carriage raised to stop, Nicosia, 11.1.58; DBF
XG251	66/14/Cv FGA.9/1	Sold 31.10.69; to Singapore ADC as No.507
XG252	66/Cv FGA.9/54/ MoA/54/8/45/ TWU/1 TWU/ 2 TWU/1 TWU	To 8840M 25.10.84 at Cosford
XG253	66/Cv FGA.9/1	Engine flamed out; abandoned 37m E of Khormaksar, 28.10.62
XG254	54/Cv FGA.9/Hdlg Sqn/54/229 OCU/ TWU/2 TWU/ 1 TWU	To 8881M 9.12.85 at Coltishall
XG255	66/43/Cv FGA.9/ 8/208/8-43	Sold to RJAF 7.9.67 as No.825
XG256	66/Cv FGA.9/43/8/ 8-43/208/43/208/ 8/208/229 OCU	Hit TV mast and abandoned, Caradon Hill, near Liskeard, Cornwall, 27.3.73

XG257	66/93	To RJAF 5.10.62 as No.812
XG258	93	Flew into ground during aerobatic display, Bitburg, 17.5.57
XG259	54	Collided with bus while taxying at night, Nicosia, 27.7.58; to RJAF as GI airframe 4.10.58
XG260	Cv FGA.9/54/MoA/ 54/ MinTech/ 229 OCU	Sold 1.10.69; to Singapore ADC as No.501
XG261	54/43/1/54/ Cv FGA.9/54/8&43/ 208/8/45/58/45/ TWU/2 TWU	Abandoned after control lost during combat practice near Dufftown, Banff, 25.5.80
XG262	4	Sold to R Jordanian AF 9.9.60 as No.712
XG263	4	To R Jordanian AF 5.7.62 as 805
XG264	54/Cv FGA.9/54/45/ 58/229 OCU/TWU/ 2 TWU	To 8715M 2.2.82 at Brawdy
XG265	66/Cv FGA.9/20	Caught fire in air and abandon-ed, Labuan, Borneo, 1.3.64
XG266	66/Cv FGA.9/20	Sold 5.5.71; to Singapore ADC as No.521
XG267	4	Sold to R.Jordanian AF 29.6.62 as No.801
XG268	4	Sold to R.Jordanian AF 7.9.62 as No.806
XG269	4	Sold to R.Jordanian AF 31.7.62 as No.807
XG270	4	Engine flamed out; forcelanded on beach with undercarriage partly down, Baltrum, Friesian Is., 31.5.57
XG271	54/Met Sector/54/ Cv FGA.9/54	Hit barrier during abandoned take-off, Sylt; caught fire, 13.7.61
XG272	93/Cv FGA.9/43/20	Sold 31.5.70; to Swiss AF as J-4111
XG273	54/66/Cv FGA.9/ 1/54	Collided with XF446 on app-roach to El Adem, abandoned 4m ESE of Tobruk, 18.4.67
XG274	14/229 OCU/4 FTS	To 8710M 30.11.81 at Halton
XG289	93	Lost hydraulics and abandoned take-off; overshot and hit trees 1½m ENE of Sylt, 29.11.57
XG290	AAEE	To MOD(PE) 1.3.71, ret'd 25.5.78;
	4 FTS/SF Laarbruch	To 8711M 20.10.81 at Halton
XG291	14/Cv FGA.9/28/20/ 45/58/229 OCU/ TWU/2 TWU/1 TWU	Sold 2.83; to Chilean AF as No.752
XG292	14/26/Cv FGA.9/ 43/208/8	Sold 1.4.70; to Singapore ADC as No.512
XG293	4/26/Cv FGA.9/ 43/20	Engine cut during aerobatics; abandoned over Tengah, 21.4.64
XG294	93/2	To RRAF 5.4.63 as No.122
XG295	14	To RRAF 2.3.63 as No.121
XG296	93/Cv FGA.9/43/ 8 & 43/43/229 OCU	Sold 23.10.69; to Singapore ADC as No.510
XG297	4/Cv FGA.9/ 20/28/20	Sold 12.2.76 to HAS; to G-9-452
XG298	4/Cv FGA.9/43/ 208/8 & 43	Sold 7.9.67; to R.Jordanian AF as No.826

* * * * * * * * * *

XG303		Saro Skeeter G-AMTZ for MoA trials at AAEE

* * * * * * * * * *

20 pre-production EEC Lightnings (P.1B) to Contract 6/Acft/10351 for Ministry of Aviation trials

XG307	Mkrs & AAEE	To MoA 30.10.59
XG308	Mkrs/AAEE/RAE	To MoA 25.3.59
XG309	Mkrs/AAEE/RAE	To MoA 28.1.60
XG310	Mkrs/AAEE/ Mkrs	Cv F.3 prototype To MoA 3.12.59
XG311	Mkrs & AAEE	Crashed on test flight in Ribble Estuary, Lancs., 31.7.63
XG312	-	To MoA 25.11.59
XG313	-	To MoA 3.12.59
XG325	AAEE/DH	To MoA 3.12.59
XG326	Mkrs & AAEE	To MoA 3.12.59
XG327	AAEE/RAE	To 8188M 22.11.71 at St Athan
XG328	Mkrs/AAEE/RAE/ AAEE	To MoA 7.3.60
XG329	Mkrs/AAEE/DH/ AAEE	To 8050M 8.7.69 at Cranwell
XG330	Mkrs	To MoA 29.3.60
XG331	Mkrs & AAEE	To MoA 22.12.59
XG332	Mkrs/DH	Caught fire in air and control on approach; abandoned, Hatfield, 13.9.62
XG333	Mkrs & AAEE	To static test airframe 7.68; SS 23.11.70
XG334	AFDS	Abandoned when undercarriage jammed off Wells-next-the- Sea, Norfolk, 5.3.60
XG335	AFDS/AAEE	Undercarriage jammed; abandoned and crashed, Woodborough, Wilts., 11.1.65
XG336	AFDS/Mkrs/AAEE	To 8091M 5.70 at Halton
XG337	AAEE/Mkrs	To 8056M 1.70 at Cosford

*   *   *   *   *   *   *   *   *   *

XG331 allotted in error to Dakota G-AMSL

XG336 originally allocated to cancelled Thin-Wing Javelin

*   *   *   *   *   *   *   *   *   *

Two Hawker Hunter F.4s delivered in July 1956 by Hawker, Blackpool, to Contract 6/Acft/10344

XG341	43/RAFFC	Sold 20.6.68; to Abu Dhabi AF 6.11.70 as No.702
XG342	92/111/222/ 229 OCU	SS 11.9.63

*   *   *   *   *   *   *   *   *   *

Temporary serials allotted to civil aircraft
Vikings: XG349 : G-AHPM   XG350 : G-AJCD

XG354 - XG398; XG419 - XG441	Cancelled Bristol 191s for Royal Navy to Contract 6/Acft/10838

*   *   *   *   *   *   *   *   *   *

26 Bristol Belvedere HC.1s delivered between March 1959 and May 1962 to Contract 6/Acft/10839 (XG447-468) and 10842 (XG473-476)

XG447	Mkrs & AAEE	MoA aircraft
XG448	Mkrs & AAEE/66	SOC 3.7.69; preserved at Changi
XG449	72/MoA/72/MoA/66	SOC 21.3.69
XG450	AAEE & Mkrs	Sold to MoA 30.11.64
XG451	Mkrs/66	SOC 13.11.67
XG452	MoA	To 7997M 8.12.67 at Cosford
XG453	BTU/66/72/26/66	Engine caught fire starting up, Seletar, 18.3.69; not repaired
XG454	BTU	Nose rose in hover and tail hit ground; undercarriage coll- apsed in heavy landing, Farnborough, 30.8.61; rebuilt for MinTech; to 8366M at RAF Museum
XG455	72	SOC 19.3.69
XG456	BTU/66	SOC 1.8.68
XG457	BTU/66/72/26/66	SOC 14.5.68
XG458	66/72/26/66	SOC 21.3.69
XG459	66/72/26/66	SOC 21.3.69
XG460	AAEE/Hdlg Sqn/ 66/72/66	SOC 21.3.69
XG461	66/72/26	Lost cyclic pitch control on rear rotor; rolled and front rotor hit ground; caught fire, Khormaksar, 31.12.64
XG462	66/72	Rear engine caught fire; crashlanded 3m SW of Bomba, Libya, 5.10.63
XG463	66/72/26	Forward engine exploded and damaged controls; crashed and caught fire 20m NNW of Khormaksar, 30.10.64
XG464	66/72/26/66	SOC 21.3.69
XG465	66/72	Engine lost power; dived into ground after take-off, Warendorf, 4m NW of Gutersloh, 30.7.62
XG466	72/26/66	SOC 13.5.68
XG467	72/26/66	SOC 21.3.69
XG468	AAEE/72/26/66	SOC 21.3.69
XG473	66	Yaw control cable failed; crashed in jungle, Trusan River, 20m SW of Labi, Sarawak, 4.5.63
XG474	66/26/66	To 8367M 2.6.69 for RAF Museum
XG475	66	SOC 15.3.67
XG476	66	SOC 13.6.68

*   *   *   *   *   *   *   *   *   *

XG480 - XG484		Cancelled Swift F.4s to Contract 6/Acft/8509
XG487 - XG492		Allotted to ML U-120 drones
XG496		DH.104 Devon C.1 G-ANDX for Royal Aircraft Establishment to Contract 6/Acft/8509

*   *   *   *   *   *   *   *   *   *

36 Bristol Sycamore HR.14s delivered between February 1955 and July 1956 to Contract 6/Acft/10943

XG500	JEHU/225	Lost tail rotor on landing, Bender, Somalia, 14.12.61; abandoned as inaccessible
XG501	275	Tail rotor hit mast on Bell Rock Lighthouse; fell on to rocks and caught fire, 15.12.55
XG502	JEHU/TCCF/JEHU/ 72/118/CFS/MCS/32	SOC 29.8.72; preserved at Museum of Army Flying
XG503	Bristols/CFS/MCS/ HDU/CFS/MCS	SOC 27.3.68; to Odiham for fire practice
XG504	Aden CS/SF Khormaksar/ Aden SAR Flt/ CFS/MCS/32	Sold 14.8.72 to Endon Service Station; preserved
XG505	275	Ditched after engine lost power on winching exercise 2m NE of North Coates, 25.6.56

XG506	275/118/225/118/ 72/MCS/HDU	To 7852M 16.6.64 at Halton
XG507	JEHU/MCS/225/ CFS	Damaged in heavy landing, Ternhill, 10.7.64; not repaired
XG508	275/110	SOC 30.6.67
XG509	275/228/CFS	Hit ground in turn and rolled over, Ternhill, 13.2.62; to 7745M
XG510	194	Wheel caught on landing mat on take-off; rotors hit ground, Paddy's Ladang, Perak, Malaya, 5.2.56; DBR
XG511	SF Nicosia/Levant CF/103	Hit mast of ship during rescue and ditched off Famagusta, Cyprus, 7.12.60
XG512	275/284/SF El Adem/103	Nosewheel collapsed on landing and rotor hit ground, Tobruk, Libya, 4.7.63; DBR
XG513	APS Sylf	Lost power on tail rotor and spun; sank into ground and rolled over, Sylt, 16.9.57
XG514	275/CFS	Rolled while practising landing on slope and rotor hit ground, Ternhill, 10.1.64
XG515	JEHU/MCS/ 225/CFS	To 8008M 1.5.68 at Halton
XG516	Levant CS/ISF Nicosia/284	Sank on landing and rotor hit trees; rolled over, Platres, Cyprus, 18.2.57
XG517	SF Nicosia/103	Rolled on landing and rotor hit ground, Tobruk, Libya, 23.8.63
XG518	SF Amman/SF Habbaniya/SF El Adem/SAR Flt Khormaksar/CFS	To 8009M 7.5.68 at Halton
XG519	194/110	Crashlanded avoiding trees and caught fire 8m W of Fort Kemar, Malaya, 24.1.64
XG520	CFS	Developed resonance and over- turned on landing, South Cerney, 11.3.60; not repaired
XG521	275/118/225/118	Rotor hit ground on landing, rolled over, Aldergrove,13.10.61
XG522	194/110	Sank after take-off from clearing and rolled over, Cameron Highlands, Malaya, 4.4.61
XG523	JEHU/CFS	Damaged in heavy landing, Ternhill, 25.9.62; to 7793M at Ternhill
_____		
XG538	194/110	Rolled on take-off and rotor hit wall, Na Plang, Thailand, 14.9.60
XG539	ISF Nicosia/284	Tail rotor hit cables; crash- landed in orchard, Kakopetria, Cyprus, 1.8.58
XG540	CFS/Bristols/MCS	Engine cut; overturned in forced landing, Henton, near Chinnor, Oxon., 23.7.65; to 7899M at Ternhill; to 8345M 7.3.73
XG541	ISF Nicosia/284	Lost height and hit ground ½m SE of Palendria, Cyprus, 20.7.58; DBR
XG542	ISF Nicosia/284	Tail rotor hit bush; rolled over 6m N of Limassol, Cyprus, 4.6.58
XG543	194	Tail rotor hit tree trunk; rolled over 12m NE of Fort Kemar, Malaya, 23.9.58
XG544	275/228/MCS/118/ 72/MCS/32	SOC 10.8.72; preserved
XG545	275	Lost height during winching practice and ditched ½m E of Happisburgh, Norfolk, 16.7.57

XG546	JEHU/ISF Nicosia/ 284	Rotor hit ground during ground resonance, Platres, Cyprus, 31.5.57; DBR
XG547	284/103/1563 Flt/ 1564 Flt/CFS	To 8010M 12.3.68 at Kemble
XG548	JEHU	Nosewheel jammed; rolled over after landing, Middle Wallop, 10.7.57; DBR
XG549	194	Lost power on approach and crashlanded, Fort Langkap, Malaya, 16.4.58

* * * * * * * * * *

**Canberra B(I).6 delivered in February 1956 to Contract No.
6/Acft/5786 and 6445**

XG554	CFE/213	Sold to BAC 8.12.69

* * * * * * * * * *

**Six Scottish Aviation Pioneer CC.1s delivered between December 1954
and March 1955 to Contract 6/Acft/10851**

XG558	267/209	SOC 7.6.63
XG559	267	Hit downdraught on approach; hit bank and undercarriage collapsed, Bidor, Malaya, 28.1.57
XG560	267/209	Engine lost power; hit tree in forced landing, Rengam, Malaya, 26.8.60
XG561	267/SF Seletar/ 267/209	Hit mast on take-off in bad weather and lost wing, Ipoh, Malaya, 23.10.59
XG562	267	SOC 7.2.58
XG563	267	Undercarriage collapsed on landing; swung off strip, Fort Shean, Malaya, 15.4.57

* * * * * * * * * *

Temporary serials allotted to civil aircraft:

Vikings: XG567 : G-AKBH   XG568 : G-AIVO

XG572 - XG588	Whirlwind HAR.3s for Royal Navy to Contract 6/Acft/10586; XG577 to 9050M
XG589 - XG597	Whirlwind HAS.7s for Royal Navy to Contract 6/Acft/10586

* * * * * * * * * *

**De Havilland Heron C.2 delivered in September 1954 to Contract
6/Acft/10859**

XG603	Brit Jt Services Mission, Washington	Sold 10.68; became OY-DNJ

* * * * * * * * * *

XG606 - XG638; XG653 - XG680	Sea Venom FAW.21s for RN to Contract 6/Acft/10501
XG681 - XG702; XG721 - XG737	Sea Venom FAW.22s for RN to Contract 6/Acft/10501
XG742 - XG748 XG765 - XG777	Sea Vampire T.22s for RN to Contract 6/Acft/10521

XG783 - XG798		Gannet AS.1/AS.4s for RN to
XG825 - XG855		Contract 6/Acft/10545

XG869 - XG890		Gannet T.2/T.5s for RN to
		Contract 6/Acft/10545

Serials allotted to civil aircraft

XG895	Viking G-AJBO	XG896	Viking G-AIVH
XG897	York G-AMRJ	XG898	York G-ANRC

XG900; XG905	Short SC.1s for Ministry of
	Aviation to Contract
	6/Acft/11094

XG912 - XG924	Cancelled Shackleton MR.3s
	To Contract 6/Acft/11106

Serial allotted to civil aircraft:	York: XG929 : G-ANSY

XG934 - XG947;	Cancelled Sea Hawk FGA.4s
XG961 - XG992	for RN to Contract 6/Acft/11127

* * * * * * * * *

Nine Blackburn Beverley C.1s delivered between November 1956 and May 1957 to Contract 6/Acft/11153

XH116	53/47&53/34	SOC 1.10.67
XH117	53	Engine cut due to fuel leak; second engine lost power; hit HT cables on emergency approach and cartwheeled, Sutton Wick, 2m S of Abingdon, 5.3.57
XH118	30	Two engines cut; swung on down-wind landing and over-turned on sand dune, Beihan, 4.2.58
XH119	30	SS 3.1.68
XH120	30/34/30/84	SS 7.1.69
XH121	53/47 & 53/84	SS 7.1.69
XH122	30/84	To 8045M 1.12.68 at Bicester
XH123	30/84/30/47	SS 8.3.68
XH124	30/84/30/ 242 OCU/47	To 8025M 27.6.68 for preservation at RAF Museum

* * * * * * * * *

Nine EEC Canberra PR.9s delivered between September 1958 and January 1960 by Short Bros. & Harland, Belfast, to Contract 6/Acft/11158

XH129	-	To MoS 11.9.58
XH130	AAEE/13	Stalled on approach to Luqa and flew into ground near Hal Far, 25.3.69
XH131	MoA/39/13/39/ 1 PRU/39	
XH132	-	To MoS 31.3.60 for conversion to Short SC.9; later to 8915M
XH133	MoA/13/MinTech/ 13/39/1 PRU	SS 4.94
XH134	MoA/58/39/ MoD(PE)/ 39/1 PRU/39	
XH135	Hdlg Sqn/MoA/58/ 13/39/1 PRU/39	
XH136	MoA/58/13/39/ AAEE	To 8782M 8.2.83 at Cosford
XH137	58/13/39	Control lost on asymmetric overshoot; hit house on approach, Oxmore Estate, Wyton, 3.5.77

* * * * * * * * *

XH138 - XH151	
XH158 - XH163	Cancelled Canberra B(I).6s

* * * * * * * * *

14 EEC Canberra PR.9s delivered between January 1960 and October 1961 by Short Bros. & Harland, Belfast, to Contract 6/Acft/11158

XH164	58/13	Rolled on approach and dived into ground 1½m ENE of Luqa, 7.1.69
XH165	58/13/39/1 PRU	SS 4.94
XH166	58/13/39/1 PRU	Sold to Chile 15.10.82 as 342
XH167	58/39/13/39/1 PRU	Sold to Chile 15.10.82 as 343
XH168	58/39/MoD(PE)/39 MoD(PE)/39/1 PRU/ 39	
XH169	58/39/MoD(PE)/39/ 1 PRU/39	
XH170	58/MoA/39	To 8739M as display aircraft, Wyton, 27.1.82
XH171	58/MoA/39/13/39	To 8746M 13.7.82 at Cosford
XH172	58/39/13	Stalled in formation and dived into sea 3m ESE of Akrotiri, 6.10.72
XH173	58/39/13/39/1 PRU	Sold to Chile 15.10.82 as 341
XH174	58/39/MinTech/ 39/13/39/1 PRU	SOC 9.94
XH175	58/39/1 PRU	SS
XH176	58/39	Abandoned after control lost on test flight with A&AEE, Chilmark, Wilts., 25.5.78
XH177	58/13	SOC 31.1.70
XH178 to XH186	-	Cancelled

* * * * * * * * *

25 EEC Canberra B(I).8s delivered between August 1956 and September 1958 by English Electric, Preston, to Contract 6/Acft/11158

XH203	-	To Indian AF as IF896
XH204	59/3	Aileron jammed; rolled and abandoned 8m NE of Wesel, W.Germany, 9.5.67
XH205	-	To Indian AF as IF897
XH206	-	To Peruvian AF as 478
XH207	59	Flew into ground in bad visibility 3m S of Sorpe Dam, W.Germany, 4.3.59
XH208	59/3	SOC 13.8.71; to 8167M at Bruggen
XH209	AAEE/59/16	To 8201M 22.5.72 at Gutersloh as decoy
XH227	-	To Indian AF as IF899
XH228	59/3	SOC 22.2.73; to Catterick for fire practice
XH229	-	To Indian AF as IF900
XH230	-	To Indian AF as IF901
XH231	59/3/88/3	Flew into high ground in bad visibility, Gross Freeden, 5m NE of Bad Iberg, W.Germany, 3.2.65
XH232	-	To Indian AF as IF902
XH233	-	To Indian AF as IF903
XH234	59/3/16	Sold to Marshalls 22.1.74 for Peru as No.252
XH235	-	To Indian AF as IF904
XH236	-	To Indian AF as IF905
XH237	-	To Indian AF as IF907
XH238	-	To Indian AF as IF908
XH239	-	To Indian AF as IF909
XH240	-	To Indian AF as IF910
XH241	-	To Indian AF as IF911
XH242	-	To Indian AF as IF912

40

Canberra   *Vampire*

| XH243 | - | To Indian AF as IF913 |
| XH244 | - | To Venezuelan AF as 4-A-39 |

* * * * * * * * * *

| XH249 | | Cancelled Fairey Rotodyne to Contract 6/Acft/5831 |
| XH255 to XH260 | | Cancelled Vickers V.1000s to Contract 6/Acft/11190 |

* * * * * * * * * *

66 de Havilland Vampire T.11s delivered between July 1955 and May 1956 to Contract 6/Acft/11204

XH264	SF Tengah/SF Butterworth/28	Engine failed and cowling flew off; abandoned as uncontrollable and crashed in sea, Tat Hong Channel, Hong Kong, 10.4.59
XH265	-	To RNZAF 18.10.55 as NZ5707
XH266	-	To RNZAF 18.10.55 as NZ5708
XH267	SF Geilenkirchen	SS 27.2.61
XH268	-	To RRAF 17.10.55 as RR128
XH269	-	To RRAF 17.10.55 as RR129
XH270	-	To RRAF 17.10.55 as RR130
XH271	-	To RNZAF 6.12.55 as NZ5709
XH272	RAFC	SS 5.10.60
XH273	608/SF Horsham St Faith/SF Coltishall/ RAFC	To 7830M 28.2.64 (cockpit only)
XH274	8 FTS/4 FTS/ 8 FTS/CATCS	SOC 31.12.69
XH275	-	To RRAF 17.10.55 as RR131
XH276	8 FTS	SS 3.6.65
XH277	RAFC/3-4 CAACU/ 8 FTS	SS 23.11.65
XH278	RAFC	To 7866M 9.11.64 at Upwood; later 8595M at 2482 Sqn ATC Henlow
XH292	SF Fassberg/ SF Wunstorf	Sold 7.1.69 to HSA; preserved at Belgian Air Museum, Brussels
XH293	ITS West Raynham	SS 10.10.60
XH294	FWS/FLS	SS 30.6.60
XH295	8 FTS/CNCS	SOC 23.10.62; to Linton-on-Ouse for fire practice
XH296	233 OCU/SF Middleton St.George	Engine cut; overshot landing and undercarriage raised to stop, Dishforth, 10.6.58
XH297	RAFC	Abandoned after elevator controls failed, Kneesall, 6m NW of Newark, Notts., 5.3.56
XH298	RAFC/CNCS	To 7760M 3.12.62 at 2356 Sqn ATC Scathby
XH299	112	Caught fire while being refuelled, Bruggen, 13.3.57
XH300	8 FTS	Abandoned take-off and undercarriage raised to stop, Swinderby, 29.11.56
XH301	ITS West Raynham/ APS Sylt	Sold 22.12.64 to HSA for Swiss AF
XH302	SF Oldenburg/SF Ahlhorn/APS Sylt	SS 5.3.64
XH303	7 FTS/CNCS	SS 5.3.64
XH304	79/SF Gutersloh/ 3 CAACU/CFS	Retained at CFS as demonstration aircraft. Collided with Meteor WA609 in formation and crashed, Mildenhall, 25.5.86
XH305	8 FTS	SOC 6.2.62
XH306	RAFC/5 FTS/4 FTS	SS 31.3.65
XH307	89/Stradishall	SS 10.10.60
XH308	RAFC	Sold to HSA 18.12.64 for Swiss AF as U-1234

XH309	71/SF Bruggen	SS 27.2.61
XH310	APS Sylt	SOC 21.6.60
XH311	APS Sylt/3-4 CAACU	SS 30.6.64
XH312	DH/8 FTS	Sold to HSA 23.11.67; preserved
XH313	111/SF Wattisham/ CATCS	Sold 17.12.70 to St.Albans Technical College
XH314	7 FTS/1 FTS	SS 5.3.64
XH315	4 FTS	SS 10.10.60
XH316	4 FTS/1 FTS	Sold 30.12.63 to HSA
XH317	-	To RNZAF 15.4.56 as NZ5710
XH318	RAFC	To 7761M 23.10.62 at 424 Sqn ATC at Calmore
XH319	7 FTS	Hit flock of seagulls, 10.4.57; not repaired
XH320	233 OCU/229 OCU/ RAFC	Sold to HSA 10.2.64 for Austrian AF as 5C-VF
XH321	8 FTS	Collided with XE990 and crashed into house, Colwick, 2m E of Nottingham, 16.1.58
XH322	500/CFS	SOC 27.8.62
XH323	APS Sylt	Lost cowling and collided with WZ575 off Sylt, 27.8.56; SOC on return
XH324	FECS	SOC 20.12.57
XH325	FECS	SS 30.6.60
XH326	SF Geilenkirchen/ SF Jever/2	SS 5.3.64
XH327	SF Tengah	SS 30.6.60
XH328	60/14 RNZAF/ 3 CAACU	Sold to Exeter Airport, 22.6.71
XH329	SF Biggin Hill/ SF Acklington/ 3-4 CAACU	Sold to Exeter Airport 16.12.71
XH330	RAFC	Sold to HSA 20.2.64
XH357	98	SS 10.10.60
XH358	14 RNZAF/FECS/60	To 7763M 10.62 at Seletar
XH359	45	SOC 29.9.59
XH360	60/FECS/60/FECS	SS 10.10.60
XH361	118/93	SS 5.3.64
XH362	DH/1 FTS/7 FTS/ 8 FTS/CNCS/ CATCS	SOC 12.6.70; to Shawbury for fire practice
XH363	5 FTS/8 FTS	Sold to BEA 9.12.68
XH364	APS Sylt	SS 21.4.64
XH365	Levant CF/8	SOC 25.11.59
XH366	-	To RNZAF 7.6.56 as NZ5711
XH367	RAFC	SS 5.3.64
XH368	7 FTS	SS 31.3.65

* * * * * * * * * *

De Havilland Heron CC.3 delivered in May 1955 to Contract 6/Acft/11217

| XH375 | Queens Flt | Sold 4.11.68; became CF-YAP |

* * * * * * * * * *

Bristol 173 prototype G-AMJI for Ministry of Aviation trials to Contract 6/Acft/1597

| XH379 | Mkrs | Hit downwash from passing Beverley and hit ground, Filton, 16.9.56; had been restored to G-AMJI 11.9.56 |

* * * * * * * * * *

Temporary serial allotted to civil aircraft

Bristol 170 Mk.31E   XH385 : G-AMSA

* * * * * * * * * *

20 Gloster Javelin T.3s delivered between May 1958 and June 1959 by Gloster, Hucclecote, to Contract 6/Acft/11262

XH390	Mkrs & AAEE/60	SOC 1.5.68
XH391	Hdlg Sqn/228 OCU	SS 25.6.64
XH392	228 OCU/JIRS/ 228 OCU	SOC 20.11.67; to Catterick for fire practice
XH393	228 OCU/5/29	SOC 20.11.67; to Catterick for fire practice
XH394	228 OCU/11	SOC 20.11.67; to Catterick for fire practice
XH395	46/25/29/226 OCU/ JIRS/228 OCU	SOC 23.11.67; to Wattisham for fire practice
XH396	228 OCU/29	SOC 23.11.67; to Coltishall for fire practice
XH397	41/226 OCU/ JIRS/228 OCU	SS 21.3.68
XH432	23/JIRS	SS 11.3.65
XH433	29/FCIRS/AAEE	SS 31.3.65
XH434	72/64	SS 25.6.64
XH435	85/64/JIRS/ 228 OCU	SS 21.3.68
XH436	151/FCIRS/ 226 OCU	Caught fire on start-up, Leuchars, 14.5.64; not repaired
XH437	33/23	Caught fire starting up, Leuchars, 19.8.64; DBR
XH438	72/FCIRS	SS 11.3.65
XH443	25/FCIRS/226 OCU/ JIRS	SOC 20.3.64
XH444	3/11/FCIRS	SOC 25.6.64
XH445	87/60/64	Brakes failed; swung off runway into drain, Tengah, 11.7.66; DBR
XH446	3/228 OCU/MoA/ 60/64/60	SOC 1.5.68
XH447	5	SS 25.6.64

* * * * * * * * *

XH451		Cancelled Vickers N.9/47 (N.113) to Contract 6/Acft/11268
XH455, XH463		Beavers for MoA trials
XH469		Pioneer G-ANRG. Temporary serial for trials

* * * * * * * * *

20 Avro Vulcan B.1s delivered between January 1958 and April 1959 to Contract 6/Acft/11301. All later converted to B.1A

XH475	230 OCU/101/ Cv B.1A/101/ Wadd Wg	To 7996M 21.11.67 at Waddington
XH476	101/Cv B.1A/101/ 44/Wadd Wg	SS 21.1.69
XH477	83/44/Cv B.1A/ 44	Flew into Hill of St.Colm, 10m WSW of Banchory, Aberdeenshire, on low-level navex, 12.6.63
XH478	MoS/Cv B.1A/101/ Wadd Wg/MoA/ Akrotiri Wg	To 8047M 1.11.70 at Akrotiri;
XH479	101/Cv B.1A/101 Wadd Wg	To 7974M 13.6.67 at Halton
XH480	44/Cv B.1A/44/ Wadd Wg	SS 19.9.68
XH481	101Cv B.1A/101/ Wadd Wg	SOC 8.1.68; to Cottesmore for fire practice
XH482	617/50/Cv B.1A/ 101/50/Wadd Wg	SS 19.9.68
XH483	617/Cv B.1A/50/ Wadd Wg	SOC 3.8.67; to Manston for fire practice

XH497	617/50/Cv B.1A/50/ Wadd Wg	Nosewheel detached; landed on mainwheels, Scampton, 3.7.58; not repaired and SS 21.1.59
XH498	617/50/Cv B.1A/50/ Wadd Wg	To 7993M 19.10.67 at Finningley
XH499	617/50/44/Cv B.1A/ 44/Wadd Wg/MoA	SOC 11.11.65 at HSA
XH500	617/Cv B.1A/617/ 50/Wadd Wg	To 7994M 1.1.68 at Scampton
XH501	617/Cv BN.1A/44/ Wadd Wg	SS 8.11.68
XH502	617/50/Cv B.1A/ Wadd Wg	SOC 10.1.68; to Waddington for fire practice
XH503	44/Cv B.1A/ Wadd Wg	SS 8.11.68
XH504	230 OCU/Cv B.1A/ 101/Wadd Wg	SOC 4.1.68
XH505	230 OCU/Cv B.1A/ 617/50/44/ Wadd Wg	SOC 9.1.68; to Finningley for fire practice
XH506	101/Cv B.1A/617/ 50/Wadd Wg	SS 8.11.68
XH532	230 OCU/101/ Cv B.1A/101/ Wadd Wg	SS 8.11.68

* * * * * * * * *

17 Avro Vulcan B.2s delivered between September 1959 and December 1960 to Contract 6/Acft/11301

XH533	Mkrs & AAEE	To 8048M 15.10.70 at St Athan
XH534	MoA/230 OCU/27	SS 16.2.82
XH535	AAEE	Yawed during low speed handling demonstration; abandoned and spun into ground, Chute, Hants., 11.5.64
XH536	MoA/Coningsby Wg	Flew into Fan Bwlch Clwyth, Brecon Beacons, on low-level exercise, 11.2.66
XH537	MoA/230 OCU/27	To 8749M 25.3.82 at Abingdon
XH538	Mkrs/Scampton Wg/ Wadd Wg /230 OCU/ 27 & 230 OCU/35/ Wadd Wg/35 Wadd Wg/35	SS 31.8.81
XH539	Avro	To MoA charge, 25.5.61
XH554	83/230 OCU	To 8694M 9.6.81; to Catterick for fire practice
XH555	27/230 OCU	SOC 1.10.71
XH556	BSE/27/230 OCU	Undercarriage collapsed while starting engines, Finningley, 18.4.66; not repaired
XH557	MoA/Cott Wg/ Wadd Wg/Akrotiri Wg/Wadd Wg	SS 12.82
XH558	230 OCU/Wadd Wg/ 27/230 OCU/27/ Wadd Wg/AAEE/ Wadd Wg/50/Cv K.2	SOC 18.9.84 for display at Waddington; became G-VLCN
XH559	230 OCU	SS 29.1.82
XH560	230 OCU/MoA/12/ 230 OCU/Cott Wg/ Wadd Wg/Cott Wg/ Akrotiri Wg/27/ Wadd Wg/50/Cv K.2	SOC 5.1.84 for spares
XH561	230 OCU/Wadd Wg/ Cott Wg/Akrotiri Wg/35/50/Cv K.2	To 8809M 13.6.84 at Waddington

XH562	230 OCU/35/230 OCU/35/230 OCU/ Cott Wg/50/Wadd Wg/Cott Wg/Akrotiri Wg/Wadd Wg/230 OCU/35/Wadd Wg	To 8758M 19.8.82 at Catterick
XH563	83/12/230 OCU/ Wadd Wg/230 OCU/MinTech/ 230 OCU/27	To 8744M 31.3.82 at Scampton

* * * * * * * * * *

Four English Electric Canberra B.6s delivered between February and April 1955 by English Electric, Preston, to Contract 6/Acft/11313

XH567	RRE/DRA	MoA aircraft; became G-BXOD 11.11.97
XH568	RAE	MoA aircraft; became G-BVIC 25.10.93
XH569	RRF	Lost power on approach and crashlanded, Bells Farm, Woodhurst, near Wyton, 24.7.56
XH570	139/249/Cv B.16/ 249/Akrotiri Wg	SOC 1.10.71

* * * * * * * * * *

Two English Electric Canberra T.4s delivered in March and May 1955 by English Electric, Preston, to Contract 6/Acft/11313

XH583	SF Gaydon/232 OCU/SF Bruggen/ 213/.SF Laarbruch	To BAe 12.10.81 as G-29-374
XH584	231 OCU	SOC 12.7.66

* * * * * * * * * *

25 Handley Page Victor B.1s (first eight) and B.1As delivered between October 1958 and February 1959 to Contract 6/Acft/11307 (first 8) and 11303 (remainder)

XH587	HP/AAEE/15/ Cv K.1A/57	SOC 17.4.75
XH588	15/55/57/Cv K.1A/ 214/55/57	SOC 30.7.75; to Machrihanish for fire practice
XH589	15/55 & 57/TTF/ Cv K.1A/55/57/ 55/214	SOC 9.7.76; to St Athan for fire practice
XH590	15/Cv K.1A/55/ 57/55	SOC 3.7.75; to Manston for fire practice
XH591	15/55/55 & 57/57/ Cv K.1A/55/57/214	SOC 5.11.76
XH592	15/55 & 57/232 OCU/ TTF/232 OCU	To 8429M 17.10.74 at Cosford
XH593	15/57/55 & 57/ TTF/232 OCU	To 8328M 17.10.74 at Cosford
XH594 ____	15/55 & 57/ 232 OCU/TTF/ 232 OCU	SOC 31.5.74
XH613	15	Lost power on all engines and abandoned on approach to Cottesmore 5m W of Castle Bytham, Lincs., 14.6.62
XH614	57/55/55 & 57/TTF/ 57/Cv K.1A/55/ AAEE/55/214/ 55/214	SOC 7.9.76
XH615	232 OCU/10/55 & 57/ Cv K.1A/55/TTF/ 232 OCU/55/ 232 OCU/55/214	SOC 4.10.74; to Leeming for fire practice

XH616	57/15/90/232 OCU/ TTF/Cv K.1A/57	SOC 20.1.76
XH617	57	Shaft pierced fuel tank; caught fire in air and abandoned, Oakley, 2½m ESE of Diss, Norfolk, 19.7.60
XH618	15/HP&AAEE/ Cv K.1A/57	Collided with Buccaneer XV156 during refuelling; damaged tailplane, bunted and broke up 95m E of Sunderland, Co.Durham, 24.3.75
XH619	57/55 & 57/57/ Cv K.1A/55/214	SOC 30.6.75; to Marham for fire practice
XH620	55/57/15/90/ Cv K.1A/55 & 57/ 55/57/TTF/57/ 232 OCU/ 57/55/57	SOC 24.6.76
XH621	57/Cv K.1A/57/214	SOC 22.12.76
XH645	57/55/Cv K.1A/55	SOC 9.9.74
XH646	55/Cv K.1A/TTF	Collided with Canberra WT325 in bad weather and crashed, Kelling Heath, near Holt, Norfolk, 19.8.68
XH647	57/55/Cv K.1A/ TTF/232/214/232 OCU/57/232 OCU	SOC 26.11.74
XH648	57/15/55 & 57/ Cv K.1A/55/TTF/ 55/57	To IWM Duxford, 2.6.76
XH649	57/55 & 57/HP/ AAEE/Cv K.1A/57	SOC 27.7.76
XH650	55/55 & 57/Cv K.1A/ 55/214/55/214	SOC 12.2.76; to Manston for fire practice
XH651	57/15/HP/Cv K.1A/ 57/214	SOC 26.1.77
XH667	57/55 & 57/Cv K.1A/ 55 & 57/55/214	SOC 23.9.75; to Hal Far for fire practice

* * * * * * * * * *

Seven Handley Page Victor B.2s delivered between December 1959 and March 1961 to Contract 6/Acft/11303

XH668	AAEE	Lost pitot head; dived into sea off Milford Haven, Pembs., 20.8.59
XH669	HP/Wittering Wg/ Cv K.2/57/55	Caught fire in air, 21.6.90; not repaired and to 9092M; to Waddington for fire practice
XH670	HP/AAEE/HP/ Cv SR.2/543/HSA	SOC 31.10.75 and nose preserved
XH671	HP/Wittering Wg/ Cv K.2/57/55/57/55	Damaged during cabin pressure test, Marham, 15.3.93; SOC
XH672	HP/AAEE/Cv SR.2/ 543/Cv K.2/57/55	Allotted 9242M To Cosford Museum 26.3.94
XH673	AAEE/139/Wittering Wg/Cv K.2/57	To 8911M 2.7.86 for display at Marham
XH674	AAEE/Cv SR.2/543/ Victor Flt, Wyton	Blue Steel testbed; SOC 22.6.76
XH675	MoA/Wittering Wg/ Cv K.2/57/55	SOC 6.91

* * * * * * * * * *

Bristol Sycamore 3 acquired in July 1954 for MoA tests

XH682	RAE/ETPS	Ex G-ALSR. Rolled over on take-off, Farnborough, 13.3.58; not repaired

* * * * * * * * * *

Six Gloster Javelin FAW.5s delivered between April and June 1957 to Contract 6/Acft/11329

XH687	151	SS 25.9.63
XH688	151/228 OCU/11	SS 11.3.63
XH689	151/228 OCU/11	SS 21.9.64
XH690	151/5	SS 21.9.64
XH691	228 OCU	SS 21.9.64
XH692	228 OCU	Caught fire after landing, Leeming, 4.5.61; not repaired

* * * * * * * * *

11 Gloster Javelin FAW.6s delivered between September 1957 and February 1958 to Contract 6/Acft/11329

XH693	89/85	SS 14.6.63
XH694	89/85	SOC 30.7.62
XH695	89/85/FTU	SS 24.6.63
XH696	89/85	SS 24.6.63
XH697	29	SS 24.6.63
XH698	29	SS 20.3.63; 7743M NTU
XH699	29	SS 17.12.62
XH700	29	SS 17.12.62
XH701	29	SS 24.6.63
XH702	46/89/85/AFDS	SS 29.3.63
XH703	29	SS 24.6.63

* * * * * * * * *

142 Gloster Javelin FAW.7s delivered between February 1957 and June 1959 by Gloster Aircraft (85) and Armstrong Whitworth (57) to Contract 6/Acft/11329. AW aircraft were XH785-XH795, XH833-XH849 and XH871-XH899

XH704	Mkrs & AAEE	SS 8.4.62
XH705	Mkrs & AAEE	SS 17.10.61
XH706	Mkrs & AAEE	SS 8.4.62
XH707	A-S/Cv FAW.9/ 23/60/64/60	SOC 12.12.67
XH708	Mkrs & AAEE/ Cv FAW.9/64	Collided with XH896 and spun into ground 10m NW of Tengah, 30.5.67
XH709	Deld as FAW.9/ 64	Abandoned after controls jammed, New Skudai Estate, 2m W of Johore Bahru, Malaya, 14.6.66
XH710	Mkrs & AAEE	To 7748M 15.5.62 at Melksham
XH711	AAEE/Cv FAW.9/29/ 60/64	SOC 20.7.67
XH712	AAEE & DH/ Cv FAW.9/23/29	SS 19.4.68
XH713	AAEE/Cv FAW.9/ 33/5/228 OCU	SOC 29.11.67; to Manston for fire practice
XH714	AAEE	Ejection seat fired of own accord and pilot blown out; crashed, Sandford, near Ringwood, Hants., 26.2.58
XH715	33/Cv FAW.9/ 33/5/228 OCU	SOC 31.1.68
XH716	33/Cv FAW.9/ 25/11/228 OCU	SOC 31.1.68
XH717	64/Cv FAW.9/60	Caught fire starting up, Butterworth, 26.4.66; not repaired
XH718	33	SOC 6.3.62
XH719	33/Cv FAW.9/60	SOC 12.10.67
XH720	33	Brake locked on landing; swung and undercarriage collapsed, Nicosia, 14.10.59
XH721	33/Cv FAW.9/60	SOC 20.7.67
XH722	AAEE/Cv FAW.9/60	SOC 20.7.67
XH723	64/Cv FAW.9/29	Engine lost power on take-off; overshot and caught fire, Nicosia, 30.1.64
XH724	64/Cv FAW.9/60	Brakes failed; swung on landing into drain and caught fire, Tengah, 3.4.64
XH725	64/Cv FAW.9/ 29/60/64/60	SOC 1.5.68
XH746	C(A)	As Sapphire 7R testbed; to MoA 1.10.61; cv FAW.9
XH747	AWDS/64/ Cv FAW.9/60	Lost tailplane tab and abandoned 15m NNW of Pontian, Johore, 10.2.64
XH748	AWDS/33	SOC 6.2.62
XH749	AWDS/AFDS/64/ Cv FAW.9/29/60	Tyre burst on landing; swung off runway and ground-looped, Butterworth, 17.11.65; not repaired
XH750	33	Struck by lightning and caught fire; abandoned 5m W of Horsham St.Faith, 9.7.59
XH751	33/Cv FAW.9/60	SOC 20.7.67
XH752	AWDS/64/ Cv FAW.9/ 29/5/11/29	SOC 13.1.67; to West Raynham for fire practice
XH753	Mkrs/AAEE/ Cv FAW.9/ 11/5/11	Sapphire testbed; SS 30.11.67
XH754	RAE & Mkrs & AAEE	To MoA 7.5.65
XH755	AWDS/23/ Cv FAW.9/33	Abandoned in uncontrollable spin 7m E of Tynemouth, Northumberland, 18.5.62
XH756	AWDS/23/ Cv FAW.9/33/5/11	SOC 2.12.66; to Leeming for fire practice
XH757	AAEE/CV FAW.9/ 33/5	7903M NTU; SOC 28.3.66
XH758	AWDS/23/Cv FAW.9/33/5	Engine blew up and tail control lost; abandoned 2m W of Zonhoven, W.Germany, 17.10.63
XH759	Cv FAW.9/AAEE & Mkrs/64/60	SOC 12.2.68
XH760	Cv FAW.9/25/11	To 7892M 10.65 at Cranwell
XH761	Cv FAW.9/Mkrs	Overshot abandoned take-off after warning lights came on and overshot runway, Moreton Valence, 22.10.59
XH762	Cv FAW.9/64/5/ 64/29	SOC 19.4.68
XH763	Cv FAW.9/23/64/60	SOC 1.5.68
XH764	Cv FAW.9/64/29	Damaged in heavy landing, Manston, 11.5.67; to 7972M; preserved at Manston
XH765	Cv FAW.9/23/64	Overshot abandoned take-off, Kalaikunda, India, 5.11.63
XH766	Cv FAW.9/64/ 60/64/60	SOC 1.5.68
XH767	Cv FAW.9/25/11/ 228 OCU	To 7955M 10.7.67; to 187 Sqn ATC at Perdiswell, Worcester
XH768	Cv FAW.9/25/11/29	To 7929M 12.1.67 at Cranwell; preserved in Germany
XH769	Cv FAW.9/25/11/60	SOC 20.7.67
XH770	Cv FAW.9/25/11/64	SOC 20.7.67
XH771	Cv FAW.9/25/11	SOC 30.11.67
XH772	Cv FAW.9/25/11/ 228 OCU	SOC 20.9.67; to Catterick for fire practice
XH773	Cv FAW.9/33/5/11	SS 30.11.67
XH774	23/Cv FAW.9/29	Engine cut on take-off and caught fire, Akrotiri, 20.5.64; not repaired
XH775	23	Collided with XH781 over Brundall, Norfolk, during night interception and abandoned, 1.9.59
XH776	Cv FAW.9/25/11/29	SOC 23.5.67

XH777	23/FAW.9/29/60	SOC 1.12.68; to Singapore ADC as GI airframe SAFTECH9
XH778	23/Cv FAW.9/29	SOC 18.8.64
XH779	23/Cv FAW.9/29/60	SOC 20.7.67
XH780	FRL/Cv FAW.9/ 33/5/11	SOC 11..4.67; to Cottesmore for fire practice
XH781	23	Collided with XH775 over Brundall, Norfolk and crashed, 1.9.59
XH782	GWTS/25/64	To 7797M 2.10.63 at Halton
XH783	AAEE/GWTS/ 23/64	To 7798M 31.7.63 at Halton
XH784	GWTS/25/64	To 7799M 2.10.63 at Halton
XH785	64/Cv FAW.9/60	Abandoned after engine caught fire on air test 5m NW of Tengah, 4.4.66
XH786	33	SOC 16.2.62
XH787	64/Cv FAW.9/60	Undercarriage leg jammed up; swung off runway on landing, Butterworth, 5.4.67; not repaired
XH788	64/Cv FAW.9/60	Broke up in air during roll near Tengah, 11.10.67
XH789	64	Overshot landing after hydraulic failure, Akrotiri, 30.7.59; not repaired
XH790	AWDS/33	To 7808M 19.3.63 at Yatesbury
XH791	64/Cv FAW.9/ 12 Gp Ferry Unit	Engine blew up; abandoned in spin over Manga River, Ganges Delta, East Pakistan, 5.8.61
XH792	AWDS/64/Cv FAW.9/ 29/60/64/60	SOC 20.7.67
XH793	Cv FAW.9/23/64/60	SOC 1.12.68; to Singapore ADC as GI airframe, SAFTECH 8
XH794	64/Cv FAW.9/33	Overshot landing after hydraulic failure and overturned, Wildenrath, 9.3.62
XH795	33	To 7757M 21.2.62 at 2155 Sqn ATC, Hamilton
XH833	33/Cv FAW.9/60	Engine caught fire on take-off; overshot runway, Butterworth, 3.3.65; not repaired
XH834	64/Cv FAW.9/29/64	SOC 20.7.67
XH835	33/Cv FAW.9/60	SOC 20.7.67
XH836	33/Cv FAW.9/60	Engine blew up; abandoned in spin 12m S of Mersing, Malaya, 3.12.62
XH837	33	Nose to 8032M 21.2.62 at 114 Sqn ATC Ruislip
XH838	33	Tyre burst on take-off; swung and undercarriage leg collapsed, Middleton St.George, 20.9.60; not repaired
XH839	33/Cv FAW.9/60	SOC 1.12.68; to SAFTECH 10
XH840	64/Cv FAW.9	Damaged during refuelling, Luqa, 27.9.61; to 7740M
XH841	64/Cv FAW.9/60	SOC 1.5.68
XH842	64/Cv FAW.9/60	SOC 20.7.67
XH843	Cv FAW.9/64/60	Engine blew up on starting up, Tengah, 16.2.68; DBR
XH844	Cv FAW.9/64	Engine blew up on starting, Waterbeach, 13.4.62
XH845	Cv FAW.9/AAEE/23	Engine blew up on take-off and caught fire, Leuchars, 28.8.64; not repaired
XH846	64/Cv FAW.9/60	SOC 20.7.67
XH847	Cv FAW.9/23/29	Wheel locked on landing; swung off runway and under-carriage leg torn off, Khormaksar, 27.6.66
XH848	Cv FAW.9/23/64/29	Stalled in slipstream on approach and abandoned near Akrotiri, 14.12.66
XH849	Cv FAW.9/23/64/ 29/AAEE/29	To 7975M 1.9.67 at Bicester
XH871	Cv FAW.9/AAEE/64	SOC 17.4.64 at Bovingdon for fire practice
XH872	Cv FAW.9/64/60	SOC 1.12.68; to SAFTECH 7
XH873	Cv FAW.9/64/23/29	SS 19.4.68
XH874	Cv FAW.9/64/ AAEE/64	Damaged on ground, Kuching, 4.8.64; not repaired
XH875	Cv FAW.9/64	Engine blew up on starting, Nicosia, 31.5.61; not repaired
XH876	Cv FAW.9/64/ 60/64	Lost power on approach and abandoned near Tengah, 25.8.66
XH877	Cv FAW.9/64/ 60/64	Abandoned after engine explosion 20m NE of Tawau, Sabah, 22.6.65
XH878	Cv FAW.9/64	Abandoned after controls lost power 11½m SW of Waterbeach, 27.11.61
XH879	Cv FAW.9/64/ 60/64/60	SOC 9.10.67
XH880	Cv FAW.9/25/11/FE	SOC 20.7.67
XH881	Cv FAW.9/25/11/FE	SOC 20.7.67
XH882	Cv FAW.9./25/11	SOC 30.11.67
XH883	Cv FAW.9/25/11/ 228 OCU	SS 31.1.68
XH884	Cv FAW.9/25/11/29	SOC 24.2.67
XH885	Cv FAW.9/23/60/64	Caught fire starting up, Tengah, 15.11.66; not repaired
XH886	23/Cv FAW.9/23/ 64/29/IRF	SS 19.6.68
XH887	Cv FAW.9/23/ 64/60/64	Undercarriage jammed up at night; abandoned off Changi, 8.11.65
XH888	Cv FAW.9/23/ 64/29	Nosewheel jammed up; landed on mainwheels, Akrotiri,18.1.67; not repaired
XH889	Cv FAW.9/23/64/29	SS 19.4.68
XH890	Cv FAW.9/23/29	Skidded on landing and under-carriage collapsed, N'dola, Zambia, 2.6.66
XH891	Cv FAW.9/23/64/ 29/AAEE	Damaged by fire, Boscombe Down, 12.9.67; to Chivenor for fire practice
XH892	Cv FAW.9/23/64/29	To 7982M at Colerne; preserved at Duxford
XH893	Cv FAW.9/23/ 64/60/64/60	SOC 1.12.68; to SAFTECH 6
XH894	Cv FAW.9/23/29	SS 19.4.68
XH895	Cv FAW.9/23/64/60	SOC 1.12.68; to SAFTECH 5
XH896	Cv FAW.9/64/AAEE/ 64/60/64	Collided with XH708 and abandoned 10m NW of Tengah, 31.5.67
XH897	25/Cv FAW.9/33/ 5/BSE/AAEE	To IWM 24.1.75; preserved at Duxford
XH898	25/Cv FAW.9/ 25/11/228 OCU	SS 31.1.68
XH899	25/Cv FAW.9/23/29	SS 18.4.68
XH900	GWTS/23/64/AAEE	To 7811M 15.5.63 at St Athan
XH901	GWTS/23/64	To 7800M 16.9.63 at Weeton
XH902	GWTS/23/64	To 7801M 1.1.64 at Weeton
XH903	23/Cv FAW.9/29/ 33/5	To 7938M 8.67; preserved at Innsworth
XH904	23/Cv FAW.9/ 29/33/5	SS 30.11.67
XH905	25/Cv FAW.9/ 33/5/228 OCU	SS 31.1.68
XH906	25/Cv FAW.9/25	Collided with Canberra WD995 on practice night interception and blew up 2½m N of Akrotiri, 26.10.61

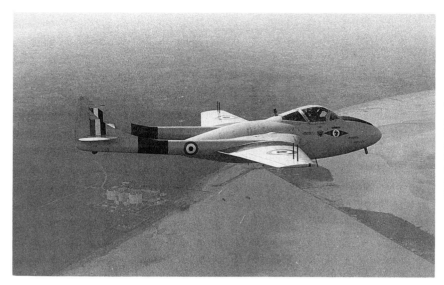

Vampire T.11 XH304 was the last of the Royal Air Force's Vampires to remain in service. It entered service in December 1955 and became a display aircraft with the Central Flying School until it collided with a Meteor and crashed in May 1986

Victor B.1A XH618 was converted to a K.1A refuelling tanker and served with No.57 Squadron until it collided with a Buccaneer during refuelling over the North Sea and crashed on 24 March 1975.

Javelin T.3 was one of a batch of operational trainers delivered in 1958/59.

Although not allotted to No.46 Squadron, XH443 carried the squadron's emblem under the cockpit when this photograph was taken.

(Peter Corbell)

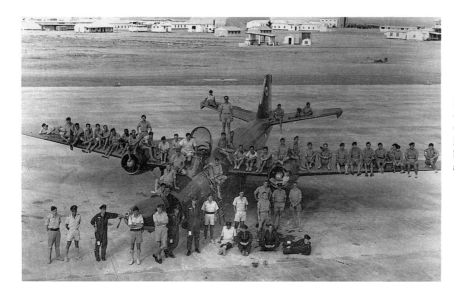

Reminiscent of old photographs of
wings being tested by having the
workforce sit on them, Canberra
PR.9 XH167 of No.39 Squadron
has the squadron personnel posed
around it at Luqa, Malta

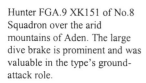

Hunter FGA.9 XK151 of No.8
Squadron over the arid
mountains of Aden. The large
dive brake is prominent and was
valuable in the type's ground-
attack role.

Victor B.2 XL512 of No.139
Squadron with a Blue Steel stand-
off missile under the belly. Painted
in an anti-reflective colour scheme,
the roundels and markings are pale
to avoid attracting heat and radiation
from nuclear explosions

XH907	25/Cv FAW.9/ 33/5/228 OCU	SS 31.1.68
XH908	25/Cv FAW.9/ 60/64/60	SOC 1.5.68 to Tengah for fire practice
XH909	25/Cv FAW.9/ 25/11/228 OCU	Overstressed in turn 9m N of Leuchars, 20.10.66 and SOC
XH910	25/Cv FAW.9/29/60	SOC 20.7.67
XH911	25/Cv FAW.9/33/5	Caught fire starting up, Geilenkirchen, 3.9.65; DBR
XH912	25/Cv FAW.9/ 33/5/228 OCU	SS 31.1.68
XH955	25/33/Cv FAW.9/60	Tyre burst on landing; swung off runway and undercarriage leg collapsed, Labuan, 29.3.64
XH956	25/23/Cv FAW.9/ 33/29/33/29/64/60	SOC 20.7.67
XH957	25/Cv FAW.9/33/5	SS 30.11.67
XH958	23/Cv FAW.9/33/ 29/33/29/33/5 228 OCU	Undercarriage leg jammed up; swung off runway on landing, Leuchars, 11.10.66; DBR
XH959	25/Cv FAW.9/ 29/60/64	Flew into sea on ASR search at night 5m E of Changi, 8.11.65
XH960	23/Cv FAW.9/ 29/60	SOC 20.7.67
XH961	25/Cv FAW.9/ 29/60/64/60	Brakes failed; swung on landing and hit bank, Tengah, 8.2.68
XH962	23/Cv FAW.9/29	Swung on take-off and undercarriage collapsed, Nicosia, 27.6.63
XH963	23/Cv FAW.9/ 29/60/64	SOC 20.7.67
XH964	23/Cv FAW.9/ AAEE/29/60	SOC 20.7.67
XH965	Mkrs & AAEE/RAE	Prototype FAW.9; to MoA 31.12.61

* * * * * * * * * *

47 Gloster Javelin FAW.8s delivered between July 1958 and August 1960 to Contract 6/Acft/11329

XH966	Mkrs & AAEE/41	SS 26.11.64
XH967	AAEE/41	SS 26.11.64
XH968	AAEE & Mkrs/85/41	SS 26.11.64
XH969	AAEE/41	DBR at Wattisham, 17.12.63
XH970	Mkrs & AAEE	SS 26.11.64
XH971	41	Broke up in air during formation break over Geilenkirchen, 29.8.61
XH972	AFDS	To 7834M 23.7.64 at Newton
XH973	41	SS 11.3.65
XH974	41	SS 11.3.65
XH975	AFDS	SS 11.3.65
XH976	AFDS	SS 11.3.65
XH977	41	Engine exploded on start-up; caught fire, Gutersloh, 9.4.62; not repaired; SS 11.3.65
XH978	41	SOC 27.11.64; to Abingdon for fire practice
XH979	AFDS	SS 11.3.65
XH980	41	To 7867M 20.11.64 for display at Stafford
XH981	41	SS 11.3.65
XH982	41	SOC 1.2.65; to Finningley for fire practice
XH983	41	SOC 22.1.65; to Cottesmore for fire practice
XH984	41	SS 11.3.65
XH985	41	SS 11.3.65
XH986	41	To 7842M 17.12.63 at Swanton Morley
XH987	41	SS 11.3.65

XH988	41	Electrics failed and fuel ran out; abandoned and crashed, Crowstone Farm, Durdar, Cumberland, 9.3.60
XH989	41	SS 11.3.65
XH990	41	Undercarriage leg jammed up; swung off runway on landing, Marham, 2.8.63
XH991	85	To 7831M 28.2.64 at Cranwell
XH992	85	To 7829M 21.2.64 at Cosford
XH993	85/41	SS 21.1.65
XJ112	-	Static test airframe
XJ113	41	Engine cut on take-off; swung off runway and caught fire, Wattisham, 11.9.63
XJ114	85	SS 11.3.65
XJ115	85	SS 11.3.65
XJ116	85	To 7832M 13.7.64 at Newton
XJ117	85	To 7833M 13.7.64 at Newton
XJ118	85	SS 11.3.65
XJ119	85	SS 11.3.65
XJ120	85	SS 11.3.65
XJ121	85	SS 11.3.65
XJ122	85	SS 21.1.65; 7863M NTU
XJ123	85	SS 26.11.64
XJ124	85	SS 26.11.64
XJ125	C(A)	Sapphire 7R testbed; SOC 11.3.65
XJ126	85	SS 21.1.65; 7837M NTU
XJ127	41	SS 26.11.64
XJ128	85	Caught fire starting up, West Raynham, 12.7.62; not repaired
XJ129	41	SS 26.11.64
XJ130	41	SS 26.11.64
XJ165	41	SS 26.11.64
XJ166 to XJ178	-	Cancelled

* * * * * * * * * *

XJ183 - XJ188; XJ217 - XJ226; XJ241 - XJ244		Cancelled Swift F.4s to Contract 6/Acft/8509

* * * * * * * * * *

Two English Electric Canberra B(I).8s delivered in March and April 1956 by EEC Preston to Contract 6/Acft/5786 to replace WJ779 and WJ784

XJ249	213	Flew into trees in snowstorm on low level navex 1m NE of Silberborn, West Germany, 30.12.57
XJ257	213	Undercarriage jammed; belly-landed, Ahlhorn, 9.4.57; not repaired

* * * * * * * * * *

Serials allotted temporarily to civil aircraft:

XJ264 York G-ANVO;		XJ269 Hermes G-ALDP;
XJ276 Hermes G-ALDX;		XJ281 Hermes G-ALDK;
XJ288 Hermes G-ALDU;		XJ304 Viking G-AJPH;
XJ309 Hermes G-ALDI		
XJ314		Rolls-Royce Thrust Measuring Rig for Ministry of Aviation
XJ319 - XJ324; XJ347 - XJ350		Sea Devon C.20s for Royal Navy to Contract 6/Acft/11260

XJ355		Saro Skeeter 6 G-ANMH allotted serial for evaluation at A&AEE, November 1954 under Contract 6/Acft/11479

* * * * * * * * * *

Ten Bristol Sycamore HR.14s delivered between March 1955 and October 1956 to Contract 6/Acft/11386

XJ361	SF Eastleigh/84/ SF Khormaksar	Ex G-AMWU. Lost tail rotor after take-off and spun into ground, Khormaksar, 2.9.58
XJ362	JEHU	Resonance built up on landing ½m SW of Bulford Camp, Wilts., 27.6.56; not repaired
XJ363	275	Engine ran away after torque limiting switch failed; force-landed at North Coates, 20.5.57; not repaired
XJ364	275/225/HDU/ CFS/HDU/CFS	SOC 20.3.68; to Old Sarum for fire practice
XJ380	275/Hdlg Sqn/ MoA/CFS	SOC 22.3.68; became 8628M for display at Finningley
XJ381	194	Sank into ground and blades hit ground in heavy landing 10m E of Tanah Ratah, Malaya, 7.8.57
XJ382	194/110	Hit obstruction during forced landing after fire warning 15m E of Kuala Nerang, Malaya, 9.7.62
XJ383	284	Yawed on take-off and rotor blades hit tree 3m NW of Ayios Nikolaios, Cyprus, 26.7.57
XJ384	284/103/1563 Flt/ CFS	SOC 3.4.68; to Catterick for fire practice
XJ385	284/CFS	Engine caught fire; forcelanded at Hinstock, 25.10.63; DBF

* * * * * * * * * *

XJ389		Fairey Jet Gyrodyne (formerly XD759) for Ministry of Aviation to Contract 6/Acft/7240
XJ393 - XJ402		Whirlwind HAR.3s for Royal Navy to Contract 6/Acft/9410

* * * * * * * * * *

20 Westland Whirlwind HAR.2s (XJ429, XJ430, XJ432-XJ436) and HAR.4s (remainder) delivered between November 1954 and May 1955 to Contract 6/Acft/9409 and 11357
XJ407 - XJ414 were originally XD777 - XD784; XJ426 – XJ437 were XD795 – XD806

XJ407	155/22/Cv HAR.10/ 110/103/32	Sold 27.4.82; became G-BKHB 25.8.82
XJ408	155	Control lost due to hydraulic failure; crashlanded, Kuala Lumpur, 26.8.55
XJ409	155/275/228/Cv HAR.10/1310 Flt/ MinTech	Sold to MoD(PE) 20.12.71
XJ410	155/Cv HAR.10/ 22/BSE/22	Hit cables over river during ASR search and ditched ½m S of Long Bridge, Bideford, Devon, 21.9.65
XJ411	Mkrs/110/225/CFS/ Cv HAR.10/110/103	To RAE 10.5.76 for fire practice
XJ412	155/228/Cv HAR.10/ MoA/103/110	Tail rotor failed in hover, sank into ground, Tinkers Hill, Sarawak, 5.11.66; abandoned as inaccessible

XJ413	155	Lost tail rotor and dived into trees 5m NNE of Slim River, Padang, Malaya, 20.9.57
XJ414 ____	155/Cv HAR.10/ 228/202	Lost rotor blade and broke up; crashed in sea off Gt. Yarmouth racecourse, 22.6.67
XJ426	155/Cv HAR.10/22	Ditched after fire warning 6m SE of Lundy Island, 22.8.71
XJ427	155	SOC 13.5.57
XJ428	155/110/Cv HAR.10/ 22/228	Lost power and crashlanded 2m S of Bridlington, Yorks., 10.9.63; to 7821M
XJ429	AAEE/22/Cv HAR.10/22	SOC 16.6.76
XJ430	22/Mkrs/22/275/ Cv HAR.4/228/ Cv HAR.10/1310 Flt/202	SOC 16.11.79; to Manston for fire practice
XJ431	155	Engine cut; forcelanded on beach and overtaken by tide 5m N of Port Dickson, Malaya, 1.8.58
XJ432	22/QF/22/Cv HAR. 10/110/103/28	Engine lost power; ditched, Sai Kung, Hong Kong, 18.1.71
XJ433	22/Mosaic Force/ 22/Cv HAR.10/110	Lost power on approach; forcelanded in scrub, Pa Umor, Borneo, 20.2.64; DBR
XJ434	22	Lost power and ditched during winching practice, Thorney Channel, Sussex, 1.10.55
XJ435	22/Cv HAR.10/ 1563 Flt/32/CFS	To 8671M 12.2.81 at Halton
XJ436	22	Engine cut during ASR demonstration 10m SW of Selsey Bill, Sussex, 30.8.55
XJ437	155/225/228/ Cv HAR.10/SAR Flt/ 22/202/22/84	To 8788M 2.9.83 at Akrotiri

* * * * * * * * * *

XJ440		Prototype Fairey Gannet AEW.3 to Contract 6/Acft/11497
XJ445		Westland Whirlwind HAR.5 for Royal Navy to Contract 6/Acft/10586

* * * * * * * * * *

Four Scottish Aviation Pioneer CC.1s delivered between May and October 1955 to Contract 6/Acft/11407 by SAL, Prestwick

XJ450	267/209	Hit by squall on landing and tipped up, Fort Kemar, Malaya, 4.10.60
XJ451 ____	267	Swung on take-off and crash-landed, Fort Langkap, Malaya, 10.4.58
XJ465	267/209/20	SOC 1.1.70; to Singapore ADC as GI airframe
XJ466	267/209	SOC 26.11.64

* * * * * * * * * *

XJ470		Bristol Freighter 31C G-18-193 delivered to AAEE in February 1955 to Contract 6/Acft/11544

XJ474 to XJ494;
XJ513 to XJ528;   Sea Vixen FAW.1s for Royal
XJ556 to XJ586;   Navy to Contract 6/Acft/10865
XJ602 to XJ611

* * * * * * * * * *

Two Hawker Hunter T.7 prototypes for Ministry of Aviation to Contract 6/Acft/11595

XJ615	Mkrs & AAEE/ETPS	Flew into high ground and broke up 1½m SE of Haslemere, Surrey, 24.6.64
XJ627	Mkrs & AAEE/ Martin-Baker	Sold to HSA 27.9.68 for Chilean Air Force as J-721

* * * * * * * * * *

45 Hawker Hunter F.6s delivered between January and May 1957 by Hawker, Kingston, to Contract 6/Acft/11617

XJ632	93/26/Cv FGA.9/ 208/8 & 43/208	Sold 5.11.69; to Singapore ADC as No.505
XJ633	4/66/Cv FR.10/ 4/2	Sold 3.3.71; to Singapore ADC as No.534
XJ634	93/229 OCU/TWU/ Cv F.6A/1 TWU	To 8684M 14.4.81 at Cranwell
XJ635	93/Cv FGA.9/ 54/208/TWU	Abandoned after control lost in cloud 2m E of Aberystwyth, Cardigan, 4.5.76
XJ636	4/26/14/Cv FGA.9/ 54/208/229 OCU/ TWU	Abandoned after engine failure 1m W of Mathry, Pembs., 25.10.76
XJ637	4/2/229 OCU/TWU/ Cv F.6A/TWU/ 1 TWU	Abandoned when engine cut on low-level navex near Talfarn, Pembs., 14.3.79
XJ638	4	To RRAF 5.4.63 as No.123
XJ639	4/2/229 OCU/ TWU/Cv F.6A/TWU	To 8687M 14.4.81 at Cranwell
XJ640	4/Cv FGA.9/1/ 229 OCU/1 & 54/ W.Raynham/HCT	Sold 17.1.75; to Lebanese AF as L-285
XJ641	93	Presumed crashed in sea after radio failure off Friesian Islands, 11.11.59
XJ642	14/Cv FGA.9/54/ SF West Raynham	Sold 10.2.70; to Singapore ADC as No.518
XJ643	14/Cv FGA.9/ 208/28/20	Sold 28.1.70; to Singapore ADC as No.515
XJ644	14/Cv FGA.9/54/ SF West Raynham	Sold 21.1.75; to Lebanese AF as L-284
XJ645	93/Cv FGA.9/208/ 8 & 43/43	Sold 10.4.68; to RJAF as No.831
XJ646	14/Cv FGA.9/ 8 & 43/8	Sold 24.4.68; to Indian AF as A-968
XJ673	14/Cv FGA.9/20	Engine cut on approach to Clark Field; abandoned and crashed in Manila Bay, Philippines, 2.4.69
XJ674	4/26/Cv FGA.9/20	Undercarriage leg jammed after hydraulic failure; rolled and abandoned 1m S of Tengah 22.7.68
XJ675	93	Engine flamed out; abandoned 5m NE of Aurich, West Germany, 8.1.60
XJ676	93/2/229 OCU/ TWU/Cv F.6A/ TWU/1 TWU	To 8844M 9.1.85 at Lyneham
XJ677	-	To Iraqi AF 15.4.57 as No.394
XJ678	-	To Iraqi AF 15.4.57 as No.395
XJ679	-	To Iraqi AF 15.4.57 as No.396
XJ680	20/Cv FGA.9/43/ 8 & 43/43/8	Sold 4.12.69; to Singapore ADC as No.511
XJ681	-	To Iraqi AF 15.4.57 as No.397
XJ682	-	To Iraqi AF 15.4.57 as No.398
XJ683	93/Cv FGA.9/43/20/ TWU/1 TWU/ 2 TWU/1 TWU	To Zimbabwe AF 5.10.87 as 1813
XJ684	20/Cv FGA.9/43/ 8-43/8	Sold 4.12.69; to Singapore ADC as No.513
XJ685	20/Cv FGA.9/43/20	Sold 15.8.69; to Singapore ADC as No.502
XJ686	20/Cv FGA.9/43/20/ 45-58/TWU/2 TWU/ 1 TWU	Sold to Chile 23.4.82 as 746
XJ687	66/Cv FGA.9/208/8/ 208/8-43/208/ 229 OCU/TWU/ 1 TWU	Sold to Chile 6.1.83 as 753
XJ688	20/26/Cv FGA.9/ 208/8-43/208/ 208/8/229 OCU/ TWU/2 TWU/ 1 TWU	Sold to Chile 5.82 as 748
XJ689	14/Cv FGA.9/8-43/8	Sold to HSA 1.4.70 for Singapore ADC as 517
XJ690	14/Cv FGA.9/20	Sold 12.2.76 to HAS; to G-9-451
XJ691	14/Cv FGA.9/208	Radio failed; crashed in sea 18m SE of Bahrein, 27.4.67; cause not known
XJ692	20/Cv FGA.9/43/ 8-43/43/8	Sold to Indian AF 5.4.68 as A969
XJ693	20	Undercarriage jammed; belly-landed, Gutersloh, 3.10.60; not repaired
XJ694	MoA/34-208/ Cv FR.10/ MoA/4&2	Sold to Indian AF 16.2.71 as S1389
XJ695	20/14/Cv FGA.9/20/ 45/58/229 OCU/ TWU/1 TWU	Flew into flock of birds and forcelanded, Brize Norton, 16.11.78; to 8738M 1.4.81 at Cranwell; later to 8738M and 9183M at Manston
XJ712	20/14/1	Sold to HSA 1.4.66 for R Saudi AF as 60-601
XJ713	20/14/1/SF West Raynham/229 OCU	Sold to HSA 11.9.69 for Chile as J-722
XJ714	C(A)/208/56/ Cv FR.10/4/8	Sold to HSA 7.6.71 for Singapore ADC as 531 17.1.73
XJ715	111/229 OCU	Sold to HSA 6.4.66 for R.Saudi AF as 60-604
XJ716	20	To RRAF 19.4.63 as 124
XJ717	20/26/14/54/SF W,Raynham/54	Sold to HSA 5.7.67 for Chilean AF as J-717
XJ718	93	To RRAF 15.12.62 as 117

* * * * * * * * * *

19 Westland Whirlwind HAR.2s and HAR.4s delivered between September 1955 and April 1956 to Contract 6/Acft/11387 Mk.4s shown *

XJ723*	155/Cv HAR.10/ 228/202	Sold 29.3.79; to 2288 Sqn ATC at Montrose
XJ724*	155/SAR Flt Khorm-aksar/225/CFS/ Cv HAR.10/228/202	To 8613M 8.1.79; to Catterick for fire practice
XJ725	22	Engine cut during winching practice; ditched off Ramsgate, Kent, 11.10.61
XJ726	22/Antler TG/22/ Cv HAR.4/Cv HAR.10/SAR Flt ME/ CFS	To Nene Valley Aviation Society 4.2.81
XJ727*	22/228/Cv HAR.10/ 1310 Flt/CFS	To 8661M 27.11.80 at Halton

XJ728	22	Tail rotor cable snapped during winching exercise; rotated into water, Padstow Estuary, Cornwall, 20.1.60
XJ729*	22/Cv HAR.10/22/ MoA/228/202/22	To 8732M 1.8.84 at Finningley
XJ730*	22	Engine lost power; crashed in sea off Felixstowe RAF station, 15.5.58
———		
XJ756	CFS/22	Flew into ground in bad weather, Whitehorse Wood, 4m NNW of West Malling, 12.12.56
XJ757	22/1360 Flt/217/Cv HAR.10/225/22/CFS	Flew into ground during practice autorotative landing, Ternhill, 19.9.66; to 7921M at Ternhill
XJ758	22/1360 Flt/217/ Cv HAR.10/CFS/ 230/CFS	To 8464M 10.2.76 at Shawbury
XJ759	ETPS	MoS aircraft. Rotor blades hit tail cone during practice auto-rotative landing, Farnborough, 1.8.66; not repaired
XJ760	22/Cv HAR.10/110	Lost power on approach and forcelanded in jungle, Long Bangar, Borneo, 10.9.64
XJ761*	155/275/228	Engine lost power during winching practice; hit water and sank off Great Yarmouth, Norfolk, 27.7.60
XJ762	Buffalo Force/22/ 1360 Flt/217/Mkrs	Damaged while with Westlands Yeovil, and not repaired, 11.1.61
XJ763	Antler TG/1362 Flt/ 22/Cv HAR.10/110/ 103/32	Sold 27.4.82; became G-BKHA 25.8.82
XJ764	JEHU/225/Cv HAR.10/CFS/ 22/1564 Flt/ 1563 Flt/22/84	SOC 3.9.76
XJ765	JEHU/225	Control rod broke; dropped into ground and caught fire ½m S of Upavon, 1.6.61
XJ766	ISF Cyprus/284/22	Engine cut during SAR search; ditched off Constantine Bay, Cornwall, 31.7.59

* * * * * * * * * *

Six de Havilland Vampire T.11s delivered between February and November 1955 from Royal Norwegian Air Force order

XJ771	8 FTS/CNCS/ CATCS	Sold to BEA 9.12.68
XJ772	RAFC/8 FTS/ 1 FTS/CATCS	To Brooklands Tech College as GI airframe, 3.2.71
XJ773	8 FTS	Sold to HSA 8.12.64 for Swiss AF
XJ774	CNCS/CATCS	8123M NTU; Sold to Chilean AF 10.11.72 as J-05
XJ775	Met Res Flt/8 FTS	SOC 6.6.63
XJ776	8 FTS	SS 30.6.64

* * * * * * * * * *

Eight Avro Vulcan B.2s delivered between January and May 1961 to Contract 6/Acft/11830

XJ780	83/12/230 OCU/ Wadd Wg/Cott Wg/ Akrotiri Wg/Wadd Wg/Akrotiri Wg/ Wadd Wg/27	SS 11.82

XJ781	83/12/230 OCU/ Wadd Wg/Akrotiri Wg	Undercarriage leg jammed up; swung on landing into gully, Shiraz, Iran, 23.5.73; salvage impracticable
XJ782	83/12/230 OCU/ Wadd Wg/Cott Wg/ Akrotiri Wg/Wadd Wg/27/Wadd Wg	To 8766M 6.9.82 at Finningley
XJ783	83/9/230 OCU/ Wadd Wg/ Akrotiri Wg/35/ 230 OCU/35	SS 11.82
XJ784	MoA/230 OCU/ Akrotiri Wg/Wadd Wg/Akrotiri Wg/ Wadd Wg	SS 12.82
———		
XJ823	27/35/230 OCU/ Wadd Wg/Akrotiri Wg/Wadd Wg/27/ 35/Wadd Wg	SS 21.1.83; preserved at Carlisle
XJ824	27/9/230 OCU/ Cott Wg/Wadd Wg/ Akrotiri Wg/35/ 230 OCU/Wadd Wg	To IWM Duxford 15.3.82
XJ825	27/35/Cott Wg/ Wadd Wg/Cott Wg/ Akrotiri Wg/35/27/ 35/Wadd Wg/50/ Cv K.2	To 8810M 5.4.84 at Waddington

* * * * * * * * * *

Two Miles Marathon 1As delivered in February and March 1955 by W S Shackleton to Contract 6/Acft/11571

XJ830	RAE	Ex G-AMHS; sold 6.10.58; to G-AMHS 18.9.58
XJ831	RAE	Ex G-AMHV; sold 2.10.58; to G-AMHV 18.9.58

* * * * * * * * * *

XJ836 - XJ842; XJ877 - XJ887	Cancelled P.376 Javelins to Contract 6/Acft/11776

* * * * * * * * * *

Nine Bristol Sycamore HR.14s delivered between October 1956 and January 1957 by Bristol, Weston-super-Mare, to Contract No.6/Acft/11899

XJ895	275/284/SF El Adem/ 103/ 1564 Flt/CFS	SOC 3.4.68; to Catterick for fire practice
XJ896	284	Flew into high ground 2m WSW of Makheras, Cyprus, 10.2.58; cause not known
XJ897	284/103/1563 Flt/ CFS	SOC 27.5.68; to Wattisham for fire practice
XJ898	284/103/1563 Flt/ SAR Flt Aden/CFS	SOC 15.5.68; to Leuchars for fire practice
XJ915	275/CFS	Rolled while taking off in cross-wind; rotor hit ground, Ternhill, 17.2.66; 7910M NTU; to 7915M
XJ916	275/SAR Flt Aden/ CFS	SOC 21.5.68; to Manston for fire practice
XJ917	275/CFS	Sold 12.12.72; preserved
XJ918	275/AAEE/Kuala Lumpur/Seletar/ 110/MCS/32	To 8190M 15.12.71 at Cosford

XJ919	275/225/AAEE/ Hdlg Sqn	Tail rotor struck ground in hover; rolled over, Boscombe Down, 27.2.63

* * * * * * * * * *

XJ924, XJ928, XJ930, XJ936		Fairey Ultralight helicopter prototypes for MoA to Contract 6/Acft/9912
XJ941		Auster J/5G Autocar (ex G-ANVN) acquired for spraying tests by Colonial Insecticides Research Unit
XJ945 - XJ958; XJ971 - XJ997; XK103 - XK111		Cancelled Hunter F.6s to Contract 6/Acft/12132

* * * * * * * * * *

53 Hawker Hunter F.6s delivered between August and October 1957 by Hawkers, Kingston, to Contract 6/Acft/12133

XK136	74/Cv FGA.9/20	Abandoned in spin and crashed in swamp 32m WNW of Tengah, 19.10.64
XK137	20/Cv FGA.9/43/ 54/SF W.Raynham/ 208/45/Hunter Wg/ TWU/2 TWU/1 TWU	Sold; to Chile 22.5.82 as No.749
XK138	20/Cv FGA.9/20/ 45/Hunter Wg/ TWU/2 TWU/1 TWU	Sold; to Chile 22.5.82 as No.750
XK139	66/Cv FGA.9/ 1/208	Collided with XE647 during practice low level attack and crashed off Dasa Is., Persian Gulf, 30.6.64
XK140	C(A)/74/Cv FGA.9/ 54/208/8/45/Hunter Wg/TWU/2 TWU	Abandoned after control lost on low level exercise off Lochinver, Highland, 3.7.79
XK141	74/229 OCU/TWU/ Cv F.6A/TWU/ 1 TWU	Sold; to Chile 6.1.83 as No.754
XK142	74/Cv FGA.9/20	Sold to HSA 11.5.71 for Singapore ADC as No.522
XK143	-	To Iraqi AF as No.400 19.12.57
XK144	-	To Iraqi AF as No.401 19.12.57
XK145	-	To Iraqi AF as No.402 19.12.57
XK146	-	To Iraqi AF as No.403 19.12.57
XK147	-	To Iraqi AF as No.404 20.12.57
XK148	Hdlg Sqn	Sold to HSA 11.7.67 for Chilean AF as J-715
XK149	CFE/14/1/54/ 229 OCU/TWU/ Cv F.6A/TWU/ 1 TWU	To 8714M 5.11.81 at Cranwell
XK150	AFDS/Cv FGA.9/ 208/8 & 43/8	Sold to RJAF 26.1.68 as 818
XK151	AFDS/Cv FGA.9/8/ 208/8 & 43/8/208/ 8/45/Hunter Wg/ TWU/2 TWU	Flew into Cuillan Hills in cloud on low level exercise, Skye, 12.2.80
XK152	-	To Iraqi AF as No.405 19.12.57
XK153	-	To Iraqi AF as No.406 20.12.57
XK154	-	To Iraqi AF as No.407 20.12.57
XK155	-	To Iraqi AF as No.408 20.12.57
XK156	-	To Iraqi AF as No.409 20.12.57
XK157 to XK176	-	To Indian AF as BA201-BA220
XK213 to XK224	-	To Indian AF as BA221-BA232

XK225 to XK241	-	Cancelled
XK257 to XK306	-	Cancelled
XK323 to XK355	-	Cancelled

* * * * * * * * * *

Four Scottish Aviation Pioneer CC.1s delivered in November and December 1955 to Contract 6/Acft/11823

XK367	215/209	SOC 11.8.67
XK368	267/209	SOC 27.9.62
XK369	215	Hit fence on down-wind take-off and crashed into ditch, Barnard Castle, Co.Durham, 23.7.56
XK370	Benson/215/230/ RAF Muscat/SOAF/ 209/20	SOC 1.1.70; to Singapore ASDC as GI airframe

* * * * * * * * * *

25 Auster AOP.9s delivered between February 1956 and March 1957 by Auster Aircraft, Rearsby, to Contract 6/Acft/11436

XK374	656	To AAC 1.9.57
XK375	656	To AAC 1.9.57
XK376	Mkrs	To AAC 25.8.58
XK377	656	To AAC 1.9.57
XK378	656	To AAC 1.9.57
XK379	656	To AAC 1.9.57
XK380	656	To AAC 1.9.57
XK381	LAS	To AAC 1.9.57
XK382	LAS	To AAC 1.9.57
XK406	-	To AAC 11.10.57
XK407	656	To AAC 1.9.57
XK408	657	To AAC 1.9.57
XK409	-	To AAC 22.10.57
XK410	160 Wg/Christ- mas Is	SOC 13.2.62
XK411	-	To AAC 31.10.57
XK412	Hdlg Sqn	To AAC 26.11.59
XK413	-	To AAC 1.9.57
XK414	-	To AAC 16.11.57
XK415	-	To AAC 22.11.57
XK416	LAS/651	To AAC 1.9.57; later to 7855M
XK417	LAS/652	To AAC 1.9.57
XK418	LAS	To AAC 1.9.57; later to 7976M
XK419	LAS	To AAC 1.9.57; later to 8058M
XK420	-	To AAC 5.2.60
XK421	LAS	To AAC 1.9.57; later to 8365M

* * * * * * * * * *

XK426		Rolls-Royce Thrust Measuring Rig to Contract 6/Eng/7814
XK429, XK434, XK436		Cancelled Bristol 188s to Contract 6/Acft/12176
XK440 - XK443; XK467 - XK473		Cancelled Canberra PR.9s to Contract 6/Acft/12164

* * * * * * * * * *

Four Saro Skeeter AOP.10/T.11 delivered in December 1956 and January 1957 to Contract 6/Acft/12206

XK479	Hdlg Sqn/CFS	Built as T.11; SOC 5.7.62
XK480	651/6 IL Flt/AACC/ CFS/AACC/ AACTDC	To AAC 1.9.57

Skeeter

XK481	651/1906 Flt/	
	1 IL Flt/AACC	SOC 15.12.62
XK482	Mkrs/Hdlg Sqn/	To 7840M 5.3.64; became G-BJWS
	Mkrs/AACC	30.11.82

*   *   *   *   *   *   *   *   *   *

XK486 - XK491;	Buccaneer S.1s for Royal Navy
XK523 - XK536	to Contract 6/Acft/11790
	XK526 to 8648M; XK527 to
	8818M NTU XK531 to 8403M;
	XK532 to 8867M
XK542 - XK548;	Cancelled Grasshopper TX.1s
XK569 - XK571	to Contract 6/Acft/12291
XK577	Javelin T.3 for Ministry of
	Aviation to Contract 6/ACFT/11262

*   *   *   *   *   *   *   *   *   *

24 de Havilland Vampire T.11s delivered between May and November 1956 by D.H., Chester to Contract 6/Acft/12202

XK582	CFS	SS 31.3.65
XK583	MCCF/SF Wroughton	SS 11.7.60
XK584	7 FTS	Abandoned in spin,
		Wanddeusant, 5m E of
		Holyhead, Anglesey, 24.4.61
XK585	8 FTS	SS 21.4.64
XK586	CFS	SS 30.6.64
XK587	SLAW/MCCF/	
	SF Wroughton	SS 11.7.60
XK588	MCCF/7 FTS/1 FTS/	
	7 FTS/5 FTS/8 FTS	SOC 11.9.63
XK589	7 FTS/RAFC	SOC 2.3.62; to Driffield for fire
		practice
XK590	7 FTS/4 FTS/	Sold 6.2.70 to W Oxford Tech
	CATCS	College
XK623	5 FTS	Sold 6.12.68 to HSA as GI airframe
XK624	7 FTS/AAEE/CFS/	
	23 Gp CF/83 Gp CF/	
	23 Gp CF/1 FTS/	
	7 FTS/3 FTS/CFS	Sold 14.12.71 to Lytham Museum
XK625	7 FTS/1 FTS/4 FTS	Sold 4.12.68 to HSA
XK626	RAFC	Engine flamed out after take-off; crash-
		landed 2m W of Cranwell, 16.6.60
XK627	CFS/DH/CFS/8 FTS	Sold 3.12.68 to HSA
XK628	CFS/RAFC	SS 30.6.60
XK629	CFS	To 7553M 20.12.57 at Hornchurch
XK630	CFS	To 7560M 13.3.58 at Cranwell
XK631	CFS	Engine flamed out and radio
		failed; abandoned 3½m ENE of
		Bromyard, Herefordshire, 7.4.59
XK632	CFS/3-4 CAACU	Sold 6.1.72 to Exeter Airport
XK633	CFS/1 FTS	Veered on take-off and under-
		carriage collapsed, Rufforth,
		10.7.63; DBR
XK634	229 OCU/	Sold to HSA 4.2.64 for
	3-4 CAACU	Austrian AF as 5C-VE
XK635	8 FTS	SS 5.3.64
XK636	RAFC	Sold 15.12.64 to HSA
XK637	7 FTS/4 FTS	Sold 30.11.67 to HSA

*   *   *   *   *   *   *   *   *   *

English Electric Canberra B.2 delivered in May 1956 by EEC, Preston, to Contract 6/Acft/12265

| XK641 | SF Binbrook/12/ | Rolled and dived into hill, |
| | Cv B.15/45 | Taseh Chini, Pahang, 4.4.66 |

*   *   *   *   *   *   *   *   *   *

Two English Electric Canberra T.4s built by EEC, Preston, to Contract 6/Acft/12265

| XK647 | - | To Indian AF as IQ994 |
| XK650 | - | To Indian AF as IQ995 |

*   *   *   *   *   *   *   *   *   *

13 de Havilland Comet C.2s, R2s and T.2s delivered between June 1956 and February 1958 to Contracts 6/Acft/11808 (first three) and 11809

XK655	Mkrs/Cv R.2/	R.2 ex G-AMXA. Sold 1.8.74
	192/51	and preserved
XK659	192/51	R.2 ex G-AMXC; SOC 13.5.74
XK663	192/51	R.2 ex G-AMXE; caught fire in
		hangar, Watton, 3.6.59; DBR
XK669	216/Cv C.2/216	T.2 ex G-AMXB; *Taurus*
		SOC 24.4.66
XK670	216/Cv C.2/216	T.2 ex G-AMXF; *Corvus*
		To 7926M 29.11.66 at Lyneham
XK671	216/51	C.2 ex G-AMXG; *Aquila*
		To 7927M 14.11.66 at Topcliffe
XK695	216/Cv R.2/51	C.2 ex G-AMXH; *Perseus*;
		to IWM 10.1.75 and preserved;
		to 9164M 11.92
XK696	216	C.2 ex G-AMXI; *Orion*
		SOC 27.10.66
XK697	216/51	C.2 ex G-AMXJ; *Cygnus*
		SOC 20.12.72
XK698	216	C.2 ex G-AMXL; *Pegasus*
		to 8031M 4.69 at Shawbury
XK699	216	C.2; *Sagittarius*
		to 7971M 6.67; preserved
XK715	216/51/216	C.2; *Columbo*; to 7905M 4.66 at
		Cosford
XK716	216	C.2; *Cepheus*; to 7958M 5.67 at Halton

*   *   *   *   *   *   *   *   *   *

| XK720 | Cancelled Rolls-Royce VTOL |
| | testbed to Contract 6/Eng/8606 |

*   *   *   *   *   *   *   *   *   *

Six Folland Gnat F.1s for Ministry of Supply delivered by Folland Aircraft to Contract 6/Acft/12292

XK724	AAEE	Ex G-39-2; to 7715M 25.2.61 at
		Henlow
XK739	BSE	
XK740	BSE	To 8396M 2.8.61 at Cosford
XK741	AAEE	Preserved
XK767	Mkrs	Abandoned on test flight and dived
		into ground, Stapleford, Wilts.,
		15.10.58; believed controls failed
XK768	-	To Indian AF as IE1059

*   *   *   *   *   *   *   *   *   *

XK773	Skeeter 6 G-ANMG for evaluation
	to Contract 6/Acft/12533, November
	1955
XK776, XK781,	M.L.Utilities for trials with
XK784	Army to Contract 6/Acft/11887
XK788 - XK791;	Grasshopper TX.1 gliders for ATC and
XK819 - XK824	CCF to Contract 6/Acft/12291
XK831 - XK835;	Vickers Wild Goose variable
XK850 - XK854	geometry models for trials to
	Contract 6/Acft/11393

*   *   *   *   *   *   *   *   *   *

Six Percival Pembroke C.1s delivered between February and October 1956 by Hunting-Percival Aircraft to Contract 6/Acft/12518

XK859	SF El Adem	Ran out of fuel and belly-landed on road 10m NW of El Adem, 28.5.57; not repaired
XK860	SF Amman/ SF Habbaniya	SOC 15.4.59
XK861	AAFCE/BCCF/ Hdlg Sqn/2 TAF CS	Bellylanded in error during asymmetric landing, Bruggen, 25.10.61; not repaired
XK862 ____	MECS/SF Gibraltar/ WCS/SF El Adem/ 70/21	8191M NTU; to 8194M 23.3.72 at St Athan
XK884	MECS/SF Nicosia/ MECS/70/SCS/207/ 21/60	Sold 15.6.87; to G-BNPG
XK885	267/209/S & TTF Seletar/B & TTF Seletar/WCS/21/60	To 8452M 22.8.75 at St Athan

* * * * * * * * * *

XK889		Percival P-74 prototype to Contract 6/Acft/7054; not flown
XK895 - XK897		Sea Devon C.20s for Royal Navy to Contract 6/Acft/12821
XK902, XK903		Sycamore HR.51s for Royal Australian Navy to Contract 6/Acft/12606
XK906 - XK912 XK933 - XK945		Whirlwind HAS.7s for Royal Navy to Contract 6/Acft/12725 XK943 to 8796M

* * * * * * * * * *

Four English Electric Canberra B(I).8s delivered in September and October 1956 by English Electric, Preston, to Contract 6/Acft/6445 and to Contract 6/Acft/11158 (XK959)

XK951	88/14/16/3	Sold to Marshalls 22.10.73 for Peru as No.248
XK952	59/3/16/MoA/ 16/14/16	SOC 6.4.73; to Manston for fire practice
XK953	-	To Indian AF as IF895
XK959	-	To Indian AF as IF898

* * * * * * * * * *

XK964		Skeeter 6 G-ANMI for evaluation, January to May 1956, to Contract 6/Acft/12975

* * * * * * * * * *

Nine Westland Whirlwind HAR.2s delivered between May and December 1956 by Westlands, Yeovil, to Contract 6/Acft/12881

XK968	JEHU/225/22/ Cv HAR.10/110/ 103/28	To 8445M 24.7.75; preserved
XK969	JEHU/225/CFS/ Cv HAR.10/228/ 202/230/202/ SAR Wg	To 8646M 16.11.79; to Manston for fire practice
XK970 _____	JEHU/225/228/ Cv HAR/10/MoA/ SAR Flt/CFS/ 230/84	To 8789M 7.82 at Odiham
XK986	JEHU/225/228/ Cv HAR.10/230/84	To 8790M 7.82 at Odiham

Whirlwind

XK987	22/1360 Flt/217/ 22/228/Cv HAR.10/ 110/103	To 8393M 3.10.73 at Brize Norton
XK988	JEHU/225/CFS/ Cv HAR.10/103/ 110/103	To A2646 for Royal Navy, 1.7.75; preserved
XK989	22	Lost height and ditched during winching practice, Thorney Creek, 1m off Thorney Island, 26.2.57; to 7415M 16.4.57 at Halton
XK990	JEHU/Cv HAR.10/ 228/202	Engine failed during landing practice; hit ground and rotors cut off tail cone ¼m N of Acklington, 27.10.67
XK991	JEHU/Cv HAR.10/ 228	Rotor hit mast of pinnace while winching; ditched in Bridlington Bay, 7.5.63; 7810M allotted but not used

* * * * * * * * * *

Five Westland Whirlwind HAR.4s delivered between November 1956 and February 1957 by Westland Helicopters, Yeovil, to Contract 6/Acft/12881

XL109	MoS/CFS/Cv HAR.10/MoA/ 110/28	Engine cut in turbulence; ditched 2m NE of Sai Kung, Hong Kong, 17.10.70
XL110	Mkrs/217/228/ Cv HAR.10/ 230/84	Lost rotor in low hover and hit ground, Nicosia, 6.2.73
XL111	RRE/QF/ CFS/225/22/Cv HAR.10/22/SAR Flt Khormaksar	Engine cut; forcelanded in soft sand and rolled over, Khormaksar, 1.4.67; to 8000M at St Athan
XL112	217/228/Cv HAR.10/ 1563 Flt/1564 Flt/ SAR Flt Khormaksar/ 22/202	Control lost in cloud; crashed, Gazing Nook Farm, Patrick Brompton, Yorks., 20.11.70
XL113	228	Engine cut during winching exercise; ditched in Cullercoats Bay, Northumberland, 5.8.61

* * * * * * * * * *

Eight Blackburn Beverley C.1s delivered between May and October 1957 by Blackburns, Brough, to Contract 6/Acft/12264

XL117	-	To XL130
XL118.	-	To XL131
XL119	-	To XL132
XL130	30/242 OCU/30/84	SS 29.8.69
XL131	30/47	SS 29.8.69
XL132	242 OCU	Engine caught fire and dropped out on approach to Thorney Island; control lost and ditched in Chichester Harbour, Sussex, 17.5.62
_____		
XL148	242 OCU/30	SS 25.3.70
XL149	242 OCU/84/30	To 7988M 7.11.67 at Finningley
XL150	RAE/84/47 & 53/34	Flew into high ground in cloud at night 72m N of Seletar, 15.12.67
XL151	47 & 53/84	Flew into sand dunes during search and blew up 15m NE of Khormaksar, 11.10.60
XL152	30	SS 25.3.70

* * * * * * * * * *

18 Handley Page Victor B.2s delivered between November 1961 and February 1962 by Handley Page, Radlett, to Contract 6/Acft/12996

XL158	AAEE/139/Witt Wg/ VTF Wyton/Witt Wg/ Cv K.2/55/57/55	SOC 1.94

XL159	AAEE	Stalled and dived into house, Stubton, Notts., 23.3.62
XL160	R-R/100/Witt Wg/ Cv K.2/55/57/55/57	To 8910M 2.7.86 for BDR trg at Marham
XL161	Avro/Cv SR.2/543/ Cv K.2/55/57/55	To Lyneham as 9214M 27.9.93
XL162	AAEE/139/Witt Wg/ Cv K.2/57/55/ 57/55	To CTE Manston, 15.8.91 as 9114M
XL163	139/100/Witt Wg & VTF/Cv K.2/ 232 OCU/55/57/ 55/57/55	To 8916M 2.9.86 at St Athan
XL164	HP&AAEE/Cv K.2/ 57/55/57/55	To 9215M 27.9 at Brize Norton
XL165	15/100/232 OCU/ AAEE/Çv SR.2/543/ VTF Wyton	SOC 30.10.75
XL188	232 OCU/Witt Wg/ VTF/Witt Wg/AAEE/ HSA/Cv K.2/55/57/55	To 9100M for BDR trg, Kinloss, 25.6.91
XL189	232 OCU/Witt Wg/ VTF/HSA/Cv K.2/ 232 OCU/55/57/ 55/57	To 8912M 2.7.86 at Waddington
XL190	139/Witt Wg/ Cv K.2/232 OCU/ 55/57/55	To 9216M 27.9.93 at St Mawgan
XL191	139/Witt Wg/ Cv K.2/232 OCU/55	Undershot approach in bad visibility; bounced and flew into ground, Hamilton, Ont., 19.6.86; DBR
XL192	100/232 OCU/Witt Wg & VTF/Cv K.2/ 57/55	To 9024M 7.7.88 for spares recovery 1.89
XL193	100/232 OCU/ Cv SR.2/543/ Victor Flt Wyton	SOC 10.11.75
XL230	IFTU/232 OCU/ Cv SR.2/543	Bounced during asymmetrical landing; yawed on attempted overshoot; hit ground and blew up, Wyton, 10.5.73
XL231	139/Witt Wg/VTF/ Witt Wg/HSA/ Cv K.2/AAEE/HSA/ 57/232 OCU/57/55	To Yorkshire Air Museum 25.11.93
XL232	139/100/232 OCU/ Witt Wg/Cv K.2/ 55/232 OCU/55/ 57/55/57/55	Engine blew up on take-off and caught fire; stopped but fire spread to airframe, Marham, 15.10.82; DBF
XL233	AAEE/Witt Wg & VTF/Cv K.2/232 OCU/55/AAEE/55	SS 25.9.88

* * * * * * * * * *

XL237 - XL241	Sea Hawk FB.50s for
XL269 - XL276	Royal Netherlands Navy to
XL305 - XL313	Contract 6/Acft/13024

* * * * * * * * * *

24 Avro Vulcan B.2s delivered between July 1961 and November 1962 by Avro, Woodford, to Contract 6/Acft/12305
(Ak = Akrotiri Wing; Cott = Cottesmore Wing; Scam = Scampton Wing; Wadd = Waddington Wing)

XL317	MoA/617/Scam/230 OCU/Scam/230 OCU/ 617/230 OCU/617	To 8725M 1.12.81 at Akrotiri
XL318	617/Scam/230 OCU/ Wadd/230 OCU/617	To 8733M for RAF Museum 4.1.82
XL319	617/Scam/230 OCU/ 617/230 OCU/35/ Wadd	To NE Avn Museum 20.1.83
XL320	617/Scam/230 OCU	SS 31.8.81
XL321	617/Scam/230 OCU/ 617/230 OCU/Wadd/ 230 OCU/35/617/ 35/50	To 8759M 19.8.82 at Catterick
XL359	617/Scam/230 OCU/ 35	To Scampton for display 1.3.82; 8744M NTU; SS 11.82
XL360	617/Scam/230 OCU/ Wadd/230 OCU/617/ 35/101	To Midlands Aircraft Museum, Coventry, 26.1.83
XL361	617/Scam/230 OCU/ Scam/230 OCU & 27/ 617/35	To Happy Valley AFB Goose Bay, 21.12.81
XL384	230 OCU/Scan/Wadd/ Scam/230 OCU/Scam & 230 OCU	To 8505M 14.1.75 at Scampton later to 8670M
XL385	9/Scam/617	Two engines exploded on take-off; caught fire, Scampton, 6.4.67
XL386	9/Scam/230 OCU/ Wadd	To 8760M 20.8.82 at Manston
XL387	230 OCU/Scam/617/ 230 OCU/Wadd	To 8748M 28.1.82 at St Athan
XL388	9/Scam/230 OCU/ 617/230 OCU/617/ Wadd	To 8750M 2.4.82 at Honington
XL389	230 OCU/Scam/230 OCU/617 & 230 OCU/Wadd	SS 31.8.81
XL390	9/Scam/230 OCU/ 617	Stalled during low run during display practice and crashed, Glenview NAS, Ill., USA, 11.8.78
XL391	MoA/BCDU/MoA/ Ak/Wadd	SOC 11.2.83; preserved Blackpool
XL392	83/Scam/617/35	To 8745M 1.3.82 at Valley
XL425	83/Scam/617-27/617	SS 4.1.82
XL426	83/Scam/27/230 CU/617/230 OCU/ 50/Waddington	Sold 22.12.86 to Southend Airport for display; to G-VJET 7.7.87
XL427	83/Scam/617/230 OCU/27/230 OCU/ 27/Wadd	To 8756M 13.8.82 at Machrihanish
XL443	27/Wadd/Cott/Ak/ Wadd/35/230 OCU/ 35/44/50	To Scampton 4.1.82 for RAF Museum; SS 4.82
XL444	27/Scam/230 OCU/ Scam/617 & 230 OCU/617/35/Wadd	SS 12.82
XL445	27/Wadd/Ak/Wadd/ 230 OCU/35/44/ Cv B.2K/50/Cv K.2	To 8811M 5.4.84 at Lyneham
XL446	27/Wadd/230 OCU/ Ak/35/Wadd/617/35	SOC 1.3.82

* * * * * * * * * *

XL449 - XL456	Fairey Gannet AEW.3s
XL471 - XL482	for Royal Navy to Contract
XL493 - XL503	6/Acft/12876; XL450 became 8601M; XL502 became 8610M
XL507	Sycamore HR.51 ex XK903 for Royal Australian Navy to Contract 6/Acft/13096

* * * * * * * * * *

Three Handley Page Victor B.2s delivered between July and September 1963 by Handley Page, Radlett, to Contract 6/Acft/12996

XL511	139/Witt Wg & VTF/ Cv K.2/55/57/55/57	SOC 2.7.86 at Manston for fire practice
XL512	139/Witt/Cv K.2/ 55/57/55	SS 3.94
XL513	139/VTF/100-139/ Cv K.2/55/232 OCU/ 55	Overshot abandoned take-off after hitting bird on take-off; caught fire, Marham, 28.9.76

*   *   *   *   *   *   *   *   *   *

Ten Scottish Aviation Pioneer CC.1s delivered between May and July 1956 by Scottish Aviation, Prestwick, to Contract 6/Acft/13190

XL517	78/230/209	Ex G-AOGK. Stalled and hit trees in turn on to approach and crashed, Long Pa Sia, Borneo, 15.7.66
XL518	78/SMOAF	SOC 30.10.62
XL519	78	SOC 10.7.57
XL520	78	Failed to become airborne due to sand drag; hit ridge and tipped up, Beihan, Aden, 13.9.57
XL553	78	Blown over by gust on landing, hit runway and tipped up, Wadi Ain, Aden, 19.9.57
XL554	78	To SOAF 5.8.59
XL555	230	Stalled on take-off and dived into ground, Upavon, 29.4.60
XL556	215/Hdlg Sqn/ 215/230	Undercarriage collapsed in heavy landing, Middle Wallop, 22.9.58; not repaired
XL557	215/230	Wing hit ground in gust on approach; undercarriage collapsed, Watchfield, 9.8.60
XL558	215/230/209	Damaged in storm, Vientiane, Laos, 10.4.68; not repaired

*   *   *   *   *   *   *   *   *   *

55 Hawker Hunter T.7s delivered between December 1957 and February 1959 by Hawkers, Kingston, to Contract 6/Acft/12626

XL563	C(A)/MoA/ I Av Med	MoA aircraft; to 9218M 7.10.93
XL564	Mkrs/229 OCU/ Hdlg Sqn	To MoD(PE) 1.4.76 for ETPS
XL565	Mkrs/8/1417 Flt/ 208/1417 Flt/8/ SF West Raynham/ 8/208/4 FTS/237 OCU/IavM/237 OCU IAvM/237 OCU -	To Royal Navy 23.11.81 Retd to RAF To Honington 12.7.88; sold 10.93
XL566	AAEE/43/1417 Flt/ 208/4 FTS/SF Laarbruch	To Royal Navy 23.11.81; became 8891M 3.4.86 at Bruggen
XL567	229 OCU/19/4 FTS/ SF Laarbruch	To 8723M 23.2.82 at Chivenor
XL568	Hdlg Sqn/74/ Cv T.7A/MoA/ 74/MinTech/12/ 237 OCU/15/SF Laarbruch/237 OCU/ SF Laarbruch/237 OCU/216/12/237 OCU/208/12/208/ 237 OCU/12/237 OCU	To 9224M 19.11.93
XL569	229 OCU/TWU/ 1 TWU/2 TWU/ 1 TWU	To 8833M 2.9.84 at Cosford
XL570	229 OCU	Dived into sea after take-off 3½m W of Chivenor, 25.9.58; cause not known
XL571	229 OCU/FCIRS/ 92/2/229 OCU/ TWU	Abandoned over sea after engine cut 1m W of Strumble Head, Dyfed, 8.9.77
XL572	229 OCU/TWU/ 2 TWU/1 TWU	To 8834M 23.8.84 at Cosford
XL573	FCS/229 OCU/4 FTS/ 237 OCU/SF Laarbruch/237 OCU/12/ 237 OCU/12/237/ OCU/12/237 OCU/ RAE/12/IAvM/12/ 237 OCU/12	Sold 12.93; to G-BVGH
XL574	C(A)	To MoD(PE) 1.4.61
XL575	229 OCU/FCIRS/ 229 OCU	Flew into high ground in bad weather 2m E of Devils Bridge, Aberystwyth, 8.11.71
XL576	229 OCU/TWU/ 1 TWU	To 8835M at Cosford 9.84
XL577	229 OCU/TWU/ 1 TWU/237 OCU/ 2 TWU	To 8676M 16.3.81 at Cranwell
XL578	229 OCU/TWU/ 1 TWU	To LTS at St Athan 26.7.84; SS
XL579	229 OCU/ETPS	To MoA 14.12.65. Engine flamed out on approach to Boscombe Down; abandoned and crashed, Winterbourne Gunner, Wilts., 22.1.76
XL580	-	To Royal Navy as T.8
XL581	-	To Royal Navy as T.8
XL582	-	To Royal Navy as T.8
XL583	229 OCU/1 TWU	Engine lost power on approach; abandoned and crashed 1½m N of Brawdy, 1.12.81
XL584	-	To Royal Navy as T.8
XL585	-	To Royal Navy as T.8
XL586	229 OCU/1 TWU/ 2 TWU/1 TWU	To MoD(PE) 28.4.83 at Warton
XL587	229 OCU/1 TWU/ 237 OCU/208/12/ 237 OCU/SF Laarbruch	To 8807M 2.3.84 at Scampton
XL591	FCS/229 OCU/ 4 FTS/RAE/4 FTS/ 237 OCU/208/ 237 OCU/208/ 237 OCU/208/237 OCU/208/237 OCU/ 208	Sold 10.93
XL592	229 OCU/TWU/ 1 TWU	To 8836M 31.8.84 at Scampton
XL593	FCS/229 OCU/ TWU/1 TWU/ 2 TWU/1 TWU	Compressor blade detached and engine lost power; abandoned 4½m NW of Carmarthen, Dyfed, 5.8.82
XL594	FCS/19	Hit ground recovering from dive during aerobatic practice and blew up ¼m NNW of Carnaby, 16.4.64
XL595	FCS/DFCS/229 OCU/TWU/ 2 TWU/1 TWU	To LTS 26.7.84; to G-BTYL 29.11.91
XL596	54/1 & 54/HCT/ 4/4 FTS	Flew into trees on approach and crashed, Besford Wood, near Shawbury, 2.11.73
XL597	66/208/1417 Flt/ 208/8/4/20/4 FTS/ 237 OCU	Engine lost power and blew up; abandoned ½m S of Little Saxham, Suffolk, 29.5.80
XL598	-	To Royal Navy as T.8
XL599	-	To Royal Navy as T.8

Hunter

XL600	65/111/4 FTS/ 237 OCU/SF Laarbruch/TMTS Scampton	To Royal Navy 17.10.84 as A2729
XL601	1/SF West Raynham/ 1/4 FTS/229 OCU/ 4 FTS/237 OCU/ 208/237 OCU	To Royal Navy 16.10.84 as A2617
XL602	-	To Royal Navy as T.8
XL603	-	To Royal Navy as T.8
XL604	-	To Royal Navy as T.8; later to Kenya AF as No.802
XL605	92/229 OCU	Sold to HSA 6.4.66 for R.Saudi AF as 70-617; returned 5.72 as XX467
XL609	56/4 FTS/237 OCU/ 216/12	To 8866M 24.7.85 at Lossiemouth
XL610	111/56	Stalled, rolled and hit ground 1m S of North Kelsey, Lincs., 7.6.62
XL611	43/CFS/Cv T.7A/ 56/19/MoA	To MinTech 22.12.67
XL612	APS Sylt/1417 Flt/8	To MinTech 19.2.70 for ETPS
XL613	8/208/8/1417 Flt/ 8/1417 Flt/208/ 8/45/4 FTS/237 OCU/SF Laarbruch/ 237 OCU/IAvM/ 237 OCU/12/237 OCU/208/237 OCU	Sold 12.93; to G-BVMB 26.4.94
XL614	APS Sylt/Cv T.7A/ 111/RAE/12/RAE/ 237 OCU/ SF Honington	Sold to MinTech 22.12.67
	237 OCU/12/237 OCU	Retd 3.3.71; to 9235M 28.3.94 but NTU; to N613XL 29.3.96
XL615	8	Flew into ground at night 13½m W of Khormaksar, 1.6.60; cause not known
XL616	APS Sylt/Cv T.7A/ 23/19/MoA	Sold to MinTech 22.12.67
	SF Laarbruch/208/ 237 OCU/208/237 OCU/12/237 OCU/ 12/237 OCU/208/ 237 OCU/AAEE	Retd 19.3.80
		To 9223M 19.11.93; to G-BWIE 17.10.95
XL617	4/SF Jever/SF Gutersloh/229 OCU/ 54/229 OCU/TWU/ 1 TWU	To 8837M 2.9.84 at Cosford later to G-HHNT 7.7.89
XL618	14/229 OCU/TWU/ 1 TWU/2 TWU	To Royal Navy 23.11.81; Retd to RAF; to 8892M 3.4.86 at Cottesmore
XL619	20/14/20/45/ Hunter Wg/TWU/ 2 TWU/1 TWU	Abandoned in inverted spin 50m SW of Brawdy, 21.10.81
XL620	66/74	To HSA 13.4.66 for R.Saudi AF as 70-616; returned to RAF as XX466; sold to HSA 31.3.66
XL621	MoD(PE) 237 OCU/RAE	To RAF charge 5.5.83; Sold 12.86; became G-BNCX 9.1.87
XL622	93/SF Jever/ SF Sylt/111/ 229 OCU/4 FTS	Flew into hill in low flying area and blew up, Glanaber, 3m NE of Blaenau Ffestiniog, Merioneth, 17.5.71
XL623	65/54/92/43/1/ 19/74/54/229 OCU/ TWU/1 TWU	To 8770M 3.12.82 at Cosford

*   *   *   *   *   *   *   *   *   *

Two English Electric Lightning T.4 prototypes for Ministry of Aviation to Contract 6/Acft/13620

XL628	Mkrs	Fin collapsed in turn on test flight; control lost and abandoned over Irish Sea, 1.10.59
XL629	Mkrs & AAEE	Preserved at Boscombe Down

*   *   *   *   *   *   *   *   *   *

Ten Bristol Britannia C.1s delivered between May 1959 and April 1960 by Short Bros & Harland, Belfast, to Contract 6/Acft/12829

XL635	All pooled between 99 and 511 Sqns	*Bellatrix*; sold 5.9.75; became OO-YCA
XL636		*Argo*; sold 6.5.76; became OO-YCE
XL637		*Vega*; sold 8.3.76; became OO-YCH
XL638		*Sirius.* Overshot landing at Khormaksar, 12.10.67; not repaired
XL639		*Atria*; sold 10.2.76; became EI-BDC
XL640		*Altares*; sold 13.1.76; became EI-BCI
XL657		*Rigel*; sold 31.12.75; became 9U-BAD
XL658		*Adhara*; sold 26.5.76; became EI-BBY
XL659		*Polaris*; sold 5.9.75; became OO-YCB
XL660		*Alphard;* sold 14.5.76; became G-BEMZ

*   *   *   *   *   *   *   *   *   *

12 Scottish Aviation Pioneer CC.1s delivered between September 1956 and February 1957 by Scottish Aviation, Prestwick, to Contract 6/Acft/13670

XL664	Sc Avn/230/ Sc Avn/AAEE	Engine cut; undershot forced landing into wood 6m WNW of Kidderminster, Worcs., 16.6.61
XL665	78/Hdlg Sqn/ 230/209	SOC 26.10.67
XL666	Sc Avn/230/209/20	SOC 1.1.70; to Singapore ADC as GI airframe
XL667	230	Wingtip hit ground on approach; slewed on to strip ½m S of Kingussie, Fife, 12.5.62
XL668	-	Diverted to Ceylon AF
XL699	209	Sank back after take-off; overshot and overturned, Bareo, Sarawak, 24.7.60
XL700	MoS/209	Failed to gain height on take-off; hit trees, Patik, Labuan, 10.2.63
XL701	78	Collided with Landrover after landing at night, Awabi, Muscat, 1.7.58
XL702	230/MoA/209/20	SOC 1.1.70; to Singapore ADC as GI airframe
XL703	230/SF Odiham/209	To 8034M 1.10.68; preserved in RAF Museum
XL704	209	SOC 18.4.67
XL705	78/209	SOC 11.8.67
XL706	78/SOAF/209	SOC 25.7.68

*   *   *   *   *   *   *   *   *   *

De Havilland (Canada) DHC-3 Otter allotted serial for 1956 British Commonwealth Trans-Antarctic Expedition

XL710	BCTAE	To BuAer 147574; to RNZAF as NZ6081

* * * * * * * * * *

XL714 - XL717		Tiger Moth T.2s for Royal Navy

* * * * * * * * * *

Sikorsky S-58 to Contract 6/Acft/13323 allocated serial for development trials

XL722	Mkrs & AAEE	Ex BuAer 141602; SOC 7.63; to RN as A2514

* * * * * * * * * *

XL727 - XL729		Wessex HAS.1s for Royal Navy to Contract 6/Acft/13323
XL734 - XL740		Saro Skeeter AOP.12s for Army Air
XL762 - XL772		Corps to Contract 6/Acft/13919
XL806 - XL814		XL738 became 7860M; XL762 became 8017M; XL764 became 7940M; XL769 became 7961M; XL770 became 8046M;

* * * * * * * * * *

Ten Bristol Sycamore HR.14s delivered between February and December 1957 by Bristols, Filton, to Contract 6/Acft/13888

XL820	284/CFS	Lost rotor blade and crashed, Ternhill Railway Station, 25.3.64; DBF
XL821	275/110	SOC 30.6.67
XL822	194/110	Engine cut; crashlanded in thicket 8m ENE of Tanahrata, Sarawak, 8.11.58
XL823	228/CFS	SOC 22.5.68; to Acklington for fire practice
XL824	284/103/ 1564 Flt/CFS	To 8021M 2.7.68; preserved in RAF Museum
XL825	194/110	Rotor blade hit tail which broke off; caught fire and fell into trees, Malakoff Estate, Malaya, 28.9.62
XL826	275/CFS	Rolled on take-off and rotor hit ground, Ternhill, 28.2.66; 7909M NTU; to 7916M at Ternhill
XL827	APS Sylt/MCS/ HDU/CFS	SOC 16.8.68; to Wroughton for fire practice
XL828	Hdlg Sqn/Bristols/ SAR Flt Aden	Rotor blades shattered on landing due to resonance 32m NNE of Ahwar, Aden, 18.12.59
XL829	SF El Adem/ SF Khormaksar/ SAR Flt Aden/ MCS/32	Sold to Bristol Museum 18.12.71

* * * * * * * * * *

XL833 - XL854		Whirlwind HAS.7s for Royal Navy
XL867 - XL884		to Contract 6/Acft/13955
XL896 - XL900		XL898 became 8654M
XL905 - XL907;		Cancelled Saro SR-177s from
XL920 - XL925		Contract 6/Acft/12672

* * * * * * * * * *

Seven Percival Pembroke C.1s delivered between February and September 1958 by Hunting-Percival, Luton, to Contract 6/Acft/13975

XL929	BCCS/FCCS/TCCS/ SCCS/2207/60	Sold 16.6.87; to G-BNPU 30.6.87
XL930	2 TAFCS/MoA/ RAFG CS/AAFCE/ CS Wildenrath/60	SOC 18.8.70
XL931	2 TAF CS/60	SOC 18.8.70
XL953	2 TAF CS/NCS/ RAFG CS/60	Caught fire during servicing, Wildenrath, 16.5.80; not repaired
XL954	2 TAF CS/RAFG CS/60	To 9042M 5.90; NTU and sold to USA as N4234C 5.90
XL955	78/152/SF Khor- maksar/Gulf CF/ SF Muharraq	SOC 17.3.69
XL956	152/70/SF El Adem/ MinTech	SOC 1.10.71; to Catterick for fire practice

* * * * * * * * * *

De Havilland Heron 2 for Royal Tour of Africa during September and October 1956

XL961	QF	Ex G-AMTS; reverted to G-AMTS

* * * * * * * * * *

12 Scottish Aviation Twin Pioneer CC.1s delivered between February and November 1958 by Scottish Aviation, Prestwick, to Contract 6/Acft/14074

XL966	AAEE/21/78/21	Flew into rising ground on supply drop, Mount Meru, Tanganyika, 2.3.61
XL967	AAEE/209	Both engines cut; crash- landed on approach, Kota Tinggi, Malaya, 19.4.60
XL968	AAEE/21/78/21	SOC 18.12.67; to Andover for fire practice
XL969	209	SOC 12.10.67
XL970	SF Katunayake/209	SOC 20.12.68
XL991	FSS/78/209	Both engines cut; ditched 3m E of Tiomar airstrip, Malaysia, 29.9.67
XL992	78/21/152	SOC 30.10.68
XL993	78/21	To 8388M 6.2.69 for RAF Museum
XL994	78/152	Dived into ground in circuit 1m W of Bu Hafafa, Oman, 18.4.63
XL995	209	SOC 20.12.68
XL996	230/SF Odiham/152	SOC 30.10.68
XL997	209	SOC 1.10.68

* * * * * * * * * *

Ten Blackburn Beverley C.1s delivered between November 1957 and May 1958 by Blackburn, Brough, to Contract 6/Acft/13088

XM103	242 OCU/30/ 242 OCU/84	SS 29.8.69
XM104	30/48/34	SOC 14.2.68
XM105	47 & 53/30	SS 25.9.69
XM106	84	Taxied over land mine and under- carriage blown off, Habulaya, Aden, 21.6.67; not repaired; on loan to 30 Sqn
XM107	84	SS 1.11.67
XM108	84/30	SS 25.3.70
XM109	84/30	SS 25.3.70
XM110	47 & 53/84	Damaged by time-bomb, Bahrein, 6.10.61; not repaired and SOC 28.10.61

XM111	84/47 & 53/84/	
	MoA/84/47/30/84	SS 29.8.69
XM112	30/48/34	SOC 14.2.68

* * * * * * * * * *

XM117 - XM126	Hunter T.7s diverted to R.Neth AF, March to May 1959 as N311-N320 to Contract 6/Acft/14171

* * * * * * * * * *

XM129	Jet Provost T.2 G-AOBU to Contract 6/Acft/14260 for trials

* * * * * * * * * *

48 English Electric Lightning F.1s delivered between March 1960 and August 1961 by English Electric, Preston, to Contract 6/Acft/12715 and F.1As (from XM160) to Contract 6/Acft/15445

XM134	Mkrs & AFDS/ Hdlg Sqn/AAEE/ 74/226 OCU	Undercarriage leg jammed up; abandoned 30m E of Happis- burgh, Norfolk, 11.9.64
XM135	AFDS/74/226 OCU/ Leuchars TFF/ Wattisham TFF	SOC 20.11.74; preserved at IWM Duxford
XM136	AFDS/74/226 OCU/ Wattisham TFF	Abandoned on approach after engine lost power and tailplane control jammed, Coltishall, 13.9.67
XM137	AFDS/74/226 OCU/ FCTU/Binbrook TFF/ 5/Wattisham TFF	SOC 8.11.74; to Leconfield for fire practice
XM138	AFDS	Caught fire after landing due to fire bottle explosion, Coltishall, 16.12.60; SOC 31.8.61
XM139	74/226 OCU/ Leuchars TFF/BAC/ Wattisham TFF	To 8411M 28.5.74 at Wattisham
XM140	74/226 OCU/111	SS 16.12.66
XM141	74/226 OCU	SS 16.12.66
XM142	74	Abandoned after hydraulic failure off Cromer, Norfolk, 26.4.63
XM143	74/226 OCU	SS 16.12.66
XM144	74/226 OCU/ Leconfield TFF/ 60 MU/Wattisham TFF/Leuchars TFF/ 23/LTF	To 8417M 28.5.74 at Leuchars
XM145	74/226 OCU/ Leuchars TFF	SOC 27.6.74
XM146	74/226 OCU/111	SS 16.12.66
XM147	74/226 OCU/ Wattisham TFF	To 8412M 28.5.74 at Wattisham
XM163	AFDS/74/226 OCU/ Wattisham TFF	SS 23.5.74
XM164	74/226 OCU/FCTU/ 5/Binbrook TFF/ Leuchars TFF	SOC 12.6.74
XM165	74/226 OCU	SS 16.12.66
XM166	74/226 OCU	SS 16.12.66
XM167	74/226 OCU	SS 16.12.66
XM168	-	Used as static test airframe
XM169	Mkrs/111/Binbrook TFF/226 OCU/23	To 8422M 13.6.74 at Leuchars
XM170	Mkrs	To 7877M 6.4.65 at Newton
XM171	56/226 OCU	SOC 29.3.74
XM172	56/226 OCU	To 8427M 10.7.74 at Coltishall
XM173	56/226 OCU/ Leuchars TFF/23/11	To 8414M 28.5.74 at Binbrook

XM174	56/226 OCU/ Leuchars TFF	Caught fire and abandoned over sea; crashed, Balmullo Quarry, 2m W of Leuchars, 29.11.68
XM175	56	To BAC for test rig 6.4.73
XM176	56	SOC 3.5.74
XM177	56/226 OCU/ Leuchars TFF/ Wattisham TFF/ Leuchars TFF/ Wattisham TFF	SOC 22.3.74
XM178	56/226 OCU/ Leuchars TFF/23	To 8418M 28.5.74 at Leuchars
XM179	56	Collided with XM181 during bomb-burst and abandoned, Great Bricett, Suffolk, 6.6.63
XM180	56/226 OCU	To 8424M 10.7.74 at Binbrook
XM181	56/111/56/ Binbrook TFF	To 8415M 28.5.74 at Binbrook
XM182	56/226 OCU/23/ Binbrook TFF/ 226 OCU/Leuchars TFF	To 8425M 10.7.74 at Binbrook
XM183	56/226 OCU/ Binbrook TFF/5/ Binbrook TFF	To 8416M 28.5.74 at Binbrook
XM184	111/226 OCU	Caught fire on landing, Coltishall, 17.4.67; not repaired
XM185	111	Undercarriage and airbrakes jammed; abandoned 1m N of Lavenham, Suffolk, 28.6.61
XM186	111	Abandoned in spin during aerobatic display 1m W of Wittering, 18.7.63
XM187	111	Bounced on landing and under- carriage collapsed, Wattisham, 19.11.63; to 7838M 28.2.64 at Newton
XM188	111/226 OCU	Throttle jammed open while taxying; hit hangar, Coltishall, 21.6.68
XM189	111/226 OCU	To 8423M 9.7.74
XM190	111/56/226 OCU	Abandoned after fire warning 5m N of Cromer, Norfolk, 15.3.66
XM191	111	Engine caught fire on approach; landed safely, Wattisham, 9.6.64; not repaired and nose to 7854M (later 8590M) at Abingdon
XM192	111/226 OCU/ Binbrook TFF/ Wattisham TFF	To 8413M 28.5.74 at Wattisham
XM213	111/56/226 OCU	Undercarriage prematurely retracted on take-off; veered off runway and hit fence, Coltishall, 6.5.66
XM214	111/226 OCU	To 8420M 19.6.74 at Gutersloh
XM215	111/226 OCU	To 8421M 14.6.74 at Gutersloh
XM216	111/226 OCU	To 8426M 10.7.74 at Gutersloh
XM217 and		
XM218	-	Not built

* * * * * * * * * *

XM223	Devon C.1 delivered in December 1957 for RAE to Contract 6/Acft/14188

XM228, XM229	Cancelled Canberra T.4s to Contract 6/Acft/12265

* * * * * * * * * *

Hunter T.7 XL609 leads three Hunter F.6s of No.4 Flying Training School, Valley, over the Snowdon massif.

The unit badge on the fin includes a palm tree in memory of No.4 FTS's long service in Egypt before the Second World War.

Britannia C.1 XL660 'Alphard' comes in to land at the Royal Australian Air Force station at Amberley, Queensland.

As Nos.99 and 511 Squadrons pooled their aircraft, it carries no unit markings.

Devoid of any unit markings, Pembroke C.1 XL930 was delivered in 1958 and served with the Royal Air Force until 1970.

A highly-polished Heron CC.4 of the Queen's Flight, XM296, awaits its passengers at Gatwick on 29 May 1958.

Unusually the serial has a hyphen between the letters and numbers.

Pioneer CC.1 XL702 of No.230 Squadron operating from a dusty airstrip during the overseeing of elections in the Cameroons in 1960.

At this time, the squadron were operated both Pioneers and Twin Pioneers.

XN983 was one of the six original Buccaneer S.2s received from the Royal Navy.

It went first to No.12 Squadron and remained in service until 1994.

This angle shows well the famous rotating bomb bay.

Heron

20 English Electric Canberra B(I).8s delivered between August 1958 and March 1959 by EEC Preston to Contract 6/Acft/6445 (XM244/245) and 11158 (remainder)

XM244	16/3/16/3/16	To 8202M 22.5.72 at Gutersloh
XM245	B-P & AAEE/14/ AAEE/3/16	SOC 6.6.72; to Nordhorn as target
XM262	16/3	SOC 23.3.73; to Catterick for fire practice
XM263	16/3	Sold to Marshalls 13.3.74 for Peru as No.255
XM264	16/3/14/16	To 8227M 19.6.72; to Laarbruch for fire practice
XM265	16/AAEE/16	To 8199M 22.5.72 at Nordhorn
XM266	59/3	Engine flamed out at night; dived into canal 2m E of Tiverton, Devon, 21.11.61
XM267	16/3	Lost power; rolled on overshoot and wing hit ground; broke up, Akrotiri, 15.12.70
XM268	16/3	SOC 8.3.73; to Catterick for fire practice
XM269	SF Wildenrath/ 88/14/16	SOC 6.6.72; to Nordhorn as target
XM270	88/16	Abandoned and spun into ground on approach to Gutersloh near Rheda, 6.6.66
XM271	59/3/MoA/3/16	To 8204M 14.6.72 at Newton
XM272	SF Wildenrath/ 88/14/16	SOC 20.6.72; to Marham for fire practice
XM273	88/14/3	Sold to Marshalls 6.2.74 for Peru as No.253
XM274	SF Bruggen/3/16	To 8170M 26.8.71
XM275	SF Laarbruch/ 16/3/16	SOC 20.6.72; to Wattisham for fire practice
XM276	59/3/RAE/3	8178M 8.10.71 NTU; sold to Marshalls 18.4.74 for Peru as No.256
XM277	SF Geilenkirchen/ 88/14/3/16	SOC 23.6.72; to Chivenor for fire practice
XM278	16/14/3	Sold 3.4.74 for spares
XM279	16/3	Sold to Marshalls 19.3.74 for Peru as No.257

* * * * * * * * *

Eight Scottish Aviation Twin Pioneer CC.1s delivered between July and October 1958 by Scottish Aviation, Prestwick to Contract 6/Acft/14074

XM284	FSS/78/21/152	SOC 27.11.67; to Muharraq for fire practice
XM285	230/SF Odiham/ 225/SRCU	Sold 29.11.69 to Scottish Avn; became G-AYFA 15.6.70
XM286	78/152/21/152	SOC 30.10.68
XM287	78	Both engines cut; overturned in forced landing 30m W of Khormaksar, 8.4.59
XM288	78	Both engines cut on approach; ditched ½m W of Khormaksar, 8.4.59
XM289	152/78/21/152	SOC 30.10.68; to Muharraq for F ire practice
XM290	152/21	Tipped up after landing, Kalimikui, Kenya, 13.3.63; not repaired
XM291	152/78/152/ 21/152	SOC 30.10.68

* * * * * * * * *

Two de Havilland Heron CC.4s delivered by D.H.Chester in March and April 1958 to Contract 6/Acft/14194

XM295	QF	Sold 4.11.68; became CF-XOK
XM296	QF/RAFG CS/60	To Royal Navy 7.72

* * * * * * * * * *

XM299 - XM301		Wessex HAS.1s for Royal Navy
XM326 - XM331		to Contract 6/Acft/13323

* * * * * * * * * *

Gloster Javelin T.3 delivered in August 1959 by Glosters, Hucclecote, to Contract 6/Acft/15318

XM336	FCIRS/226 OCU/ FCIRS	Both engines cut; abandoned and crashed in Saujac, near Orange, France, 5.11.63
XM337 to XM341	-	Cancelled

* * * * * * * * * *

100 Hunting Jet Provost T.3s delivered between June 1958 and July 1960 by Hunting, Luton, to Contract 6/Acft/14157

XM346	MoS/AAEE/H-P/ CFS/6 FTS/RAFC	SOC 9.6.69; to Thorney Island for fire practice
XM347	C(A)/AAEE/2 FTS	Engine flamed out; abandoned near Wragby, Lincs., 23.3.61
XM348	Mkrs & AAEE	Forcelanded in field after false fire warning; hit road and caught fire, Barge Farm, Twyford, Berks., 4.9.58
XM349	AAEE/2 FTS/CFS/ RAFC/CFS/1 FTS/ CFS	To 9046M 12.89 at Cosford
XM350	AAEE/RAFC/1 FTS/ 7 FTS	To 9036M 11.89 at Church Fenton
XM351	Hdlg Sqn/2 FTS/ 7 FTS/1 FTS/3 FTS	To 8078M 25.2.70 at Halton
XM352	AAEE & Mkrs/ 3 FTS/1 FTS/ 7 FTS/1 FTS	Sold; to USA as N35378 8.11.94
XM353	BSE	SS 3.9.68
XM354	2 FTS/1 FTS	SOC 8.8.74
XM355	CFS/7 FTS/1 FTS	To 8229M 17.10.73 at Halton
XM356	CFS/7 FTS	SOC 3.12.69; to Linton-on-Ouse for fire practice
XM357	CFS/3 FTS/1 FTS	To USA as N27357 12.7.94
XM358	2 FTS/7 FTS/CFS/ RAFC/CFS/1 FTS/ 3 FTS/1 FTS	To 8987M 1.89 at Halton
XM359	CFS/7 FTS/2 FTS/ 6 FTS/2 FTS	SOC 28.5.76; to Sennybridge as target
XM360	CFS	Flew into high ground in cloud on low-level navex, Brown Clee Hill, Abdon, Salop., 24.1.69
XM361	CFS/7 FTS/RAFC	SOC 8.8.74
XM362	2 FTS/3 FTS	To 8230M 21.3.73 at Halton
XM363	2 FTS	SOC 6.8.69; to Leeming for fire practice
XM364	2 FTS/CFS	SOC 28.5.76; to Army Apprentices College, Arborfield
XM365	H-P/2 FTS/ 3 FTS/1 FTS	Sold; to G-BXBH 29.1.97
XM366	2 FTS/CFS/RAFC/ 7 FTS/CFS	Engine flamed out during aerobatics; undershot approach and abandoned near Holme-on-Spalding Moor, Yorks., 22.10.81
XM367	2 FTS/3 FTS	To 8083M 2.2.70 at Halton
XM368	2 FTS/3 FTS/ 2 FTS	Abandoned in spin 2½m SW of Pateley Bridge, Yorks., 29.4.63
XM369	2 FTS	To 8084M 19.3.70 at Halton

XM370	2 FTS/3 FTS/1 FTS/ 7 FTS/1 FTS	Sold; to G-BVSP 31.8.94
XM371	2 FTS/3 FTS/CFS/ RAFC/CFS	To 8962M 27.4.88 at Halton
XM372	2 FTS/1 FTS	Bellylanded at Dishforth, 6.12.85; to 8917M 10.10.86 at Linton-on-Ouse
XM373	2 FTS	Stalled on take-off and sank back on to runway; undercarriage collapsed, Syerston, 29.6.61; to 7726M 26.7.61 at Cranwell
XM374	2 FTS/CFS/3 FTS/ 1 FTS/RAFC/7 FTS/ 1 FTS	Sold; to USA as N374XM 11.4.95
XM375	2 FTS/CFS/3 FTS/ RAFC	To 8231M 21.3.73 at Halton
XM376	2 FTS/RAFC/ CATCS/3 FTS/ 1 FTS/RAFC/ 7 FTS/1 FTS	Sold; to G-BDWR 6.6.95
XM377	2 FTS	Radio aids failed; bellylanded due to fuel shortage, Syerston, 4.2.60
XM378	2 FTS/CFS/1 FTS/ CFS/7 FTS/1 FTS	Sold; to G-BWZE 29.11.96
XM379	2 FTS/6 FTS/3 FTS	SOC 28.5.76; to GI airframe at Army Apprentice College, Arborfield
XM380	2 FTS	Engine flamed out; abandoned after fire warning 1m S of Seagrave, Leics., 29.7.63
XM381	2 FTS/RAFC	To 8232M 21.3.73 at Halton
XM382	2 FTS	Abandoned in spin during stalling practice 3½m NNE of Melton Mowbray, Leics., 17.6.60
XM383	2 FTS/AAEE/2 FTS/ BSE/6 FTS/RAFC/ 1 FTS/7 FTS	To spares recovery, 1990
XM384	2 FTS	Collided with XP631 over Woodborough, Notts., and abandoned, 26.5.66
XM385	2 FTS	Undershot landing after engine failed to pick up on overshoot, Syerston, 8.3.60
XM386	2 FTS/CFS	To 8076M 2.2.70 at Halton
XM387	2 FTS/3 FTS/CFS	Sold; to USA as N387TW 19.7.95
XM401	2 FTS/CFS/3 FTS/ 1 FTS	
XM402	2 FTS/6 FTS	To 8055AM 21.11.69 at Halton
XM403	2 FTS/1 FTS/CFS/ 3 FTS/CFS	To 9048M at Cosford
XM404	2 FTS/3 FTS	To 8055BM 21.11.59 at Halton
XM405	2 FTS/1 FTS/RAFC/ 1 FTS	Sold; became G-TORE 14.6.91
XM406	2 FTS	Abandoned in spin 1m SSW of Clipstone, Notts., 12.11.65
XM407	2 FTS/6 FTS	SOC 31.10.69
XM408	2 FTS/MoA	To 8233M 21.3.73 at Halton
XM409	2 FTS	To 8032M 13.5.70 at Halton
XM410	2 FTS/7 FTS/RAFC	To 8054AM 23.10.69 at Halton
XM411	CFS	To 8434M 10.11.74 at Halton
XM412	2 FTS/3 FTS/1 FTS	To 9011M 8.89 at Halton
XM413	CFS/7 FTS/2 FTS	SOC 28.5.76 to GI airframe at Army Apprentices College, Arborfield
XM414	2 FTS/RAFC/6 FTS/ 1 FTS/RAFC/7 FTS	To 8996M 4.89 at Halton
XM415	2 FTS/3 FTS	SOC 28.5.76; to target at Sennybridge
XM416	2 FTS/7 FTS/2 FTS/ 6 FTS/3 FTS	SOC 28.5.76; to target at Sennybridge
XM417	2 FTS/7 FTS/6 FTS	To 8054BM 23.10.69 at Halton
XM418	2 FTS/CFS/6 FTS/ 3 FTS	Engine caught fire on runway awaiting take-off, Leeming, 25.3.71; not repaired and to 8593M
XM419	2 FTS/RAFC/6 FTS/ RAFC/3 FTS/CFS/ RAFC/CFS/3 FTS/ 7 FTS	To 8990M 4.89 at St Athan
XM420	2 FTS/6 FTS	SOC 18.12.69; to Catterick for fire practice
XM421	2 FTS/CFE/7 FTS	Abandoned after control lost in cloud 2m NW of Church Fenton, 13.12.63
XM422	2 FTS/CFS/6 FTS	Flew into ground during aerobatic display practice ½m WSW of Acklington, 8.5.62
XM423	CFS	Engine cut on night navex; abandoned 3m SE of Kidderminster, Worcs., 30.8.61
XM424	CFS/6 FTS/RAFC/ 3 FTS/1 FTS	Sold; to G-BWDS 6.6.95
XM425	CFS/3 FTS/RAFC/ 1 FTS/7 FTS	To 8995M 4.89 at Halton
XM426	CFS/6 FTS/ 2 FTS/3 FTS	SOC 28.5.76
XM427	RAFC	Flew into ground on night approach 1½m NNE of Waddington, 16.10.62
XM428	CFS/3 FTS	Collided with XN631 and abandoned 1½m E of Northallerton, Yorks., 20.4.65
XM451	RAFC	SOC 8.8.74
XM452	RAFC	Tip tank struck by lightning; abandoned after control lost 1m S of Rauceby Hospital, Lincs., 5.4.62
XM453	RAFC/3 FTS & 26/ CFS/3 FTS	Hit birds and engine lost power at low level; abandoned and flew into hill 2m SSE of Ribblehead Viaduct, Ingleton, N.Yorks., 21.11.83
XM454	RAFC	SOC 8.8.74
XM455	RAFC/3 FTS/26/ 3 FTS/26/3 FTS/ 26 & 3 FTS/1 FTS/ CFS	To 8960M 21.4.88 at Cosford
XM456	RAFC/Hunting	Failed to recover from spin on test flight and abandoned near Histon, Cambs., 22.8.62
XM457	2 FTS/7 FTS/1 FTS	SOC 8.8.74
XM458	RAFC/BSE/3 FTS/ 26/3 FTS/1 FTS/ CFS	To spares recovery and target 1990
XM459	RAFC/3 FTS/26/ 3 FTS/7 FTS/CFS	Sold
XM460	RAFC/CFS	Bounced on landing, overshot, hit power cables and crashed, Little Rissington, 14.12.64
XM461	RAFC/3 FTS/CFS/ 3 FTS/1 FTS	Sold in USA as N6204H 2.6.93
XM462	RAFC	SOC 18.12.69; to Little Rissington for fire practice
XM463	RAFC/1 FTS	To RAF Museum for preservation
XM464	RAFC/3 FTS/1 FTS	SS 1.93
XM465	RAFC/1 FTS/7 FTS/ 1 FTS	
XM466	RAFC/1 FTS/CFS/ 1 FTS/7 FTS/1 FTS	Sold; to USA as N7075U 2.6.93
XM467	RAFC/1 FTS/6 FTS	To 8085M 25.2.70 at Halton
XM468	1 FTS/6 FTS	To 8081M 6.5.70 at Halton
XM469	RAFC/1 FTS	Abandoned in spin 5m NNE of York, 5.5.61
XM470	1 FTS/6 FTS/2 FTS/ CFS/3 FTS/CFS/ 1 FTS	Sold; to G-BWZZ 5.9.96

XM471	CFS/6 FTS/RAFC/ 2 FTS/3 FTS/CFS/ 1 FTS/7 FTS	To 8968M 16.5.88 at Cosford
XM472	CFS/7 FTS/1 FTS/ 3 FTS/1 FTS/7 FTS	To 9051M 1990 at Sealand
XM473	1 FTS/3 FTS/CFS/ 1 FTS/7 FTS/1 FTS/ 7 FTS	To 8974M 9.6.88 at Halton
XM474	CFS/6 FTS/MoA/ 6 FTS/MinTech	To 8121M 15.12.70 at Shrewsbury
XM475	2 FTS/7 FTS/RAFC/ TWU/RAFC/26/ RAFC/7 FTS	To CTE Manston 14.8.91 as 9112M
XM476	2 FTS/7 FTS	Collided with XN466 while landing in bad visibility, Church Fenton, 29.1.63; DBR
XM477	1 FTS	Abandoned after fire warning 2m S of Dishforth, 28.3.61
XM478	1 FTS/7 FTS/1 FTS	8983M NTU; to G-BXDL 18.3.97
XM479	RAFC/1 FTS	Sold; to G-BVEZ 13.10.93
XM480	1 FTS/6 FTS	To 8080M 21.4.70 at Halton

*   *   *   *   *   *   *   *   *   *

XM484, XM485	Jet Provost T.3s to Contract 6/Acft/15226 not built

*   *   *   *   *   *   *   *   *   *

Ten Bristol Britannia C.1s delivered between October 1959 and December 1960 by Short Bros & Harland, Belfast, to Contract 6/Acft/14293 (first three) and 15527 (remainder)

XM489	All pooled between 99 and 511 Sqns	*Denebola*; sold 10.2.76; became OO-YCC
XM490		*Aldebaran*; sold 29.10.75; became G-BDLZ
XM491		*Procyon*; sold 8.9.75; became EI-BBH
XM496		*Regulus*; sold 6.1.76; became G-BDUP
XM497		*Schedar*; sold 23.4.76; became OO-YCF
XM498		*Hadar*; sold 9.4.76; became OO-YCG
XM517		*Avior*; sold 21.10.75; became 9Q-CAJ
XM518		*Spica*; sold 4.3.76; became OO-YCD
XM519		*Capella*; sold 13.2.76; became G-BDUR
XM520		*Arcturus*; sold 16.9.75; became 9G-ACE

*   *   *   *   *   *   *   *   *   *

XM524 - XM530	Skeeter AOP.12s for Army
XM553 - XM565	to Contract 6/Acft/15410 XM527 became 7820M; XM529 became 7979M; XM555 became 8027M; XM556 became 7870M; XM561 became 7980M; XM565 became 7861M

*   *   *   *   *   *   *   *   *   *

40 Avro Vulcan B.2s delivered between February 1963 and January 1965 by Avro, Woodford, to Contract 6/Acft/12305 and KD/B/01

Most of these aircraft were pooled in Wings according to station and are shown as Ak - Akrotiri Wing; Cott - Cottesmore Wing; Scam - Scampton Wing and Wadd - Waddington Wing

XM569	27/Wadd/Cott/ Ak/27/Wadd	To Wales Aircraft Museum 21.1.83

XM570	27/Wadd/Cott/ Ak/27/35/230 OCU/ 35/617/35	SS 29.1.82
XM571	83/Cott/Wadd/ Cott/Ak/27/35/Wadd/ 35/Wadd/35/617/ Wadd/617/101/ AAEE/44/AAEE/ Wadd/Cv K.2/50	To 8812M 10.5.84 at Gibraltar
XM572	83/Wadd/Ak/35/9	SS 11.82
XM573	83/Wadd/230 OCU/ Ak/Wadd/230 OCU/ Wadd	To Offutt AFB 6.82
XM574	27/Scam/Wadd/ Ak/617	SS 29.1.82
XM575	617/Scam/Wadd/ Scam/617/Wadd	Registered G-BLMC To E.Midlands Airport 25.1.83
XM576	Scam	Wing hit ground on overshoot; swung and skidded into control tower, Scampton, 25.5.65
XM594	27/Scam/Wadd	To Newark Air Museum 19.1.83
XM595	617/Scam/230 OCU/ 617/230 OCU & 617/ 35	SS 11.82
XM596	-	Fatigue testing airframe
XM597	12/Cott/Watt/50	To Museum of Flight, East Fortune, 12.4.84
XM598	12/Cott/Watt	To 8778M 19.1.83 at Cosford
XM599	35/Cott/Wadd	SS 29.1.82
XM600	35/Cott/Wadd	Caught fire in air and abandoned near Spilsby, Lincs., 17.1.77
XM601	9	Wingtip hit ground during asymmetric approach; broke up, Coningsby, 7.10.64; DBF
XM602	12/Cott/Wadd/ 230 OCU/35/Wadd	To 8771M 16.3.83 at St Athan
XM603	9/Cott/Wadd/BAe	To Woodford for preservation 12.3.82
XM604	35/Cott/9	Compressor failed and controls severed; flew into ground on approach to Cottesmore, Cow Close Farm, Burley, Rutland, 30.1.68
XM605	9/Cott/Wadd	To Castle AFB 2.9.81 for display
XM606	12/Cott/MoA/ Cott/Wadd	To Barksdale AFB 14.6.82 for display
XM607	35/Cott/Wadd	To 8779M 19.1.83 at Waddington
XM608	9/Cott/Wadd	SS 2.12.82
XM609	12/Cott/230 OCU/ Cott/Wadd	SS 31.8.81
XM610	9/Cott/Wadd	Engine caught fire on low-level exercise; abandoned and crashed, Wingate, Co.Durham, 8.1.71
XM611	9/Cott/Wadd	SOC 27.1.82
XM612	Cott/Wadd	To Norwich Air Museum 19.1.83
XM645	Cott/Wadd/230 OCU/ Wadd/Cott/Wadd	Undershot landing at Luqa, bounced and undercarriage leg damaged fuel tanks; blew up attempting overshoot, Zabbar, Malta, 14.10.75
XM646	Cott/Ak/Wadd	SS 29.6.83
XM647	Cott/Ak/Wadd	To 8765M 17.9.82 at Laarbruch
XM648	Cott/Wadd	SS 12.82
XM649	Cott/Wadd	SS 2.12.82
XM650	Cott/Wadd	SOC 21.5.82
XM651	Cott/Ak/Wadd	SS 11.82
XM652	Cott/Wadd/50	SS 20.2.84
XM653	Cott/Wadd	SS 28.7.81
XM654	Cott/Ak/Wadd	SS 12.82
XM655	Cott/Wadd/50	Sold 11.2.84; became G-VULC
XM656	Cott/Wadd	To 8757M 9.8.82 at Cottesmore

Vulcan

XM657	Cott/Wadd	To 8734M 5.1.82 at Manston

*   *   *   *   *   *   *   *   *   *

XM660 - XM669	Whirlwind HAS.7s for Royal Navy
XM683 - XM687	Contract 6/Acft/15633

*   *   *   *   *   *   *   *   *   *

14 Folland Gnat T.1s delivered between February 1961 and January 1962 by Folland Aircraft, Hamble, to Contract 6/Acft/15260 (XM691-698) and 15434 (XM704-709)

XM691	Mkrs	MoA aircraft
XM692	Mkrs	MoA aircraft
XM693	Mkrs	To 7891M 8.65; preserved
XM694	Mkrs & BSE	MoA aircraft
XM695	BSE	MoA aircraft
XM696	AAEE	Lost tyre on take-off; bellylanded, Boscombe Down, 12.10.62; DBR
XM697	Mkrs	MoA aircraft
XM698	MinTech	To 8090M 1.5.70; later 8497M
XM704	CFS	Bounced on landing and undercarriage leg collapsed; slewed off runway, Kemble, 28.9.66; nose to 7992M 8.12.67 at Cranwell
XM705	CFS/4 FTS/ CFS/4 FTS	To 8574M 21.12.77 at Bruggen
XM706	CFS/4 FTS	To 8572M 2.12.77 at Halton
XM707	CFS	Abandoned after tailplane control lost 2½m WNW of Kemble, 30.6.67
XM708	Hdlg Sqn/CFS/ 4 FTS	To 8573M 2.12.77 at Halton; to Locking for display 10.86
XM709	CFS/4 FTS	To 8617M 4.3.79 at Halton

*   *   *   *   *   *   *   *   *   *

Five Handley Page Victor B.2s delivered between January and May 1963 by Handley Page, Radlett, to Contract 6/Acft/15566, later KD/C/08

XM714	100	Stalled after night take-off and spun into ground 3½m ENE of Wittering, 20.3.63
XM715	139/100/232 OCU/ Cv SR.2/543/Cv K.2/ 232 OCU/55	Sold; to Bruntingthorpe 19.11.93
XM716	139/100/232 OCU/ Cv SR.2/543	Overstressed and lost tail after high speed run; bunted and blew up 3m N of Wyton, 29.6.66
XM717	100/Witt Wg/ Cv SR.2/543/ Cv K.2/55/57/55	Nose to RAF Museum
XM718	100/Cv SR.2/ 543/232 OCU	SOC 31.3.76
XM719 to XM721	-	Cancelled
XM745 to XM756	-	Cancelled
XM785 to XM794	-	Cancelled

*   *   *   *   *   *   *   *   *   *

XM797, XM819	Edgar Percival EP.9s to Contract KD/M/01 for trials with Army Air Corps

*   *   *   *   *   *   *   *   *   *

Two de Havilland Comet 1XBs for Ministry of Aviation to Contracts 6/Acft/15321 and 15417 respectively

XM823	DH/HSA	Ex G-APAS/G-5-23 for Dectra trials. SOC 8.4.68; to 8351M 3.7.73 for RAF Museum
XM829	AAEE	Ex G-AOJU; SOC 20.2.64

*   *   *   *   *   *   *   *   *   *

XM832 - XM845	Wessex HAS.1s for Royal Navy
XM868 - XM876	to Contract 6/Acft/15487
XM915 - XM931	XM927 to 8814M

*   *   *   *   *   *   *   *   *   *

English Electric Canberra B(I).8 delivered in March 1959 by EEC, Preston, to Contract KD/E/01

XM936	59/3	Sold to Marshalls 11.2.74 for Peru as No.254

*   *   *   *   *   *   *   *   *   *

12 Scottish Aviation Twin Pioneer CC.1s delivered between October 1958 and January 1959 by Scottish Aviation, Preston, to Contract 6/Acft/14074 and KC/K/08

XM939	152/78/21/209	SOC 9.10.68
XM940	Sc Avn/AAEE/Sc Avn/230/SF Odiham/SRCU/ 78/21/152	Cv CC.2 SOC 30.10.68
XM941	224 Gp Supp Flt/ 209	Both engines cut; forcelanded in clearing and tipped up 4m W of Paloh, Johore, Malaya, 9.3.60
XM942	209	Hit soft patch on landing and undercarriage broke off, Long Akah, Borneo, 29.5.64
XM943	78	Hit by whirlwind on landing; swung off strip and hit tree stumps, Manawa, Aden, 16.9.64; SOC 16.12.74
XM957	78/21/AAEE/209	SOC 20.7.67
XM958	21/152	SOC 30.10.68
XM959	21/152	Ran into ruts on runway on landing and tipped up, Tayibah, Oman, 14.9.67; not repaired
XM960	21/78/21	SS 3.9.68
XM961	21/230/SF Odiham/ SRCU	Cv CC.2; to 7978M 28.7.67 at Halton; became G-BBVF 17.12.73
XM962	Alvis/209	Cv CC.2; SOC 9.10.68
XM963	21/78/21/209	Damaged tailwheel on landing, Grik, Malaysia, 10.2.68; SOC 14.8.68 as not worth repairing

*   *   *   *   *   *   *   *   *   *

20 English Electric Lightning T.4s delivered between June 1962 and January 1963 by EEC Preston to Contract 6/Acft/15445

XM966	MoA/Cv T.5/Mkrs	Crashed in Irish Sea on test flight 12m off St.Bee's Head, Cumbria, 22.7.65
XM967	RAE	Built as T.5 prototype; to 8433M
XM968	AAEE/226 OCU/92	Abandoned after hydraulic failure near Gutersloh, 24.2.77; 8541M NTU
XM969	LCS/226 OCU/ 92/226 OCU	To 8592M 19.6.74 at Binbrook
XM970	LCS/226 OCU/19	To 8529M 1.1.77 at Bruggen
XM971	LCS/92/LCS/ 226 OCU	Radar fairing came off and ingested into engine; abandoned, Tunsted, 2m E of Coltishall, 2.1.67

Lightning

XM972	LCS/226 OCU	SOC 11.6.74; to Waddington for fire practice
XM973	AFDS/226 OCU/ 111/CFE/23/226 OCU/19	To 8528M 1.1.77 at Bruggen
XM974	74/226 OCU/ 65/226 OCU	Engine cut; caught fire and abandoned off Happisburgh, Norfolk, 14.12.72
XM987	LCS/226 OCU	SOC 25.6.74; to Coningsby for fire practice
XM988	19/74/92/226 OCU	Abandoned in spin 23m NE of Great Yarmouth, Norfolk, 5.6.73
XM989	56	Sold to BAC 7.4.66 for R.Saudi AF as 54-650
XM990	LCS/226 OCU	Abandoned after control lost during Battle of Britain display, Little Plumstead, Norfolk, 19.9.70
XM991	LCS/226 OCU/19	Caught fire on ground, Gutersloh, 3.5.74; to 8456M 5.11.75 NTU
XM992	111/19/111	Sold to BAC 12.2.66 for R.Saudi AF as 54-651
XM993	LCS	Undercarriage collapsed on landing, swung and rolled over, Middleton St.George, 12.12.62; DBF
XM994	19/LCS/226 OCU	SOC 29.4.74; to West Raynham for fire practice
XM995	19/92	To 8542M 1.4.77 at Wildenrath
XM996	LCS/226 OCU	SOC 2.7.74; to Machrihanish for fire practice
XM997	LCS/226 OCU/ 92/226 OCU	SOC 22.11.74; to Leconfield for fire practice
XN103 to XN112	-	Cancelled

* * * * * * * * * *

Hunting Jet Provost T.3 prototype (ex T.2 G-23-1)

XN117	AAEE	Used for ground-attack trials in Aden; reverted to makers

* * * * * * * * * *

Folland Gnat F.1 for trials

XN122	AAEE	Used for ground-attack trials; to Indian AF as IE1064 9.58

* * * * * * * * * *

Two Westland Whirlwind HCC.8s delivered in August and November 1959 by Westlands, Yeovil, to Contract KC/2N/01

XN126	QF/Cv HAR.10/110/ 103/CFS/21/CFS/ 2(A) FTS	To 8655M 3.9.80 at Halton
XN127	QF/Cv HAR.10/ CFS/2(A) FTS	Rotor control lost; rolled into ground and cart-wheeled, Shawbury, 8.5.80

* * * * * * * * * *

XN132; XN133		Alouette AH.2s G-WIPG and G-WIPH for Army Air Corps evaluation to Contract KF/2J/01; XN133 to 7702M

* * * * * * * * * *

Hunting Jet Provost T.3 delivered in August 1960 by Hunting, Luton, to Contract 6/Acft/14157 as replacement for XM348

XN137	CFS/3 FTS	SOC 28.5.76

* * * * * * * * * *

XN142		DHC Beaver 2 G-ANAR for evaluation by Army Air Corps; formerly XH463
XN146 - XN157 XN183 - XN189		Slingsby Sedbergh TX.1 gliders for ATC and CCF to Contract KF/2R/04 XN185 to 8942M
XN194 - XN199 XN236 - XN253		Slingsby Cadet TX.3 gliders for ATC and CCF to Contract KF/2R/05 XN195 to 7845M; XN239 to 8889M
XN258 - XN264 XN297 - XN314		Whirlwind HAS.7s for Royal Navy to Contract KF/2N/015 XN302 to 9037M

* * * * * * * * * *

Four Scottish Aviation Twin Pioneer CC.2s delivered in July and August 1959 by Scottish Aviation, Prestwick, to Contract KC/K/018

XN318	230/209	Flew into trees and hit cliff; fell into river 6m N of Long Semodo, Sarawak, 14.2.63
XN319	209	SOC 9.10.68
XN320	209	SOC 20.12.68
XN321	209	Engine cut on take-off; undercarriage collapsed in forced landing, Butterworth, 28.4.67

* * * * * * * * * *

Folland Gnat F.1 delivered in February 1959 to Contract KD/2M/01 for trials

XN326	AAEE	Ex G-39-11; to Finland as GN-113

* * * * * * * * * *

XN332 - XN334		Saro P.531 to Royal Navy for evaluation to Contract KF/2Q//01
XN339 - XN355		Skeeter AOP.12s for Army Air Corps to Contract KF/Q/021; XN341 to 8022M; XN344 to 8018M; XN348 to 8024M
XN357 - XN362 XN379 - XN387		Whirlwind HAS.7s for Royal Navy to Contract KF/2N/015; XN387 to 8564M

* * * * * * * * * *

Three Bristol Britannia C.2s delivered in October, March and April 1959 respectively by Short Bros. & Harland, Belfast, to Contract 6/Acft/11804

XN392	All pooled between 99 and 511 Sqns	*Acrux*; ex G-APPE; sold 18.12.75
XN398		*Altair*; ex G-APPF; sold 11.9.75; became 9Q-CPX
XN404		*Canopus*; ex G-APPG; sold 17.12.75

* * * * * * * * * *

XN407 - XN412 XN435 - XN443		Auster AOP.9s for Army Air Corps to Contract KC/N/034 XN443 to 7977M

XN448 - XN450   Sycamore HR.51s for Royal Australian
Navy to Contract 6/Acft/7461

*   *   *   *   *   *   *   *   *   *

De Havilland Comet 2E for Ministry of Aviation

XN453	AAEE/RAE	Ex G-AMXD; to ground experiments, 1973

*   *   *   *   *   *   *   *   *   *

100 Hunting Jet Provost T.3s delivered between August 1960 and February 1962 by Hunting, Luton, to Contract KC/E/031

Serial	Units	Notes
XN458	1 FTS	To 8234M 21.3.73 at Halton
XN459	1 FTS/MoD(PE)/ 1 FTS/CFS	Sold; to G-BWOT 25.3.96
XN460	2 FTS	Abandoned in spin, Castle Bytham, Lincs., 1.2.61
XN461	1 FTS/7 FTS/ 3 FTS/1 FTS	Sold; became G-BVBE 21.7.93
XN462	1 FTS/2 FTS/CFS/ 3 FTS/7 FTS/CFS/ 1 FTS	To FAA Museum
XN463	AAEE/BSE/AAEE	Engine lost power; crash-landed into trees, Teffont Evias, Wilts., 26.10.60
XN464	CFS/6 FTS	SOC 31.7.69; to Linton-on-Ouse for fire practice
XN465	CFS/3 FTS	Abandoned in spin 1m N of Easingwold, Yorks., 24.2.71
XN466	1 FTS/7 FTS/ 1 FTS	Collided with XM476 while landing in bad visibility, Church Fenton, 29.1.63; to 1005 ATC Sqn Radcliffe
XN467	Mkrs & AAEE/CFS	Blt as T.4; to 8559M 1.2.78 at Halton
XN468	BSE/1 FTS/ RAFC/CFS	Blt as T.4 SOC 1.10.71
XN469	1 FTS	Engine cut; undercarriage collapsed in forced landing at disused airfield, East Moor, 22.6.70; not repaired and to Catterick for fire practice
XN470	1 FTS/7 FTS/1 FTS	Sold; to G-BXBJ 29.1.97
XN471	1 FTS/RAFC/TWU/ 3 FTS/RAFC/1 FTS	Sold 2.93; became N471XN 7.7.93
XN472	CFS/1 FTS/CFS/ RAFC/7 FTS/1 FTS/ 7 FTS	To 8959M 16.3.88 at Cosford
XN473	RAFC/7 FTS	Abandoned take-off to avoid hitting birds and nosewheel collapsed, Cranwell, 15.8.84; nose to 8862M; to Church Fenton for fire practice
XN492	RAFC/6 FTS	To 8079M 18.3.70 at Halton
XN493	RAFC/7 FTS/ 3 FTS	SOC 28.5.76; nose for exhibition use
XN494	RAFC/1 FTS	To 9012M 3.90 at Halton
XN495	RAFC/7 FTS/2 FTS/ 1 FTS/RAFC/7 FTS	Engine lost power on roller landing and wing hit ground, Church Fenton, 30.3.83; to 8786M 13.10.83 at Halton
XN496	RAFC	SS 10.7.69
XN497	RAFC/3 FTS/1 FTS	WFU 6.91
XN498	RAFC/3 FTS/1 FTS	WFU 8.94
XN499	RAFC/3 FTS/ 1 FTS/CFS	Sold to USA as N7075X 2.6.93
XN500	RAFC/3 FTS/26/ 3 FTS/RAFC/7 FTS/ 1 FTS	To GI airframe at Oxford Air Training School. Kidlington, 26.1.93
XN501	1 FTS/CFS	To 8958M 3.3.88 at Cosford
XN502	1 FTS/2 FTS/CFS	Sold; to N502GW 24.1.95
XN503	AAEE/6 FTS/ MinTech/2 FTS/ 4 FTS/MinTech	SOC 28.5.76; nose to RAFEF Abingdon
XN504	1 FTS	Engine lost power in circuit; abandoned on approach ½m N of Rufforth, 14.3.63
XN505	1 FTS/RAFC/1 FTS	Sold
XN506	1 FTS/7 FTS/RAFC/ 3 FTS/6 FTS/ 3 FTS/3 FTS & 26/ CFS/RAFC/7 FTS/ 1 FTS/7 FTS/1 FTS	Sold; to N77506 5.93 Sold 2.93
XN507	1 FTS	SOC 8.8.74
XN508	1 FTS/CFS/3 FTS/ 7 FTS/1 FTS	To DARA St Athan
XN509	1 FTS/6 FTS/RAFC/ 1 FTS/7 FTS/2 FTS/ 1 FTS	Sold 20.1.93; to USA
XN510	1 FTS/7 FTS/RAFC/ 3 FTS/1 FTS	Sold; to G-BXBI 29.1.97
XN511	CFS/1 FTS/CFS	SOC 28.5.76; nose to Blackpool Apt
XN512	CFS	To 8435M 10.11.71 at Halton
XN547	RAFC/1 FTS	Control lost in inverted spin; abandoned, Great Habton, 3m NW of Malton, N. Yorks., 8.3.89
XN548	CFS/RAFC/7 FTS	To 9014M 7.6.88 at Halton
XN549	CFS/1 FTS	To 8335M 21.3.73 at Halton (carried 8235M)
XN550	CFS	SOC 28.5.76; nose to 730 Sqn ATC Truro
XN551	RAFC/6 FTS/3 FTS/ 1 FTS/RAFC/7 FTS	To 8984M 4.89 at St Athan
XN552	RAFC/CFS/7 FTS/ 1 FTS	Sold; to N68354 12.7.94
XN553	RAFC/1 FTS/ SF St.Athan	Sold; to N57553 25.4.94
XN554	CFS	To 8436M 17.11.71 at St Athan
XN555	RAFC	SOC 8.8.74
XN556	1 FTS/6 FTS/ 1 FTS	Stalled on overshoot and hit runway, Linton-on-Ouse, 17.3.70
XN557	CFS/7 FTS/2 FTS	SOC 8.8.74
XN558	RAFC/3 FTS	Ingested bird; abandoned on approach, Dishforth, 29.6.71
XN559	RAFC/7 FTS/RAFC	SOC 1.2.74; to Catterick for fire practice
XN573	CFS/1 FTS	SOC 28.5.76; nose to Blackpool Apt
XN574	3 FTS/1 FTS/7 FTS	To Scampton as GI airframe, 27.10.88; preserved in France
XN575	1 FTS/7 FTS/ 3 FTS	Stalled on take-off and wing hit ground; cart-wheeled, Leeming, 30.9.69
XN576	CFS	Engine cut; abandoned over Northleach and crashed, Yandon, Glos., 4.9.69
XN577	RAFC/7 FTS/ 1 FTS/7 FTS	To 8956M 22.2.88 at Cosford
XN578	RAFC/6 FTS	SOC 18.12.69; to Valley for fire practice
XN579	RAFC/TWU/RAFC/ 1 FTS/7 FTS/1 FTS	To 9137M 4.92 at N Luffenham
XN580	RAFC	Caught fire on air test and abandoned, Scopwick, Lincs., 15.6.64
XN581	RAFC/7 FTS/6 FTS/ 3 FTS/CFS/RAFC/ CFS/3 FTS/CFS	SOC 7.91
XN582	RAFC/3 FTS/1 FTS/ 7 FTS	To 8957M 11.3.88 at Cosford
XN583	RAFC/7 FTS	Flew into wood during aerobatics, Hill Top Farm, 2½m S of Harrogate, Yorks., 17.9.64
XN584	RAFC/TWU/RAFC/ CFS/RAFC/CFS	To 9014M 9.90 at Halton
XN585	RAFC/3 FTS/ 1 FTS	Abandoned after fire warning on take-off, Linton-on-Ouse, 28.3.79

XN586	RAFC/2 FTS/CFS/ 1 FTS/7 FTS	To 9039M 5.90 at Cosford
XN587	RAFC	To GI airframe, Cranwell, 27.12.69; no M-serial allotted
XN588	RAFC/1 FTS	Dived into ground out of cloud near Wharram-le-Street, Yorks., 18.5.67
XN589	RAFC/1 FTS	To 9143M for display at Linton-on-Ouse
XN590	6 FTS/RAFC	Hit birds and lost power after roller landing; abandoned near Elvington, Yorks., 31.7.80
XN591	CFS/1 FTS/7 FTS/ 1 FTS/MoA	SOC 18.3.70; to Army Apprentices College, Arborfield
XN592	6 FTS/1 FTS/2 FTS	SOC 28.5.76; nose to 1105 ATC Sqn Winchester
XN593	2 FTS/1 FTS/7 FTS	To 8988M 5.89 at Cosford
XN594	2 FTS/7 FTS/6 FTS	To 8077M 21.4.70 at Halton
XN595	2 FTS/CFS/3 FTS/ 7 FTS/1 FTS	Sold; to N4436P 9.98
XN596	6 FTS	To Singapore AF as GI airframe SAFTECH 1, 4.9.69
XN597	2 FTS	Nosewheel collapsed in heavy landing, Wymeswold, 28.6.67; nose to 7984M at 196 Sqn ATC
XN598	3 FTS/1 FTS	Control lost when wingtip hit water in turn; crashed in Gouthwaite Reservoir, Pateley Bridge, Yorks., 1.6.78
XN599	6 FTS	Swung off runway and skidded into bank, Acklington, 27.3.62
XN600	3 FTS	SOC 28.5.76; nose to 168 ATC Sqn Leeds
XN601	6 FTS	Lost power on take-off and hit ground ½m W of Acklington, 16.10.62
XN602	6 FTS	To 8088M 2.3.70; preserved at Brampton
XN603	6 FTS	Abandoned after fire warning on approach 2m SW of Acklington, 29.7.65
XN604	6 FTS	Abandoned after false fire warning 5m S of Acklington, 9.5.62
XN605	6 FTS/1 FTS/RAFC/ CFS/1 FTS/CFS	SS 4.89
XN606	3 FTS/6 FTS/1 FTS/ 7 FTS/1 FTS	To 9121M at Brawdy
XN607	3 FTS	SOC 28.5.76
XN629	3 FTS/RAFC/ MoD(PE)/RAFC/ CFS/1 FTS/ 7 FTS/1 FTS	Sold; became G-BVEG
XN630	3 FTS/RAFC/ 1 FTS/7 FTS	Sank back on take-off and bellylanded, Biggin Hill, 23.7.69
XN631	3 FTS	Collided with XM428 and lost tail 1½m E of Northallerton, Yorks., and abandoned, 20.4.65
XN632	3 FTS	To 8352M 16.7.73 at St Athan
XN633	3 FTS	To 8353M 16.7.73 at Bicester
XN634	6 FTS/RAFC/1 FTS/ 7 FTS/1 FTS	SOC .81; to 8704M at Abingdon
XN635	RAFC/3 FTS	To GI airframe 16.7.73 at Aldergrove; no M-serial
XN636	RAFC/1 FTS	To 9045M at Halton
XN637	3 FTS	SOC 11.3.74; preserved as G-BKOU
XN638	6 FTS	SOC 18.12.69; to Church Fenton for fire practice
XN639	6 FTS	SOC 31.10.69; to Manston for film work

XN640	6 FTS/CFS/3 FTS/ RAFC/7 FTS	To 9016MB 1.90 at Cosford
XN641	3 FTS/RAFC/1 FTS	Bounced on landing and ran into barrier, Linton-on-Ouse, 11.5.84; not repaired; to 8865M 26.11.85 at Newton
XN642	3 FTS	Abandoned after flame-out on take-off 2m from Leeming, 19.2.63
XN643	3 FTS/CFS/3 FTS & 26/1 FTS	Engine flamed out during aerobatics; abandoned 2m N of Snainton, Yorks., 30.7.81

*   *   *   *   *   *   *   *   *   *

XN635		Sycamore HR.51 renumbered XR592
XN647 - XN658 XN683 - XN710		Sea Vixen FAW.1s for Royal Navy to Contract 6/Acft/15244; XN652 to 8817M; XN658 to 8223M; XN685 to 8173M; XN688 to 8141M; XN691 to 8243M; XN699 to 8224M; XN700 to 8138M; XN705 to 8225M; XN707 to 8144M
XN714, XN719		Hunting H.126s for Ministry of Aviation to Contract KD/2B/01; XN719 not built

*   *   *   *   *   *   *   *   *   *

44 English Electric Lightning F.2s delivered between September 1962 and October 1963 by EEC Warton, to Contract KC/2D/03

XN723	R-R	Caught fire on test flight and abandoned, Keyham, Leics., 25.3.64
XN724	BAC/Cv F.2A/19	To 8513M 8.12.76 at Laarbruch
XN725	Cv F.3/Mkrs/ Cv F.3A/Mkrs & AAEE/RAE	Used for barrier trials; to PEE 3.9.74
XN726	CFE/19/92	SOC 1.4.77; 8545M NTU and airframe to PEE
XN727	19/92	SOC 1.4.77; 8547M NTU
XN728	92	To 8546M 1.4.77 at Wildenrath
XN729	AFDS	Sold to BAC 25.1.67; to R Saudi AF as 52-659
XN730	19/92	To 8496M 8.7.76 at Gutersloh
XN731	92/19	To 8518M 1.1.77 at Laarbruch
XN732	92	To 8519M 1.1.77 at Laarbruch
XN733	92/19/92/19	To 8520M 1.1.77 at Laarbruch
XN734	Cv F.3/Mkrs & AAEE & R-R/ Cv F.3A/AAEE	To 8346M 25.5.73; later to G-27-239
XN735	92/19/92	To 8552M 1.4.77 at Wildenrath
XN767	-	Sold to BAC 10.5.66 for R.Saudi AF as 52-655
XN768	92	To 8347M 1.6.73
XN769	92/19/92	To 8402M 28.6.74 for display at West Drayton
XN770	-	Sold to BAC 5.5.66; to R.Saudi AF as 52-656
XN771	CFE/19	SOC 1.4.77; to PEE Shoeburyness
XN772	MoA/92	Abandoned in spin 1½m E of Diepholz, West Germany, 28.1.71
XN773	MoA/92	To 8521M 1.1.77 at Laarbruch
XN774	19/92	To 8551M 1.4.77 at Coningsby
XN775	19/92	To 8448M 18.6.75
XN776	19	To 8535M 1.4.77 at Leuchars
XN777	AFDS/CFE/19	To 8536M 1.4.77 at Wildenrath
XN778	19/92	To 8537M 1.4.77 at Wildenrath

XN779	19	To 8348M 1.6.73
XN780	19/92	Caught fire on ground during engine run, Gutersloh, 29.9.75; not repaired
XN781	19	To 8538M 1.4.77 at Leuchars
XN782	19/92	To 8539M 1.4.77 at Wildenrath
XN783	92/19	To 8526M 1.1.77 at Bruggen
XN784	19	To 8540M 1.4.77 at Bruggen
XN785	92	Ran out of fuel and crash-landed 5m N of Leconfield, 27.4.64
XN786	92/19/92/19	Jet pipe separated from engine; aircraft damaged by fire near Gutersloh, 4.8.76; SOC as not worth repair; to 8500M
XN787	19/92	To 8522M 1.1.77 at Laarbruch
XN788	92	To 8543M 1.4.77 at Bruggen
XN789	92/19	To 8527M 1.1.77 at Bruggen
XN790	92/19	To 8523M 1.1.77 at Laarbruch
XN791	92	To 8524M 1.1.77 at Bruggen
XN792	92	To 8525M 1.1.77 at Bruggen
XN793	92/19/92	To 8544M 1.1.77
XN794	92/19	To 8349M 1.6.73
XN795	Mkrs & AAEE	Sold to MinTech 21.12.67
XN796	-	Sold to BAC 29.4.66; to R.Saudi AF as 62-657
XN797	-	Sold to BAC 29.4.66; to R.Saudi AF as 62-658
XN798 to		
XN803	-	Cancelled

* * * * * * * * * *

XN808, XN809	GAF Jindivik 102 drones; retained RAAF serials A92-105 and 106

* * * * * * * * * *

20 Armstrong Whitworth Argosy C.1s delivered between December 1961 and April 1964 by Armstrong Whitworth, Bitteswell, to Contracts KU/K/031 (first seven) and KD/2K/01 (remainder)

XN814	Mkrs/Cv E.1/115	To MoD; SS 10.77
XN815	MoA/114/242 OCU/ 114/115	SS 12.9.75
XN816	MoA/Cv E.1/115	To 8489M 30.3.75 at Cosford
XN817	MoA/Cv E.1/115	Sold to MinTech 21.5.70
XN818	MoA/267/242 OCU/ 267/215/70/114	SS 12.9.75
XN819	MoA/105/267 & 114	8198M NTU; to 8205M 10.7.72 at Finningley
XN820	114/105/114 & 267/70	SS 18.8.75
XN821	AOCU/242 OCU/ 114-267/242 OCU/ 70	SS 22.5.75
XN847	AOCU/105/AOCU/ 114/MoA/114/ 267/70	SOC 21.8.72; allotted 8220M at St Athan
XN848	AOCU/242 OCU/ 267/114/70/AEAES	To 8195M 10.4.72 at Topcliffe
XN849	AOCU/105/114/ 105/114 & 267	SS 15.6.73
XN850	AOCU/242 OCU/ 114	SS 25.4.75
XN851	AOCU/242 OCU/ 114/215/115	SS 10.2.76
XN852	AOCU/114/105/ 114 & 267/114/ SF Benson	SS 22.5.75
XN853	114	SS 18.8.75
XN854	114/AOCU/ 242 OCU/114	SS 22.5.75

XN855	114/AOCU/242 OCU/Cv E.1/115	To 8556M 3.8.77 at Manston
XN856	114	SS 18.8.75
XN857	114	SS 18.8.75
XN858	114/242 OCU/70	SS 7.10.75

* * * * * * * * * *

XN862 - XN876	Northrop Shelduck D.1 target
XN893 - XN917	drones to Contract KF/5R/01
XN922 - XN935	Buccaneer S.1s for Royal Navy
XN948 - XN983	to Contract KC/2F/05; XN925 to 8087M; XN928 to 8179M; XN929 to 8051M; XN930 to 8180M; XN953 to 8182M; XN956 to 8059M; XN962 to 8183M; XN972 to 8181M

* * * * * * * * * *

Ten Blackburn Buccaneer S.2As and S.2Bs delivered by Hawker-Siddeley, Holme-in-Spalding-Moor, for Royal Navy as S.2s. Six subsequently transferred to RAF and modified to S.2A and S.2B standard

XN975	RAE	Control lost avoiding helicopter; abandoned in spin near Oelde, West Germany, 14.6.78
XN976	237 OCU/12/237 OCU/12/237 OCU/ 12/208/12/208	Hit sea avoiding fighter radar during simulated attack on ship 38m E of Leuchars, 9.7.92
XN977	12/237 OCU/ Cv S.2B/15	Engine caught fire after explosion during bombing on Nordhorn ranges, 8.3.82; not repaired
XN978	12	Control lost in cloud during air-to-air refuelling demonstration at low altitude for Paris Air Show and abandoned over Forêt de Compiègne, 5.6.71
XN981	12/RN/12/Cv S.2B/ 208 12	To RN 19.2.73 – 19.9.78 Retd to RAF; SS 4.94
XN983	12/237 OCU/15/16/ 15/12237 OCU//208/ 12/237 OCU/208	SS 4.94

* * * * * * * * * *

XP000		Carried by Beaver at AAC Centre made up from XP812 and XP815 as GI airframe, June 1974; sold; to G-BMGE 14.10.85
XP103-XP118		Westland Wessex HAS.1s for
XP137-XP160		Royal Navy to Contract KF/M/047 XP140 to 8806M; XP159 to 8877M
XP165-XP167		Westland Scout AH.1s for Army
XP188-XP192		Air Corps to Contract KF/2Q/04
XP197-XP199;		Fairey Gannet AEW.3s for Royal
XP224-XP229		Navy to Contract KC/L/017
XP232-XP254;		Auster AOP.9s for Army Air
XP277-XP286		Corps to Contract KC/N/047 XP244 to 7864M; XP248 to 7822M; XP283 to 7859M

RAF use:

XP278	38 Gp CF	Swung on landing and under-carriage leg collapsed, Benson, 23.8.66; DBR

XP289, XP290		Canberra B(I).12s for RNZAF to Contract KD/E/01

* * * * * * * * * *

Three Scottish Aviation Twin Pioneer CC.2s delivered between March and May 1961 by Scottish Aviation, Prestwick, to Contract KC/K/030

XP293	Hdlg Sqn/209	SOC 20.12.68
XP294	SF Odiham/AAEE/209	Skidded into ditch on landing on wet strip and undercarriage leg collapsed, Bario, Borneo, 11.9.64
XP295	230/SF Odiham/ 1310 Flt/Sc Avn/ AAEE/SF Odiham/ Sc Avn/AAEE/Sc Avn/SF Odiham	Sold 26.8.70 to Scottish Avn; to G-AZHJ
XP296	-	Cancelled

* * * * * * * * * *

52 Westland Whirlwind HAR.10s delivered between July 1961 and November 1962 by Westland Helicopters, Yeovil, to Contracts KF/2N/037 (first twelve) and KF/2N/042 (remainder)

XP299	MoA/CFS/230/QF/ 1563 Flt/230/ 22/SAR Wg	To 8726M; preserved by RAF Museum at Cosford, 9.12.81
XP300	MoA/1563 Flt/ 1564 Flt/CFS	SOC 14.7.77; to Portland for fire practice
XP301	MoA & Mkrs/ 225/103/28	SOC 9.3.76
XP302	CFS/230/84	To 8443M 22.7.75 at Halton
XP303	MoA/110/103/ 110/28	Rolled over during hover and caught fire, Peak Alpha, Hong Kong, 24.1.71; DBF
XP327	225	Lost tail rotor and crashed into hill near Serian, Sarawak, 25.9.65
XP328	225/110/225/ 110/28/21/32	Sold 27.4.82; to G-BKHC 25.8.82
XP329	225/110/103-110/ 230/84	SOC 7.82; to 8791M at Episkopi
XP330	225/110/230/ 32/21	Sold to CAA 26.1.76
XP331	CFS	To 8649M 8.2.80 at Upavon
XP332	225/103/28	Engine cut; ditched 1m E of Brothers Island, Hong Kong, 13.5.69
XP333	CFS	To 8650M 8.2.80 at Odiham
XP338	225/CFS/HDU/CFS	To 8647M 17.1.80 at Shawbury
XP339	225/103/32	Sold 10.5.76; preserved at Pryton Hill, Oxon.
XP340	225/103/28	Damaged 19.11.68; SOC 6.2.76
XP341	CFS	To 8340M 7.3.73 at Cranwell
XP342	CFS	Flew into HT wires; lost tail cone and crashed, Llyn Rhuddwyn, 4m W of Oswestry, Salop., 2.6.66
XP343	CFS	Rotor blades hit roof on take-off; tail hit ground and broke off, Valley, 26.11.69
XP344	CFS/SAR Wg/22	To 8764M 20.10.82 at Cranwell
XP345	CFS/202/ 1563 Flt/84	To 8792M 2.9.83 at Dekhelia
XP346	225/22/84	To 8793M 2.9.83 at Akrotiri
XP347	225/22	Tail rotor failed on landing on ferry flight; hit ground and rolled over, Koksijde, 3.6.81; to 8688M at Guterloh
XP348	225/22	Lost blade; flew into ground 2m SW of Midhurst, Sussex, 3.6.64
XP349	225/22	Engine lost power; ditched in Holyhead Harbour, Anglesey, 13.12.72
XP350	225/22/SAR Wg	To Cornwall Aero Park, Helston, 3.3.82
XP351	22/SAR Wg/2 FTS	To 8672M 9.2.81 at Shawbury
XP352	22/202/SAR Wg	To 8701M 31.7.82 at Abingdon
XP353	22/1564 Flt/ 1563 Flt/202/ SAR Wg	To 8720M 3.11.81 at Catterick
XP354	22/202	To 8721M 4.11.81 at Halton
XP355	CFS/MinTech/21	To 8463M 6.2.76; to G-BEBC 25.6.76
XP356	CFS/MoD(PE)/CFS	Sold to MoD(PE) 17.11.75
XP357	225/110/230/22	Forcelanded on Newgale Sands, Dyfed, and overtaken by tide, 13.6.76; to 8499M at Manston
XP358	225/103/110/ 103/28	To RAE 10.5.76
XP359	225/103/110/103	To 8447M 12.6.75 at Abingdon
XP360	225/CFS	Sold 31.3.76; preserved Fawkham Green
XP361	225/110/103/ 22/SAR Wg	To 8731M 25.10.82 at Chivenor; later preserved at Boulmer
XP362	225/230/103	SOC 26.2.76
XP363	230/103/110/ 103/28	To 8228M 30.4.73 at Halton
XP392	-	Crashed before delivery, 20.6.62
XP393	225/103/28	To RAE 10.5.76 for fire practice
XP394	CFS	To Royal Navy 10.12.79
XP395	230/22	To 8674M 2.2.81 at Halton
XP396	230	Tail rotor drive failed; yawed and flew into ground, Fleckney, 7m SE of Leicester, 7.6.69
XP397	230	Lost power and tail rotor hit ground in forced landing ½m N of Gutersloh, 17.8.64
XP398	225/110/103/202/ 1563 Flt/22	To 8794M 2.9.83 at St John's School, Cyprus
XP399	230/1563 Flt/32	Sold 10.5.76; preserved at Pryton Hill, Oxon.
XP400	230/110/103	To 8444M 23.7.75 at Halton
XP401	230/110/103/28	SOC 6.2.76
XP402	230	Engine lost power; ditched and sank off Shell Pier, Victoria, Labuan, 3.7.65
XP403	228/202/SAR Wg/ 22	To 8590M 31.10.81 at Bruggen
XP404	228/202/SAR Wg/ 22	To 8682M 10.82 at Finningley
XP405	CFS	To 8656M 3.9.80 at Halton

* * * * * * * * * *

20 Armstrong Whitworth Argosy C.1s delivered between April 1962 and March 1963 to Contract KD/2K/011

XP408	105/114-267/114	SS 15.6.73
XP409	105/114-267/70	8197M NTU; to 8221M 9.72 at Halton
XP410	105/114-267/70	SS 15.6.73
XP411	105/114-267/ 70/6 FTS	To 8442M 22.5.75 at Cosford
XP412	105/114-267/ 115/70	Sold 22.5.75; to G-BDCV 9.5.75
XP413	105/242 OCU/ Cv E.1/115	SOC 1.5.76
XP437	105/114-267	SS 7.10.75
XP438	105/114	SS 7.10.75
XP439	105/Cv E.1/115	To 8558M 13.9.77 at Lossiemouth
XP440	105/114/SF Benson	SS 22.5.75
XP441	114/267/114	Bounced on landing and wing-tip hit ground; broke up, Benson, 4.6.70

XP442	114/MoA/114/	
	114-267/114/	Cv T.2
	SF Benson/MoD(PE)	To 8454M 2.10.75 at Halton
XP443	114	SS 18.8.75
XP444	267/215/70	To 8455M 3.11.75 at Cosford
XP445	267/215/70	SS 15.6.73
XP446	267/215/70	Sold 26.1.76; to 9Q-COE
XP447	267/215/70/Cv T.2	Sold 10.2.76; to N1430Z
XP448	267/215/Cv E.1/115	SOC 18.1.78; to Catterick for fire practice
XP449	267/215/70/	
	Cv E.1/115	SS 13.10.75
XP450	267/215/70/Trials	
	Flt Cottesmore/70	Sold 22.5.75; to RP-C-1192 7.75

* * * * * * * * * *

XP454-464; XP487-495		Slingsby Grasshopper gliders To Contract KF/2R/012

* * * * * * * * * *

30 Hawker-Siddeley Gnat T.1s delivered between November 1962 and July 1963 to Contract KC/2B/05

XP500	4 FTS	To 8557M 24.8.77 at St Athan
XP501	CFS	Undershot after hydraulic failure; bounced and crash-landed, Fairford, 13.6.69
XP502	4 FTS	To 8576M 25.1.78 at St Athan
XP503	4 FTS	To 8568M 31.10.77 at Halton
XP504	4 FTS/CFS/4 FTS	To 8618M 4.3.79 at Halton
XP505	MoA/CFS/MoA	Sold to MinTech 7.1.69; to Science Museum 18.11.84
XP506	4 FTS	SOC 15.5.77
XP507	4 FTS	Flew into sea on approach and broke up, Valley, 13.4.66
XP508	4 FTS	Engine lost power on take-off; control lost and abandoned ¼m SW of Valley, 6.9.73
XP509	4 FTS	Airbrake selected in error for undercarriage; bellylanded, Valley, 14.12.67; not repaired
XP510	4 FTS	Abandoned after control lost in dive off Nevin, Caernarvon, 14.11.68
XP511	4 FTS/CFS/4 FTS	To 8619M 4.3.79 at Halton
XP512	4 FTS	Abandoned after tailplane control lost; crashed on beach, Rhoscolyn, 1m SSW of Valley, 23.8.67
XP513	4 FTS/MoD(PE)	Sold to MoD(PE) 5.12.78
XP514	4 FTS/CFS/4 FTS/ CFS	To 8635M 19.9.79 at Cosford
XP515	CFS/4 FTS/CFS/ 4 FTS/CFS/4 FTS/ CFS/4 FTS	To 8614M 12.3.79 at 1331 Sqn ATC, Wattisham
XP516	4 FTS/CFS/4 FTS/ CFS/4 FTS	To 8580M 8.2.78 at Valley
XP530	CFS/4 FTS	To 8606M 29.9.78 at Halton
XP531	CFS/4 FTS/CFS	Flew into power cables near Kemble, 16.2.76; not repaired and SOC 12.3.76
XP532	4 FTS/CFS/4 FTS	8577M 9.3.79 NTU; to 8615M at Farnborough
XP533	4 FTS/CFS	To 8632M 21.9.79 at Cosford
XP534	CFS/4 FTS/CFS/ 4 FTS/CFS/4 FTS	To 8620M 31.3.79 at Halton
XP535	CFS/4 FTS/CFS	To A2679 (SAH-1) for Royal Navy 21.9.79 at Culdrose
XP536	CFS/4 FTS/ CFS/4 FTS	Collided with XR983 and crashed 3m E of Dolgellau, Merioneth, 30.4.76

XP537	CFS/4 FTS/CFS/ 4 FTS/CFS/4 FTS	SOC 15.5.78
XP538	4 FTS/CFS/4 FTS/ CFS/4 FTS/CFS/ 4 FTS	To 8607M 29.9.78 at Halton
XP539	4 FTS/CFS/4 FTS/ CFS/4 FTS/CFS	Engine cut due to fuel pipe blockage; abandoned near Leeming, 22.5.79
XP540	4 FTS/MoA/4 FTS	To 8608M 12.10.78 at Halton
XP541	4 FTS/CFS/4 FTS/ CFS/4 FTS/CFS/ 4 FTS	To 8616M 4.79 at Abingdon
XP542	4 FTS/CFS/4 FTS	To 8575M 5.1.78 at St Athan

* * * * * * * * * *

100 Hunting Jet Provost T.4s delivered between October 1961 and December 1962 to Contract KC/E/041

XP547	AAEE/RAFC/ CATCS/MoD(PE)/ CATCS/SRF/1 TWU	To 8992M 4.89 at Cosford
XP548	Hdlg Sqn/RAFC/ 6 FTS	8404M NTU SOC 25.1.74; to Brawdy for fire practice
XP549	CFS/CAW	SS 22.11.68
XP550	CFS/2 FTS	SS 22.11.68
XP551	CFS/CAW	SS 22.11.68
XP552	CFS/3 FTS	SOC 1.10.71
XP553	CFS	SS 20.11.68
XP554	CFS	SS 22.11.68
XP555	RAFC	SOC 1.10.71; to Manby for fire practice
XP556	RAFC/6 FTS/ SRF/CATCS	To 9027M at Halton
XP557	RAFC/6 FTS	To 8494M 30.6.76 at Halton
XP558	RAFC/3 CAACU/ CAW/MoD(PE)	To Royal Navy as GI airframe A2628, 13.5.74 at Culdrose; later to 8627M
XP559	RAFC	SOC 16.1.70
XP560	RAFC/6 FTS	SOC 22.12.75; to Finningley for fire practice
XP561	RAFC/1 FTS	Abandoned after control lost in cloud 15m SW of Linton-on-Ouse, 21.2.68
XP562	RAFC/3 FTS	SS 18.12.70
XP563	RAFC/CATCS/ 6 FTS/SRF/CATCS	To 9028M at Halton
XP564	RAFC/3 FTS/ CATCS/6 FTS/ CATCS/1 TWU	Abandoned after engine lost power when throttle linkage disconnected; crashed, Nant-y-Moch Reservoir, Llandeilo, Dyfed, 22.4.82
XP565	RAFC	SOC 14.8.72; to Shawbury for fire practice
XP566	RAFC	Flew into ground on night approach 2m NW of Cranwell, 30.4.70
XP567	RAFC/6 FTS/ CATCS	To 8510M 30.3.77 at Halton
XP568	RAFC	SOC 1.10.71; to Hatfield Polytechnic
XP569	RAFC/2 FTS	Spun into ground, East Drayton, near Retford, Notts., 30.12.66; cause not known
XP570	CFS/RAFC/6 FTS	SS 22.11.68
XP571	CFS/6 FTS	SS 22.11.68
XP572	CFS	SS 22.11.68
XP573	CFS/1 FTS/BSE	To 8336M 21.3.73 at Halton; painted as 8236M
XP574	3 FTS	SS 17.2.70
XP575	CFS/RAFC/CAW	SS 11.11.69
XP576	3 FTS	Abandoned after engine flamed out on approach; crashed on bank of Swale 1¼m E of Leeming, 16.3.70

XP577	3 FTS	SS 18.12.70
XP578	3 FTS	SS 17.2.70
XP579	3 FTS	SS 13.5.69
XP580	3 FTS/1 FTS/CAW	SOC 7.1.69 for camouflage trials at 431 MU
XP581	3 FTS	SS 11.11.69
XP582	3 FTS	SS 22.11.68
XP583	RAFC/6 FTS/ CAW/4 FTS	To 8400M 11.1.74 at Valley
XP584	RAFC	SOC 1.10.71
XP585	RAFC/6 FTS/RAFC	To 8407M 7.10.74 at St Athan
XP586	RAFC	SS 14.8.72
XP587	3 FTS	SS 13.5.69
XP588	CFS	Abandoned after fire warning ½m N of Chedworth, Glos., 2.5.63
XP589	1 FTS	SS 18.12.70
XP614	2 FTS	SS 18.12.70
XP615	1 FTS	SS 15.2.71
XP616	1 FTS	Flew into hill in bad weather, Newgate Bank, 4½m NW of Helmsley, Yorks., 14.9.66
XP617	3 FTS/7 FTS/2 FTS	SS 18.12.70
XP618	3 FTS	SS 15.2.71
XP619	2 FTS	SS 17.2.70
XP620	2 FTS	SOC 1.10.71
XP621	1 FTS/3 FTS	Abandoned after fire warning and flew into hill 5m SW of Catterick Camp, Yorks., 15.11.65
XP622	2 FTS	Engine cut on take-off from roller landing; undercarriage collapsed in heavy landing on grass, Wymeswold, 20.9.63
XP623	2 FTS	Abandoned in spin, Thrussington, Leics., 19.4.63
XP624	2 FTS/RAFC/2 FTS	SS 15.2.71
XP625	2 FTS/CAW	Engine cut after ingesting bird; abandoned 2m E of North Frodingham, Yorks., 27.7.66
XP626	1 FTS	SS 15.2.71
XP627	1 FTS/3 FTS/6 FTS	SOC 1.10.71
XP628	2 FTS	SS 18.12.70
XP629	2 FTS/CAW/CATCS/ 6 FTS/SRF/CATCS	To 9026M at Halton
XP630	2 FTS	SOC 1.10.71
XP631	2 FTS	Hit by XM384 in formation and collided with XP617; abandoned over Woodborough, Notts., 26.5.66
XP632	CFS/CAW	SOC 8.5.72; to Church Fenton for fire practice
XP633	1 FTS	SS 17.8.71
XP634	6 FTS/1 FTS	SS 17.8.71
XP635	6 FTS	Abandoned after fire warning, Whitton Shields, near Morpeth, Northumberland, 18.4.63
XP636	6 FTS/3 FTS	SS 15.2.71
XP637	1 FTS	SS 17.2.70
XP638	6 FTS/CAW/CATCS/ 1 TWU/CATCS/ 1 TWU/CATCS	To 9034M at Halton
XP639	CFS/Hdlg Sqn/ CFS	Collided with XR670 during formation aerobatics and abandoned 1m N of Moreton-in-Marsh, 12.3.64
XP640	3 FTS/CFS/CAW/ 6 FTS/CATCS	To 8501M 13.9.76 at Halton
XP641	CFS/2 FTS	SS 15.2.71
XP642	CFS/2 FTS	SS 14.8.72
XP661	6 FTS	Overstressed 27.3.63; SOC and to 7819M (NTU); later to 8594M at Linton-on-Ouse
XP662	6 FTS/1 FTS/ 2 FTS/1 FTS	SS 15.2.71

XP663	3 FTS	SOC 1.10.71
XP664	2 FTS	SOC 1.10.71
XP665	2 FTS	SS 17.8.71
XP666	7 FTS	Sold to BAC 30.8.67 for South Yemen AF as T.52 No.107
XP667	3 FTS/RAFC	SS 15.2.71
XP668	7 FTS/RAFC/1 FTS	SS 17.8.71
XP669	2 FTS	SOC 14.8.72
XP670	7 FTS	Abandoned in spiral dive during instrument flying practice near Coxwold, Yorks., 5.4.66
XP671	RAFC/1 FTS	SS 17.8.71
XP672	2 FTS/CAW/CATCS/ CAW/SRF	To 8458M 19.12.75 at Halton
XP673	2 FTS/RAFC	SS 18.12.70
XP674	6 FTS/3 FTS	SS 15.2.71
XP675	7 FTS/CFS	Collided with XS229 near Hauling, near Guiting Power, Glos., 26.2.68; landed safely but not repaired; SS 22.11.68
XP676	6 FTS/3 FTS	SS 15.2.71
XP677	2 FTS	SOC 1.10.71; nose to 8587M at Abingdon
XP678	7 FTS/1 FTS	SS 17.8.71
XP679	7 FTS/CFS/ 1 FTS/3 FTS	SS 17.8.71
XP680	6 FTS/CAW	To 8640M 21.12.75 at St Athan
XP681	7 FTS/1 FTS	SS 15.2.71
XP682	7 FTS	Hit power cable on low-level exercise and lost wing, Scotton, 6m S of Scunthorpe, Lincs., 27.7.64
XP683	6 FTS/1 FTS	SS 14.8.72
XP684	7 FTS	Sold to BAC 30.8.67 for South Yemen AF as T.52 No.105
XP685	7 FTS/2 FTS	SS 14.8.72
XP686	3 FTS/CAW/ CATCS/CAW/ 6 FTS/CATCS	8401M NTU; to 8502M 23.9.76 at Halton
XP687	3 FTS	SS 15.2.71
XP688	RAFC/CAW/SRF/ CATCS	To 9031M

*   *   *   *   *   *   *   *   *   *

47 BAC Lightning F.3s delivered between May 1963 and November 1964 by BAC, Preston to Contract KC/2T/019

XP693	AAEE/Cv F.6/Cv F.3A/AAEE/BAe	MoA aircraft To G-FSIX 31.12.92
XP694	BAC & AAEE/29/ TDFF Wattisham/ 29/111/29/56/5/ LTF/5-11/LTF/ 5-11	SOC 21.9.87
XP695	CFE/FCTU/56/ 29/5-11	SOC 6.1.83; to 8808M for display at Binbrook
XP696	CFE/AAEE/ 226 OCU/ 111/29	SOC 28.11.74
XP697	BAC/Cv F.3A/ Cv F.6/AAEE	Sold to MinTech 23.2.70
XP698	Hdlg Sqn/74/ TDFF Wattisham/56/ Wattisham TFF/ 56/29/111/29	Collided with XP747 and crashed in sea 60m E of Harwich, Essex, 16.2.72
XP699	AAEE/56/Wattisham TFF/56	Abandoned after fire warning 2m N of Wethersfield, 3.3.67
XP700	74/56/111/29	Caught fire on take-off and abandoned 9m SW of Wattisham; crashed at Gt. Waldingfield, Suffolk, 7.8.72

XP701	AAEE/29/111/29/ 56/11/5/LTF/5/LTF	To 8924M 9.2.86 at Binbrook
XP702	74/56/29/56/ LTF/5/11	SOC 21.9.87
XP703	74/56/29	To MoD(PE) 23.5.75
XP704	74	Stalled and spun into ground during aerobatic display practice, Leuchars, 28.8.64
XP705	74/Wattisham TFF/ 56/23/Wattisham TFF/29	Abandoned after engine fire 35m S of Akrotiri, Cyprus, 8.7.71
XP706	74/111/23/LTF/ 5/11/LTF	To 8925M 9.2.87 at Binbrook
XP707	23/29/226 OCU/ 5/11/LTF	Abandoned in inverted spin during aerobatic practice, Binbrook, 19.3.87
XP708	23/Wattisham TTF/29	SOC 31.3.76
XP735	23/Wattisham TFF/29	SOC 16.10.75
XP736	23/29	Dived into sea 40m NE of Great Yarmouth, Norfolk, 22.9.71; cause not known
XP737	23/29/226 OCU/ 11/5	Undercarriage jammed up; abandoned off Valley, 17.8.79
XP738	111/Wattisham TFF/111	Bellylanded in error at night, Wattisham, 10.12.73; SOC for spares 7.1.74
XP739	111	Abandoned after both engines flamed out, Battisford Hall, Needham Market, Suffolk, 29.9.65
XP740	111/TFF Wattisham/ 111	SOC 28.11.74
XP741	111/TDFF Wattis- ham/111/TDFF Wattisham/111/ 5/11/LTF5/LTF/5	To 8939M 1.10.87; to Manston for fire practice
XP742	111/Wattisham TFF/111	Engine caught fire; abandoned off Great Yarmouth, Norfolk, 7.5.70
XP743	56/Wattisham TFF/ 56/29/56/29	SOC 16.10.75
XP744	56/Wattisham TFF/56	Abandoned after fire warning 15m W of Akrotiri, 10.5.71
XP745	56/Wattisham TFF/56/29	To 8453M 25.9.75 for display at Boulmer
XP746	56/Wattisham TFF/56/111	SOC 28.11.74
XP747	56/29	Collided with XP698 at night and abandoned 60m E of Harwich, Essex, 16.2.72
XP748	56/Wattisham TFF/56/111	SOC 28.4.75; to 8446M for display at Binbrook; to RAE 12.5.88 for weapons trials
XP749	CFE/111/TDFF Wattisham/111/ 5/LTF/11/LTF/11	8926M NTU; SS 21.12.87
XP750	CFE/111/TDFF Wattisham/111/ 23/LTF/5/LTF	To 8927M 9.2.87 at Binbrook
XP751	74/23/111/23/ LTF/5/LTF/5-11/ LTF	To 8928M 9.2.87 at Binbrook
XP752	74/Wattisham TFF/23/111	Collided with Mirage IIIE over Colmar, 3.5.71; landed safely; to 8166M 12.8.71 at Coltishall
XP753	74/TDFF Wattisham/ 111/TDFF Wattis- ham/56/11-5/LTF	Dived in sea during flypast, Castle Cliff, Scarborough, Yorks., 26.8.83
XP754	74/Wattisham TFF/56/111/29/ 111/29	SOC 28.11.74

XP755	74/Wattisham TFF/ 56/29	SOC 16.10.75
XP756	23/29	Abandoned after fire warning off Great Yarmouth, 25.1.71
XP757	23/29	SOC 13.11.75
XP758	23/111/29	SOC 13.11.75
XP759	23/Wattisham TFF/ 56/111/29/111	SOC 28.11.74
XP760	23	Engine would not relight and elevators jammed up; abandon- ed off Seahouses, Fife, 24.8.66
XP761	23/111/11	To 8438M 20.2.75 at Binbrook
XP762	111/Wattisham TFF/ 11129	SOC 13.11.75
XP763	23/Wattisham TFF/29	Damaged on ground, 29.3.74; SOC 11.4.74
XP764	74/56/23/29/5/11/ LTF/5/LTF	To 8929M 9.2.87
XP765	56/Wattisham TFF/56/29	SOC 21.11.74

* * * * * * * * * *

XP769 - XP780		DHC-2 Beavers AL.1s
XP804 - XP827		for Army Air Corps

* * * * * * * * * *

Two Hawker-Siddeley P.1127s for Ministry of Aviation to Contract KD/2Q/02

XP831	Mkrs	To 8406M and preserved in Royal Air Force Museum
XP836	Mkrs	Front nozzle became detached; rolled on approach and abandoned, Yeovilton, 14.12.61

* * * * * * * * * *

XP841		Handley Page H.P.115 for Ministry of Aviation to Contract KD/2N/02
XP846 - XP857		Westland Scout AH.1s for Army
XP883 - XP910		Air Corps to Contract KF/2Q/06 XP854 to 7898M; XP919 to 8163M; XP921 to 8226M

* * * * * * * * * *

De Havilland Comet 3B for Ministry of Aviation delivered in February 1961 ex-G-ANLO

XP915	BLEU	To HSA Woodford, 22.8.73

* * * * * * * * * *

XP918 - XP925		Sea Vixens for Royal Navy
XP953 - XP959		to Contract 6/Acft/15244
XP966, XP967		Sud Alouette AH.2s for Army Air Corps to Contract KF/2T/05

* * * * * * * * * *

Four Hawker-Siddeley P.1127s for Ministry of Aviation first flown between July 1961 and February 1964 to Contract KC/2Q/03

XP972	RAE & AAEE	Crashlanded after engine fire, Tangmere, 30.11.62
XP976	Mkrs/BSE/RAE	To test rig, 1971
XP980	Mkrs/AAEE/RAE	To trials airframe; became A2700 with Royal Navy

Whirlwind HAR.10 XP399 was passed on to No.32 Squadron for communications use after its search-and-rescue days were over.

It is seen here hovering in front of a hangar at Northolt where the squadron was based.

Whirlwind HAR.10 XP352 of No.202 Squadron in full yellow search-and-rescue colours.

The squadron's mallard emblem is carried on its badge on the sliding door.

Argosy C.1 XR141 of No.114 Squadron visits Biggin Hill on 20 September 1969 for Battle of Britain Day.

With XN819, it provided back-up for the Falcons parachute team. (John Ware)

Belfast C.1 XR371, named
'Enceladus' of No.53 Squadron, at
Sharjah on 15 December 1970 while
moving No.84 Squadron personnel
and equipment to Muharraq.
   In the background is Vulcan B.2
XJ783 of No.35 Squadron from
Akrotiri.
(Don Neate)

Wessex HC.2 XR507 of No.18
Squadron in tactical camouflage
scheme..
   The squadron's Pegasus badge is
carried on the tail rotor mount.

Wessex HC.2 XR518 converted for
search-and-rescue duties with No.72
Squadron.
   Although No.72 was a tactical
support unit, it also played a SAR
role in Northern Ireland.

| XP984 | Mkrs & RAE | Control lost in cross-wind landing; crashlanded, Bedford, 31.10.75; to A2658 with Royal Navy |

*   *   *   *   *   *   *   *   *   *

16 Armstrong Whitworth Argosy C.1s delivered between March and December 1963 to Contract KU/K/01

XR105	AAEE & Mkrs/267	To MoA 11.11.70 for ETPS. Wing dropped on asymmetric approach; hit hangar and rolled into ground, Boscombe Down, 27.4.76
XR106	267/215/114	SS 18.8.75
XR107	267/215/70	To 8441M 14.5.75 at Cosford
XR108	267/215/114	SS 25.4.75
XR109	267/105/114-267/114	SS 22.5.75
XR133	267	Wing hit ground during flypast; flew into runway, cartwheeled and blew up, Got-el-Afraq airstrip, Libya, 7.5.68
XR134	267/114	SS 18.8.75
XR135	114	SS 18.8.75
XR136	114	Sold 26.1.76; became 9Q-COA
XR137	267/242 OCU/115/Cv E.1/AAEE/115	SOC 10.1.78; to Northolt for fire practice
XR138	267/114	SS 18.8.75
XR139	267/114/SF Benson	SS 22.9.75
XR140	114/242 OCU/114/Cv E.1/115	To 8579M 18.1.78 at Halton
XR141	114/SF Benson	SS 22.5.75
XR142	114	SS 18.8.75
XR143	267/115/Cv E.1/115	Sold; became G-BFVT 29.6.78

*   *   *   *   *   *   *   *   *   *

XR148 - XR162 XR185 - XR209		Northrop Shelduck D.1 target drones to Contract KF/5R/07
XR213 - XR216		Beaver AL.1s for Army Air Corps to Contract KC/25/03 for Sultan of Oman Air Force
XR219 - XR227		Cancelled TSR.2s to Contract KD/2L/02; XR220 to 7932M 11.4.67
XR232		Alouette AH.2 ex F-WEIP for Army Air Corps to Contract KF/2T/05
XR236 - XR246 XR267 - XR271		Auster AOP.9s for Army Air Corps to Contract KC/N/058
XR290 - XR315 XR331 - XR336 XR345 - XR356		Northrop Shelduck D.1 target drones to Contract KF/5R/01 and KF/5R/011

*   *   *   *   *   *   *   *   *   *

Ten Short Belfast C.1s delivered between January 1966 and January 1969 by Short Brothers and Harland, Belfast

XR362	53	*Samson*; sold 29.3.77; became G-BEPE 30.3.77
XR363	53	*Goliath*; sold 8.78 to R-R; to G-OHCA 11.9.81
XR364	53	*Pallus*; sold 8.78 to R-R
XR365	53	*Hector*; sold 8.78 to R-R; to G-HLFT 11.9.81
XR366	53	*Atlas*; sold 8.78 to R-R
XR367	53	*Heracles*; sold 8.78 to R-R became G-BFYU 13.11.78
XR368	53	*Theseus*; sold 6.4.77 became G-BEPS
XR369	53	*Spartacus*; sold 4.4.77 became G-BEPL
XR370	53	*Ajax*; sold 8.78 to R-R
XR371	53	*Enceladus*; sold 8.78 to R-R preserved at Cosford

*   *   *   *   *   *   *   *   *   *

| XR376 - XR387 | | Alouette AH.2s for Army Air Corps to Contract KK/X/01 |

*   *   *   *   *   *   *   *   *   *

One de Havilland Heron C.4 delivered in June 1961 by D.H., Chester to Contract KU/J/01

| XR391 | QF/AAEE/60 | Sold 16.1.72; became CF-CNT |

*   *   *   *   *   *   *   *   *   *

Five de Havilland Comet C.4s delivered between December 1961 and February 1962 by D.H., Chester to Contract KD/G/054

XR395	AAEE/216	Sold 1. 9.75; to G-BDIT
XR396	216	Sold 1.9.75; to G-BDIU; later to 8882M
XR397	216	Sold 1.9.75; to G-BDIV
XR398	216	Sold 1.9.75; to G-BDIW
XR399	216	Sold 1.9.75; to G-BDIX

*   *   *   *   *   *   *   *   *   *

XR404 - XR428		Radioplane OQ-19 Drones to Contract KF/5R/011
XR431 - XR433		Fairey Gannet AEW.3s for Royal Navy to Contract KC/L/037
XR436		Scout AH.1 for Army Air Corps To Contract KF/2Q/04
XR441 - XR445		Sea Heron C.1s for Royal Navy Purchased from W S Shackleton
XR447 - XR450		Northrop Shelduck D.1 drones for Royal Navy

*   *   *   *   *   *   *   *   *   *

15 Westland Whirlwind HAR.10s delivered between November 1962 and May 1964 to Contract KK/K/04

XR453	CFS/1563 Flt/230/CFS	To MoD(PE) 12.12.79; became 8873M for display at Odiham
XR454	103/230/84	Engine cut and boom broke off in forced landing 3m E of Mt. Troodos, Cyprus, 27.1.75; not repaired
XR455	103/225/110/28	To 8219M 31.5.72 at Halton
XR456	230/110/103	Engine cut; forcelanded in trees and rolled over 7m W of Mersing, Malaya, 5.11.68
XR457	230/103/22/Upavon	SOC 7.5.81; to 8644M as target at Otterburn
XR458	103/110/28/CFS	To 8662M 27.11.80 at Halton
XR477	103/28	Hit cables and lost rotor blade; caught fire and crashed near Fanling, Hong Kong, 30.10.69

XR478	103/110/230	Sank into ground during practice power-off landing and rolled over, Odiham, 7.8.67; not repaired
XR479	103/110/103	To RAE 10.5.76 for fire practice
XR480	103	Shot down by Indonesian light flak 5m W of Stass, Sarawak, 17.11.65
XR481	103/110/103	SOC 14.7.77; to Wroughton for fire practice
XR482	103/110/103/ 110/28	SOC 29.10.75 for NBC trials
XR483	110/103/22	Sold 27.7.81 to Autair; to N2979G
XR484	103	To Royal Navy 14.2.77 for fire practice
XR485	CFS	Sold to Norfolk & Suffolk Museum, 29.1.81

* * * * * * * * * *

Two Westland Whirlwind HCC.12s delivered in May 1964 to Contract KK/K/04

XR486	QF/32/Cv Mk.10/ 32	To 8727M 9.12.81 at St Athan; later to G-RWWW
XR487	QF	Rotor head failed; lost blades and dived into ground, Brightwalton, 5m WNW of Newbury, Berks., 7.12.67

* * * * * * * * * *

XR493		Saro P.531 Scout for MoA ex G-APVM; became 8040M

* * * * * * * * * *

30 Westland Wessex HC.2s delivered between February 1963 and December 1964 to Contract KF/N/019

XR497	AAEE/78/103/ 72/Cv SAR/22/ SARTU/22/72	
XR498	AAEE/72/60/72	
XR499	WTU/18/72/SF Odiham/72/HOCF/ 72	To AESS Gosport as A2710(3)
XR500	WTU/72/78/28	Flew into sea in fog during winching practice, Mirs Bay, Hong Kong, 19.4.79
XR501	AAEE/WTU/18/ 72/Cv SAR/22/ SARTU/22	To AESS Gosport as A2642(4)
XR502	WTU/18/WTF/ 72/60/72/60/72/60	Sold 16.3.00
XR503	MoA/AAEE/RAE/ DRA	To AESS Gosport as A2705(2)
XR504	WTU/18/SARTS/ 22/SARTU/22/84	
XR505	WTU/72/18/2 FTS	To Uruguayan Navy 8.1.98 as 081
XR506	18/72/60/72	
XR507	18/SARTS/22/ SARTU/22/SARTU/ 22	Sold to USA 11.5.99
XR508	18/72/78/72/103/28	To AESS Gosport as A2615(4)
XR509	18/72/240 OCU/72	Rolled over while running up, Benson, 16.10.81; to 8752M
XR510	18/HOCF	Hit by rotor of XT679 and broke up, Odiham, 12.11.70
XR511	18/72/60/72	
XR515	18/28/78/28	To Uruguayan Navy .97
XR516	18/2 FTS	To AESS Gosport as A2709(2)
XR517	18/72/60	To storage 2.97

XR518	18/72/18/ Cv SAR/22/72/60	To storage 27.1.97
XR519	18/2 FTS	Oscillated during test run and rolled over, Shawbury, 7.12.90; not repaired
XR520	72/22/SARTU/22	To AESS Gosport as A2708(2)
XR521	72/18/2 FTS	To Uruguayan Navy 8.1.98 as 082
XR522	72/84/28/72/78/SAR Flt/HOCF/ATS/ 240 OCU/72/ SF Benson/84/28	To Uruguayan Navy .97
XR523	72/60	To storage 27.1.97
XR524	72/SF Benson/Cv SAR/22/SARTU/ 22/SARTU/22	Tail rotor failed; dived into Llyn Pardan, Llanberis, Gwyned, 12.8.93
XR525	72/SF Benson/SAR Wg/SF Benson/72/ 60/72	
XR526	72	Damaged by ground resonance, Odiham, 27.5.70; to 8147M 11.6.70
XR527	72/78/28/72/60/72/60	To storage 7.97
XR528	72/78/HOCF/ATS/ 240 OCU/28/72/60	To 9268M 12.3.97; to Culdrose for fire practice 5.12.00
XR529	72/78/18/CATCS/ 2 FTS/72/SARTU/72	

* * * * * * * * * *

20 Hawker-Siddeley Gnat T.1s delivered between May and November 1963 by HSA, Hamble, to Contract KC/2B/05

XR534	CFS/4 FTS/ CFS/4 FTS	To 8578M 2.12.77 for display at Valley
XR535	4 FTS	To 8569M 17.11.77 at Halton
XR536	4 FTS	Hit obstruction during forced landing after fire warning, Sealand, 18.10.63
XR537	4 FTS/CFS/ 4 FTS/CFS	To RAE 20.9.79; to 8643M 10.83 at Cosford
XR538	4 FTS	To 8621M 11.3.79 at Halton
XR539	4 FTS	Abandoned in spin 5m NE of Porthmadog, Gwynedd, 13.5.66
XR540	MoA/4 FTS/Hdlg Sqn/CFS	To 8636M 18.9.79 at Cranwell
XR541	4 FTS/CFS/4 FTS/ CFS/4 FTS/CFS	Overshot landing into barrier and nosewheel collapsed, Mona, 7.2.78; to 8602M 7.12.78 at St Athan
XR542	4 FTS	Engine lost power; abandoned on approach, Valley, 9.3.65
XR543	Hdlg Sqn/MoA/4 FTS	Dived into lake on approach to Valley, Lake Maelog, Rhosneigr, Anglesey, 19.7.65
XR544	4 FTS/CFS/4 FTS	Engine flamed out on approach; abandoned and crashed on beach, Valley, 26.4.78
XR545	4 FTS/CFS	Collided with XR986 during practice crossover and abandoned, Kemble, 20.1.71
———	4 FTS/CFS	Lost fin and rudder after rolling at low level; hit ground, Upper Heyford, 13.12.71
XR567	4 FTS	(see above)
XR568	4 FTS	Engine lost power and cut on approach; undershot into marsh, Valley, 14.1.65; to 7874M 5.2.65 at Bicester
XR569	CFS/4 FTS/ CFS/4 FTS	To 8560M 13.10.77 at Halton
XR570	4 FTS	Hit HT cables over Llyn Celyn and abandoned; flew into hill, Llyn Celyn, Merioneth, 23.5.66
XR571	4 FTS	To 8493M 11.75 at Brampton

XR572	4 FTS/CFS	To Royal Navy as GI airframe A2676, 19.9.79 at Culdrose
XR573	4 FTS/CFS	Hit trees regaining formation during practice display and crashed, Kemble, 26.3.69
XR574	4 FTS/CFS/4 FTS/ CFS/4 FTS/CFS/ 4 FTS/CFS	To 8631M 8.10.79 at Halton

* * * * * * * * * *

Westland Wessex HC.2 prototype delivered to RAF in February 1968 to Contract KF/N/026

XR588	Mkrs & AAEE/28/ 103/Cv HAR.2/22/ SARTU/22/SARTU/ 22/SARTU/22/84	

* * * * * * * * * *

XR592		Sycamore HR.51 for RAN to Contract 6/Acft/7461 ex G-AMWI; became VH-BAW
XR595 - XR604		Scout AH.1s for Army Air Corps
XR627 - XR640		to Contract KF/2Q/09

* * * * * * * * * *

50 Hunting Jet Provost T.4s delivered between January and October 1963 by Hunting Aircraft, Luton, to Contract KC/E/057

XR643	6 FTS/RAFC/ 3 CAACU	To 8516M at Halton
XR644	6 FTS/2 FTS	SOC 1.10.71; to Little Rissington for fire practice
XR645	7 FTS	Control lost in cloud; abandoned and dived into ground, Stellingfleet, 3½m NE of Church Fenton, 4.10.66
XR646	7 FTS/6 FTS/ 3 FTS/6 FTS	SOC 1.10.71; to Hatfield for fire practice
XR647	2 FTS/CAW/6 FTS	Collided with XS216 in formation and abandoned, Norton-le-Clay, 1½m SE of Dishforth, Yorks., 7.5.73
XR648	2 FTS	SS 18.12.70
XR649	6 FTS/CAW	SOC 14.3.72; to Ouston for fire practice
XR650	7 FTS/CAW/3 FTS/ CATCS/CAW/SRF	To 8459M 19.12.75 at Halton
XR651	7 FTS/3 FTS/ CATCS/CAW/SRF	To 8431M 17.1.75 at Halton
XR652	6 FTS	Sold to BAC 30.8.67 for South Yemen AF as T.52 No.106
XR653	7 FTS/CAW/CATCS/ CAW/SRF/CATCS	To 9035M 3.91 at Halton
XR654	6 FTS/RAFC/ 3 FTS/CAW	SOC 25.11.71; preserved
XR655	7 FTS/1 FTS	SOC 1.10.71
XR656	6 FTS/RAFC	SOC 1.10.71
XR657	7 FTS/1 FTS	SS 15.2.71
XR658	7 FTS/CAW/6 FTS	Airframe overstressed during Aerobatics; crashlanded 4m ENE of Gainsborough, Lincs., 26.10.71; to 8192M 29.12.71 at Abingdon
XR659	6 FTS/3 FTS	SS 17.8.71
XR660	6 FTS/CAW/ CATCS/4 FTS	To 8374M 17.8.72 at Linton-on-Ouse for display
XR661	7 FTS/3 FTS	Sold to BAC 30.8.67 for South Yemen AF as T.52 No.108

XR662	7 FTS/6 FTS/CAW/ RAFC/CATCS/ CAW/SRF	To 8410M 6.6.74 at Halton
XR663	6 FTS	SOC 6.12.68 after airframe over-stressed 25.3.68; to 431 MU for camouflage trials
XR664	6 FTS	Hit bird and engine flamed out; abandoned 3m NE of Jedburgh, Rox., 30.9.64
XR665	1 FTS	SS 15.2.71
XR666	6 FTS/1 FTS	SS 17.8.71
XR667	2 FTS/3 FTS/ CATCS/CAW/ 6 FTS	SOC 12.12.73
XR668	1 FTS	SS 22.11.68
XR669	MoA	To 8062M 26.11.69 at Halton
XR670	CFS/7 FTS/2 FTS/ 1 FTS/3 FTS/ CATCS/SRF/ CAW/SRF	To 8498M 30.7.76 at Halton
XR671	CFS/2 FTS/CFS	SS 18.12.70
XR672	1 FTS/3 FTS/ CATCS/CAW/ 6 FTS/SRF	To 8495M 14.6.76 at Halton
XR673	2 FTS/RAFC/6 FTS/ CATCS/SRF/CATCS	To 9032M 3.91 at Halton
XR674	1 FTS/3 FTS/CATCS/ CAW/CATCS/SRF/ CATCS	To 9030M 3.91 at Halton
XR675	6 FTS/3 FTS/RAFC	SS 17.8.71
XR676	7 FTS/3 FTS	SS 17.8.71
XR677	3 FTS	SS 17.8.71
XR678	CFS	SS 11.1.64
XR679	RAFC/CAW/ 3 CAACU/CAW/ SRF/CATCS/1 TWU	To 8991M 4.89 at Cosford
XR680	6 FTS/CFS	SOC 8.5.72; to Church Fenton for fire practice
XR681	RAFC/6 FTS/ CATCS	SOC 1.10.71; nose to 8588M at Abingdon
XR697	3 FTS	SS 18.12.70
XR698	3 FTS	Stalled on approach to practice forced landing and bellylanded, Leeming, 3.1.64
XR699	1 FTS	SS 15.2.71
XR700	1 FTS/3 FTS/ CATCS	SOC 1.10.71; nose to 8589M at Abingdon
XR701	1 FTS/27 MU/CAW/ SRF/AAEE/CATCS/ MoD(PE)/CATCS/ 1 TWU/CATCS	To 9025M at Halton
XR702	3 FTS	SS 18.12.70
XR703	3 FTS	SS 15.2.71
XR704	CFS/CAW/6 FTS	To 8506M 28.3.78 at Halton
XR705	CFS/CAW	SOC 17.10.73; to Manston for fire practice
XR706	6 FTS/2 FTS/CFS	SOC 1.10.71; to Catterick for fire practice
XR707	2 FTS/RAFC	Fuselage to Hatfield for structural tests 25.10.71; to 8193M 20.1.72

* * * * * * * * * *

44 BAC Lightning F.3s and F.6s delivered between December 1964 and August 1966 by BAC Warton to Contract KD/2T/079
XR766 onwards built as F.6s

XR711	111/Wattisham TFF/111	Undercarriage retracted prematurely on take-off; skidded into barrier and caught fire, Wattisham, 29.10.71; not repaired

XR712	111	Engine blew up during display at Exeter; began to break up and abandoned over Watergate Bay, Cornwall, 26.6.65
XR713	111/TDFF Wattisham/111/5/LTF/11/LTF/5/11/5/LTF	To 8935M 9.3.87 at Leuchars
XR714	111	Undercarriage prematurely retracted on take-off; sank back on to runway, Akrotiri, 27.9.66; not repaired
XR715	111/Wattisham TFF/29	Abandoned after fire warning, Blyford Green, near Southwold, Suffolk, 13.2.74
XR716	111/TDFF Wattisham/111/226 OCU/29/56/LTF/5/11/5/LTF/5	To 8940M 1.10.87 at Cottesmore
XR717	56/29/56/AAEE	SOC 29.3.74; to Boscombe Down for fire practice
XR718	56/29/226 OCU/5/LTF/5/LTF/11/5/LTF/5/11/LTF/11/LTF	To 8932M 9.2.87 at Wattisham
XR719	56/Wattisham TFF/56/226 OCU	Damaged in heavy landing, Coltishall, 5.6.73; SOC 1.3.74 for fire practice
XR720	56/TDFF Wattisham/56/29/11/LTF	To 8930M 3.87 at Binbrook
XR721	56	Engine flamed out and hood jammed; bellylanded in field and hit wall, Elm Farm, Helmingham, Suffolk, 5.1.66
XR722	-	Sold to BAC 21.3.68 for cv to F.53 53-666 for Saudi AF
XR723	Cv F.6/11/23/11/23/5	Engine caught fire; abandoned 15m S of Akrotiri, 18.9.79
XR724	Cv F.6/11/LTF/5/11/5/11/5/Trials Flt	To BAe 11.4.88 for MoD Sold; to G-BTSY 25.7.91
XR725	Cv F.6/23/5/74/56/5/LTF/11	SS 24.6.88
XR726	Cv F.6/5/11/LTF/11/LTF/11/LTF/11	SS 24.6.88
XR727	Cv F.6/23/11/5/11/5/11	To 8963M 10.5.88 at Wildenrath
XR728	Cv F.6/23/11/23/56/5/LTF/11/5/11/5/11	SS 22.6.88
XR747	Cv F.6/23/111/5/11/5/11/5	SS 24.6.88
XR748	Wattisham TFF/56/111	Abandoned after hydraulic failure 5m off Great Yarmouth, Norfolk, 24.6.74
XR749	Wattisham TDFF/56/5/11/5/LTF/5/LTF/5/LTF/5/11/LTF/11/5/LTF/11	Overstressed 17.2.86; to 8934M at Leuchars
XR750	56/226 OCU/111/29/111	SOC 28.11.74
XR751	Mkrs/226 OCU/29/5/11/5/11/5/11/LTF	SS 21.6.88
XR752	Cv F.6/FCTU/23/11/23/111/5/11/5/11	SS 24.8.87
XR753	Cv F.6/FCTU/23/5/23/5-11/11	To 8969M 25.5.88 at Leeming
XR754	Cv F.3A/AAEE/5/Cv F.6/23/5-11/11	To 8972M 3.5.88 at Honington
XR755	Cv F.3A/5/Cv F.6/5/11/5/11	SS 21.6.88
XR756	5/Cv F.6/23/11/23/11/23/5-11/LTF/5/LTF/11	SOC 12.5.88; to RAE for weapons trials, then PEE
XR757	5/23/5-11/11	SS 24.6.88
XR758	5/TDFF Leuchars/23/11/74/23/5-11/LTF/11	To 8964M 11.5.88 at Laarbruch
XR759	5/74/56/5-11	SS 24.6.88
XR760	5/23/5/LTF/11/5/11	Abandoned after engine fire 7m N of Whitby, Yorks., 15.7.86
XR761	5/23/5/74/56/5-11/LFS/5	Abandoned after engine fire 10m off Spurn Head, Yorks., 8.11.84
XR762	5/23/11	Spun into sea during tailchase off Akrotiri, 7.4.75
XR763	5/23/11/23/5-11/5	Abandoned on approach after engine failure due to ingesting part of target drogue 2m from Akrotiri, 1.7.87
XR764	5/74/56	Abandoned after catching fire 35m SE of Akrotiri, 30.9.71
XR765	5/23/11/23/11/5	Control lost after engine caught fire; abandoned over sea 30m E of Spurn Head, 23.7.81
XR766	FCTU/23	Abandoned in spin 51m ENE of Leuchars, 7.9.67
XR767	FCTU/23/5/74	Flew into sea at night about 50m NW of Singapore, 26.5.70
XR768	74/5	Engine flamed out and caught fire; abandoned 13m E of Saltfleet, Lincs., 29.10.74
XR769	74/5-11/5/11	Abandoned after engine fire 5m E of Easington, off Spurn Head, 11.4.88
XR770	74/23/56/5-11/11	SOC 10.6.88 for preservation
XR771	74/56/5/11/5/11/5/11	SS 21.6.88
XR772	74/5/11/LTF/5-11	Spun into sea after control lost 20m NE of Skegness, Lincs., 6.3.85
XR773	74/56/5/11/5/11/LTF/11/5/11/Trials Flt	To MoD 27.6.88 To Lightning Flying Club, 23.12.92 as G-OPIB

*   *   *   *   *   *   *   *   *   *

Two Vickers Viscounts for Ministry of Aviation delivered in January 1962 to Contract KU/D/01

XR801 ex G-APKK;   XR802 ex G-ARUU. Both used by ETPS

*   *   *   *   *   *   *   *   *   *

Five Vickers VC-10 C.Mk.1s delivered between July 1966 and April 1967 by Vickers, Weybridge, to Contract KD/2R/02

XR806	10/Cv C.1K/10	*George Thompson VC*; tipped on tail while being defuelled and rear fuselage damaged, Brize Norton, 18.12.97; not repaired
XR807	10/Cv C.1K/10	*Donald Garland VC and Thomas Gray VC*
XR808	10/Cv C.1K/10	*Kenneth Campbell VC*
XR809	10	*Hugh Malcolm VC.* To Rolls-Royce 17.4.69; became G-AXLR as RB-211 testbed
XR810	10/Cv C.1K/10	*David Lord VC*

*   *   *   *   *   *   *   *   *   *

XR814		Britten-Norman Cushioncraft CC.2 for Ministry of Aviation to Contract KC/2T/010

XR818 - XR842; XR861 - XR890;		Northrop Shelduck D.1 target drones to Contract KK/T/05
XR894 - XR898; XR916 - XR923;		Northrop Shelduck D.1 target drones to Contract KK/T/016
XR927 - XR938		Northrop Shelduck D.1 target Drones to Contract KK/T/014
XR942, XR943, XR944		Wallis WA-116s for AAC trials To Contract KK/2A/01

*   *   *   *   *   *   *   *   *   *

41 Hawker-Siddeley Gnat T.1s delivered between December 1963 and July 1964 by HSA, Hamble, to Contract KC/2B/031

XR948	4 FTS	Abandoned after engine caught fire 3m NE of Llanbedr, 14.3.72
XR949	4 FTS	Abandoned after hood fractured and student thought instructor had ejected 3m W of Bala, Gwynedd, 27.5.64
XR950	4 FTS	Collided with XS108 in formation and dived into ground, Carmel, Caernarvon, 22.4.65
XR951	4 FTS/CFS/4 FTS/ CFS/4 FTS	To 8603M 23.6.78 at Halton
XR952	4 FTS	Abandoned in spin near Betws-y-Coed, Caernarvon, 13.6.69
XR953	4 FTS	To 8609M 12.10.78 at Halton
XR954	4 FTS/CFS/4 FTS	To 8570M 17.11.77 at Halton
XR955	4 FTS/CFS	To RN as GI airframe A2678, 21.9.79 at Culdrose
XR976	4 FTS	Undershot practice forced landing and undercarriage broke off; abandoned over Rhosneigr, Anglesey, 12.10.64
XR977	4 FTS/CFS/RAE	To 8640M 20.9.79; preserved at Cosford
XR978	4 FTS	Abandoned in inverted spin, Pont ar Gelyn, 2½m NW of Bala, Merioneth, 22.7.64
XR979	4 FTS	Sank back on formation take-off; skidded off runway and caught fire, Valley, 6.9.65
XR980	4 FTS/CFS/4 FTS/ CFS/4 FTS	To 8622M 11.3.79 at Halton
XR981	4 FTS/CFS	Hit ground during aerobatics, Kemble, 3.3.78
XR982	4 FTS	To MoD 1.5.72 for static Testing; SOC 3.8.73
XR983	4 FTS/CFS/4 FTS	Collided with XP536 and crashed 3m E of Dolgellau, Merioneth, 30.4.76
XR984	4 FTS	To 8571M 2.12.77 at Halton
XR985	4 FTS	Engine lost power; bounced on landing and undercarriage collapsed, Valley, 5.4.65; nose to 7886M 6.5.65
XR986	4 FTS/CFS	Collided with XR545 and crashed, Kemble, 20.1.71
XR987	4 FTS/CFS	To 8641M 19.11.79 at Cosford
XR991	4 FTS/CFS	To 8637M 18.9.79 at Cranwell
XR992	4 FTS/CFS	Abandoned after fire warning and crashed at Latton, Glos., 16.12.69
XR993	4 FTS/CFS	To RN as GI airframe A2678, 21.9.79; later allotted 8878M at Hendon
XR994	4 FTS/CFS	Caught fire in air during aerobatics and abandoned 1½m ESE of Kemble, 13.11.70
XR995	4 FTS/CFS	Caught fire and abandoned 1m S of Kemble, 16.12.69
XR996	4 FTS/CFS/ 4 FTS	Flew into ground on approach, Shawbury, 8.10.76
XR997	4 FTS	Dived into ground on take-off from Valley, Llanfaelog, Anglesey, 3.1.70
XR998	4 FTS/CFS/4 FTS	To 8623M 11.3.79 at Halton
XR999	4 FTS	Controls jammed; abandoned and crashed in sea 8½m SW of Valley, 8.6.68
XS100	4 FTS	To 8561M 14.11.77 at Halton
XS101	CFS	To 8638M 17.9.79 at Cranwell; became G-GNAT 14.4.82
XS102	4 FTS	To 8624M 31.3.79 at Halton
XS103	4 FTS/CFS	Collided with Italian F-104S MM6774 near Leck, 3.9.75; SOC on return
XS104	4 FTS/CFS/4 FTS	To 8604M 7.8.78 at Cosford
XS105	4 FTS/CFS/4 FTS/ CFS/4 FTS	To 8625M 25.3.79 at Cosford
XS106	4 FTS/CFS/4 FTS	Control lost in spin; crashed 1m N of Llanrwst, Gwynedd, 16.10.75
XS107	4 FTS/CFS	To 8639M 21.9.79 at Cosford
XS108	4 FTS	Collided with XR950; belly-landed and broke up, Valley, 22.4.65
XS109	4 FTS/CFS/4 FTS/ CFS/4 FTS	To 8626M 25.3.79 at Cosford
XS110	4 FTS/CFS/4 FTS/ CFS/4 FTS/CFS/ 4 FTS	To 8562M 31.10.77 at Halton
XS111	CFS	Brakes failed; undercarriage raised to stop, Kemble, 24.6.76

*   *   *   *   *   *   *   *   *   *

| XS115 - XS128;
XS149 - XS154 | | Westland Wessex HAS.1s for
Royal Navy to Contract KK/M/029
XS120 to 8653M |
| XS159 - XS172 | | Hiller HT.2s for Royal Navy to
Contract KK/M/013 |

*   *   *   *   *   *   *   *   *   *

35 Hunting Jet Provost T.4s delivered between October 1963 and September 1964 by Hunting Aircraft, Luton, to Contract KC/E/070

XS175	7 FTS/CFS	Sold to BAC 7.7.71
XS176	2 FTS/3 FTS/ CATCS/CAW/ SRF/CATCS	To 8514M 24.3.77 at Halton
XS177	RAFC/2 FTS/ 3 FTS/CATCS/ CAW/SRF/TWU/ CATCS/TWU/ CATCS	To 9044M at Valley
XS178	7 FTS/CFS/RAFC/ CATCS/1 TWU	To 8994M 4.89 at Cosford
XS179	RAFC/CAW	To 8337M 9.8.73 at Halton; painted as 8237M
XS180	6 FTS/CAW	To 8338M 6.8.73 at Halton; painted as 8238M
XS181	3 FTS/RAFC/ CATCS/1 TWU/ CATCS	To 9033M at Halton
XS182	CFS/RAFC/6 FTS/ 2 FTS/3 FTS	SOC 1.10.71; to Hatfield for fire practice
XS183	2 FTS	SOC 1.10.71
XS184	3 FTS	SOC 1.10.71
XS185	3 FTS/RAFC	SS 15.2.71
XS186	CAW	To 8408M 7.10.74 at St Athan
XS209	CAW	To 8409M 7.10.74 at St Athan

Jet Provost

XS210	CAW	To 8339M 21.3.73 at Halton; painted as 9239M
XS211	CAW/CATC/SRF	Abandoned on overshoot after engine flamed out ½m N of Leeming, 13.2.76
XS212	CAW/CFS	SS 18.12.70
XS213	CAW/CFS	To 8097M for Kenya AF 18.6.70
XS214	CAW	SOC 11.3.74; to Cranwell for fire practice
XS215	CAW/CATCS/SRF	To 8507M at Halton
XS216	CAW/6 FTS	Collided with XR467 1½m SE of Dishforth, 7.5.73; landed safely but SOC 5.6.73
XS217	RAF/CFS/CATCS/ 6 FTS/SRF	To 9029M at Halton
XS218	3 FTS/27 MU/CAW/ SRF	To 8508M 23.2.77 at Halton
XS219	CAW/CATCS/ CAW/SRF/CATCS/ 1 TWU	To 8993M 4.89 at Cosford
XS220	3 FTS	SS 18.12.70
XS221	JP Trials Unit	Hit trees during FAC trials and crashed in jungle near Alor Star, Malaya, 10.2.66
XS222	RAFC/CFS	SOC 1.10.71
XS223	JP Trials Unit	Sold to BAC 13.1.67 for South Yemen AF as T.52 No.101
XS224	JP Trials Unit	Sold to BAC 16.1.67 for South Yemen AF as T.52 No.102
XS225	1 FTS/CFS	SOC 1.10.71
XS226	CAW/CFS	SOC 1.10.71
XS227	-	Sold to BAC 18.1.67 for South Yemen AF as T.52 No.103
XS228	-	Sold to BAC 18.1.67 for South Yemen AF as T.52 No.104
XS229	3 FTS/CFS	Collided with XP675 and abandoned near Hauling, Glos., 26.2.68
XS230	-	To MoA as prototype T.5; sold to MinTech 31.1.70 for ETPS
XS231	-	Ex G-ATAJ; prototype BAC-166 for MoA

* * * * * * * * *

XS235		De Havilland Comet 4C for Ministry of Aviation to Contract KU/L/038
XS238		Auster AOP.9 for Army Air Corps to Contract KC/N/047; replacement for XP254
XS241		Westland Wessex HU.5 prototype for RN trials under Contract KC/M/011; to 9102M 1.91 at Benson
XS246 - XS257; XS273 - XS290; XS294 - XS311; XS335 - XS346		Northrop Shelduck D.1 target drones to Contract KK/T/022
XS349		Hughes 269A G-ASBL for AAC evaluation
XS352 - XS381; XS398 - XS408		Northrop Shelduck D.1 target drones

* * * * * * * * *

One Westland Whirlwind HAR.10 delivered in October 1962 to Contract KF/2N/042 as replacement for XP392

XS412	230	Engine cut; forcelanded in wood 4m SW of Basingstoke, Hants., 18.6.68; to 8030M at St Athan

* * * * * * * * * *

20 BAC Lightning T.5s delivered between March and December 1965 to Contract KC/2D/064

XS416	MoA/226 OCU/74/ 11/LTF/5&LTF/5	SS 24.6.88
XS417	226 OCU/23/11/23/ 56/LTF/11/5/11/5/ LTF	SOC 29.7.88; preserved at Winthorpe
XS418	Hdlg Sqn/226 OCU/5	To 8531M 22.9.76 at Binbrook
XS419	226 OCU/23/5/11/ LTF/5/LTF/5/LTF	SS 24.6.88
XS420	226 OCU/LTF/ 5/LTF	SS 16.6.88
XS421	226 OCU/111/23	To MoD(PE) 14.9.76
XS422	226 OCU/111/29/ 111/29/56	To MoD(PE) 28.3.77
XS423	226 OCU/23/ 226 OCU	To 8532M 22.9.76 at Binbrook
XS449	226 OCU	To 8533M 5.1.77 at Binbrook
XS450	111/226 OCU/5	To 8534M 22.9.76 at Binbrook
XS451	5/226 OCU/11/LTF	To 8503M 7.76 at St Athan
XS452	226 OCU/111/29/ 111/29/111/56/ 11/LTF/5/LTF/11/ 5/11/LTF/11/5/11/ LTF/11/LTF/11	Sold 24.6.88 to A Glass, Jersey; to Regd G-BPFE 26.10.88
XS453	226 OCU	Undercarriage jammed; abandoned ¼m S of Happisburgh, Norfolk, 1.7.66
XS454	74/226 OCU/ MinTech//226 OCU/11	To 8535M 5.1.77 at Binbrook
XS455	226 OCU/5	Hydraulics failed; abandoned after controls froze 10m N of Spurn Head, Yorks., 6.9.72
XS456	56/TDFF Wattisham/ 56/11/LTF/11/LTF	SS 13.7.88
XS457	226 OCU/11/LTF/ 5/11/5	SOC 21.9.87
XS458	226 OCU/5/LTF/ 5-11/LTF/11/ LTF	Sold 24.6.88 to A Glass, Jersey
XS459	226 OCU/29/56/ LTF/5	Sold 21.6.88 and preserved
XS460	-	Diverted to Saudi AF as T.55 55-710

* * * * * * * * * *

XS463, XS476		Westland Wasp HAS.1 for Royal Navy trials to Contract KK/N/014
XS479 - XS500; XS506 - XS523		Westland Wessex HU.5s for Royal Navy to Contract KK/M/020; XS479 to 8819M 8.6.84 at Brize Norton; XS486 to 9272M at Wroughton; XS488 to 9056M at Halton; XS491 to 8920M at Stafford; XS509 to RN as A2597; NTU;

* * * * * * * * * *

Six Westland Wessex HU.5s received from Royal Navy between September 1983 and May 1984

XS479	-	To 8819M 8.6.84 at Brize Norton

XS485	84	To RN as A2635 at Gosport, 2.97
XS498	84	To RN as A2641 at Gosport 2.97
XS509	ETPS/AAEE/ETPS	To RN as A2597
XS517	84	To RN as A2625 at Gosport 2.97
XS518	84	Flew into sea at night off Limassol, Cyprus, 5.11.86

* * * * * * * * *

XS527 - XS545; XS562 - XS572		Westland Wasp HAS.1s for Royal Navy to Contract KK/N/011 XS572 to 8845M at Stafford
XS574		Northrop Shelduck D.1 for display at Yeovilton from parts
XS576 - XS590		Sea Vixen FAW.2s for Royal Navy to Contract KK/R/0180 XS583 to 8397M NTU; XS587 to 8828M NTU

* * * * * * * * *

31 Hawker-Siddeley Andover C.1s delivered between January 1967 and February 1968 to Contract No. KU/11/013

XS594	AAEE/46	SOC 24.1.80
XS595	AAEE/46/84/ SAR Flt	SOC 28.1.80; to Brize Norton for fire practice
XS596	AAEE/46/ATS/ SF Abingdon/ SF ThorneyIsland/ 46/115/Cv R.4/60/ Cv C.1(PR)/AAEE/ DRA/DTEO/DERA	
XS597	AAEE/SF Abingdon/ SF Thorney Island/ 46/32/SF Brize Norton/32/115/60/32	Sold 8.7.93; to G-BVNJ 19.5.94
XS598	Hdlg Sqn/SF Abing- don/AOCU/46	Engine cut on take-off; swung and undercarriage raised to stop, Abingdon, 5.7.67
XS599	SF Abingdon/AOCU/ 242 OCU/46	To RNZAF 16.3.77 as NZ7620
XS600	SF Abingdon/AOCU/ 242 OCU/46	To RNZAF 20.4.77 as NZ7621
XS601	SF Abingdon/ AOCU/46	SOC 29.3.83
XS602	SF Abingdon/ AOCU/46	To RNZAF 19.11.76 as NZ7622
XS603	SF Abingdon/46/ AOCU/46/EWETU/ 115/Cv E.3/115	To Hunting Air Services 12.10.94 to P4-PVS 10.96
XS604	SF Abingdon/46	To RNZAF 26.1.77 as NZ7623
XS605	SF Abingdon/46/ 242 OCU/46/SF Brize Norton/115/ Cv E.3/115	To Hunting Air Services 12.10.94 to Northolt for fire practice
XS606	SF Abingdon/46/ 52/SF Abingdon/ SF Thorney Island/	To MoD(PE) 1.8.75 for AAEE
XS607	SF Abingdon/46/ 52/46/SF Thorney Island/46	To MoD(PE) 1.4.76; SOC 15.9.95; temp to G-BEBY 2.8.76 - 9.76
XS608	46/52/SF Thorney Island/46/SF Thor- ney Island/46/115	To RNZAF 18.10.76 as NZ7624
XS609	46	Engine cut on take-off and wing hit ground; caught fire, Ampugnano, Italy, 8.4.72

XS610	46/242 OCU/46/ 242 OCU/46/SF Brize Norton/ Cv E.3/115	To Hunting Air Services 16.12.94; to P4-BLL 10.96
XS611	46/21/MECS/84/ 46/84/AAEE/RAE	To RNZAF 16.3.77 as NZ7625
XS612	46/52/SF Abingdon/ 46	To RNZAF 26.1.77 as NZ7626
XS613 ———	46/52/46/SF Thor- ney Island/46/ 242 OCU/46	To RNZAF 22.4.77 as NZ7627
XS637	46/52/SF Abingdon/ SF Thorney Island/ 32/SF Brize Norton/ Oslo for CinC AFNth/ 32/115/60/32	Sold 8.7.93; to G-BVNK
XS638	46/242 OCU/46	To RNZAF 30.12.76 as NZ7628
XS639	46/32/115/ Cv E.3A/115/32	To 9241M 13.7.94 at Cosford
XS640	46/MinTech/46/ MoD(PE)/46/115/ Cv E.3/115	To Hunting Air Services 18.10.94; to P4-TBL 10.96
XS641	84/SAR Flt/84/ 46/115/Cv E.3A/ 115/60/115/Cv C.1(PR)/60	To 9198M 1.94 at Cosford
XS642	84/SAR Flt/84	To 8785M 18.1.83; to Benson for fire practice
XS643	84/115/Cv E.3A/ 115/32/AAEE	To 9278M 15.7.97 at Manston
XS644	AOCU/ATS/Thorney Island/242 OCU/46/ EWETU/MoD(PE)/ EWAU/115/EWAU/ 115/Cv E.3A/115/32	Sold; to VR-BOI 6.94
XS645	46/84/SF Thorney Island/46	To RNZAF 28.4.77 as NZ7629
XS646	46/84/SAR Flt/ 84	To MoD(PE) 1.8.75 for RAE
XS647	AAEE	Sold to BAe 1.81 as mock-up for ATP

* * * * * * * * *

XS650 - XS652		Slingsby Swallow TX.1 gliders to Contract KK/7/09; XS650 to 8801M at St Athan
XS655		Westland SR-N3 hovercraft for trials to Contract KC/3A/08
XS660 - XS670		Cancelled TSR-2s to Contract KD/2L/013

* * * * * * * * *

Six Westland Wessex HC.2s delivered between March and May 1965 by Westland Helicopters, Yeovil, to Contract KK/M/64

XS674	72/78/72/18/72/ SF Benson/72	Sold
XS675	72/78/103/Cv SAR/ 22/SARTU/22/84	
XS676	72/SRCU/HOCF/ ATS/240 OCU/ WTF/2 FTS/ 72/2 FTS	To Uruguayan Navy 8.1.98 as 083
XS677	72/SRCU/HOCF/ ATS/240 OCU/ WTF/2 FTS	To storage 9.97

XS678	72/SMOAF/ ETPS	Lost height in transition and crashed near Boscombe Down, 19.3.76; to Australia as test airframe
XS679	AAEE/18/72/18/ CATCS/2 FTS	To Uruguayan Navy 8.1.98 as 084

* * * * * * * * * *

XS681 - XS683		Brantley B-2A G-ASHK and B-2Bs G-ASEH and G-ASHJ for AAC trials
XS684, XS685		Hughes 269As G-ASBL and G-ASBD for AAC trials

* * * * * * * * * *

**Nine Hawker-Siddeley Kestrel FGA.1s delivered between December
1964 and August 1965 by HSA, Kingston to Contract KC/2Q/016**
USAAF serials 64-18262 to 16270 allotted to this batch

XS688	TES	To German AF 11.1.66
XS689	TES	To MoA 2.12.65; to US as 64-18263
XS690	TES	To US as 64-18264 11.1.66
XS691	TES	To German AF 11.1.66
XS692	TES	To US as 64-18266 11.1.66
XS693	TES/AAEE	Engine cut; abandoned 2m SW of Boscombe Down, 21.9.67
XS694	TES	To US as 64-18267 11.1.66
XS695	TES	To MinTech 15.12.67; to RN as A2619
XS696	TES	Caught fire on take-off, West Raynham, 1.4.65; DBR

* * * * * * * * * *

XS700 - XS706		Hiller HT.2s for Royal Navy to Contract KK/191/023

* * * * * * * * * *

**20 Hawker-Siddeley Dominie T.1s delivered between September 1965
and May 1966 by D.H., Chester to Contract KU/E/10**

XS709	1 ANS/CAW/1 ANS/ 6 FTS/MoD(PE)/ 6 FTS/3 FTS/55R	Ex G-37-65
XS710	CAW/RAFC/6 FTS/ 3 FTS	To 9259M 7.10.96 at Cosford
XS711	Hdlg Sqn/1 ANS/ Hdlg Sqn/MinTech/ CAW/6 FTS/3 FTS/ 55R	
XS712	Hdlg Sqn/1 ANS/ MinTech/1 ANS/6 FTS/ 3 FTS/55R	
XS713	1 ANS/CAW/1 ANS/ CAW/1 ANS/6 FTS/ 3 FTS/55R	
XS714 ⎯⎯⎯	1 ANS/CAW/1 ANS/ CAW/1 ANS/6 FTS/ 3 FTS	To 9246M 21.9.95 at Manston
XS726	1 ANS/MinTech/ 1 ANS/CAW/1 ANS/ 6 FTS/A-S/CAW/ RAFC/MoD(PE)/ CAW/6 FTS/ 3 FTS	To 9273M 24.6.97 at Cosford
XS727	1 ANS/6 FTS/ MoD(PE)/6 FTS/ 3 FTS/55R	
XS728	1 ANS/6 FTS/RAFC/ 6 FTS/Cv T.2/DTEO/ 55R	

XS729	1 ANS/6 FTS/ MoD(PE)/6 FTS/ 3 FTS	To 9275M 24.6.97 at Cosford
XS730	1 ANS/6 FTS/3 FTS/ 55R	
XS731	1 ANS/6 FTS/3 FTS/ 55R	
XS732	CAW/1 ANS/6 FTS/ MoD(PE)/6 FTS/ MoD(PE)/6 FTS/ 3 FTS	SOC 1.89
XS733	CAW/RAFC/6 FTS/ 3 FTS	To 9276M 20.6.97 at Cosford
XS734	CAW/1 ANS/6 FTS/ 3 FTS	To 9260M 7.10.96 at Cosford
XS735	CAW/RAFC/6 FTS/ 3 FTS	To 9264M 28.10.96 at Cranwell
XS736	CAW/RAFC/6 FTS/ 3 FTS/55R	
XS737	Hdlg Sqn/1 ANS/ 6 FTS/55R	
XS738	1 ANS/6 FTS/ MoD(PE)/ 6 FTS/3 FTS	To 9274M 24.6.97 at Cosford
XS739	1 ANS/6 FTS/ 3 FTS/55R	

* * * * * * * * * *

**22 Beagle B.206Zs (first two) and Basset CC.1s delivered between
February 1965 and September 1966 by Beagle Aircraft, Shoreham, to
Contract KU/S/02**

XS742	AAEE	To MoA for ETPS
XS743	AAEE	To MoA for ETPS
XS765	Hdlg Sqn/MoA/ NCS/SCS/MCS/ 32/207/26	To MoD(PE) 16.9.74 for ETPS; to G-BSET 3.12.86
XS766	WCS/NCS/MinTech/ NCS/TCCS/26	Sold 16.7.74; became G-BCJE
XS767	NCS/TCCS/26	Sold 12.7.74; became G-BCIS
XS768	NCS/TCCS/26	Sold 9.7.74; became G-BCJT
XS769	NCS/MoA/NCS/ SCS/MCS/32	Sold 12.8.74 as spares
XS770	NCS/TCCS/26/ QF/32	To MoD(PE) 17.1.75; preserved at Cosford
XS771	NCS/TCCS/26	Sold 15.7.74; became G-BCJA
XS772	NCS/SCS/MCS/32	Sold 15.7.74; became G-BCJB
XS773	NCS/TCCS/32	Sold 1.7.74; became G-BCJF
XS774	SCS/MoA/SCS/ MCS/32	Sold 9.7.74; became G-BCMW
XS775	SCS/SCCS/207/26	Sold 12.8.74 for spares
XS776	SCS/SCCS/207	Sold 12.8.74; became G-BCJG
XS777	SCS/SCCS/207/32	Sold 12.7.74; became G-BCIV
XS778	SCS/SCCS/207/32	Sold 9.7.74; became G-BCIX
XS779	SCS/SCCS/207	Sold 15.7.74; became G-BCJC
XS780	SCS/SCCS/207	Sold 12.7.74; became G-BCIU
XS781	SCS/NCS/SCS/ SCCS/207	Sold 19.7.74; became G-BCIY
XS782	SCS/BCCS/207	Sold 15.7.74; became G-BCJD
XS783	MoA/26	Filled up with wrong fuel; lost power on take-off and crashed 4m SE of Valley, 5.7.73
XS784	SCS/SCCS/207	Sold 18.7.74; became G-BCIZ

* * * * * * * * * *

**Six Hawker-Siddeley Andover CC.2s delivered between July 1964 and
September 1965 to Contract KU/11/015**

XS789	QF/32	Sold 31.3.95; became D2-MAG 4.95
XS790	QF/DRA/DTEO	Nose preserved at Boscombe Down .99

XS791	SF Abingdon/ MECS/FECS/48/ FEAF VIP Flt/ 60/32/SF Brize Norton/32	Sold 28.11.94
XS792	SF Abingdon/ FECS/48/FEAF VIP Flt/32/SF Brize Norton/32	Sold 28.11.94; became G-BVZS 8.3.95
XS793	SF Abingdon/ MECCF/21/152/ QF/32/60/QF/ 60/CinC RAFG	Damaged on landing; Northolt; to 9178M 2.93 at Cosford
XS794	MoA/SF Abingdon/ MCS/32/SF Brize Norton/32	Sold 31.3.95; became D2-MAF 4.95

* * * * * * * * * *

XS798		Vickers VA-1 hovercraft for trials to Contract KC/3A/05; used G-14-252 and serial cancelled
XS802 - XS812		Cancelled Westland Wasps for
XS834 - XS852		Royal Navy to Contract KK/N/49
XS856		Vickers VA-2 hovercraft for trials to Contract KC/3A/19
XS859		Slingsby Swallow TX.1 glider ex-BGA.1136 for ATC presented by The MacRobert Trust
XS862 - XS889		28 Westland Wessex HAS.1s for Royal Navy to Contract KK/M/68 XS871 to 8457M

* * * * * * * * * *

33 BAC Lightning F.6s delivered between November 1966 and August 1967 by BAC Preston to Contract KD/2T/0139

XS893	74	Undercarriage jammed; abandoned 18m E of Changi, 12.8.70
XS894	5	Flew into sea 6m NNE of Flamborough Head, Yorks., 8.9.70
XS895	74/5/23/111/23/ 5-11/LTF/11	To RAE 12.5.88 for weapons trials
XS896	74	Caught fire on approach and spun into ground 4m NE of Tengah, 12.9.68
XS897	74/56/11/5/11/5/11/5	SOC 5.2.88; sold 24.6.88 and preserved
XS898	5/11	Sold 24.6.88 to Cranfield and preserved
XS899	5/23/5/11/5/11	Sold 24.6.88 to Cranfield and preserved
XS900	5	Caught fire; abandoned after controls jammed 6m SE of Lossiemouth, 24.1.68
XS901	5/56/11/5/11/5/11	To 8965M 10.5.88 at Bruggen
XS902	5	Abandoned after engine caught fire 15m NE of Grimsby, Lincs., 26.5.71
XS903	5-11/11	SOC 18.5.88; preserved at Elvington
XS904	11/5/11/5/11/ Trials Flt	To BAe 12.4.88 for MoD
XS918	11	Caught fire and abandoned 9m E of Leuchars, 5.3.70
XS919	11/56/5/11/5/11	SOC 4.88; preserved at Farnsfield
XS920	74/11/5/11/5/11/5/5	Hit HT cables during combat practice with A-10A 15m N of Hemslingen, Germany, 13.7.84

XS921	74/56/5-11/11	Controls failed; abandoned and crashed 50m E of Flamborough Head, 19.9.85
XS922	5/56/5-11/11	To 8973M 14.6.88 at Wattisham
XS923	5/5-11/LTF/11/	Sold 24.6.88 to A Glass, Jersey
XS924	5	Control lost during flight refuelling; dived into ground 4m SW of Binbrook, 29.4.68
XS925	5-11	To 8961M for RAF Museum 26.4.88
XS926	5	Abandoned after loss of control 75m E of Whitby, Yorks., 22.9.69
XS927	74/11/23/5-11	To RAE 12.5.88 for weapons trials
XS928	11/5/74/56/ 11/56/5-11	To BAe 13.6.88 for display at Warton
XS929	11/56/11/LTF/5/11/ 5/11	To 8970M 20.5.58 for display
XS930	11/74	Spun into ground on take-off ½m S of Tengah, 27.7.70
XS931	11/5	Controls jammed after take-off; crashed in sea off Flamborough Head, Yorks., 25.5.79
XS932	11/56/11/5/11/5	SS 24.6.88; nose preserved
XS933	11/56/5/BAe/5/11/5	SS 21.6.88; preserved
XS934	11/56	Caught fire and abandoned 20m NNE of Akrotiri, 3.4.73
XS935	23/5/11/5	SS 24.6.88
XS936	23/11/5/LTF/5&11/ LTF/11/5	Sold 21.6.88; preserved Liskeard
XS937	23/11	Undercarriage jammed; abandoned off Flamborough Head, Yorks., 30.7.76
XS938	23/5/23	Caught fire on take-off and abandoned 12m E of Leuchars, 28.4.71

* * * * * * * * * *

XS941		Miles Student G-APLK for evaluation by MoA; reverted to G-APLK 25.9.64
XS944 - XS954		Cancelled TSR.2s to
XS977 - XS995		Contract KD/2L/16
XT101 - XT250		Agusta-Westland Sioux AH.1s for AAC to Contract KK/191/033 XT133 to 7923M; XT141 to 8509M
XT255 - XT257		Wessex HAS.3s for Royal Navy to Contract KK/M/017 XT255 to 8751M; XT257 to 8719M
XT261 - XT266		Cancelled HS.681s

* * * * * * * * * *

18 Hawker-Siddeley Buccaneer S.2As and S.2Bs diverted to RAF from Royal Navy Contract KC/2F/048

XT269	-	Written off 15.2.72 and not transferred
XT270	Cv S.2B/12/ 237 OCU/12/237 OCU/12/237 OCU/ 208	To storage 11.9.80; SS 10.91
XT271	12/237 OCU/208/ 237 OCU/15/16/15/ 16/15/16/237 OCU/ 12/237 OCU/12/ 237 OCU	SOC .97
XT272	Mod(PE) on loan	To MoD(PE) 11.1.80 for RAE

Buccaneer

XT273	Cv S.2A/237 OCU/ 208/237 OCU/12/ 208/12/208/12	SOC 7.91
XT274	Cv S.2A/12/237 OCU/12/237 OCU/ 208/237 OCU	To 8856M 21.5.85 at Abingdon
XT275	208/15	To storage 15.8.80; SS 10.91
XT276	Cv S.2B/12/237 OCU/12/15/16	To Catterick for fire-fighting 13.6.86
XT277	Cv S.2A12//237 OCU/12/237 OCU	To 8853M 21.5.85; preserved
XT278	Cv S.2A/208/12/15/ 208/237 OCU	SOC 31.3.83; to Catterick for fire practice
XT279	12/237 OCU/ Cv S.2B/15/16/ 208/SFLossiemouth/ 208	SOC 5.92
XT280	Cv S.2B/237 OCU/ 16/12/208/12/208	SS 4.94
XT281	Cv S.2B/237 OCU/12	To 8705M 18.8.81 at Lossiemouth
XT282	-	SOC 31.8.70 and not transferred
XT283	Cv S.2A/208/ 237 OCU/AAEE	To MoS(PE) 24.9.87
XT284	Cv S.2A/208/15/ 237 OCU	To 8855M 21.5.85 at Abingdon
XT285	Mkrs/RAE	Control lost in circuit after take-off during radar trials, West Freugh, 5.7.78
XT286	237 OCU/12/ 16/208/16/208	SOC 8.93
XT287	Cv S.2B/237 OCU/ 15/16/12/208/237 OCU/12/208/ 237 OCU	SOC 5.91
XT288	Cv S.2B/12/237 OCU/12/237 OCU/ 12/208/12	To 9134M 4.91; preserved at East Fortune

*   *   *   *   *   *   *   *   *   *

XT293 - XT323	Northrop Shelduck D.1 drones for Royal Navy to Contract KK/T/36
XT357 - XT410	
XT414 - XT443	Wasp HAS.1s for Royal Navy to Contract KK/N/49
XT448 - XT487	Wessex HU.5s for Royal Navy to Contract KK/M/70 XT456 to 8941M 11.11.87

*   *   *   *   *   *   *   *   *   *

Six Wessex HU.5s transferred from Royal Navy between October 1982 and September 1984

XT463	84	To RN as A2624 at Gosport 2.97
XT466	-	To 8921M 22.10.86 at Cosford
XT467	-	To 8922M 22.10.86 at Gutersloh
XT469	-	To 8920M 22.10.86 at Stafford
XT475	-	Not transferred; to 9108M 8.91
XT479	EMAU/AAEE/84	To 9271M 21.5.97
XT486	-	To 8919M 22.10.86 at JATE

*   *   *   *   *   *   *   *   *   *

XT492, XT493	Westland SR-N.5 hovercraft for trials to Contract KK/3A/25
XT498 - XT516	Westland Sioux AH.1s for AAC to Contract KK/191/033
XT540 - XT570	

XT575	Viscount 837 (ex OE-LAG) for Ministry of Technology, October 1964 to Contract KU/D/7
XT580 - XT589	Northrop Shelduck D.1 drones for Royal Navy to Contract KK/T/38
XT592	SRN-5 hovercraft 004 for evaluation

*   *   *   *   *   *   *   *   *   *

Four McDonnell Douglas Phantom FG.1s delivered as development aircraft to Contract RAF/A.236/78

XT595	-	Nose only to RAF as 8550M, 3.77; later renumbered 8851M
XT596	R-R/BSE/BAe	Preserved in FAA Museum
XT597	AAEE	MoD(PE) aircraft
XT598	111/43/111	Flew into sea on approach to Leuchars east of Bell Rock, 23.11.78

*   *   *   *   *   *   *   *   *   *

Seven Westland Wessex HC.2s delivered between June and October 1966 to Contract KK/M/111

XT601	78/Muharraq SAR Flt/78/72/18/72/240 OCU/72/WTF/22/ SARTU/22	To 9277M 1.7.97 at Odiham
XT602	78/Muharraq SAR Flt/78/72/ Cv SAR/22/60	To A2706(2) at AESS Gosport 8.98
XT603	78/Muharraq SAR Flt/78/103/18/72/ 18/CATCS/2 FTS	To Uruguayan Navy 8.1.98 as 085
XT604	78/Muharraq SAR Flt/78/103/Cv SAR/ 22/SARTU/22/ SARTU/22	Sold 16.3.00
XT605	72/28	To Uruguay .97
XT606	72/84/Cv SAR/22/ 2 FTS	To storage 9.97
XT607	72/240 OCU/72	

*   *   *   *   *   *   *   *   *   *

Scottish Aviation Twin Pioneer CC.2 delivered in March 1965 to Contract KC/K/74

XT610	ETPS/AAEE	SOC 11.2.75; became G-BCWF

*   *   *   *   *   *   *   *   *   *

XT614 - XT649	Scout AH.1s for Army Air Corps to Contract KK/N/80
XT653	Slingsby Swallow TX.1 for ATC from The MacRobert Trust
XT657	Westland SR-N6 hovercraft for trials to Contract KC/3A/34
XT661	Viscount 838 (ex 9G-AAV) delivered to Ministry of Technology for RSRE in February 1965

*   *   *   *   *   *   *   *   *   *

15 Westland Wessex HC.2s delivered between October 1966 and July 1967 by Westlands, Yeovil, to Contract KK/M/111

XT667	72/28	Engine cut during rescue; ditched in South China Sea off Hong Kong and sank, 17.9.93
XT668	72/SOAF/MoD(PE)/ 72	
XT669	72	Hit radio mast on take-off, Forkhill, Co.Armagh, 25.10.85; to 8894M
XT670	72/Cv SAR/22	To AESS at Gosport
XT671	72/60	Sold; became G-BYRC 23.9.99
XT672	72/SF Benson/2 FTS	Sold 12.5.99 for spares
XT673	72/28	To Uruguay 6.97
XT674	SF Odiham/SRCU/ HOCF/ATS/ 240 OCU/WTF/ Cv SAR/SARTS/ 22	Crashed on take-off in snowstorm during mountain rescue, Ben More, Perthshire, 1.2.87
XT675	72/SMOAF/72/ SF Benson/84/28	To Uruguay 6.97 as 071
XT676	18/72/18/72/ WTF/SF Benson/ 72/60/72	
XT677	18	Flew into ground in fog at night on approach, Rheinsehlen Camp, 25.4.68; to 8016M 20.5.68 at Lyneham
XT678	18/28	To Uruguay 6.97
XT679	SF Odiham/SRCU/ HOCF	Rotor hit XR510; broke up and crashed, Odiham, 12.11.70
XT680	78/103/Cv SAR/ 22/SARTU/22/84	
XT681	18/WTF/72	To 9279M 23.9.97 at Benson

*   *   *   *   *   *   *   *   *   *

XT685 - XT703	Northrop Shelduck D.1 drones
XT717 - XT747	to Contract KK/T/41
XT752	Gannet T.5 for Royal Navy to Contract KC/L/72; ex-WN365
XT755 - XT774	Wessex HU.5s for Royal Navy to Contract KK/M/120 XT755 to 9053M; XT766 to 9054M; XT770 to 9055M; XT772 to 8805M; XT773 to 9123M
XT778 - XT795	Wasp HAS.1s for Royal Navy to Contract KK/N/93
XT798 - XT820	Westland Sioux AH.1s for Army
XT824 - XT849	Air Corps to Contract KK/2C/2
XT852, XT853	Phantom FGR.2s for Ministry of Defence (PE); XT853 became 9071M

*   *   *   *   *   *   *   *   *   *

16 of batch of 20 McDonnell Douglas Phantom FG.1s transferred to RAF from Royal Navy

XT857	POTF/111	Ran off runway on landing and nosewheel collapsed, Leuchars, 7.85; nose to 8913M 10.9.86 at Leuchars
XT858	43	SOC 7.11.72 for fatigue testing
XT859	43/111/43/111	To 8999M at Leuchars
XT860	43/111/43	Flew into sea on interception exercise 28m E of Leuchars, 20.4.88; cause not known
XT861	POTF/43/ 111/43	Collided with XT872 during formation practice and crashed in sea 55m E of Leuchars, 7.9.87
XT862	-	Not transferred
XT863	111/43/111/43	SOC 24.2.89
XT864	111	To 8998M for preservation at Leuchars
XT865	111	SOC 8.91
XT866	POTF/43	Rolled on final approach and hit ground; abandoned and crashed, Leuchars, 9.7.81
XT867	111	To 9064M 10.91 at Leuchars
XT868	-	Not transferred
XT869	-	Not transferred
XT870	111/43/111/43/111	SOC 4.92
XT871	-	Not transferred
XT872	111	SOC 4.4.91
XT873	RN/43/111	SOC 1.4.92
XT874	43/111/43/111	To 9068M
XT875	43/111/43	SOC 8.91
XT876	-	Not transferred

*   *   *   *   *   *   *   *   *   *

24 McDonnell Douglas Phantom FGR.2s delivered between July 1968 and July 1969

XT891	54/6/228 OCU/6/ 56/56/228 OCU/29/ 228 OCU/29/228 OCU/29/228 OCU/ 56/228 OCU/74	To 9136M as display airframe, Coningsby, 6.92
XT892	228 OCU/111/ 228 OCU/56/ 228 OCU/74/56/ 228 OCU	To display airframe 30.10.92 at Wattisham
XT893	228 OCU/111/23/ 228 OCU/92/228 OCU/29/228 OCU/ 56	Abandoned over North Sea 48m E of Flamborough Head, 24.4.89
XT894	228 OCU/17/29/ 228 OCU/56	SOC 13.4.92
XT895	228 OCU/6/228 OCU/ 111/228 OCU/29/ 228 OCU/74	To 9171M at Valley 9.92
XT896	6/228 OCU/19/228 OCU/29/228 OCU/ 74	SOC 6.10.92 and scrapped 8.95
XT897	228 OCU/31/14/ 228 OCU/19/228 OCU/56/228 OCU/ 19/228 OCU/29/228 OCU/56/74/56	SOC 6.10.92 and scrapped 8.95
XT898	228 OCU/31/14/ 228 OCU/2/19/ 228 OCU/29/ 228 OCU/29/228 OCU	SOC 6.10.92 for spares
XT899	228 OCU/92/ 228 OCU/ 23/56/19/92/19	To Czechoslovakia as display airframe, 16.1.92
XT900	AAEE/228 OCU/ 14/31/228 OCU/ 56/228 OCU/74	To 9099M 17.6.91 at Honington
XT901	228 OCU/17/2/17/2/ MoD(PE)/2/19/ 228 OCU/19/228 OCU/19/228 OCU 56/228 OCU/74	SOC 7.91
XT902	228 OCU/54/228 OCU/54/111/ 228 OCU/BAe/ 228 OCU/29/ 228 OCU/19	SOC 11.91

XT903	228 OCU/2/228 OCU/29/228 OCU/ 23/56/23/228 OCU/ 29/228 OCU/92/ 228 OCU/56	To Leuchars as decoy Nose preserved by RAF Museum
XT904	228 OCU	Abandoned after control lost in spin off Cromer, Norfolk, 15.10.71
XT905	228 OCU/17/14/ 31/17/31/228 OCU/ 23/228 OCU/HSA/ 228 OCU/74	To Coningsby as decoy; to GI airframe at N Luffenham 7.5.00
XT906	228 OCU/2/ 228 OCU/29/ 228 OCU/56/ 228 OCU/56	SOC 9.92
XT907	228 OCU/6/54/ 228 OCU/MoD PE/ 228 OCU/BAe/56/ 228 OCU/74	To 9151M for display at Chattendon
XT908	228 OCU/6/29/228 OCU23/228 OCU/ 23/56/23/56/92/19/ 228 OCU/29/228 OCU29/228OCU/19/ 92/19/56/228 OCU	Control lost due to illness of pilot; crashed in sea 52m E of Dundee, 9.1.89
XT909	228 OCU/31/14/31/ 228 OCU/29/56/ 228 OCU/MoD(PE)/ 228 OCU/23/56/ 228 OCU/23/228 OCU/56/228 OCU/ 29&228 OCU/19	SOC 7.92
XT910	228 OCU/2/228 OCU/ 29/228 OCU/56/228 OCU/92/19/92/19/ 92/228 OCU/29/228 OCU/19/56/228 OCU/56	SOC 6.10.92 and scrapped 8.95
XT911	228 OCU/19/92	SOC 9.91
XT912	228 OCU/14/17/ 14/31/14/31/14/2/ 14/111/23/29/ 228 OCU	Collided with XT903 after take-off from Coningsby and abandoned near Billinghay, Lincs., 14.4.82
XT913	228 OCU	Abandoned after controls jammed 1m N of Happisburgh, Norfolk, 14.2.72
XT914	228 OCU/14/228 OCU14/17/228 OCU/ 56/228 OCU/92/228 OCU/56/228 OCU/ 56/92/228OCU/74	To Leeming as decoy 5.10.92; to 9269M 17.3.97 at Brampton
XT915 to XT928	-	Cancelled

* * * * * * * * * *

XT931-XT947; XT953-XT985		Northrop Shelduck D.1 drones To Contract KK/T/41

* * * * * * * * * *

Nine Vickers VC-10 C.1s delivered by BAC Weybridge between February 1967 and July 1968 to Contract KU/C/11

XV101	10/Cv C.1K/ AAEE/10	*Lanoe Hawker VC*
XV102	10/Cv C.1K/10	*Guy Gibson VC*
XV103	10/Cv C.1K/10	*Edward Mannock VC*; SOC 11.12.00
XV104	10/Cv C.1K/10	*James McCudden VC*
XV105	10/Cv C.1K/10	*Albert Ball VC*
XV106	10/Cv C.1K/10	*Thomas Mottershead VC*
XV107	10/Cv C.1K/10	*James Nicolson VC*

XV108	10/Cv C.1K/10	*William Rhodes-Moorhouse VC*
XV109	10/Cv C.1K/10	*Arthur Scarfe VC*
XV110 to XV114	-	Cancelled

* * * * * * * * * *

XV118 - XV141		Scout AH.1s for Army Air Corps to Contract KK/N/102; XV118 to 9141M
XV144		Comet 2E G-AMXK delivered to Ministry of Technology for BLEU in November 1966

* * * * * * * * * *

Two Hawker-Siddeley Nimrod trials aircraft for Ministry of Technology modified from Comet 4Cs and delivered in May and July 1967 to Contract KD/G/64

XV147	Mkrs/RAE	To BAe 5.3.94
XV148	AAEE/Mkrs/AAEE/ RRE/RSRE	To BAe

* * * * * * * * * *

12 of batch of 17 Hawker-Siddeley Buccaneer S.2As and S.2Bs to Contract KC/2F/125 transferred from Royal Navy to RAF between October 1969 and March 1975

XV152	Cv S.2A/208/ 237 OCU	To 8776M 31.3.83 at Swanton Morley
XV153	-	Written off 6.10.66 and not transferred
XV154	Cv S.2A/237 OCU/ 12	To 8854M 21.5.85 at Lossiemouth
XV155	Cv S.2B/12/ 237 OCU/12	To MoD(PE) 6.1.84; later to 8716M
XV156	Cv S.2A/208/ 237 OCU	To 8773M 31.3.83 at St Athan
XV157	Cv S.2B/12/237 OCU/208/12	To LTS 13.10.80; SOC 10.91
XV158	-	Written off 20.5.68 and not transferred
XV159	-	Written off 3.3.69 and not transferred
XV160	Cv S.2B/237 OCU/ 208/12/16	Stalled recovering from attack and abandoned in spin, Capo Frasca ranges, Sardinia, 20.9.82
XV161	Cv S.2A/208/ Cv S.2B/208/12	To 9117M 4.91 at Lossiemouth
XV162	Cv S.2B/12	Flew into sea in bad visibility 8m E of Hornsea, Yorks., 13.6.72
XV163	Cv S.2A/208/ 237 OCU/208/ 237 OCU	SOC; nose to Phoenix Avn 1.95
XV164	-	Written off 16.9.65 and not transferred
XV165	12/Cv S.2B/12/237 OCU/12/237 OCU/ Cv S.2D/12	SOC Nose to Staverton
XV166	Cv S.2A/237 OCU/ Cv S.2B/16/15	Stalled after control lost on approach; abandoned, Honington, 3.3.76
XV167	-	Written off 29.1.70 and not transferred
XV168	Cv S.2B/12/208/ 237 OCU/12/237 OCU/208/12	To Brough for preservation, 15.10.93

* * * * * * * * * *

Jet Provost T.4 XS213 served with the College of Air Warfare at Manby

Andover C.1 XS612 comes in to land at Southend on 26 April 1970.

The squadron's three arrowheads emblem is carried on the fin.

One useful feature of the Andover was its 'kneeling' undercarriage that brought the cargo doors close to the ground for loading and unloading. (John Ware)

Kestrel FGA.1 XS691 in hovering mode.

To evaluate the type and its unique method of operation, a Tripartite Evaluation Squadron was formed and manned by British, German and American personnel.

The flash on the fin is a combination of the colours of these countries.

Dominie T.1 XS730 was a navigation trainer of No.1 Air Navigation School at Stradishall and is photographed shortly after going into service in 1966

Beagle Basset CC.1 XS782 was one of twenty-two of the type delivered in 1965/66.

In this era, the V-bomber force could disperse widely in times of crisis, with normally four aircraft at each dispersal site.

The Basset was originally intended to carry complete V-bomber crews and their equipment to and from their home bases and dispersal sites.

Comet C.4 XR397 of No.216 Squadron was delivered at the end of 1961 and used on fast strategic transport routes around the world.

XV172		Britten-Norman Cushioncraft CC.2 hovercraft for trials at FVRDE

*　*　*　*　*　*　*　*　*　*

48 Lockheed Hercules C.1s delivered between December 1966 and January 1968
USAF serials 65-13021to 65-13044 and 66-8850 to 8873

These aircraft were pooled at Lyneham for use by all units based there and are shown as LTW (Lyneham Tactical Wing) except in cases when aircraft were allocated elsewhere.

XV176	242 OCU/LTW	Cv C.3/C.3P; to Lockheed 4.3.00
XV177	AAEE/24-6/ LTW	Cv C.3/C.3P
XV178	AAEE/LTW	Cv C.1P; to Lockheed 26.11.00
XV179	242 OCU/30-7/ 48/LTW	Cv C.1P
XV180	242 OCU/30	Engine went into reverse thrust after take-off ; dropped wing and dived into ground, Fairford, 24.3.69
XV181	24-36/242 OCU/ LTW/AAEE/LTW	Cv C.1P
XV182	242 OCU/30-47/ 242 OCU/70/LTW	Cv C.1P; to Lockheed 12.11.00
XV183	242 OCU/39-47/ 24-36/70/LTW	Cv C.3/C.3P
XV184	242 OCU/Fairford Wg/F'ford Wg/LTW	Cv C.3/C.3P
XV185	242 OCU/LTW/ DERA	Cv C.1P
XV186	242 OCU/70/LTW/ 242 OCU/LTW	Cv C.1P
XV187	242 OCU/LTW/ 70/LTW/1312 Flt	Cv C.1P; to Lockheed 28.1.01
XV188	242 OCU/LTW	Cv C.3/C.3P
XV189	242 OCU/LTW/70/ 70	Cv C.3/C.3P; to Lockheeds 10.12.00
XV190	36/24-36/LTW	Cv C.3/C.3P
XV191	36/24-36/Lyneham Wg/AAEE/LTW	Cv C.1P
XV192	36/24-36/Lyneham Wg/70/LTW/1312 Flt/ LTW/1312 Flt/LTW	Cv C.1K
XV193	36/24-36/Lyneham Wg/LTW/242 OCU/ LTW	Cv C.3/C.3P. Stalled after cargo drop; crashed and caught fire, Glen Tilt, 8m N of Pitlochry, Grampian, 27.5.93; DBF
XV194	36/24-36/48/ Lyneham Wg/24	Swung on landing; overshot runway into ditch, Tromso, 12.9.72; DBR
XV195	36/24-36/70/ Lyneham Wg/ 70/LTW	Cv C.1P To Lockheed 28.1.01
XV196	36/24-36/Lyneham Wg/LTW	Cv C.1P
XV197	36/24-36/Lyneham Wg/242 OCU/LTW	Cv C.3/C.3P
XV198	48/30-47/48	Engine cut on take-off from roller landing; dived into ground, Colerne, 10.9.73
XV199	48/242 OCU/LTW	Cv C.3/C.3P
XV200	48/24-36/LTW	Cv C.1P
XV201	48/Lyneham Wg/ Fairford Wg/242 OCU/LTW/242 OCU/ LTW/1312 Flt/ LTW/1312 Flt	Cv C.1K; SOC 29.3.96
XV202	48/24-36/Lyneham Wg/242 OCU/LTW	Cv C.3
XV203	48/30-47/Lyneham Wg/LTW/1312 Flt/ LTW/1312 Flt	Cv C.1K To Sri Lanka 6.9.00 as CR880
XV204	48/24-36/Lyneham Wg/LTW/AAEE/ LTW/1312 Flt/LTW	Cv C.1K To Cambridge 29.3.96 and reduced to spares
XV205	48/24-36/Lyneham/ 70/LTW/1312 Flt/ LTW	Cv C.1P
XV206	48/24-36/LTW/ 70/LTW/1312 Flt/	Cv C.1P
XV207	48/Lyneham Wg/ LTW	Cv C.3/C.3P To Lockheeds 26.11.00
XV208	48/AAEE/Met Res Flt	Cv W.2
XV209	48/24-36/Lyneham Wg/LTW/70/LTW	Cv C.3/C.3P.
XV210	36/24-36//LTW/ AAEE/LTW	Cv C.1P To Lockheeds 10.12.00
XV211	36/24-36//Lyneham Wg/70/Lyneham Wg/ 242 OCU/LTW/ AAEE/LTW	Cv C.1P
XV212	36/24-36/70//LTW	Cv C.3/C.3P
XV213	36/24-36/48/ Lyneham Wg/LTW/ 1312 Flt/LTW/1312 Flt/LTW	Cv C.1K To Cambridge 30.3.96 and to Sri Lanka 8.99 as CR881
XV214	36/24-36/Lyneham Wg/Fairford Wg/ Lyneham Wg/LTW	Cv C.3/C.3P
XV215	36/24-36/Lyneham Wg//LTW	Cv C.1P; to Lockheed 12.11.00
XV216	36/24-36/242 OCU/ Lyneham Wg/24	Flew into sea during night parachute exercise 17½m WSW of Pisa 9.11.71
XV217	36/24-36/Lyneham Wg/LTW	Cv C.3/C.3P
XV218	30-47/Fairford Wg/ Lyneham Wg/70/ LTW/1312 Flt/LTW	Cv C.1P To Lockheed 10.12.00
XV219	47/24-36/Fairford Wg/Lyneham Wg/ LTW	Cv C.3/C.3P To Lockheed 26.11.00
XV220	36/24-36//Lyneham Wg/70/Lyneham Wg/ 242 OCU/LTW	Cv C.3/C.3P
XV221	47/40-47/Lyneham Wg/242 OCU/LTW	Cv C.3/C.3P
XV222	47/30-47/Fairford Wg/Lyneham Wg/ LTW	Cv C.3/C.3P
XV223	47/30-47/24-36/ Fairford Wg/242 OCU/LTW/ L'heed Boscombe Down/AAEE/LTW	Cv C.3/C.3P; to Lockheed 12.11.00

*　*　*　*　*　*　*　*　*　*

38 Hawker-Siddeley Nimrod MR.1s delivered between July 1968 and August 1972 by HSA, Woodford to Contract KD/G/64
Aircraft pooled at Kinloss (K) and St.Mawgan (SM)

XV226	MinTech/K&SM/	Cv MR.2/K&SM
XV227	K/Cv MR.2/K&SM/	AAEE/K
XV228	MinTech/203/K/42/	Cv MR.2/206/42/ K&SM
XV229	MinTech/K/Cv MR.2/	AAEE/42/K/SM/K
XV230	236 OCU/42/K/	Cv MR.2/K
XV231	236 OCU/203/K/42/	Cv MR.2/K//K&SM

Nimrod

XV232	203/K/Cv MR.2/ K&SM	
XV233	236 OCU/K/42/ Cv MR.2/K&SM	To BAe for cv to MRA.4 ZJ520
XV234	236 OCU/SM/42/ 203/42//Cv MR.2/ 42/K&SM	To BAe for cv to MRA.4 ZJ518
XV235	236 OCU/SM/K/ Cv MR.2/42/K&SM	
XV236	K/203/K/Cv MR.2/ 42/K&SM	
XV237	SM/203/Cv MR.2/ K/42/SM&K	Broken up for spares 1992
XV238	K/Cv MR.2/K/42/K	SOC and broken up 1991
XV239	K/42/K/Cv MR.2/ K/AAEE/K	Stalled at low altitude during display and dived into Lake Ontario ½m off Toronto, 2.9.95
XV240	K/203/K/42/K/ Cv MR.2/K/42/ K&SM	
XV241	K/203/K/Cv MR.2/ AAEE/K/42/SM&K	
XV242	K/42/K/Cv MR.2/ K/42/AAEE/K&SM	To BAe for cv to MRA.4 ZJ517
XV243	K/Cv MR.2/K/42/ SM&K	
XV244	K/42/203/K/42 Cv MR.2/BAe/K	
XV245	K/203/K/42/ Cv MR.2/42/ K&SM	
XV246	K/203/236 OCU/ K/42/Cv MR.2/42/ K&SM	
XV247	K/42/K/Cv MR.2/K	To BAe for cv to MRA.4 ZJ516
XV248	K/203/K/Cv MR.2/ K&SM	
XV249	K/203/K/42/Cv MR.2/ 42/BAe/K&SM/ Cv R.1/51	
XV250	K/203/K/42/Cv MR.2/ K/42/K&SM	
XV251	K/42/Cv MR.2P/ MoD(PE)/42/BAe/ K&SM	To BAe for cv to MRA.4 ZJ514
XV252	42/SM/42K/203/51/ K/Cv MR.2/K	
XV253	SM/K/Cv MR.2/ K/42/K&SM	To 9118M 11.91 at Kinloss
XV254	42/SM/K/Cv MR.2/ K/AAEE/K	
XV255	SM/42/K/Cv MR.2/ 42/AAEE/KK	
XV256	SM/K/Cv MR.2/K	Hit birds on take-off and three engines lost power; crashed in Roseisle Forest, 1m W of Kinloss, 17.11.80
XV257	203/K/Cv MR.2/ K/42/K&SM	Caught fire in bomb bay, presumably due to flares, 3.6.84; not repaired
XV258	203/K/42/Cv MR.2/ 42/K&SM	To BAe for cv to MRA.4 ZJ515
XV259	236 OCU/SM/K/ Cv AEW.3/BAe	SS 10.91 Nose preserved at Carlisle
XV260	203/Cv MR.2P/K	
XV261	203/K/203/K/42/K/ 42/Cv AEW.3/BAe	To 8986M and to spares 21.12.87
XV262	K/42/Cv AEW.3/BAe	SOC 21.12.87 for spares recovery
XV263	203/42/Cv AEW.3/ JTU	To 8967M 13.7.87 at Finningley

*   *   *   *   *   *   *   *   *   *

XV268 - XV273	Beaver AL.1s for Army Air Corps to Contract KC/2S/40 XV269 to 8011M
XV276 - XV281	Pre-production Harrier GR.1s to Contract KC/3G/02 for development trials . XV277 to RN as A2600, later to Museum of Flight, East Fortune; XV278 preserved Berlin; XV279 became 8566M at Wittering
XV285	Britten-Norman Cushioncraft CC.2 hovercraft for trials to Contract KC/3A/74

*   *   *   *   *   *   *   *   *   *

18 Lockheed Hercules C.1s delivered between January and May 1968 USAF serials 66-13533 to 66-13550

XV290	47/Fairford Wg/70/ LTW	Cv C.3/C.3P
XV291	47/30&47/Fairford Wg/LTW	Cv C.1P
XV292	47/24&36/48/ Fairford Wg/ Lyneham Wg/LTW/ 1312 Flt	Cv C.1P
XV293	30&47/24&36/ Lyneham Wg/ LTW	Cv C.1P; to Lockheed 4.3.00
XV294	30&47/Fairford Wg/ 70/LTW	Cv C.3/C.3P
XV295	30&47/Fairford Wg/ 70/LTW	Cv C.1P
XV296	30&47/Fairford Wg/ LTW/1312 Flt/LTW	Cv C.1K; to Cambridge 8.96 for spares
XV297	30&47/48/Fairford Wg/242 OCU/LTW	Cv C.1P
XV298	30&47/Fairford Wg/LTW	Cv C.1P. Load shifted during night take-off; overshot runway and hit building, Kukes, Albania, 11.6.99
XV299	30&47/24&36/ Fairford Wg/ Lyneham Wg/70/ LTW	Cv C.3/C.3P
XV300	30&47/Fairford Wg/ Lyneham Wg/LTW	Cv C.1P To Lockheed 28.1.01
XV301	30&47/Fairford Wg/ 70/LTW	Cv C.3/C.3P
XV302	30&47/Fairford Wg/ LTW	Cv C.3/C.3P
XV303	30&47/Fairford Wg/ 70/LTW	Cv C.3/C.3P
XV304	30&47/Fairford Wg/ LTW	Cv C.3/C.3P
XV305	30/47/Fairford/ 70/LTW	Cv C.3/C.3P
XV306	24&36/30&47/ Fairford Wg/LTW	Cv C.1P; to Lockheed 4.3.01
XV307	242 OCU/48/ Fairford Wg/70/ Fairford Wg/LTW	Cv C.3/C.3P

*   *   *   *   *   *   *   *   *   *

XV310 - XV324	Sioux HT.2s for Army Air Corps to Contract KK/2L/8 XV312 to 8430M

*   *   *   *   *   *   *   *   *   *

Two BAC Lightning T.5s delivered in January and February 1967 by BAC, Preston, to Contract KD/2T/188 as replacements for XS453 and XS460

XV328	29/5/LTF/5/LTF/11	Sold 29.6.88 to A Glass, Jersey
XV329	74	SOC 3.5.74

* * * * * * * * *

30 Hawker-Siddeley Buccaneer S.2s for Royal Navy under Contract KC/2F/153; later 23 diverted to RAF between October 1969 and December 1978 as S.2A and S.2B/S.2C

XV332	12/237 OCU/12 216/12/208/ 237 OCU/12/208	To RN 2.4.74; returned 27.11.78 To 9232M 28.3.94 at Marham
XV333	12/237 OCU/ 16/12/208	To RN 2.4.74; returned 27.11.78 Preserved at Yeovilton
XV334	12/237 OCU/ 12/237 OCU/15	To LTS 13.2.81; SOC 10.91
XV335	-	Written off 1.7.68 and not transferred
XV336	12/Cv S.2B/237 OCU/ 208/12	To LTS 24.9.80; SOC 10.91
XV337	Cv S.2B/AAEE/208/ AAEE	To 8852M at Abingdon
XV338	Cv S.2B/12/237 OCU	Cockpit section to 8774M 31.3.83 at Honington
XV339	-	Written off 6.10.72 and not transferred
XV340	Cv S.2B/16/12/208/ 15	To 8659M 17.9.80 at Honington
XV341	12/237 OCU/Cv S.2B/ 208/12/208/12/15/16/ 12	Tailplane linkage lost on approach; abandoned and crashed, Lossie- mouth, 14.6.85
XV342	Cv S.2A/12/237 OCU/ 208/12/208/Cv S.2B/ 16/237 OCU/16/208	SOC 4.93
XV343	-	Written off 12.4.73 and not transferred
XV344	RAE/DRA	MoD(PE) aircraft
XV345	12/237 OCU/Cv S.2B/208/16/15	Lost wing in turn due to fatigue failure, Nellis ranges, Nevada, 7.2.80
XV346	-	Written off 13.2.69 and not transferred
XV347	12	Engine blew up on take-off and caught fire, Lossiemouth, 9.12.71; DBF
XV348	Cv S.2A/12/Cv S.2B/ 12/15/16/12/ 237 OCU	Hit HT cables and abandoned, Glomfjord, Norway, 31.10.77
XV349	12/Cv S.2B/15/237 OCU/12	To LTS 4.8.80; SOC 10.91
XV350	MinTech	To MoD(PE) 5.7.84
XV351	12	SOC 11.11.74
XV352	AAEE/208/237 OCU/ Cv S.2D/208/237 OCU/208	Preserved at Manston
XV353	12/237 OCU/12/ 237 OCU/Cv S.2B/12/208/SF Lossiemouth/12	To RN 28.5.73; returned 27.11.78 9144M NTU
XV354	Cv S.2A/208/237 OCU/Cv S.2B/237 OCU/12/237 OCU	8775M NTU; to 9231M 28.3.94
XV355	12/237 OCU/208/ 237 OCU/12/208	SOC 5.92
XV356	12/237 OCU/Cv S.2B/208/15	To LTS 15.8.80; SOC 10.91
XV357	208/237 OCU	To RAE 28.2.84; later to PEE
XV358	Cv S.2C	To 8658M 12.10.80 at 431 MU
XV359	Cv S.2B/12/208/12/ 208/237 OCU/208/ 12/208	To RN 20.3.94 as A2693 at Predannack; later to Culdrose for display
XV360	12/237 OCU	Abandoned after control lost off Covehithe, Norfolk, 29.7.75
XV361	Cv S.2B/15/12/208	To Ulster Aviation Society 5..4.94

* * * * * * * * * *

XV366		Vickers VA-3 hovercraft G-15-253 for trials to Contract KC/3A/67
XV370		Sikorsky SH-3D G-ATYU for Royal Navy
XV371 - XV373		Sea King HAS.1s for Royal Navy to Contract KK/M1/055
XV377		Westland SR.N5 for trials to Contract KC/3A/93; not built
XV378 - XV389		Cancelled Shelduck D.1 drones to Contract KK/T/48

* * * * * * * * * *

92 McDonnell Douglas Phantom FGR.2s delivered between December 1968 and September 1969

XV393	228 OCU/74	SOC .94
XV394	228 OCU/6/228 OCU/92/19/92	Damaged c 9.10.90 and SOC 16.9.91
XV395	228 OCU/6	Abandoned on approach to Coningsby after hydraulic control failure 1m N of Miningsby, Lincs., 9.7.69
XV396	228 OCU/14/228 OCU/23/228 OCU/ 41/228 OCU/19/ 228 OCU	SOC 7.91
XV397	228 OCU/17/31/ 17/31/17	Abandoned after instrument failure near Kempen, West Germany, 1.6.73
XV398	228 OCU/29/228 OCU/29/228 OCU/ 74	SOC 1.10.92
XV399	228 OCU/17/14/17/ 14/29/228 OCU/29/ 228OCU/56/ 228 OCU	SOC 8.91
XV400	228 OCU/6/54/228 OCU/41/29/41/29/ 19/56	SOC 7.91
XV401	228 OCU/41/111/56/ 228 OCU/29/23/228 OCU/56/19/228 OCU/74	Preserved at Boscombe Down
XV402	2/31/41/92/23/ 228 OCU/29/228 OCU/AAEE/228 OCU/29/23/56/ 29/228 OCU/56	Tyre burst in heavy landing and undercarriage caught fire, Valley, 30.4.90; not repaired and SOC 7.91
XV403	228 OCU/54/41/ 54/111/228 OCU/ 54/111/23/111	Flew into sea during practice interception 58m E of Aberdeen, 4.8.78; cause not known
XV404	54/228 OCU/54/ 111/31/228 OCU/ 29/228 OCU/23/56/ 23/56/29/228 OCU/ 29/19/92	SS 4.94
XV405	228 OCU/54/228 OCU	Abandoned after hydraulic failure off Skegness, Lincs., 24.11.75

XV406	HSA/AAEE/228 OCU/54/41/54/ 111/23/228 OCU/ 23/56/23/56/228 OCU/43/111/ 228 OCU	To Carlisle for display as 9098M, 21.11.91
XV407	6/228 OCU/6/ 228 OCU/41/29/ 228 OCU/19/ 228 OCU/19/29/228 OCU/29/56/29/228 OCU/29/228 OCU/ 19	SOC 9.92
XV408	6/228 OCU/23/228 OCU/23/56/23/29/ 229 OCU/29/92/19	To Cranwell for display as 9165M
XV409	54/228 OCU/41/ 228 OCU/41/111/ 56/111/56/228 OCU/ 29/228 OCU/29/ 228 OCU/29/228 OCU/74/1435 Flt	To 9160M 8.92; preserved at Mt.Pleasant
XV410	AAEE/111/56/ 228 OCU/29/228 OCU23/56/23/56/ 23/56	SOC 9.92
XV411	14/41/2/92/19/92/ 29/56/19	To 9103M; to Manston 11.7.91 for fire practice
XV412	54/41/228 OCU/41/ 228 OCU/92/ 19/29/228 OCU/ 29/56/29/228 OCU/ 29/92/19	To 9104M 10.7.91 at Laarbruch
XV413	6/14/2/92/228 OCU/ 29/228 OCU/29	Crashed in sea at night 70m E of Grimsby, Lincs., 12.11.80
XV414	228 OCU/54/5/54/ 111/41/111/92/ 229 OCU/92/23/ 17/23	Caught fire from fuel leak and abandoned 10m NE of Lowestoft, Suffolk, 9.12.80
XV415	AAEE/54/41/ 228 OCU/41/ 228 OCU/31/ 228 OCU/56/ 228 OCU/29/92/ 56/23/228 OCU/ 74/56	To 9163M at Boulmer
XV416	54/111	Engine lost power on take-off; abandoned and crashed in River Witham near Coningsby, 3.3.75
XV417	228 OCU/2/41/14/ 17/14/17/29	Lost wingtip and abandoned when control lost 8m off Mablethorpe, Lincs., 23.7.76
XV418	54/6/41/29/92/19/92	Control lost; dived into ground, Lohne, near Diepholz, West Germany, 11.7.80
XV419	54/228 OCU/54/ 111/14/31/14/17/31/ 111/29/228 OCU/29/ 23/56/29/228 OCU/ 23/1435 Flt/228 OCU/19	SOC 5.10.92 for BDR training
XV420	54/228 OCU/54/ 228 OCU/54/6/29/ 56/19/29/19/23/56/ 23/29/23/56/29/92/ 19/92/56/92/19/56	To 9247M 28.9.95 at Wattisham; to Neatishead 29.11.95 for display
XV421	14/228 OCU/23/228 OCU/29/228 OCU/ 29&228 OCU/92/19/ 92/1435 Flt	Dived into sea during combat practice off McBrides Head, Falklands, 30.10.91
XV422	6/31/228 OCU/23/ 228 OCU/23/92/19/ 92/19/92/19/56	To 9157M; to Stornoway for display, 6.8.92
XV423	228 OCU/6/228 OCU/6/29/23/56/ 23/56/29/23/56/29/ 56/74	To GI airframe at Leeming
XV424	6/54/6/228 OCU/54/ 6/228 OCU/6/29/ 111/56/228 OCU/ 29/228 OCU/29/ 228 OCU/92/29/ 228 OCU/56	To 9152M 12.11.92 for RAF Museum
XV425	228 OCU/54/14/17/ 29/228 OCU/29/ 228 OCU/29/228 OCU/29/56/23/56/ 228 OCU/56	To 9094M at Bruggen, 4.91
XV426	228 OCU/31/17/31/ 111/56/228 OCU/ 29/228 OCU/29/23/ 56/92/19/56	Nose preserved at Coltishall
XV427	AAEE/31/17	Flew into hill regaining formation on low-level 4m E of Bad Berleberg, West Germany, 22.8.73
XV428	228 OCU/17/14/17/ 111/19/56/23/56/ 29/228 OCU	Failed to recover from loop during display practice and hit ground, Abingdon, 23.9.88
XV429	54/111/41/228 OCU/ 41/228 OCU/29/ 228 OCU/29/HSA/ AAEE/228 OCU/29/ 228 OCU/56/MoDPE/ 56/BAe/56	SOC 8.91
XV430	2/228 OCU/29/228 OCU/23/ 19/92	SOC 11.91
XV431	31	Wings unlocked and folded on take-off; abandoned, Bruggen, 11.10.74
XV432	6/54/41/6/228 OCU/ 23/14/228 OCU/23/ 111/23/228 OCU/ 56/23/56/29/23/29/ 56	SOC 10.91
XV433	31/17/31/228 OCU/ 29/228 OCU/29/ 228 OCU/29/56/23/ 1435 Flt/74	To store 6.10.92 and SOC 8.95
XV434	HSA/6/54/41/228 OCU/17/23/228 OCU/92/19/56/29/ 228 OCU/29/228 OCU/29	Control lost; abandoned near West Burton, 12m SW of Richmond, Yorks., 7.1.86
XV435	14/228 OCU/23/ 228 OCU/92/228 OCU/29/92/19/92	To RAE Llanbedr 7.92
XV436	228 OCU/41/228 OCU/111/31/ 228 OCU/29	Overshot flapless landing after hydraulics failed and abandoned, Coningsby, 5.3.80; fuselage to 8850M
XV437	54/111/56/228 OCU/ 56/29/19/23/92/ 228 OCU/92/19/92	Lost power and abandoned near Polle, W.Germany, 18.10.88
XV438	228 OCU/6/ 228 OCU&29/ 56/23/228 OCU/23/ 1435 Flt/56	Collided with XV473 and lost part of tail, 12.8.91; SOC 13.4.92
XV439	14/2/19/92/19	SOC 2.92
XV440	31/17/31	Flew into sea at night on approach to range off Vlieland, Neth., 25.6.73
XV441	228 OCU/2/14	Engine caught fire after take-off; abandoned and crashed, Lang Hent, Netherlands, 21.11.74

XV442	AAEE/6/228 OCU/6/ 29/41/29/228 OCU &29/56/23/19/92/19/ 228 OCU/1435 Flt	To spares 10.91 at Mt Pleasant
XV460	31/228 OCU/56/19/ 228 OCU/92/228 OCU/29/228 OCU/ 29/92/19/56/74	To Wattisham for display
XV461	6/54/228 OCU/54/ 228 OCU/111/29/ 228 OCU/29/228 OCU/29/56/23/56/ 92/56/1435 Flt	SS 8.92
XV462	17/31/228 OCU/ 41/228 OCU/92/ 19/92/19/92/19	Control lost after take-off; abandoned 15m S of Akrotiri, Cyprus, 8.1.91
XV463	14/41/228 OCU/ 41	Dived into sea after control lost off Maybray, Cumberland, 17.12.75
XV464	14/17/2/19/56/23/ 56/228 OCU/29/23/ 29/56/92	SOC 11.10.91
XV465	54/41/228 OCU/ 41/31/23/29/228 OCU/29/228 OCU/ 92/19/74	SOC 5.10.92 for BDR at Leeming
XV466	6/41/14/228 OCU/92/ 56/23/56/29/228 OCU/29/23/29/ 228 OCU/56/1435 Flt	SS 8.92
XV467	2/19/92/19/92/19/ 56/92	To Benbecula for display, 6.8.92 as 9158M
XV468	17/2/19/228 OCU/19/ 56/228 OCU/29/ 228 OCU/29/ 92/19/56	To Woodvale for display, 8.92 as 9159M
XV469	17/31/17/14/17/31/ 17/2/19/56/23/56/23/ AAEE/56/92/19/56/ 92/56/74	SOC 8.95
XV470	14/17/31/228 OCU/ 56/92/228 OCU/92/ 228 OCU/29/228 OCU/19/228 OCU/ 56/228 OCU/43/111/ 228 OCU/56	To 9156M; to Akrotiri for display
XV471	17/6/29/41/228 OCU/ 29/19/92/19	Lost power on approach to Wildenrath; abandoned and crashed, Rath-Anhoven, 3.7.86
XV472	6/228 OCU/23/ 29/228 OCU/29/19/ 56/1435 Flt	SS 8.92
XV473	14/2/228 OCU/29/ 228 OCU/29/228 OCU&29/56	To Waddington for fire practice
XV474	17/31/2/19/23/ 56/23/56/29/23/ 56/74	To Duxford for display
XV475	17/2/56/19/92/19/ 92/19	To 9105M 11.7.91 at Bruggen
XV476	54/31/111/23/ 228 OCU/23/56/ 19/228 OCU/19/ 92/19/19/92/56	SOC 8.9.91
XV477	54/6	Flew into Thack Moor in cloud 9m E of Penrith, Cumberland, 21.11.72
XV478	6/41/54/111/228 OCU/41/228 OCU/ 111/23/228 OCU/ 23/56/23/29/229 OCU/29/56/19	Caught fire on ground, Wildenrath, 1.4.90; DBR
XV479	54	Engine lost power; abandoned and hit house near Karup, Denmark, 12.10.71
XV480	6/41/31/111/56/92/ 228 OCU/19/92/56	SOC 9.91
XV481	228 OCU/6/228 OCU/6/228 OCU/ 29/19/56/23/92/56	To 9135M 16.2.92 at Bruggen
XV482	54/41/54/6/228 OCU/29/56/92/19	To 9107M 12.7.91 at Leuchars
XV483	17/41/23/92	Flew into ground on practice interception, Beverungen, 8m S of Hoxter, West Germany, 24.7.78
XV484	31/2/31/14/17/14/ 228 OCU/23/2/ 19/228 OCU/29/23	Flew into Mt.Usborne 9m NNE of Goose Green, Falklands, in cloud, 17.10.83
XV485	2/29/41/228 OCU/ 111/228 OCU/29/ 228 OCU/111/228 OCU/29/228 OCU/ 23/56/23/29/228 OCU&29/19/ 92/19	To 9106M 11.7.91 at Bruggen
XV486	2/14/31/111/56/23/ 228 OCU/29/228 OCU/29/228 OCU/ 29	SOC 8.91
XV487	17/31/111/29/228 OCU/29/92/23/56/ 29/19/56/74	SOC 6.10.92
XV488	17/2/19/92/228 OCU/29/56/228 OCU/92/19/56/ 92/19/92/56	SOC 6.92
XV489	2/17/228 OCU/29/ 56/92/228 OCU/ 29/23/56/23/ 228 OCU/43/92	SOC 15.9.91
XV490	54/41/6/228 OCU/ 29/23/56/92/23/56/ 23/56/228 OCU/74/ 1435 Flt/74	SOC 1.10.92
XV491	31/17/31/111/19/29/ 228 OCU/29	Flew into sea in fog 35m N of Cromer, Norfolk, 7.7.82
XV492	6/228 OCU/29/41/ 228 OCU/29/228 OCU/23/56/23/56/ 29/92	SOC 11.10.91
XV493	228 OCU/41	Collided with Pawnee G-ASVX and crashed, Fordham Fen, 2m S of Downham Market, Norfolk, 9.8.74
XV494	2/14/17/31/228 OCU/ 111/56/23/56/23/56/ 29/19/92/19/56	SOC 1.10.92
XV495	54/6/41/111/41/228 OCU/29/56/23/56/ 228 OCU/56/29/23/ 56/29/56	SOC 1.10.92
XV496	228 OCU/41/228 OCU/17/228 OCU/ 23/92/228 OCU/ 19/92/19/92/56	SOC 9.92
XV497	6/41/228 OCU/17/ 228 OCU/56/23/ 92/228 OCU/19/29/ 92/19/92/228 OCU/ 23/1435 Flt/74	SOC 11.92; to Coningsby for fire practice
XV498	228 OCU/17/31/17/ 2/19/92/74	WFU 5.7.91; SOC 2.92

Phantom

XV499	228 OCU/6/228 OCU/29/228 OCU/ 41/92/19/23/228 OCU/29/228 OCU/ 29/92/228 OCU/19/ 74	To Leeming 5.10.92 for BDR training
XV500	54/111/56/23/43/23/ 56/23/29/228 OCU/ 29/56	To 9113M at St Athan
XV501	14/17/14/31/29/228 OCU/92/29/228 OCU/29/56/AAEE/ 56	Abandoned after control failure NE of Mayenne, France, 2.8.88
XV520 to		
XV551	-	Cancelled

* * * * * * * * * *

25 of batch of 28 McDonnell Douglas Phantom FG.1s transferred from Royal Navy to RAF

XV565	-	Not transferred
XV566	-	Not transferred
XV567	43	SOC 4.92
XV568	43/111/43	SOC 4.92
XV569	POTF/111/43/111/ Wildenrath	WFU 9.90; to 9063M at Bruggen
XV570	POTF/111	To 9069M 9.90 at Wattisham
XV571	43/111	SOC 4.92
XV572	43/111	SOC 4.92
XV573	43/111/43/111	SOC 4.92
XV574	43/111	Undershot approach and crashlanded, Yeovilton, 27.7.89; not repaired
XV575	43/111/43/111	SOC 9.91
XV576	43/111	Undershot approach and crashlanded, Yeovilton, 27.7.89; not repaired
XV577	43	To 9065M 2.91 at Leuchars
XV578	43/111	Abandoned after engine failure over sea 50m E of Montrose, Angus, 28.2.79
XV579	43/111/43	SOC 4.92
XV580	43	Abandoned after control lost during aerobatic practice, Gateside, 5m W of Forfar, Tayside, 18.9.75
XV581	43/111/43	To 9070M 9.91 at Wattisham
XV582	43/111/43/ 228 OCU	To 9066M 9.90 at Leuchars and preserved
XV583	43/111	SOC 4.91
XV584	43/111	SOC 4.91
XV585	43	SOC 4.92
XV586	43	To 9067M 8.90 at Leuchars
XV587	43/111	To 9088M 9.90 at Wattisham
XV588	-	Not transferred
XV589	111	Radome folded back on approach; abandoned, Alconbury, 3.6.80
XV590	43	SOC 9.91
XV591	111	SOC 7.12.87 for spares
XV592	111	SOC 4.91
XV604 to		
XV610	-	Cancelled

* * * * * * * * * *

XV614 - XV617	Westland SR.N6 hovercraft to Contract KC/3A/82 for trials
XV622 - XV639	Wasp HAS.1s for Royal Navy to Contract KK/N/142
XV642 - XV677 XV695 - XV714	Westland Sea King HAS.1s for Royal Navy to Contract KK/191/055

* * * * * * * * * *

13 Westland Wessex HC.2s delivered between December 1967 and July 1968 by Westlands, Yeovil, to Contract KK/M/169

XV719	72/84/72	Tail hit ground in turn, Bishops Court, 27.4.90; DBR and SOC
XV720	18/Cv SAR/22/60/22	To A2701(2) at Gosport
XV721	18/72/MoD(PE)/72/ 84/72	
XV722	18/72/18/CATCS/ 2 FTS	To storage 9.97
XV723	18/72/60/72	
XV724	18/Cv ASR/SARTS/ 22/SARTU/22/ SARTU/22	
XV725	18/72/60/72	To A2707(2) at Gosport
XV726	QF/72/60/72/60/72	
XV727	MinTech/AAEE	Flew into trees in snow cloud and crashed, Mistberget, 20m N of Gardermoen, Norway, 30.1.69
XV728	18/CATCS/2 FTS/ 72/60/72	To Newark Air Museum
XV729	MinTech/78/103/72/ Cv SAR/SARTS/ 22/Mkrs/22	Preserved at Redhill
XV730	78/103/240 OCU/ 72/22/SARTU/22/84	
XV731	78/18/240 OCU/ WTF/72	Preserved at Redhill

* * * * * * * * * *

Two Westland Wessex HCC.4s delivered in May 1969 by Westlands, Yeovil, to Contract KK/M/192

XV732	QF/32	To LTS 31.3.98
XV733	QF/32	To LTS 13.3.98

* * * * * * * * * *

60 Hawker-Siddeley Harrier GR.1s, modified to GR.1As, delivered between April 1969 and April 1971 by HSA, Kingston, to Contract KC/3G/04

XV738	HCT/3/233 OCU/1/ Cv GR.3/4	To 9074M 8.90 at Halton
XV739	1	Abandoned when aircraft dived during low-level transition, Episkopi, 24.9.73
XV740	4/1/Cv GR.3/1	To 8989M 4.89 at Abingdon
XV741	HCT/3/4/3/Cv GR.3/ 3/233 OCU/3/1/ 233 OCU	To RN as A2607 at Culdrose
XV742	Cv GR.3/AAEE/1/ 233 OCU	Probably hit by ricochet and flew into sea on Holbeach ranges, 28.10.83. Temp reg G-VSTO
XV743	HSA	Rolled during transition and abandoned, Dunsfold, 27.1.69
XV744	HCT/1/233 OCU/ Cv GR.3/223 OCU/ 3/233 OCU	To 9167M for display at Shrivenham, 4.93
XV745	HCT/233 OCU/ Cv GR.3/233 OCU	Collided with XV754 and crashed, Wardle, near Nantwich, Cheshire, 19.1.76
XV746	HCT/233 OCU/1/ Cv GR.3/1	Flew into mountain in bad visibility near Barufoss, Norway, 12.3.76
XV747	HCT/233 OCU/1/ 233 OCU/Cv GR.3/ 4/1/233 OCU	Pilot ejected on landing, Wittering, 11.11.87; to 8979M 30.9.88 at Coltishall
XV748	HCT/1/233 OCU/1/ 233 OCU/Cv GR.3/ 233 OCU/1	To GI airframe at DRA Bedford
XV749	HCT/233 OCU/1	Ingested bird and lost power; abandoned over sea off Theddlethorpe, Lincs., 26.4.72

XV750	HCT/233 OCU/20/ Cv GR.3/20	Engine cut; abandoned 4m WSW of Wildenrath, 6.9.73
XV751	HCT/233 OCU/1/233 OCU/1/233 OCU/20/ 3/Cv GR.3/1/3	To RN as A2760 16.5.91
XV752	HCT/233 OCU/1/ Cv GR.3/233 OCU/ 1317 Flt/233 OCU/ 1/3	To 9078M at Cosford
XV753	HCT/233 OCU/1/ 233 OCU/Cv GR.3/ 233 OCU/3/1/233 OCU/1	To GI 2.88; NTU and retd To 9075M 8.90 at Culdrose
XV754	HCT/233 OCU/1/ 233 OCU/1/ Cv GR.3/1	Collided with XV745 and crashed, Wardle, near Nantwich, Cheshire, 19.1.76
XV755	HCT/233 OCU/1/233 OCU/Cv GR.3/1/233 OCU/1/233 OCU/ 3/233 OCU/3/ 233 OCU	To RN as A2604 at Yeovilton
XV756	HCT/233 OCU/ OCU/Cv GR.3/ 233 OCU/1	Hit by ricochet and abandoned over Holbeach ranges, 8.11.79
XV757	HCT/233 OCU/1/233 OCU/1/233 OCU/ 1/Cv GR.3/1	Collided with XZ128 and abandoned; crashed in Wisbech, Cambs., 21.9.79
XV758	HCT/233 OCU/ Cv GR.1A/233 OCU/ Cv GR.3/3/1/233 OCU/3/4/3	To 9089M at Decimomannu
XV759	HCT/233 OCU/Cv GR.3/233 OCU/ Belize/233 OCU/1/ 233 OCU/AAEE/233 OCU/1/233 OCU	SOC 7.89; to PEE Pendine 30.3.90
XV760	HCT/233 OCU/ Cv GR.3/233 OCU/ 4/3	To RN as A2614 30.5.91
XV761	HCT/233 OCU/3/ Cv GR.3/ 4/1/4 4/1/4	Hit bird and compressor failed; abandoned ½m S of Kalenborn, 19m N of Bitburg, 28.10.80
XV762 _____	HCT/233 OCU/ Cv GR.3/233 OCU/ 1/233 OCU/1453 Flt	Flew into high ground in bad visibility, Laforia, near Goose Green, East Falklands, 19.11.83
XV776	HCT/1/Cv GR.3/ 1	Engine flamed out; abandoned, Ditton Priors, Church Stretton, Salop, 9.4.75
XV777	HCT/1	Rolled during transition and abandoned, Wittering, 1.5.72
XV778	HCT/1/Cv GR.3/1/ 1417 Flt/1/1453 Flt/ SFWittering/1	To 9001M 1.89 at Valley
XV779	1/4/20/3/Cv GR.3/20/ 3/SF Wittering/3/ 233 OCU	To 8931M 23.1.87 at Wittering
XV780	1/4	Ingested bird and engine lost power; abandoned near Hamborn, West Germany, 27.6.72
XV781	1/4/20/3/Cv GR.3/ 3/4/3	Abandoned after engine fire on approach, Gutersloh, 12.6.79
XV782	HCT/4/Cv GR.3/4/1/ 1453 Flt/4/233 OCU	To 8982M 9.5.88 at St Athan
XV783	HCT/4/Cv GR.3/4/20/ 4/233 OCU/1417 Flt/ 233 OCU/3/1/233 OCU/3/4/233 OCU	To RN as A2608 16.3.90 at Culdrose
XV784	HCT/4/Cv GR.3/4/ 1/4/233 OCU	Caught fire on ground, Wittering, 2.4.86; to 8909M 10.6.86
XV785	HCT/233 OCU/20/ 3/4/Cv GR.3/4	Became airborne after landing and abandoned, Wildenrath, 26.3.74
XV786	233 OCU/20/Cv GR.3/4/1/4/3/4/3	To A2615 5.6.91 at Culdrose
XV787	233 OCU/Cv GR.3/ 1/233 OCU/11453 Flt	Compressor failed and engine flamed out on approach; abandoned 2m E of Stanley airfield, Falklands, 22.3.83
XV788	1/Cv GR.3/1	Hit bird and engine lost power; abandoned, Belize, 1.12.75
XV789	1/4/Cv GR.3/4/1/ 4/1453 Flt/1/233 OCU/1	To 8966M 20.8.87 at Bruggen
XV790	HCT/20/Cv GR.3/ 20/4/233 OCU/4/1/3	Collided with XZ136 during practice attack and crashed, Otterburn ranges, Northumberland, 2.11.87
XV791	HCT/4/20/ Cv GR.3/20	Hit birds on take-off; abandoned as control lost, Wildenrath, 9.7.73
XV792	1/3/Cv GR.3/3	Rolled while hovering and hit ground, Gutersloh, 14.10.80
XV793	HCT/233 OCU/Cv GR.3/20/3/1/4	To 8980M 11.12.87 at St Athan
XV794	HCT/4	Ingested bird; lost power and abandoned near Hutten, West Germany, 4.5.72
XV795	1/Cv GR.3/1/3/ 233 OCU	Collided with XW926 and abandoned, Eye, near Peterborough, Cambs., 23.2.83
XV796	1	Engine flamed out on approach; abandoned, Ouston, 6.10.70
XV797	233 OCU/20/4/ Cv GR.3/4	Flap jammed down; rolled out of control and abandoned, Vredepeel, 4m W of Venraij, Netherlands, 23.1.74
XV798	233 OCU/20	Control lost during hover and abandoned; sideslipped into wood, Wildenrath, 23.4.71; DBF
XV799	233 OCU	Flew into hill after control lost in cloud, Dornie, near Kyle of Lochalsh, Highland, 12.9.72
XV800	233 OCU/20/ Cv GR.3/20/4	Engine cut after take-off on ingesting bird, Wildenrath, 16.5.74; DBR
XV801	20/4/Cv GR.3/ 4/20/3	Control lost; abandoned, Ennigerloh, 12m NE of Hamm, West Germany, 15.12.78
XV802	20	Dived into ground during low-level exercise 1m NW of Stadtoldendorf, West Germany, 21.3.72
XV803	1	Dived into ground after nozzle failure on approach, Wattisham, 3.8.71
XV804	233 OCU/Cv GR.3/ 233 OCU/1417 Flt/ 233 OCU/1417 Flt/ 233 OCU/4/3/1/3/4	To 9280M 17.12.97 at North Luffenham
XV805	20/Cv GR.3/20	Engine cut after birdstrike; abandoned 1½m SW of Coesfeld, West Germany, 30.7.73
XV806	20/4/20/Cv GR.3/ 20/4/3/4/3	To A2606(2) 4.90 at Culdrose
XV807	233 OCU/Cv GR.3/ 233 OCU/3/233 OCU/1417 Flt	Hit tree recovering from practice attack on vehicles 4m S of Georgeville, Belize, 14.7.81; elevator control had disconnected
XV808	4/20/Cv GR.3/20/ 3/233 OCU	To 9076M at Halton (later A2687)
XV809	20/4/Cv GR.3/4/1/ 233 OCU/3	Flew into cloud on take-off from Gutersloh and control lost; hit trees and broke up, 20.5.88
XV810	20/Cv GR.3/20/ 4/233 OCU/AAEE/ 233 OCU	SOC 16.1.89; to 9038M at Abingdon

XV814		de Havilland Comet 4 (ex G-APDF) for Ministry of Technology for use at RAE to Contract KU/L/129
XV818 - XV837		Northrop Shelduck D.1 drones to Contract KK/T/52
XV841 - XV855		Cancelled Chinook HC.1s
XV859		Westland SRN.6 hovercraft for trials to Contract KC/3A/137

*   *   *   *   *   *   *   *   *   *

Seven Hawker-Siddeley Buccaneer S.2Bs to Contract KC/2F/179 transferred from Royal Navy, September (XV864) and November 1983 (remainder)

XV863	16/237 OCU/208/ 237 OCU/208	9115M NTU, ex 9139M NTU To 9145M at Lossiemouth; preserved
XV864	16/237 OCU/12/208	To 9234M 28.3.94 at Manston
XV865	208/216/208/12/ 237 OCU/12/SF Lossiemouth/208	To 9226M 25.1.94 at Coningsby; preserved
XV866	16	To LTS 12.8.80; SOC 10.91
XV867	237 OCU/208/12/208/ 237 OCU/12/SF Lossiemouth/208/ 237 OCU/208/237 OCU	Undercarriage came down in turn and damaged; collapsed on landing, Leeming, 10.9.93; SOC as not worth repair
XV868	12/208/237 OCU/ 298/237 OCU/208/ 12/208/12	SS 9.92
XV869	208/12/237 OCU/ 208/237 OCU/12	SS 4.94
XV870 to XV879	-	Cancelled

*   *   *   *   *   *   *   *   *   *

XV884 - XV887	Cancelled General Dynamics TF-111Ks USAF serials 67-0151 to 67-0153 and 67-0155
XV902 - XV947	Cancelled General Dynamics F-111Ks USAF serials 67-0149, 67-0150; 67-0154; 67-1056 to 67-0158, 68-0181 to 68-0210; 68-0229 to 68-0238
XV951	Slingsby T.53B glider for ATC to Contract KK/D/2735
XV952 - XV990	Cancelled T-53Bs
XW101 - XW150 XW161 - XW170	Northrop Shelduck D.1 drones for Royal Navy to Contract KK/T/55

*   *   *   *   *   *   *   *   *   *

Two Hawker-Siddeley Harrier T.2 prototypes to Contract KK/3G/27 for Ministry of Technology

XW174	HSA/AAEE	Lost power and abandoned 6m W of Boscombe Down, 4.6.69
XW175	HSA	To MinTech 8.70 for RAE

*   *   *   *   *   *   *   *   *   *

XW179 - XW195	Sioux AH.1s for Army Air Corps to Contract KK/2C/22

*   *   *   *   *   *   *   *   *   *

Forty Westland Puma HC.1s delivered between January 1971 and June 1973 by Westland-Fairey, Hayes

XW198	HOCF/240 OCU/ 230/33/230/33/230/ 72/230	
XW199	HOCF/240 OCU/ 230/33/230/33/ 27R/72/33/230	SOC 9.12.99; to spares
XW200	HOCF/240 OCU/ 33/240 OCU/33/ 240 OCU/27R/ 230/33	Flew into hill in fog 3m SW of Kacanik, Kosovo, 9.4.01
XW201	240 OCU/230/ 240 OCU/27R/33/ 230	
XW202	240 OCU/230/240 OCU/230/AAEE/ 230/240 OCU/33/ 1563 Flt/33/1563 Flt/ 33/1563 Flt/230/ 27R/33/230	
XW203	HOCF/230/33	Flew into ground after control lost, Beacon Hill, 7m N of Whitchurch, Hants, 15.11.74
XW204	33/1563 Flt/33/1563 Flt//33/1563 Flt/33/ 1563 Flt/230/33/18/ 230/33/72/33/72/33	
XW205	HOCF/33	Door came off and hit tail rotor; spiralled into ground near Voss, Norway, 30.1.78
XW206	33/240 OCU/33/1563 Flt/33/1563 Flt/33/ 230/27R/230/33/230/ 72	
XW207	33/240 OCU/33/32/ 33/1563 Flt/33/ 1563 Flt/33/230/33	Crashed at Hipswell Moor, Catterick, 19.4.00; to spares
XW208	33/240 OCU/33/240 OCU/33/1363 Flt/33/ 240 OCU/230/33/ DERA/33/72/33/230/ 33	
XW209	33/1563 Flt/33/230/ 27R/230/72	
XW210	33/240 OCU/33/230/ 33/240 OCU/33/1563 Flt DERA/33	Tail rotor hit hangar; over-turned and caught fire, Gallon Jug airstrip, Belize, 21.5.92 Rebuilt using XW215 by 1999
XW211	33/240 OCU/33/240 OCU/33/27R/72/230/ 33	
XW212	33/230/33/240 OCU/ 33/1563 Flt/230/33/ 72/230/PASF	
XW213	33/230/240 OCU/33/ 1563 Flt/33/1563 Flt/ 33/230/72/230	
XW214	33/AAEE/33/230/ 1563 Flt/33/230/33/ 230/33	
XW215	33/240/33/230/240 OCU/230/240 OCU/ 230/33/230/22/230	Tail control failed and aircraft became uncontrollable; ditched 25m NE of Manston, 24.6.91
XW216	33/230/33/1563 Flt/ 33/230/18	
XW217	33/230/33/230/ 27R/230/33	
XW218	230/240 OCU/33/ 230/33/230/18/33/ 230/18/72/33/72/ 230/PASF/33	

Puma

XW219	230/240 OCU/230/ 240 OCU/230//33/ 230/33/230/18/ 1563 Flt/33/230/ 18/72/33/721/ 230/PASF	
XW220	230/240 OCU/230/ 240 OCU/230/33/ 230/33/27R/230	
XW221	230/33/230/33/230/ 33/230/72/33/72/33	
XW222	230/18/1563 Flt/ 27R/230/33/230/33	
XW223	230/33	
XW224	230/33/230/33/230/ 1563 Flt/18/230/72/ 33/230	
XW225	230/33/230/240 OCU/230/240 OCU/EWAU/ 240 OCU/230/240 OCU/230/240 OCU/ 230/18	Overshot landing in field into trees in snow cloud, Ursprung, Bavaria, Germany, 15.2.97
XW226	230/18/33/230/27R/ 33/72/33/230/72/ 230	
XW227	33/230/33/230/33/ 230/33/27R/72/33/ 230/72/33/230	
XW228	33/230/240 OCU/ 230/33	Flew into wires and rotor hit ground; broke up, Mtoko, S Rhodesia, 27.12.79
XW229	230//Mod(PE)/230/ 33/230/33/72/33	
XW230	MoD(PE)/230/33/ 230/1563 Flt	Engine cut; crashed in forest, Toledo, Belize, 27.8.76
XW231	230/33/240 OCU/ 33/240 OCU/33/ 1563 Flt/33/240 OCU/27R/230	
XW232	230/18/230/33/230	
XW233	AAEE/33/Mkrs/33/ 1563 Flt/33/230/33	
XW234	RAE/33/230	
XW235	230/33/1563 Flt/ 33/230/33/230/33	
XW236	33/1563 Flt/33/ 1563 Flt/230/18/33/ 27R/230/33	
XW237	33/240 OCU/33/230/ 33	

* * * * * * * * * *

Sud SA.330E Puma delivered in October 1968 as pattern aircraft

XW241	Westland/RAE	Ex F-ZJUX; SOC 11.88

* * * * * * * * * *

XW246	Westland SRN.5 hovercraft for trials to Contract KC/3A/168
XW249	Cushioncraft CC.7 hovercraft for trials to Contract KC/3A/159
XW255	British Hovercraft BH-7 for trials to Contract KC/3A/145
XW260	Hovermarine HM-2 hovercraft for trials to Contract KC/3A/180

* * * * * * * * * *

**Nine Hawker-Siddeley Harrier T.2s (later updated to T.4s) delivered
between May 1970 and July 1971 to Contract KC/3G/33**

XW264	HSA & AAEE	Control lost; flew into ground near Boscombe Down, 11.6.70; DBF
XW265	AAEE/233 OCU/20R	Cv T.4; to 9258M 3.10.96 at Cosford
XW266	233 OCU/Cv T.4/233 OCU	To Royal Navy as T.4N 21.9.88
XW267	233 OCU/Cv T.4/233 OCU/1/233 OCU/ RAE/AAEE/RAE/ SAOEU	To 9263M 23.10.96; preserved at Chetwynd Barracks, Notts.
XW268	233 OCU/Cv T.4/233 OCU/SF Wittering/ 233 OCU	To Royal Navy as T.4N 15.3.89
XW269	4/3/4/Cv T.4/4/233 OCU/1/AAEE/3/233 OCU/SAOEU	To 9267M 18.11.96 at Boscombe Down
XW270	233 OCU/Cv T.4/ 233 OCU/1/4/SF Gutersloh/233 OCU/ 20R	SOC by 5.92
XW271	1/Cv T.4/1/233 OCU/ 1/233 OCU/1/233 OCU/3/233OCU/ 20R	To RN as A2692 3.11.94 at Culdrose
XW272	20/3/20/3/20/4/20/4	Cv T.4. Flew into trees on take-off, Bergen-Hohne ranges, West Germany, 29.6.82; nose to 8783M 21.10.82 at Cranfield
XW273		Harrier T.2 to G-VTOL 27.7.70
XW274		Harrier T.2 static test airframe

* * * * * * * * * *

XW276	Aerospatiale SA.341 Gazelle delivered to Westland for compatibility purposes. Ex F-ZWRI
XW280 - XW284	Scout AH.1s for Army Air Corps to Contract KK/N/155

* * * * * * * * * *

**110 BAC Jet Provost T.5s delivered between September 1969 and
October 1972 by BAC, Luton, to Contract KC/E/124**
(93 converted to T.5As and some to T.5Bs)

XW287	CFS/RAFC/3 FTS/ 6 FTS	Sold; to USA as N4107K 12.7.94
XW288	CFS/RAFC/1 FTS	Flew into ground during roll while practising aerobatics, Linton-on-Ouse, 17.5.82
XW289	CFS/RAFC/1 FTS/ RAFC/3 FTS/1 FTS	Sold; to G-BVXT 18.1.95
XW290	CFS/RAFC/3 FTS	To 9199M at Halton
XW291	CFS/RAFC/CFS/ RAFC/3 FTS/6 FTS	Sold; to G-BWOF 18.3.96
XW292	CFS/RAFC/3 FTS	To 9128M at Cosford
XW293	CFS/6 FTS	Sold; to G-BWCS 28.4.95
XW294	CFS/1 FTS/3 FTS/ RAFC/3 FTS	To 9129M at Halton
XW295	CFS/1 FTS/RAFC/ 3 FTS	Sold; to Australia as VH-JPV 1.5.98
XW296	1 FTS/RAFC/ 3 FTS/6 FTS	Sold; to USA as N4107G 12.7.94
XW297	CFS/1 FTS	Abandoned in spin, Kipling- coates, Yorks., 17.9.70
XW298	1 FTS/3 FTS/6 FTS/ MoD(PE)/6 FTS/ BFTS Cranwell	To 9013M 7.89
XW299	1 FTS/RAFC/1 FTS	To 9146M at Halton

XW300	1 FTS	Collided with Sea Prince WP312 and crashed 2m ESE of Selby, Yorks., 2.3.71
XW301	1 FTS/7 FTS/1 FTS	To 9147M at Cosford
XW302	1 FTS/RAFC/3 FTS/ 6 FTS	Sold; to USA as N155A 22.11.95
XW303	1 FTS/7 FTS/1 FTS/ 7 FTS	To 9119M at Halton
XW304	1 FTS/3 FTS/6 FTS	To 9172M at Cosford
XW305	1 FTS/RAFC/3 FTS	Sold; to USA as N453MS 4.96
XW306	1 FTS/3 FTS/6 FTS/ MoD(PE)/6 FTS	Sold; to USA as N313A 22.11.95
XW307	1 FTS/RAFC/3 FTS/ 6 FTS	Sold; to USA as N4107U 18.8.95
XW308	1 FTS	Dived out of cloud after take-off and hit Crumlie Hill during recovery, 4m W of Leuchars, 28.1.81
XW309	1 FTS/6 FTS	To 9179M at Cosford
XW310	1 FTS/RAFC/3 FTS	Sold; to G-BWGS 14.5.97
XW311	1 FTS/3 FTS/6 FTS	To 9180M at Cosford
XW312	1 FTS	To 9109M at Cosford
XW313	1 FTS/3 FTS/RAFC/ 3 FTS/1 FTS	Sold; to G-BVTB 7.9.94
XW314	3 FTS/RAFC	Control lost in spin; abandoned near Swinderby, 8.5.80
XW315	RAFC/3 FTS/CFS/ 3 FTS/CFS	Caught fire in air, 5.7.84; not repaired and SOC 8.5.86
XW316	3 FTS/CFS/RAFC/ CFS/6 FTS/RAFC/ 7 FTS	Sold 2.93; to USA as N316HC 7.7.93
XW317	3 FTS/RAFC/ MoD(PE)/ 3 FTS/1 FTS	Sold; to USA as N355A 22.11.95
XW318	3 FTS/RAFC/3 FTS/ 1 FTS	To 9190M 15.6.93 at Cosford
XW319	3 FTS/CFS/7 FTS/ 1 FTS	Sold; to USA as N8087V 7.3.95
XW320	3 FTS/RAFC/3 FTS/ 1 FTS	To 9015M, then 9016MA at Cosford (also 9018M in error)
XW321	3 FTS/1 FTS/3 FTS/ RAFC/7 FTS/1 FTS	To 9154M 4.93 at Cosford
XW322	RAFC/6 FTS/RAFC/ 1 FTS/3 FTS/6 FTS	Sold; to USA as N8086U 7.12.95
XW323	RAFC/3 FTS/1 FTS	To 9166M for RAF Museum
XW324	3 FTS/1 FTS/6 FTS	Sold; to G-BWSG 13.5.96
XW325	3 FTS/1 FTS/3 FTS/ RAFC/3 FTS/6 FTS	Sold; to G-BWGF 10.8.95
XW326	3 FTS/CFS/1 FTS/ 7 FTS/1 FTS	Sold; to USA as N326GV
XW327	3 FTS/RAFC/1 FTS/ 7 FTS/6 FTS/ 7 FTS/CFS	To 9130M at Halton
XW328	3 FTS/RAFC/3 FTS/ 7 FTS/3 FTS/1 FTS	To 9177M at Cosford
XW329	3 FTS	Stalled during practice loss of power on take-off and flew into ground, Leeming,16.6.81; parts to 8741M 1.7.82 at Church Fenton
XW330	3 FTS/RAFC/CFS/ 7 FTS/RAFC/3 FTS/ 1 FTS	To 9195M at Cosford
XW331	3 FTS	Hit runway after simulated flame-out; nosewheel collapsed, Leeming, 11.4.73; to fire practice
XW332	3 FTS/RAFC/3 FTS	Sold 2.93; to USA as N332RC 12.7.93
XW333	3 FTS/1 FTS/3 FTS/ RAFC/CFS/1 FTS	Sold; to G-BVTC 7.7.93
XW334	1 FTS/3 FTS/RAFC/ 7 FTS/3 FTS	Sold 2.93; to USA as N334XW
XW335	RAFC/3 FTS	To 9061M at Halton
XW336	RAFC/3 FTS/CFS/ 1 FTS	Sold; to USA as N8089U 3.95

XW351	RAFC/1 FTS/RAFC/ 3 FTS	To 9062M at Halton
XW352	RAFC/3 FTS/6 FTS	Sold 11.92
XW353	RAFC/3 FTS/CFS	To 9090M and preserved at Cranwell 18.7.91
XW354	RAFC/3 FTS/1 FTS	Sold; to USA as N300LT 14.2.94
XW355	RAFC/3 FTS	Sold; to G-JPTV 2.5.96
XW356	RAFC	Abandoned after control lost in cloud, New Tupton, Derby, 12.9.72
XW357	RAFC/3 FTS	Sold; to Australia 1993
XW358	RAFC/CFS/7 FTS/ CFS	To 9181M at Cosford
XW359	RAFC/7 FTS/1 FTS/ 6 FTS/1 FTS	Sold; to USA as N400LT 14.2.94
XW360	RAFC/3 FTS/7 FTS/ 1 FTS	To 9153M at Cosford
XW361	RAFC/3 FTS/RAFC/ 7 FTS/RAFC/7 FTS/ 3 FTS/1 FTS	To 9192M at Cosford
XW362	RAFC/3 FTS	Sold; to Australia in 1993
XW363	RAFC/1 FTS/6 FTS/ RAFC/3 FTS	To BAe Warton as GI airframe 11.1.91
XW364	1 FTS/3 FTS/RAFC/ 3 FTS/CFS/RAFC	To 9188M at Cosford
XW365	RAFC/3 FTS/1 FTS/ 7 FTS/1 FTS	To 9018M at Halton
XW366	RAFC/3 FTS/1 FTS	To 9097M at Halton
XW367	RAFC/1 FTS/3 FTS	To 9193M at Cosford
XW368	RAFC/CFS/3 FTS/ CFS/6 FTS/1 FTS	Sold; to USA as N600LT 2.94
XW369	RAFC/3 FTS/1 FTS	SOC 5.4.90
XW370	3 FTS/1 FTS	To 9196M at Cosford
XW371	1 FTS/7 FTS	Flew into ground in bad weather on low-level navex 10m E of Lancaster, Lancs., 3.7.79
XW372	RAFC/1 FTS/7 FTS/ 1 FTS/7 FTS/6 FTS	Sold; to USA as N372JP 4.96
XW373	RAFC/3 FTS	Sold 2.93; to USA as N373XW
XW374	1 FTS/RAFC/3 FTS	Sold; to Australia as VH-JPE 17.11.99
XW375	3 FTS/6 FTS/CFS	To 9149M at Halton
XW404	1 FTS	To 9049M at St Athan
XW405	RAFC/1 FTS/7 FTS/ 1 FTS/6 FTS	To 9187M at Cosford
XW406	3 FTS/RAFC/3 FTS	Sold; to Netherlands 3.95
XW407	3 FTS/7 FTS	Collided with XW411 and abandoned near Helmsley, North Yorks., 6.6.86
XW408	RAFC/3 FTS/1 FTS	Sold; to Australia in 1993
XW409	1 FTS/7 FTS	To 9047M at St Athan
XW410	3 FTS/RAFC/1 FTS	To 9125M at Cosford
XW411	RAFC/3 FTS/7 FTS	Collided with XW407 and abandoned near Helmsley, North Yorks., 6.6.86
XW412	RAFC/3 FTS/1 FTS	Sold; to USA as N8088V 3.95
XW413	RAFC/1 FTS/3 FTS/ 7 FTS/1 FTS	To 9126M at Halton
XW414	CFS/3 FTS	Engine cut on approach; abandoned, Dishforth, 28.6.78
XW415	3 FTS/7 FTS/3 FTS/ CFS/1 FTS	Sold; to USA as N900LT 2.94
XW416	RAFC/7 FTS/3 FTS/ 1 FTS	To 9191M at Cosford
XW417	RAFC/1 FTS/7 FTS/ 1 FTS/7 FTS	Control lost in bad visibility; dived into trees, Lake Thirlmere, Cumbria, 9.12.82
XW418	3 FTS/CFS/7 FTS/ CFS	To 9173M at Cosford
XW419	RAFC/1 FTS/CFS/ 1 FTS/7 FTS/1 FTS/ 7 FTS	To 9120M at Halton
XW420	RAFC/3 FTS/1 FTS	To 9194M at Halton
XW421	CFS/RAFC/CFS/ 3 FTS/CFS	To 9111M at Cosford

XW422	RAFC/3 FTS	Sold; to G-BWEB 19.6.95
XW423	3 FTS/1 FTS/RAFC/ 3 FTS	Sold; to G-BWUW 18.7.96
XW424	3 FTS/1 FTS/3 FTS/ 1 FTS	Control lost during aerobatic practice; flew into ground, Linton-on-Ouse, 30.4.77
XW425	MoD(PE)/CFS/ RAFC/CFS/3 FTS/ CFS/6 FTS	To 9200M 6.7.93 at Cosford
XW426	3 FTS/1 FTS/3 FTS/ 1 FTS	Abandoned after control lost in dive, Dalby Forest, 5m ENE of Pickering, North Yorks., 23.1.78
XW427	3 FTS/7 FTS/3 FTS/ CFS/3 FTS/1 FTS/ 3 FTS	To 9124M at Halton
XW428	3 FTS/1 FTS/3 FTS/ 6 FTS	To DRA Farnborough as GI airframe; to USA as N4311M 30.12.94
XW429	3 FTS/CFS/1 FTS/ 6 FTS	Sold; to USA as N556A 5.12.95
XW430	3 FTS/CFS/6 FTS/ 1 FTS	To 9176M at Cosford
XW431	3 FTS/CFS/6 FTS	Sold; to G-BWBS 13.4.95
XW432	3 FTS/1 FTS/7 FTS/ 1 FTS	To 9127M at Cosford
XW433	3 FTS/7 FTS/3 FTS/ 7 FTS	Sold; to G-JPRO 10.8.95
XW434	CFS/3 FTS/1 FTS/ 7 FTS/1 FTS/7 FTS/ 1 FTS	To 9091M at Halton
XW435	CFS/RAFC/3 FTS	Sold; to USA as N4XW 12.98
XW436	RAFC/3 FTS/3 FTS/ CFS/1 FTS	To 9148M at Halton
XW437	CFS/RAFC/3 FTS/ 1 FTS	Sold; to USA as N80873 3.95
XW438	RAFC/3 FTS/6 FTS	To Muscat & Oman as GI airframe 1995

*   *   *   *   *   *   *   *   *   *

| XW444 - XW478; XW492 - XW516 | Northrop Shellduck D.1 drones to Contract KK/T/58 |

*   *   *   *   *   *   *   *   *   *

26 Hawker-Siddeley Buccaneer S.2Bs delivered between January 1970 and March 1973 by HSA, Brough to Contract KC/2F/258

XW525	12/237 OCU/208	Lost tailplane avoiding Hunters; abandoned and crashed into Claerwen Reservoir, Powys, 4.4.77
XW526	MinTech/12/15/ 237 OCU/16	Lost part of wing and crashed near Osnabruck, West Germany, 12.7.79
XW527	12/15/16/12/208/ 12/208	SOC 1994; nose preserved
XW528	12/15	To 8861M 21.5.85 at Coningsby
XW529	AAEE/BAe	MoD(PE) aircraft
XW530	16/MinTech/15/16/ 208/12/208/12	SS; preserved at Buccaneer Service Stn Elgin
XW531	15/12/237 OCU/ 15/12	Control lost and abandoned off Bodo, Norway, 29.10.76
XW532	15	Dived into ground after breaking up in cloud after take-off 4m SW of Laarbruch, 25.3.71
XW533	15/16/12/16/216/12/ 237 OCU/15/208/15/ 16/237 OCU/208/ 12/237 OCU/208/ 237 OCU/12/237 OCU/208/12	Bellylanded, Lossiemouth, 9.1.92 9116M NTU; to 9138M for display but scrapped 9.92

XW534	15/16 237 OCU/12/AAEE/ 12/237 OCU	To MoD(PE) 2.85-9.88 SOC 7.94
XW535	237 OCU/15/16	Control lost avoiding collision and abandoned 4½m ENE of Lubecke, near Minden, West Germany, 24.1.73
XW536	237 OCU/15/16/15	Collided with XW528 and abandoned off coast of Jutland, Denmark, 16.6.75
XW537	237 OCU/15/16/15/ 237 OCU	Stalled on approach; rolled and abandoned, Wattisham, 23.9.81
XW538	237 OCU/16	To 8660M at Lossiemouth
XW539	12	Flew into sea on low-level formation exercise 8m NW of Port Erin, Isle of Man, 4.1.72
XW540	15/208/216/12/208/ 12/208/12/237 OCU/ 12/237 OCU/12	Flew into sea at night on shipping attack exercise 17m ENE of Duncansby Head, Highland, 22.4.87
XW541	15&6/12	To 8858M 21.5.85 at Lossiemouth
XW542	15/16/15/16/216/12/ 208/MoD(PE)/203/ 12/237 OCU/12/ 237 OCU/208/237 OCU/208	SOC 2.94
XW543	15/16/208/16/237 OCU/12	Hydraulics failed; bellylanded at St.Mawgan, 14.5.92; DBR
XW544	15/16	To 8857M 21.5.85 at Cosford
XW545	15/16	To 8859M 21.5.85 at St Athan
XW546	15/16/237 OCU/ BAe/12/237 OCU	SOC 8.92
XW547	15/12/237 OCU/12/ 216/12/208/ 237 OCU/12	9095M NTU; to 9169M for display at Cosford
XW548	15/16/208/16	Engine caught fire in air on low-level exercise; abandoned near Volkel, 3.2.77
XW549	15/16/12	To 8860M 21.5.85 at Kinloss
XW550	15/16	To LTS 18.8.80; nose preserved at West Horndon, Essex

*   *   *   *   *   *   *   *   *   *

| XW555 | | Hovermarine HM-2 hovercraft for trials to Contract KC/3A/180 |

*   *   *   *   *   *   *   *   *   *

Three Sepecat Jaguar prototypes delivered by BAC Preston for Ministry of Technology

XW560	AAEE	S-06; Engine caught fire while awaiting take-off, Boscombe Down, 11.8.72; not repaired
XW563	AAEE	S-07; to 8563M at Bruggen
XW566	AAEE/RAE	B-08, prototype T.2; SOC 3.84 and stored

*   *   *   *   *   *   *   *   *   *

XW571 - XW580; XW594 - XW603	Northrop Shelduck D.1 drones to Contract KK/T/59
XW608	Hovermarine Hovercat 3 for trials to Contract KC/3A/208
XW612 - XW616	Scout AH.1s for Army Air Corps to Contract KK/N/182
XW620 - XW622	Hover Development HD.1/HD.2/HU.4 for trials

XW626		Comet 4C (ex-G-APDS) for MinTech trials as Nimrod development aircraft

* * * * * * * * * *

Hawker-Siddeley Harrier GR.1 delivered by HSA, Kingston, in June 1971 to Contract KC/3G/04. Replacement for XV743

XW630	20/Cv GR.3/20/4/ 20/3/4/3	Cv GR.1A; to A2759 15.5.91 at Yeovilton

* * * * * * * * * *

Beagle D5/180 Husky presented to Air Training Corps in June 1969 to Contract AF/5/38A

XW635	5 AEF	Ex G-AWSW; reverted to G-AWSW 19.4.89

* * * * * * * * * *

XW640		Schleicher Ka 6CR sailplane (BGA 1348) for ETPS to Contract CR/U/0262
XW644 - XW655		Hawker-Siddeley Harrier 50s for US Marine Corps as AV-8As 158384 to 158395 to Contract K2B/A/01
XW660		Hover-Air Hoverhawk III for trials to Contract K5B/14

* * * * * * * * * *

Three Hawker-Siddeley Nimrod R.1s delivered between July 1971 and approx August 1972 by HSA, Woodford, to Contract KD/G/93

XW664	51/AAEE/51	
XW665	51/MoD(PE)/51	
XW666	51	Two engines caught fire on air test due to fuel leak; ditched 4½m NE of Lossiemouth, 1.6.95; salvaged for spares

* * * * * * * * *

XW670 - XW707		Northrop Shelduck D.1 drones
XW724 - XW745		for Royal Navy to Contract K20C/6/28

* * * * * * * * * *

Hawker-Siddeley HS.748 for Ministry of Technology purchased in January 1970 to Contract K10A/18

XW750	RAE & BLEU/DRA	Ex G-ASJT

* * * * * * * * * *

Eight Hawker-Siddeley Harrier GR.1s, converted to GR.1As, delivered between November 1971 and December 1972 by HSA Kingston to Contract KC/3G/54

XW754 to		
XW762	-	Renumbered XW916 to XW924
XW763	4/Cv GR.3/3/1453 Flt/ 1/AAEE/1/233 OCU	SOC 22.3.89; 9002M NTU; to 9041M and preserved at Duxford
XW764	4/3/Cv GR.3/3	To 8981M 25.5.88 at Leeming
XW765	20/3/Cv GR.3/3/ 233 OCU/3	Hit bird and engine cut; abandoned 2½m SSE of Lampeter, Dyfed, 12.3.80

XW766	20/3/Cv GR.3/3	Lost power and abandoned and crashed in wood near Ravensberg, West Germany, 4.10.79
XW767	20/3/Cv GR.3/3/ 233 OCU/1	Compressor failed and engine flamed out; abandoned and crashed in sea off Cape Pembroke, Falklands, 6.11.82
XW768	20/3/Cv GR.3/20/ 4/1/4	To 9072M 8.90 at Halton
XW769	3/20/1/1417 Flt/ 4	Abandoned when control lost in hover during demonstration, Chièvres, 28.6.86
XW770	HSA/3/Cv GR.3/3	Engine flamed out due to blade failure; abandoned near Borken, West Germany, 6.7.76

* * * * * * * * * *

XW778 - XW780		Harrier T.2s renumbered XW925 to XW927
XW784		Mitchell-Procter Kittiwake I built by Royal Navy apprentices; became G-BBRN

* * * * * * * * * *

Four Hawker-Siddeley HS.125 CC.1s delivered in April and May 1971 by HSA Chester to Contract K49B/39

XW788	32	SOC 31.3.94; to G-BVTP 15.9.94
XW789	32	SOC 31.3.94; to G-BVTR 15.9.94
XW790	32	SOC 31.3.94; to G-BVTS 15.9.94
XW791	32	SOC 31.3.94; to G-BVTT 15.9.94

* * * * * * * * * *

XW795 - XW799		Scout AH.1s for Army Air Corps to Contract K25A/223/SW
XW800 - XW801		Cancelled Scout AH.1s
XW803 - XW832		Northrop Shelduck D.1 drones to Contract K20C/65/6
XW835 - XW839		Westland Lynx prototypes to Contract KZ/A/7

* * * * * * * * * *

60 Westland Gazelles for Army Air Corps, Royal Navy, Royal Marines and Royal Air Force delivered between June 1973 and June 1974 to Contract 69/71117-02

XW842 to XW871; XW884 to XW913

Ten HT.3s for Royal Air Force

XW852	32/Cv HCC.4/32	
XW855	32/Cv HCC.4/32	
XW858	2 FTS	
XW862	CFS/2 FTS	
XW866	CFS/2 FTS	Sold; to G-BXTH 13.3.98
XW870	CFS/2 FTS	Damaged in heavy landing, Shawbury, 8.8.95; not repaired and stored
XW898	CFS/2 FTS	
XW902	CFS/2 FTS	
XW906	CFS/2 FTS	To Apprentices School, Boscombe Down 1999
XW910	CFS/2 FTS	To G-BXZE 25.8.98

* * * * * * * * * *

Vickers VC.10 C.1 XV104 of No.10 Squadron.

The VC.10s were, appropriately, named after holders of the Victoria Cross and XV104 was 'James McCudden VC'.

Later, all nine of the batch were convered to tankers.

Nimrod MR.1 XV236 of No.201 Squadron on the apron at Luqa during Exercise 'Lime Jug' in 1971.

The Nimrod force was eventually concentrated at Kinloss and St Mawgan and lost their individual markings except for ceremonual purposes.

Hercules C.1 XV179 from the Lyneham Tactical Wing with markings toned down to make them less visible.

After serving with overseas squadrons, the Hercules were concentrated in a single wing whose squadrons used any aircraft allocated for a task.

Harrier GR.1s of No.1 Squadron shortly after their equipment with the type.

They still have the standard Fighter Command colour scheme as used on Hunters.

XV748 in the foreground was later converted to a GR.3 and survived to become a ground instructional airframe at the DRA Bedford.

The unique Hercules W.2 XV208 was used by the Meteorological Research Flight at Farnborough equipped with a long instrument probe in the nose and a variety of other sensors.

It carried out this role until 2001.

Puma HC.1 XW208 of No.33 Squadron whose badge is carried on the entrance door.

As a result of the Anglo-French Helicopter Agreement, the Puma was built in Britain by Westland for the Royal Air Force.

Nine Hawker-Siddeley Harrier GR.1s/GR.1As delivered between November 1971 and June 1972 by HSA Kingston to Contract KC/3G/54

XW916	20/3/4/3/Cv GR.3/ 20/4/233 OCU/ MoD(PE)/4/ 233 OCU	Abandoned after electrical failure on approach, Yeovilton, 17.6.86
XW917	4/3/4/3/Cv to GR.3/3	To 8975M 30.4.88 at Gutersloh
XW918	4	Abandoned out of control in cloud and dived into ground, Tuschenbroich, West Germany, 12.1.72
XW919	233 OCU/1/Cv GR.3/ 1/MoD(PE)/1/4/1/4	To GI airframe 4.90 at Cosford later to RN as A2609(2)
XW920	20/3	Engine lost power; abandoned over Cape Frasca ranges, Sardinia, 20.6.72
XW921	20/4/Cv GR.3/4/233 OCU/1417 Flt/233 OCU/4/3/4/3	Engine caught fire after take-off; abandoned and crashed in wood 1½m N of Gutersloh, 18.8.88
XW922	233 OCU/1/233 OCU/ Cv GR.3/233 OCU 1/233 OCU	Rolled while making vertical landing, Wittering, 19.11.85; to 8885M 19.2.86 with MoD(PE)
XW923	1/Cv GR.3/1/ 233 OCU/1417 Flt	Failed to gain height on vertical take-off; abandoned and hit trees, Belize Airport, 26.5.81; nose to 8724M at Wittering
XW924	20/420//Cv GR.3/4/ 233 OCU/1/233 OCU/1/3/1/4/3/4	To 9073M at Halton

* * * * * * * * * *

Three Hawker-Siddeley Harrier T.2s delivered between February 1972 and July 1972 by HSA Kingston to Contract KC/3G/54

XW925	233 OCU/Cv T.4/233 OCU/1/233 OCU/ 4/233 OCU/4/233 OCU/4	Control lost on overshoot from vertical landing; abandoned, Gutersloh, 20.6.89
XW926	3/20/3/Cv T.4/3/20/3/ 20/3/233 OCU	Collided with XV795 and crashed, Eye, near Peterborough, 23.2.83
XW927	233 OCU/Cv T.4/233 OCU/SF Wittering/ 4/233 OCU/3/ SF Gutersloh/4/ SF Gutersloh	Damaged in heavy landing, Gutersloh, 7.2.92; not repaired

* * * * * * * * * *

XW930		DH.125 Srs 1B G-ATPC for RAE to Contract CR/O/0585

* * * * * * * * * *

Two Hawker-Siddeley Harrier T.4s delivered in August and December 1973 to Contract KC/3G/33

XW933	3/4/20/3/20/3/4/3	Collided with F-104G 26+70 and abandoned, Bad Rothenfelde, West Germany, 18.2.85
XW934	1/233 OCU/1/233 OCU/Yeovilton/233 OCU/AAEE/233 OCU/1/AAEE/1/SF Gutersloh/233 OCU/ 20R/DRA	To GI airframe at Farnborough by 1.97

* * * * * * * * * *

XW938		Piper Twin Comanche G-ATMT acquired in January 1971 for College of Aeronautics; reverted to G-ATMT 22.5.75

XW941 - XW980		Northrop Shelduck D.1 drones to Contract K20C/97

* * * * * * * * * *

Slingsby T-61A Venture T.1 purchased in March 1971 ex G-AYUP to Contract K20C/85

XW983	AAEE/2 GS/ACCGS	To RAFGSA as G-AYUP; reverted to G-AYUP 9.12.80

* * * * * * * * * *

Three Hawker-Siddeley Buccaneer S.2Bs delivered to Ministry of Defence (PE) by HSA Brough to Contract K58A/316

XW986	RAE/DRA	To GI airframe 4.93
XW987	RAE/AAEE	Sold; to S Africa as ZU-BCR
XW988	RAE/AAEE	Sold; to S Africa as ZU-AVI
XW989	-	Cancelled

* * * * * * * * * *

XW990 - XW999		Northrop Chukar D.1 drones to Contract K20C/115
XX101, XX102		Cushioncraft CC-7s for trials to Contract K5B/3A/135
XX105		BAC One-Eleven Srs 201 G-ASJD acquired for RAE Bedford to Contract K10A/49

* * * * * * * * * *

Fifteen Sepecat Jaguar GR.1s, later modified to GR.1As, delivered between October 1972 and February 1974 by BAC Preston to Contract KD/3G/32

XX108	AAEE/DERA	To G-27-313 for BAe; cv GR.3
XX109	AAEE	To 8918M 17.10.86 at Coltishall
XX110	Mkrs/AAEE/6/226 OCU/6/41/6	To 8955M 3.12.87 at Cosford
XX111	JCT/JOCU/226 OCU	To BAe 3.4.79 for Indian AF as J1011
XX112	AAEE/54/6/41/6/ Cv GR.3A/6	
XX113	AAEE/226 OCU/ 41/226 OCU	Power controls jammed; abandoned out of control 1m SE of Great Malvern, Worcs., 17.7.81
XX114	JCT/JOCU/226 OCU/41/226 OCU	Flew into birds on approach and abandoned after engines lost power, Lossiemouth, 19.9.83
XX115	JCT/JOCU/226 OCU	To BAe 22.12.78 for Indian AF as J1005; retd to RAF 23.7.82
	226 OCU	To 8821M 20.6.84 at Halton
XX116	JCT/JOCU/226 OCU	To BAe 23.2.79 for Indian AF as J1008; retd to RAF 5.85
	6/226 OCU/16R/ Cv GR.1B/6Cv GR.3A/DERA	
XX117	JCT/JOCU/226 OCU	To BAe 6.12.78 for Indian AF as J1004; retd to RAF 3.12.84
	54/6/54/226 OCU/ RAE/DRA/6/16R/ Cv GR.3A	
XX118	JCT/JOCU/226 OCU/ SF Lossiemouth/6	To BAe 4.9.79 for Indian AF as J1018; retd to RAF 2.6.82
	6	To 8815M 27.3.84 at Halton
XX119	JCT/JOCU/226 OCU/ 54/17/54/6/54/AAEE/ 226 OCU/16R/54/ Cv GR.3	8898M NTU

Jaguar

XX120	JOCU/226 OCU/54	Control lost in low cloud; flew into sea off Samso Is, Denmark, 17.9.76
XX121	JOCU/54&6/226 OCU/54/6	Sale to Ecuador 7.91 NTU; preserved at Charlwood
XX122	JOCU/226 OCU/54/ 6/54/17/54/6/54/6/ 54	Flew into sea during low run over The Wash off Heacham, Norfolk, 2.4.82

* * * * * * * * * *

15 Sepecat Jaguar T.2s/T.2As delivered between June 1973 and May 1974 by BAC Preston to Contract KD/3G/32

XX136	AAEE	Abandoned after engine fire on test flight, Wimborne St.Giles, Dorset, 22.11.74
XX137	JCT/JOCU/226 OCU	Abandoned and crashed in sea after turbine failure 4m off Lossiemouth, Moray, 6.2.76
XX138	JCT/JOCU/226 OCU	To BAe 6.12.78 for Indian AF as J1001; retd and to Oman AF as No.200
XX139	JCT/JOCU/226 OCU/ 54/6/226 OCU/16R/ Cv T.4/DERA/16R	
XX140	JCT/JOCU/54/226 OCU	To 9008M at Cosford
XX141	JOCU/226 OCU/6/ 226 OCU/16R/6	To GI airframe at Cranwell
XX142	JOCU/226 OCU	Control lost after roll; yawed and dived into sea 10m N of Lossiemouth, 22.6.79
XX143	JOCU/226 OCU	To BAe 6.12.78 for Indian AF as J1002; retd to RAF 23.9.82
	226 OCU/16R/54	Engine surged after take-off; lost height and abandoned ½m off Lossiemouth, 18.9.96
XX144	JOCU/226 OCU/ 6/226 OCU/16R	
XX145	JOCU/226 OCU/31/ 226 OCU/ETPS/ 226 OCU/	To ETPS 10.3.86
XX146	JOCU/226 OCU/6/ SF Coltishall/6/41/ 54/41/6/54/6/54/ 41/6/54/6/226 OCU/ 41/54/6/41/6/41/6/ 54/6/41/6/54/6/41/ 6/54/6/54/6/41/6/ 41/54/6/41/16R/ SAOEU/54	
XX147	JOCU/226 OCU/ RAFC/2/17/14/17	Hit bird and engine temperature rose; abandoned, Sudlohn, 14m W of Coesfeld, West Germany, 26.3.79
XX148	JOCU/226 OCU	Flew into ground during dummy attack near Whittingham, Northumberland, 29.7.77
XX149	JOCU/226 OCU	Dived into ground inverted out of cloud near Cullen, Grampian, 27.4.78
XX150	6/226 OCU/54/20/ 31/14/31/20/14/31/ 17/31/14226 OCU/ 16R/DERA/16R	

* * * * * * * * * *

XX153		Lynx AH.1 for Army Air Corps to Contract K21A/13

* * * * * * * * * *

One prototype and 175 production Hawker-Siddeley Hawk T.1s delivered between November 1977 and February 1982 by HSA Kingston to Contract K87A/02; progressively converted to T.1A

XX154	Mkrs/RAE/DRA/TEE Llanbedr	To ETPS 10.00
XX156	AAEE/BAe/RAE/ AAEE/DRA/DTEO/ 19R/CFS(RA)	
XX157	AAEE/1 TWU/ 2 TWU/63/ 7 FTS/92R 208R	To FRADU 4.2.95; retd
XX158	2 TWU/19R/208R/ CFS	
XX159	AAEE/1 TWU/ 4 FTS/74R/CFS/ 19R/208R	
XX160	RAE/DRA/TEE Llanbedr/208R/ 19R/208R	
XX161	CFS/4 FTS/CFS/ 4 FTS/CFS(RA)/ 234R/208R/19R	
XX162	CFS/4 FTS/74R/ IAVM/S of AM	
XX163	CFS/4 FTS/CFS	Lost height after simulating engine failure on take-off; flew into ground and abandoned, Valley, 1.7.93; to 9243M
XX164	CFS/4 FTS/100/74R	Aileron controls unconnected; rolled into ground after take-off and abandoned, Valley, 13.2.96
XX165	CFS/4 FTS/CFS/ 74R/CFS 4 FTS	To Royal Navy 5.94; retd to RAF
XX166	CFS/4 FTS	Flew into high ground in cloud, Clagh Ouyr, North Barrule, Isle of Man, 24.6.83
XX167	4 FTS/MoD(PE)/ 4 FTS/92R/74R/19R	
XX168	4 FTS/74R/6 FTS/ 100	
XX169	4 FTS/234R/6 FTS/ 74R/19R	
XX170	4 FTS/CFS/234R/ TEE Llanbedr/208R	To FRADU 1.12.00
XX171	4 FTS/CFS/74R/ 208R/19R	To FRADU
XX172	4 FTS/234R/SF St. Athan/4 FTS/19R	
XX173	4 FTS/6 FTS	
XX174	4 FTS/74R/19R/ 6 FTS/19R	
XX175	4 FTS/CFS/19R 208R	To Royal Navy 5.94; retd to RAF
XX176	4 FTS/CFS/19R/ 92R/100/208R	
XX177	4 FTS/2 TWU/ CFS/4 FTS/ 234R/100/ 74R/208R	
XX178	4 FTS/234R/92R/ 19R	
XX179	4 FTS/92R/74R/ 19R/74R/19R	
XX180	4 FTS	Abandoned after hitting birds on take-off and engine lost power, Mona, 7.11.84
XX181	4 FTS/CFS/1 TWU/ BAe/1 TWU/100/ 208R/19R/208R	
XX182	4 FTS	Collided with XX291 and abandoned, Borth, Dyfed, 14.6.89

XX183	4 FTS/234R 208R	To Royal Navy 5.94; retd to RAF
XX184	4 FTS/CFS/4 FTS/ SF St.Athan	
XX185	4 FTS/19R/6 FTS/ 208R	
XX186	TWU/1 TWU/ 2 TWU/Cv T.1A/ 2 TWU/19R/ 208R/19R/74R	Controls jammed; abandoned over sea 20m off Valley, 30.4.98
XX187	TWU/1 TWU/ 2 TWU/Cv T.1A/ 2 TWU/1 TWU/ 4 FTS/CFS/ 6 FTS/74R	
XX188	TWU/1 TWU/ 100/74R	
XX189	TWU/1 TWU/ 2 TWU/7 FTS/ 4 FTS/74R	
XX190	TWU/1 TWU/ 2 TWU/1 TWU/ 74R/4 FTS/ 74R/208R	
XX191	TWU/1 TWU/ 234R/208R	
XX192	TWU/1 TWU	Lost power on take-off and flew into ground on approach, Brawdy, 20.9.89
XX193	TWU/1 TWU/74R/ 100	Dived into ground in turn and hit barn, Shap, Cumbria, 22.10.99
XX194	TWU/1 TWU/74R/ 100	
XX195	TWU/1 TWU/ 2 TWU/100/208R/ 19R/4 FTS/208R	
XX196	TWU/1 TWU/ 2 TWU/1 TWU/ 4 FTS/234R/ 208R	
XX197	TWU/1 TWU	Ingested bird on take-off from Brawdy and engine flamed out; abandoned and crashed, Newgale Sands, 13.5.88
XX198	TWU/1 TWU/ 2 TWU/1 TWU/ 234R/208R/19R	
XX199	TWU/1 TWU/ 2 TWU/1 TWU/ 74R	
XX200	TWU/1 TWU/ 2 TWU/1 TWU/ 234R/CFS/19R/ 100	
XX201	TWU/1 TWU/ 2 TWU/92R	
XX202	TWU/1 TWU/ 2 TWU/92R/19R	
XX203	TWU/1 TWU/ 2 TWU/4 FTS/ CFS/19R/74R/19R	
XX204	TWU/1 TWU/ 2 TWU/92R/ BAe/208R	
XX205	TWU/1 TWU/ 2 TWU/92R	To FRADU
XX217	TWU/1 TWU/ AAEE/1 TWU/ 2 TWU/RAE/ 2 TWU/RAE/ 2 TWU/19R/100	
XX218	TWU/1 TWU/ 234R/74R/208R/ 19R	
XX219	1 TWU/2 TWU/ 19R/100	
XX220	TWU/1 TWU/ CFS/19R	To FRADU
XX221	TWU/1 TWU/234R/ 208R/74R	
XX222	TWU/1 TWU/74R/ 208R/100	
XX223	4 FTS	Tyre burst on landing; swung off runway and abandoned, Valley, 7.7.86
XX224	4 FTS/CFS/4 FTS/ 74R/CFS/19R	
XX225	4 FTS/19R/208R	
XX226	4 FTS/74R/CFS/ 74R/100	
XX227	CFS(RA)	
XX228	1 TWU/2 TWU/100	
XX229	1 TWU/2 TWU/ 1 TWU	Abandoned after engine flamed out at low altitude 45m SW of Brawdy, 29.7.83
XX230	1 TWU/2 TWU/ 19R/74R	
XX231	4 FTS/RAE Llanbedr/ 4 FTS/92R/FRS.2 OEU/19R/92R/ 19R/74R	To FRADU 20.11.00
XX232	4 FTS/74R/6 FTS/ 19R	
XX233	4 FTS/CFS/4 FTS/ CFS	
XX234	4 FTS/74R/234R 208R	To Royal Navy 5.94; retd to RAF
XX235	4 FTS/CFS/74R/ 19R/208R/19R/ 208R	
XX236	4 FTS/234R/CFS/ 19R	
XX237	4 FTS/CFS(RA)	
XX238	4 FTS/CFS/7 FTS/ CFS/6 FTS/19R/ 74R/19R	
XX239	4 FTS/CFS/19R/ 208R/74R/208R/ 74R/19R/BAe	
XX240	4 FTS/6 FTS/74R/ 19R	
XX241	4 FTS/CFS(RA)	Air brake failed; collided with XX259 during display practice and abandoned 5m E of Scampton, 16.11.87
XX242	4 FTS/92R	To Royal Navy 5.94
XX243	4 FTS/CFS(RA)	Rolled and hit ground during formation aerobatic practice, Scampton, 22.1.88
XX244	4 FTS/234R/208R/ 74R/208R	
XX245	4 FTS/19R 208R	To Royal Navy 5.94; retd to RAF
XX246	1 TWU/2 TWU/19R/ 208R/74R	
XX247	1 TWU/2 TWU/ 1 TWU/100	
XX248	1 TWU/2 TWU/ 1 TWU/100	
XX249	4 FTS/CFS/4 FTS/ 100/CFS/234R/ 208R/19R/208R	
XX250	4 FTS/CFS/4 FTS/ 6 FTS/100/208R/ 100	

XX251	CFS(RA)	Hit ground recovering from loop and ejector seat fired, Akrotiri, 21.3.84
XX252	CFS(RA)	Lost height in turn on approach and abandoned, Cranwell, 17.11.98
XX253	CFS(RA)	
XX254	1 TWU/2 TWU/19R	To BAe Brough for fatigue tests, 1.11.94
XX255	1 TWU/2 TWU/ 7 FTS/4 FTS/ 74R/ETPS	To FRADU 11.97
XX256	1 TWU/2 TWU/19R/ 74R	
XX257	CFS(RA)	Abandoned after compressor failure during display 3m off Sidmouth, Devon, 31.8.84
XX258	1 TWU/CFS/19R/ 74R	
XX259	CFS(RA)	Collided with XX241 during formation aerobatics 5m E of Scampton; abandoned and crashed, Welton, Lincs., 16.11.87
XX260	CFS(RA)	
XX261	1 TWU/234R/208R/ 19R/100/208R	
XX262	CFS(RA)	Hit mast of yacht during display off Brighton; rolled and abandoned, 17.5.80
XX263	1 TWU/2 TWU/19R	
XX264	CFS(RA)	
XX265	1 TWU/2 TWU/92R/ 100	
XX266	CFS(RA)	
XX278	2 TWU/19R/100/19R	
XX279	1 TWU/2 TWU	Abandoned after loss of control and crashed in sea 7m off Lynton, Devon, 30.1.85
XX280	1 TWU/92R/234R/ 6 FTS/19R	
XX281	1 TWU/2 TWU/92R 19R	To FRADU 2.95; retd to RAF
XX282	1 TWU/2 TWU/19R/ 100/19R/100	Bird hit cockpit; abandoned near Lowick, Northumberland, 18.10.00
XX283	1 TWU/2 TWU/100/ 208R	
XX284	1 TWU/2 TWU/100/ 208R	
XX285	1 TWU/2 TWU/100	
XX286	1 TWU/19R/234R/ 208R	
XX287	1 TWU/2 TWU/ 7 FTS/92R/208R	
XX288	1 TWU/2 TWU/ 1 TWU/100/234R/ 208R	Veered off runway and hit rocks; abandoned, Mona, 10.8.95
XX289	1 TWU/2 TWU/ 19R/100	
XX290	4 FTS/CFS(RA)/ 4 FTS/234R/100/ 208R	
XX291	4 FTS	Collided with XX182 and crashed, Borth, Dyfed, 14.6.89
XX292	4 FTS/92R/19R/ CFS(RA)	
XX293	4 FTS	Abandoned after canopy blew off on take-off from Wattisham and crashed, Nedging Tye, Suffolk, 17.4.85
XX294	4 FTS/CFS(RA)	
XX295	4 FTS/6 FTS/208R	
XX296	4 FTS/74R/208R	
XX297	4 FTS/CFS/4 FTS/ CFS	Engine flamed out during aerobatics; flew into ground and abandoned on approach, Scampton, 3.11.86; to 8933M 5.2.87 at Finningley
XX298	4 FTS	Abandoned after controls seized up; crashed in Tremadoc Bay, Gwynedd, 25.10.84
XX299	4 FTS/7 FTS/92R/ 74R/208R/19R/100	
XX300	1 TWU/2 TWU	Lost power due to bird ingestion on night approach and abandoned, Chivenor, 20.10.82; to 8827M 28.2.84 at Abingdon
XX301	1 TWU/2 TWU/ 92R/19R	
XX302	1 TWU/74R	Collided with Portuguese F-16B 15120 during dummy attack on Beja airfield and abandoned, 26.5.96
XX303	1 TWU/74R/CFS/ 19R/74R	
XX304	CFS(RA)	Sank back on take-off, hit ground and caught fire; abandoned, Scampton, 24.6.88
XX305	4 FTS	Stalled on emergency approach and abandoned, Valley, 28.7.82
XX306	4 FTS/CFS(RA)	
XX307	4 FTS/CFS(RA)	
XX308	4 FTS/CFS(RA)	
XX309	4 FTS/234R/ 6 FTS/19R	
XX310	4 FTS/74R/CFS/ 19R/208R	
XX311	4 FTS/CFS/4 FTS/ 92R/FRADU/19R	
XX312	4 FTS/1 TWU/100/ 74R/19R	
XX313	4 FTS/7 FTS/19R/ CFS/19R/74R/208R	
XX314	4 FTS/2 TWU/ 4 FTS/74R/208R/ 100	
XX315	1 TWU/234R/208R	
XX316	1 TWU/234R/74R/ 234R/208R/74R	
XX317	1 TWU/4 FTS/ 234R/208R/74R/ 100	
XX318	1 TWU/CFS/ 19R/74R/19R	
XX319	1 TWU/74R/ 19R/100	
XX320	1 TWU/2 TWU/ 19R/100	
XX321	1 TWU/2 TWU/19R/ 208R/19R/100	
XX322	1 TWU/2 TWU/92R 74R	To Royal Navy 17.10.94; retd to RAF
XX323	1 TWU/74R/BAe/ 19R	
XX324	1 TWU/4 FTS/ 234R/208R/19R	
XX325	1 TWU/2 TWU/100/ 19R	
XX326	2 TWU/92R/19R	
XX327	2 TWU/RAE/	
_____	2 TWU/IAVM/ DRA/IAvM/ S of AM	
XX329	2 TWU/92R/19R/ 74R	

Hawk

XX330	2 TWU/92R/208R/19R/100	
XX331	2 TWU/100	
XX332	2 TWU/92R/74R/19R/74R	
XX333	2 TWU	Collided with XX340 during attack on Phantom and abandoned, Decimomannu ranges, Sardinia, 26.9.85
XX334	2 TWU/19R	Control lost on approach after practice engine shut-down; abandoned, Chivenor, 30.9.92; DBF
XX335	2 TWU/92R/19R/100	
XX336	2 TWU	Collided with XX353 near Bude and abandoned after power lost on approach, Chivenor, 29.7.83
XX337	2 TWU/92R	To FRADU 17.10.94
XX338	BAe/4 FTS/7 FTS/19R/208R/19R	
XX339	BAe/AAEE/1 TWU/74R/CFS/19R/74R/208R/19R	
XX340	2 TWU	Collided with XX333 during attack on Phantom and abandoned, Decimomannu ranges, Sardinia, 26.9.85
XX341	1 TWU/ETPS/Cranfield I of Tech/AAEE/ETPS	
XX342	ETPS	
XX343	ETPS	Ran off runway take-off into trees; abandoned, Boscombe Down, 8.4.97
XX344	RAE	Hit vortex on approach and rolled into runway, Bedford, 7.1.82; to 8847M
XX345	2 TWU/19R/208R/74R/BAe	
XX346	2 TWU/19R	To FRADU 11.94
XX347	CFS/4 FTS	Control lost after take-off; abandoned, Valley, 9.5.90
XX348	2 TWU/1 TWU/2 TWU/1 TWU/234R/74R	
XX349	4 FTS/2 TWU/7 FTS/100/4 FTS/74R/19R/208R/100	
XX350	1 TWU/74R	
XX351	1 TWU/234R/208R/19R/100	
XX352	2 TWU/19R/100	
XX353	2 TWU	Collided with XX336 in tail-chase near Bude and abandoned, Holsworthy, Devon, 29.7.83

*   *   *   *   *   *   *   *   *   *

Bristol Britannia 312F purchased in April 1972 to Contract K49A/125

XX367	AAEE	Ex EC-BSY; SOC 26.9.83 and sold as 9Q-CHY

*   *   *   *   *   *   *   *   *   *

XX370 - XX419; XX431 - XX462	Westland Gazelles for Royal Navy, Army Air Corps and Royal Air Force to Contract 70.71082.00

Four Hiller HT.3s to Royal Air Force

XX374	CFS/2 FTS	Flew into Snowdon during aerobatics and fell into valley, Llyn Teyrn, Gwynedd, 20.4.83
XX382	CFS/2 FTS/DHFS	
XX396	CFS/2 FTS	Tail rotor hit ground in heavy landing, Shawbury, 30.6.81; to 8718M 9.11.81 as display aircraft at Abingdon
XX406	CFS/2 FTS/7	

*   *   *   *   *   *   *   *   *   *

Two Hawker Hunter T.7s transferred from Royal Jordanian Air Force in May 1972 to Contract AV/7A/SM38

XX466	228 OCU/2 TWU/IAVM/1 TWU	Ex-No.835 and XL620 to Royal Navy 2.84 as A2738
XX467	MoD(PE)/229 OCU/2 TWU/1 TWU	Ex-No.836 and XL645; to AST 13.10.83 as GI airframe

*   *   *   *   *   *   *   *   *   *

XX469		Lynx HAS.2 for Royal Navy to Contract K21A/13

*   *   *   *   *   *   *   *   *   *

26 Scottish Aviation Jetstream T.1s delivered between August 1973 and October 1976 by Scottish Aviation, Prestwick, to Contract K/10A/92

XX475	AAEE/Mkrs	Sold 11.9.75 to Scottish Avn; to Royal Navy
XX476	Hdlg Sqn/AAEE/CFS	To Royal Navy 29.10.76
XX477	CFS	Ex G-AXXS. Both engines lost power on take-off from roller landing; crashlanded, Little Rissington, 1.11.74; fuselage to 8462M at Finningley
XX478	CFS	Ex G-AXXT. To Royal Navy, 29.10.76
XX479	5 FTS/CFS	Ex G-AXUR. To Royal Navy, 29.10.76
XX480	CFS	Ex G-AXXU. To Royal Navy, 29.10.76
XX481	5 FTS	Ex G-AXUP. To Royal Navy, 29.10.76
XX482	CFS/5 FTS/3 FTS/6 FTS/45R/3 FTS/45R	To RN 29.10.76; retd to RAF
XX483	5 FTS/CFS	To Royal Navy 29.10.76
XX484	5 FTS/CFS	To Royal Navy 29.10.76
XX485	5 FTS/CFS	To Royal Navy 29.10.76
XX486	5 FTS/CFS	To Royal Navy 29.10.76
XX487	-	To Royal Navy 29.10.76
XX488	Mkrs/METS	MoD(PE) aircraft
XX489	-	To Royal Navy 29.10.76
XX490	-	To Royal Navy 29.10.76
XX491	METS/6 FTS/45R/3 FTS/45R	
XX492	METS/6 FTS/45R/3 FTS/45R	
XX493	AAEE & Mkrs/METS/6 FTS/45R/3 FTS/45R	
XX494	METS/6 FTS/BAe/6 FTS/45R/3 FTS/45R	
XX495	METS/6 FTS/45R/3 FTS/45R	
XX496	METS/6 FTS/45R/3 FTS/45R	
XX497	METS/6 FTS/45R/3 FTS/45R	

XX498	METS/6 FTS/45R/ 3 FTS/45R	
XX499	METS/6 FTS/45R/ 3 FTS/45R	
XX500	METS/6 FTS/45R/ 3 FTS/45R	

*   *   *   *   *   *   *   *   *   *

**Two Hawker-Siddeley HS.125 CC.1s delivered in September and
October 1972 by HSA, Hatfield, to Contract KA/C/192**

XX505	32	Ex G-5-17; returned to HSA 22.5.73; became G-BAZB
XX506	32	Ex G-BABL; returned to HSA, 30.4.73; reverted to G-BABL

*   *   *   *   *   *   *   *   *   *

**Two Hawker-Siddeley HS.125 CC.2s delivered in April 1973 by HSA,
Hatfield, to Contract KA/C/193**

XX507	32	Sold; to USA 13.12.98 as N606TS
XX508	32	Sold; to USA 23.9.98 as N256WJ

*   *   *   *   *   *   *   *   *   *

XX510		Lynx HAS.2 prototype to Contract K2/A/13; to RN as A2683 at Gosport

*   *   *   *   *   *   *   *   *   *

**130 Scottish Aviation Bulldog T.1s delivered between February 1973
and August 1975 by Scottish Aviation, Prestwick, to Contract
KA/C/147**

XX513	S'ton UAS/6 FTS/ AAEE/5 MU/ Leeming/1 FTS/ CFS/3 FTS/N'umb UAS/3 FTS/CFS	
XX514	CFS/Leeming/ 1 FTS	Hit tree avoiding bird during practice forced landing and crashed, Knayton, Yorks., 29.9.86
XX515	CGS/Leeming/CFS/ N'umb UAS/ RAFCAS/3 FTS/ M&S UAS/L'pool UAS	
XX516	CFS/Leeming/ 1 FTS/CFS/CUAS/ Bristol UAS	
XX517	CFS/Leeming/ CFS/1 FTS	Abandoned after control lost in cloud during aerobatics, Great Langton, N.Yorks., 25.4.89
XX518	CFS/RNEFTS/ CUAS/OUAS/ CUAS/S'ton UAS/CUAS/L&M UAS	
XX519	CFS/RNEFTS/ CUAS/RNEFTS/ 1 FTS/RAFCAS/ 3 FTS/CFS	To USA 15.9.00
XX520	CFS/2 FTS/YUAS/ RNEFTS/CFS/ EMUAS	Damaged in heavy landing, Newton, 10.98; to storage
XX521	2 FTS/E Lowlands UAS/B'ham UAS	
XX522	CFS/RNEFTS/ 1 FTS/HQ UAS/ RAFCAS/CFS/ 3 FTS/ELUAS	

XX523	CFS/RNEFTS/ QUAS/RNEFTS/ 1 FTS/L'pool UAS/ OUAS	Sold; to G-BZFM 18.4.00
XX524	CFS/London UAS/ CFS	
XX525	RNEFTS/ELUAS/ GUAS/S'ton UAS	
XX526	CFS/RNEFTS/ OUAS	
XX527	CFS/2 FTS/N'umb UAS/RNEFTS/ 1 FTS/N'umb UAS/ QUAS/ADStA UAS/ ELUAS	Sold; to USA 15.9.00 as N527BD
XX528	CFS/RNEFTS/OUAS	Sold; to G-BZON 19.12.00
XX529	CFS/RNEFTS/1 FTS/ 6 FTS/5 AEF/CUAS/ ELUAS	Sold: to G-BZOJ 11.12.00
XX530	CFS/2 FTS/OUAS/ RNEFTS	Engine cut on low level navex; flew into rising ground, Cockayne Ridge, 10m N of Helmsley, Yorks., 21.9.78
XX531	CFS/2 FTS/N'umb UAS/RNEFTS/ CFS/RNEFTS/ 1 FTS/Wales UAS/ B'ham UAS	
XX532	CFS/2 FTS/YUAS/ RNEFTS/CFS/YUAS/ 6 FTS/YUAS/CFS/ 3 FTS/CUAS/3 FTS/ CFS/L&M UAS/ CFS/L'pool UAS	
XX533	CFS/2 FTS/RNEFTS/ 1 FTS/CFS/YUAS/ 1 FTS/N'umb UAS	
XX534	CFS/RNEFTS/ ELUAS/YUAS/ B'ham UAS	
XX535	CFS/RNEFTS/ ULAS/EMUAS/ CFS/L&M UAS	
XX536	CFS/RNEFTS/CFS/ 1 FTS/M'cr UAS/ M&S UAS/L&M UAS/L'pool UAS	
XX537	CFS/2 FTS/YUAS/ RNEFTS/ELUAS/ YUAS	
XX538	CFS/RNEFTS/ EMUAS/RNEFTS/ 1 FTS/6 FTS/ 3 FTS/CFS/A&StA UAS/ELUAS/ L&M UAS/ L'pool UAS	
XX539	CFS/RNEFTS/ ELUAS/GUAS/ B'ham UAS/ CFS/L'pool UAS	
XX540	CFS/RNEFTS/OUAS/ RNEFTS/1 FTS/ RAFCAS/3 FTS/CFS	To USA 15.9.00 as N540BD
XX541	CFS/RNEFTS/ 1 FTS/B'tol UAS	To USA 21.1.01
XX542	CFS/RNEFTS	Control lost in turbulence; abandoned near Skipton-on- Swale, Yorks., 16.11.79
XX543	CFS/RNEFTS/ YUAS/6 FTS/ YUAS	
XX544	CFS/London UAS	Sold; to G-BZLR 16.8.00

XX545	CFS/London UAS	Stalled during practice engine failure on take-off and hit ground, Abingdon, 18.9.80
XX546	CFS/London UAS/ OUAS	
XX547	CFS/London UAS/ YUAS/L&M UAS/ L'pool UAS	
XX548	CFS/London UAS/ OUAS	
XX549	CFS/M'cr UAS/ 1 FTS/CFS/S'ton UAS	
XX550	CFS/ ULAS/6 AEF/ RNEFTS/N'umb UAS/ULAS/ N'umb UAS/6 FTS/ N'umb UAS	
XX551	CFS/S'ton UAS/ 6 FTS/YUAS/ 1 FTS/London UAS/OUAS	Sold; to G-BZDP 31.3.00
XX552	CFS/S'ton UAS/ ULAS/3 FTS/ULAS	
XX553	CFS/ULAS/B'ham UAS/ULAS/N'umb UAS	
XX554	CFS/ULAS/ B'ham UAS/ ULAS	Sold; to G-BZMD 18.8.00
XX555	CFS/S'ton UAS/ RNEFTS/CFS/ CUAS/L'pool UAS	
XX556	CFS/S'ton UAS/ RNEFTS/ULAS/ YUAS/ULAS/ Bristol UAS/ Wales UAS/EMUAS/ ULAS/EMUAS/ ULAS/EMUAS/ 7 AEF/EMUAS	
XX557	CFS/Glasgow UAS	Flew into trees low flying, Torres Forest, Callender, Perthshire, 11.9.75; to St Athan as PAX trainer
XX558	CFS/S'ton UAS/ B'ham UAS	
XX559	CFS/Glasgow UAS/ G&S UAS/B'ham UAS	
XX560	CFS/Glasgow UAS/ G&S UAS/Bristol UAS	
XX561	CFS/QUAS/S'ton UAS/QUAS/A&StA UAS/ADStA UAS/ 3 FTS/CFS	Sold; to G-BZEP 4.4.00
XX562 _____	CFS/Queens UAS/ 13 AEF/QUAS/ 3 FTS/CFS/ N'umb UAS	
XX611	CFS/Glasgow UAS/ G&S UAS/EMUAS. S'ton UAS	
XX612	CFS/QUAS/ RNEFTS/ S'ton UAS/Wales UAS	
XX613	CFS/QUAS	Engine cut on approach to Sydenham; forcelanded and hit wall, Comber, Co. Down, 16.10.92
XX614	CFS/M'cr UAS/CFS/ 3 FTS/OUAS/N'umb UAS	

XX615	CFS/M'cr UAS/ M&SUAS	
XX616	CFS/M'cr UAS/ CUAS	Sold; to F-AZRM 28.7.00
XX617	CFS/M'cr UAS/ 3 FTS/CFS/3 FTS	
XX618	CFS/YUAS	Control lost in spin; abandoned and spun into beach, Birkdale, Lancs., 22.7.76
XX619	CFS/YUAS/6 FTS/ YUAS/N'umb UAS	
XX620	CFS/YUAS/6 FTS/ YUAS/ELUAS	Sold 29.11.00; to USA 15.1.01 as N621BD
XX621	CFS/YUAS/6 FTS/ 9 AEF/YUAS/B'ham UAS	
XX622	CFS/YUAS/6 FTS/ YUAS/9 AEF/YUAS	
XX623	CFS/YUAS/ EMUAS	Engine cut; damaged in forced landing 2m NW of Folkestone, 26.7.95; not repaired
XX624	CFS/YUAS/RNEFTS/ YUAS/6 FTS/N'umb UAS/CUAS/Bristol UAS	
XX625	CFS/Wales UAS/ 7 AEF/CFS/N'umb UAS/CFS	
XX626	CFS/Wales UAS	To 9290M at DARA Training School 10.00
XX627	CFS/Wales UAS/ S'ton UAS	
XX628	CFS/Wales UAS/ Bristol UAS/ S'ton UAS	
XX629	CFS/N'umb UAS/ L'pool UAS/M&S UAS	
XX630 CFS	CFS/EMUAS/ L'pool UAS/3 FTS/ Sold; to G-SIJW 31.3.00	
XX631	CFS/N'umb UAS/ 9 AEF/N'umb UAS	
XX632	2 FTS/Bristol UAS/ Wales UAS/Bristol UAS/Wales UAS/ YUAS	Sold; to USA as N632BD
XX633	2 FTS/N'umb UAS	
XX634	2 FTS/CUAS/CFS/ 3 FTS/CFS/EMUAS/ M&S UAS/L'pool UAS	
XX635	2 FTS/EMUAS	To 8767M 1982 at St Athan
XX636	2 FTS/N'umb UAS	
XX637	2 FTS/N'umb UAS	To 9197M at RAF EP&TU
XX638	2 FTS/EMUAS/ RNEFTS/1 FTS/ YUAS/CFS/3 FTS/ CFS/EMUAS/CFS	
XX639	2 FTS/EMUAS/ London UAS/YUAS/ N'umb UAS	
XX640	2 FTS/Bristol YAS/ EMUAS/London UAS/EMUAS/ QUAS/Bristol UAS/ S'ton UAS	
XX653	2 FTS/Bristol UAS	To GI airframe at Boscombe Down, 2.01
XX654	2 FTS/Bristol UAS/ 3 FTSD/CFS/3 FTS/ CFS	

XX655	2 FTS/Bristol UAS	To Colerne as GI airframe 7.00
XX656	2 FTS/Bristol UAS/ CFS/Bristol UAS/ L&M UAS/L'pool UAS	
XX657	2 FTS/CUAS	Sold; to USA as spares
XX658	2 FTS/CUAS/OUAS/ CUAS/ELUAS	Sold 29.11.00; to G-BZPS 8.1.01
XX659	2 FTS/CUAS/YUAS	
XX660	2 FTS/OUAS	Control lost in spin; abandoned near Yeldon, Oxon., 25.3.85
XX661	2 FTS/OUAS/ RNEFTS/OUAS/ 3 FTS/CFS/3 FTS	
XX662	2 FTS/London UAS/ A'deen UAS	Control lost in spin; abandoned Peat Inn, Neacham, Fife, 20.2.82
XX663	2 FTS/ULAS/ A'deen UAS/ ADSt.A UAS/ ELUAS	Sold 29.11.00; to F-AZLK 26.1.01
XX664	2 FTS/ELUAS/ N'umb UAS	
XX665	2 FTS/ELUAS/ A'deen UAS/ ADStA UAS/ ELUAS/ ADSt.A UAS/ G&S UAS	Engine lost power; forcelanded in field near Balloch, Strathclyde, 20.9.97; to 2409 Sqn ATC at Halton, 11.00
XX666	2 FTS/A'deen UAS/ RNEFTS/ADSt.A UAS/1 FTS/QUAS/ ELUAS	Lost height after practice engine cut on take-off and undercarriage collapsed, Leuchars, 5.3.99; to spares
XX667	2 FTS/A'deen UAS/ ADSt.A UAS/ G & S UAS/ADSt.A UAS/RAFCAS/ 3 FTS/CFS	Sold; to G-BZFN 18.4.00
XX668	2 FTS/B'ham UAS/ RNEFTS/ 1 FTS/ Mcr UAS/M&S UAS L'pool UAS	
XX669	2 FTS/B'ham UAS/ M'cr UAS/M&S UAS	Damaged 6.9.88; to 8997M at Cosford
XX670	RNEFTS/B'ham UAS/CFS/B'ham UAS	
XX671	2 FTS/B'ham UAS	
XX672	2 FTS/B'ham UAS	
XX685	2 FTS/L'pool UAS/ EMUAS/L'pool UAS/ADSt.A UAS/ 3 FTS/CFS	Sold; to G-BZLB 15.8.00
XX686	2 FTS/L'pool UAS/ G &S UAS/OUAS/ G & S UAS/3 FTS/ CFS	To 9291M at DARA Trg School 10.00
XX687	EMUAS/3 FTS/CFS/ N'umb UAS	
XX688	L'pool UAS/Mcr UAS/ 3 FTS/CFS/3 FTS/ CFS/Mcr UAS	
XX689	2 FTS/RNEFTS/ CUAS/RNEFTS/ CFS/3 FTS/ Bristol UAS	
XX690	2 FTS/RNEFTS/ ELUAS/RNEFTS/ Yorks UAS/CFS/ 3 FTS/ULAS/ L'pool UAS	
XX691	Yorks UAS/ULAS	Sold; to Malta as 9H-ADQ 13.2.00
XX692	CFS/YUAS/Bristol UAS	Sold; to G-BZMH 21.8.00

XX693	CFS/3 FTS/ELUAS/ Bristol UAS/ELUAS	Sold; to G-BZML 1.9.00
XX694	EMUAS	
XX695	13 AEF/ULAS/ N'umb UAS/ULAS/ N'umb UAS/ULAS/ OUAS/ULAS/L&M UAS	
XX696	CFS/Wales UAS/ 3 FTS/ULAS	Sold; to Malta as 9H-ADR 13.2.00
XX697	QUAS/Bristol UAS	
XX698	RNEFTS/CFS/ 3 FTS/CFS	Sold; to G-BZME 18.8.00
XX699	RNEFTS/1 FTS/ B'ham UAS	
XX700	RNEFTS/1 FTS/ RAFCAS/3 FTS/ CUAS/CFS/S'ton UAS	
XX701	RNEFTS/ULAS/ S'ton UAS	
XX702	Glasgow UAS/G&S UAS/CFS/7 AEF/ EMUAS/L&M UAS/ L'pool UAS	
XX703	AT&DF/E Lowlands UAS	Engine cut; crashed in forced landing near Glenrothes, Fife, 3.6.76; not repaired
XX704	RNEFTS/QUAS/ EMUAS	Sold; to USA 16.9.00 as N706BD
XX705	B'ham UAS/ S'ton UAS	To GI airframe at Boscombe Down Apprentices School 4.01
XX706	6 FTS/S'ton UAS/ RNEFTS/S'ton UAS	
XX707	RNEFTS/S'ton UAS	
XX708	RNEFTS/6 FTS/ S'ton UAS	
XX709	RNEFTS/London UAS/ADSt.A UAS/ CFS/YUAS	Sold; to Malta as 9H-ADS 13.2.00
XX710	RNEFTS/London UAS/Mcr UAS/ M&S UAS	Lost power on take-off from roller landing and crashlanded, Woodvale, 21.7.97
XX711	RNEFTS/QUAS/ 13 AEF/CFS/Glasgow UAS/13 AEF/QUAS/ OUAS/L'pool UAS	
XX712	RNEFTS/N'umb UAS/RNEFTS/ M'cr UAS/1 FTS/ Mcr UAS	Flicked off turn after take-off and spun into beach, Woodvale, 2.3.88
XX713	RNEFTS/CFS/6 FTS/ Bristol UAS/S'ton UAS	
XX714	N'umb UAS/MoD (PE)/ CFS/YUAS	Sold; to Malta as 9H-ADT 13.2.00
XX715	-	Cancelled
XX716	-	Cancelled

*   *   *   *   *   *   *   *   *   *

61 Sepecat Jaguar GR.1s delivered between March 1974 and October 1975 by BAC, Preston, to Contract KD/39/40
Progressively modified to GR.1A and GR.1B

XX719	JOCU/54/6/31/54/ 14/6/41/6	To SOAF 11.8.98 as No.226
XX720	MoD(PE)/54 54/ETPS/6/54/ Cv GR.3A	To BAe 6.12.78 for Indian AF as J1003; Retd 2.84
XX721	JOCU/54/6/54	Abandoned after both engines flamed out after take-off near Hahn, West Germany, 22.6.83

XX722	JOCU/54/6/54/ 17/54/6	Fuselage to 9252M 13.6.96 at St Athan
XX723	JOCU/54/20/54/6/ 226 OCU/54/Cv GR.3A/54	
XX724	JOCU/54/6/54/6/54/ 14/54/Cv GR.3	
XX725	JOCU/54	To BAe 23.6.79 for Indian AF as J1010; retd 4.84
	6/54/Cv GR.3A/ SAOEU	
XX726	JOCU/6/54/6/31/6	To 8947M 13.9.87 at Halton
XX727	JOCU/6/54/14/54/ 17/54/6	To 8951M 13.12.87 at Cosford
XX728	JOCU/226 OCU/6	To BAe 22.12.79 for Indian AF as J1009; retd 23.7.82
	6	Collided with XX731 in formation and abandoned, Hartside Pass, 4m SW of Alston, Cumbria, 7.10.85
XX729	JOCU/226 OCU/6	To BAe 23.2.79 for Indian AF as J1012; retd 2.6.82;
	54/6/226 OCU/54/ 41/Cv GR.3/6	
XX730	JOCU/54/654/5/14/ 6/31/6	To 8952M 3.12.87 at Cosford
XX731	JOCU/54/6/54/6	Collided with XX725 and abandoned, Hartside Pass, 4m SW of Alson, Cumbria, 7.10.85
XX732	JOCU/54/SF Lossiemouth/ 54/6/226 OCU	Flew into high ground on low level exercise, Stock Hill, 11m SW of Hawick, Borders, 27.11.86
XX733	JOCU/6/54/6/ MoD(PE)/6	Reheat not selected for take-off and hit top of barrier; crashed, Coltishall, 23.1.96
XX734	JOCU/6/17/6	To BAe 27.5.79 for Indian AF as J1014; retd 2.6.82 To 8816M 21.11.84 at Coltishall
XX735	JOCU/6	Control lost after practice loft-bombing attack; flew into ground, Eggebeck, West Germany, 15.9.76
XX736	JOCU/226 OCU/6	To BAe 27.5.79 for Indian AF as J1013; retd 2.84; to 9110M at Coltishall
XX737	JOCU/226 OCU/ 54/6/54SF Lossie-mouth	To BAe 27.5.79 for Indian AF as J1015; retd 2.6.82
	6/20/6/54/Cv GR.3/ 6	
XX738	JOCU/6	To BAe 27.4.79 for Indian AF as J1016; retd 19.4.84
	54/Cv GR.3/54	
XX739	226 OCU/6/17/6/54/ 226 OCU/54/6/20/6/ 41/6/41/226 OCU/14/ 2/54/41/6	To 8902M 27.5.86 at Halton
XX740	6	To BAe 5.6.79 for Indian AF as J1017; retd 4.84; BAe 14.10.85 for sale to Oman AF 4.11.86 as No.225
XX741	54/14/54/226OCU/ 6/54/14/6/54/6/31/ 6/17/31/17/6/2/54/ 41/6/16R	
XX742	226 OCU/6/54/6/ 54/6	Abandoned after controls failed; crashed in sea 35m NNE of Coltishall, 19.4.83
XX743	6/54/6	To 8949M 3.12.87 at Halton
XX744	AAEE/17/14/17/20/ 31/17/6/54/6	To 9251M 13.6.96 at Coltishall
XX745	226 OCU/54/20/6/54/6/ 226 OCU/6/226 OCU/ 16R/6/16R/54	
XX746	226 OCU/31/6/31/6/ 17/41/17/31/6/17/14/ 6/2/54/41/14/226 OCU	To 8895M 23.5.86 at Halton
XX747	226 OCU/54/226 OCU/MoD(PE)/17/ 31/20/6/31/6/41/6/ 41/6	To 8903M 23.5.86 at Halton
XX748	226 OCU/14/41/6/14/ SF Coltishall/54/ DTEO/54/6/54/Cv GR.3A/54	
XX749	226 OCU	Collided with XX755 during formation change at low level and crashed near Lumsden, Aberdeen-shire, 10.12.79
XX750	226 OCU/14/41/ 17/31/14	Flew into ground inverted while avoiding ground radar 90m NW of Nellis AFB, Nevada, 7.2.84, while flown by 6 Sqn
XX751	14/226 OCU	To 8937M 29.5.87 at Cosford
XX752	54/226 OCU/6/54/ 6/54/6/16R/6/16R	
XX753	6/226 OCU/54 226 OCU	Nose to 9087M at Abingdon
XX754	226 OCU/54/226 OCU/14/226 OCU/ 54/41/54/6	Flew into ridge on low level exercise 100m S of Bahrain, 13.11.90
XX755	14/226 OCU/54/ 226 OCU	Collided with XX749 during turn at low level and abandoned near Lumsden, Aberdeenshire, 10.12.79
XX756	14/226 OCU/20/14/ 6/14/41/54/14/SF Coltishall/41	To 8899M 23.5.86 at Cranwell
XX757	14/226 OCU/20	To 8948M 13.9.87 at Halton
XX758	14/226 OCU	Flew into hill in snow shower Grudie Valley, 14m NNW of Dingwall, Highland, 18.11.81
XX759	14/226 OCU	Control lost at low level; dived into ground near Selkirk, Borders, 1.11.78
XX760	14/226 OCU/14	Engine caught fire in air; aband-oned, Brora, 10m NW of Dornoch, Highland, 13.9.82
XX761	14/226 OCU	Caught fire on ground during running-up, Lossiemouth, 6.6.78; nose to 8600M
XX762	14/226 OCU	Flew into Beinn a'Chleibh on low-level exercise after pilot ejected near Dalmally, Argyll, 23.11.79
XX763	226 OCU/54/226 OCU	To 9009M at St Athan
XX764	14/226 OCU	To 9010M at St Athan
XX765	14/17/226 OCU/ AAEE/BAe	ACT trials aircraft to Loughborough University
XX766	14/17/226 OCU/54/ 226 OCU/54/6/54	
XX767	14/17/226 OCU/14/ 31/17/31/14/31/17/ 226 OCU/54/Cv GR.3/DTEO/54	
XX768	14/17/31/17	Abandoned after engine caught fire 6m S of Wildenrath and crashed at Randerath, 29.9.82
———	14/17	Caught fire in air and abandoned on approach to Bruggen ½m S of Hardt, 17.7.80
XX817		
XX818	14/17/20/31/20/31/ 17/14/31	To 8945M 4.11.87 at Halton
XX819	14/17/20	To 8923M 19.12.86 at Cosford

XX820	17/31/17/20/17/31	Engine flamed out on approach; abandoned ½m E of Bruggen, 11.6.82
XX821	17/14/31/14/31/41/ 54/41/14/41	To 8896M 23.5.86 at Cosford
XX822	14	Flew into ground on low level exercise 5m NW of Cloppenburg, 2.7.76
XX823	17	Flew into hill after control lost during aerobatics near Cagliari, Sardinia, 25.7.78
XX824	14/17/14/17/31/ 17/14	To 9019M 1.90 at Halton
XX825	14/31/17/20/31/17	To 9020M 1.90 at Halton
XX826	14/20/2	To 9021M 1.90 at Cosford
XX827	14/20/17	Rolled and flew into ground during low level exercise, Nellis ranges, Nevada, 12.2.81

* * * * * * * * * *

20 Sepecat Jaguar T.2s/T.2As delivered between November 1974 and November 1975 by BAC, Preston, to Contract KD/3G/40

XX828	226 OCU	Engines lost power due to bird-strike; abandoned and crashed, Tullo Hill, 8m NE of Kirriemuir, Tayside, 1.6.81
XX829	54/41/54/6/54/6/54/6/ 226 OCU/6/AAEE/6/ 16R/54	
XX830	226 OCU/AAEE/ ETPS	
XX831	MoD(PE)/226 OCU	Abandoned after controls jammed during low run while inverted, Lossiemouth, 30.4.75
XX832	226 OCU/ETPS/ 226 OCU/16R/6	
XX833	226 OCU/20/31/ 20/14/20/14/31/14/ 41/RAE/SAOEU	
XX834	226 OCU/2/6	Flew into HT wires, rolled and abandoned near Wildbad-Kreuth, 15m SSE of Karlsruhe, West Germany, 7.9.88
XX835	226 OCU/RAE/ Cv T.4/DRA/41/ 6/41	
XX836	14/31/14/17/2/17/ 2/17/6/41/6/226 OCU/14/17/6	
XX837	226 OCU/41/ 226 OCU	To 8978M 29.9.88 at Halton
XX838	226 OCU/17/Cv T.4/ 226 OCU/16R	
XX839	226 OCU/16R/41/54	To 9256M 20.9.96 at St Athan
XX840	14/17/226 OCU/2/ 41/Cv T.4/16R	
XX841	226 OCU/41/Cv T.4/ ETPS/6	
XX842	54/41/54/41/2/6/ 41/Cv T.4/ETPS/6/ 41/16R	
XX843	226 OCU/2/226 OCU/2/226 OCU/ 2/41/54	Collided with Cessna 152 G-BMHI and abandoned, Carno, Powys, 29.8.91
XX844	14/31/2/31/17/ 226 OCU/AAEE	To 9023M 1.90 at Cosford
XX845	17/2/14/17/31/17/ 31/17/14/2/Cv T.4/ 226OCU/41/54/ 16R/6/54/6	

XX846	226 OCU/2/226 OCU/6/226 OCU/ Cv T.4/RAE/226 OCU/41/16R/41/ 16R	
XX847	226 OCU/6/54/6/ 226 OCU//14/226 OCU/17/14/31/14/ 20/14/Cv T.4/226 OCU/41	

* * * * * * * * * *

XX850 - XX879		Shelduck D.1 drones to Contract K/GU416/186

* * * * * * * * * *

17 Hawker-Siddeley Buccaneer S.2Bs delivered between April 1974 and January May 1977 by HSA, Holme, to Contract K58A/316

XX885	16/15/12/216/208/ 12/208/12/208/12	To 9225M 25.11.93 at Lossiemouth
XX886	16/216	To GI airframe at Honington
XX887	RAE/15/16	SOC 10.91
XX888	RAE/15/16	SOC 10.91
XX889	16/15/16/12/208/ 237 OCU/12/208/ 237 OCU/12/237 OCU/12	Preserved at Staverton
XX890	15	Control lost on approach after turbine failure; abandoned, Laarbruch, 18.8.77
XX891	15/208/15/16	Stalled on approach and abandoned 4m NE of Laarbruch, 11.8.83
XX892	16/15/16/208/16/12/ 237 OCU/12/237 OCU/12/208	SOC
XX893	16/12/16/15/16/ 237 OCU/208/237 OCU/208	SS 4.94
XX894	15/16/AAEE/12/208/ 12/208/12/237 OCU/ 208	SOC .94; preserved at Kemble
XX895	12/208/15/16/237 OCU/12/237 OCU/ 12/237 OCU/12/ 237 OCU/12/208	SOC; preserved in Woking 13.1.95
XX896	12	SS 10.91
XX897	-	Sold to MoD(PE) 1.5.77
XX898	12/208/12	Abandoned after loss of power on night approach to Lossiemouth, Duffus, Grampian, 17.6.82
XX899	208/12/208/15/16/ 237 OCU/12/237 OCU/12/237 OCU/ 208	SS 10.94; nose preserved at Coventry
XX900	208/216/12/208/SF Lossiemouth/208/ 12/237 OCU/12/ 208	Preserved at Bruntingthorpe
XX901	208/12/237 OCU/ 208	To Gloucestershire Avn Collection 1.95

* * * * * * * * * *

XX904		Lynx HAS.2 for French Navy to Contract KA25A/04
XX907		Lynx AH.1 prototype to Contract KZ/A/14

XX910		Lynx HAS.2 prototype to Contract KZ/A/7
XX911		Lynx HAS.2 for French Navy to Contract KZ/A/7

*   *   *   *   *   *   *   *   *   *

Vickers VC.10 purchased by Ministry of Technology in February 1973 to Contract KA/16/150

XX914	RAE	Ex G-ATDJ; to 8777M at Brize Norton

*   *   *   *   *   *   *   *   *   *

Two Sepecat Jaguar T.2s delivered in July 1976 by BAC Warton, to Contract KD/3G/40

XX915	ETPS	Hydraulics failed; abandoned on approach to Boscombe Down and crashed, Porton Down, Wilts., 17.1.84
XX916	ETPS	Lost power after birdstrike; abandoned off Hartland Point, North Devon, 24.7.81

*   *   *   *   *   *   *   *   *   *

BAC One-Eleven 402AP delivered in May 1974 for RAE to Contract KA1B/149

XX919	RAE/DRA	Ex PI-C-1121; scrapped 6.7.00

*   *   *   *   *   *   *   *   *   *

XX923 - XX941		Shelduck D.1 drones to Contract KGW416/186

*   *   *   *   *   *   *   *   *   *

de Havilland Comet 4 delivered in July 1973 for RAE to Contract KA1c/228

XX944	RAE	Ex G-APDP; to GI airframe at Farnborough 4.75

*   *   *   *   *   *   *   *   *   *

Four Panavia Tornado prototypes delivered by BAC, Preston, to Ministry of Technology

XX946	Mkrs	To 8883M 5.2.86 at Honington; preserved at RAF Museum
XX947	Mkrs	To 8797M at Cosford
XX948	Mkrs	To 8879M 11.85 at Cosford
XX950	Mkrs	Flew into sea in mist during loft bombing trials 44m off Blackpool, 12.6.79

*   *   *   *   *   *   *   *   *   *

45 Sepecat Jaguar GR.1s delivered between October 1975 and June 1976 by BAC, Preston, to Contract KD/3G/049
Progressively modified to GR.1A and some to GR.1B

XX955	14/17/14/SF Coltishall/54	
XX956	17/14/31/17	To 8950M 3.12.87 at Halton
XX957	14/20	Struck by lightning after take-off; engine lost power and second flamed out on approach; abandoned ½m E of Bruggen, 21.10.81
XX958	14/17/41/6/41/54	To 9022M 1.90 at Cosford

XX959	14/20	To 8953M 3.12.87 at Cosford
XX960	14	Hit TV mast on low-level exercise and abandoned near Iserlohn, West Germany, 18.7.79
XX961	17	Collided with XX964 during landing break and crashed, Bruggen, 28.5.80
XX962	17/31/17/20/17/ 54/17/6	To 9257M 2.10.96 at Cranwell
XX963	14	Abandoned after accidentally hit by Sidewinder from Phantom near Wesel, 25.5.82
XX964	17	Collided with XX961 during landing break and abandoned, Bruggen, 28.5.80
XX965	14/54/6/54/226 OCU/16R	To 9254M 18.9.96 at Cranwell
XX966	17/20/AAEE/20/54/ 226 OCU/6/54/6	To 8904M 23.5.86 at Halton
XX967	17/31/14	To 9006M at Cosford
XX968	17/31/54/31/14	To 9007M at Cosford
XX969	17/31/17/31/226 OCU/17/226 OCU	To 8897M 23.5.86 at Cosford
XX970	17/14/31/17/31/14/ 31/17/226 OCU/6/ 41/Cv GR.3/6	
XX971	17/31	Engine flamed out after take-off; control lost on approach, Lahr, West Germany, 21.3.78
XX972	17/31	Dived into high ground out of cloud 2m SW of Barnard Castle, Co.Durham, 6.8.81
XX973	17/31	Stalled and spun during combat practice; abandoned 6m SW of Gutersloh, 14.4.81
XX974	31/17/31/6/41/54/ 16R/54/16R	
XX975	31/17/31/17/31/6/17/ 6/54/17/226 OCU	To 8905M 23.5.86 at Halton
XX976	17/31/17/41/54	To 8906M 22.10.86 at Halton
XX977	31/17/31/20/31	To 9132M 6.12.90 at Abingdon
XX978	31	Flew into house recovering from dive near Verden, West Germany, 14.6.77
XX979	AAEE/DTEO	To 9282M 19.12.97 at St Athan
XZ101	2/6/54/2/41/16R	
XZ102	2	Aileron came loose and control lost; abandoned 10m NE of Laarbruch, 14.12.76
XZ103	2/41/6/41	
XZ104	2/6/Cv GR.3A/41	
XZ105	2	Collided with XZ110 changing formation and abandoned in circuit, Goose Bay, Labrador, 16.6.83
XZ106	2/41/6/Cv GR.3/41	
XZ107	2/6/41/6/Cv GR.3/41	
XZ108	2/54/16R/54	Control lost during combat practice; abandoned 13m N of Cromer, 3.9.98
XZ109	2/54/6/Cv GR.3	
XZ110	2	Collided with XZ105 changing formation and abandoned in circuit, Goose Bay, Labrador, 16.6.83
XZ111	2/6/54	Damaged by birdstrike; crashed 5m NE of Dumfries, Borders, 27.10.00
XZ112	2/54/41/Cv GR.3A/ 54/SAOEU/54	
XZ113	SF Coltishall/41/ 54/6/2/Cv GR.3A/41	

XZ114	SF Coltishall/41/54/ 41/6/41/54/41/6/41/ 54/41	
XZ115	SF Coltishall/41/17/ 41/2/41/Cv GR.3/41	
XZ116	41	Collided with Tornado ZA493 on low-level exercise and abandoned, Walla Crag, 6m S of Keswick, Cumbria, 17.6.87
XZ117	41/54/6/Cv GR.3	
XZ118	41/AAEE/41/Cv GR.3/41	
XZ119	41/6/54/41/54/41	To 9266M 29.10.96 at Cranwell
XZ120	2	Control lost in turn; crashed 2m S of Nordhorn ranges, 25.2.77

* * * * * * * * * *

| XZ125 | | Hawker-Siddeley AV-8A Harrier Mk 50 158969 of U.S.Navy allotted serial for trials aboard *Jeanne d'Arc*, October 1973 |

* * * * * * * * * *

12 Hawker-Siddeley Harrier GR.3s delivered by HSA Dunsfold between March 1976 and March 1977 to Contract KA9A/31

XZ128	1	Collided with XV757 and abandoned, Wisbech, Cambs., 21.9.79
XZ129	1/233 OCU/1	To Inst. of Technology, Cranfield, 1.3.90; to RN as A2602(2) 24.4.91
XZ130	20/4/1/1453 Flt/ 3/233 OCU/3/4	To 9079M at Cosford
XZ131	4/1/4/233 OCU/ 1417 Flt/233 OCU	To 9174M (nose) for 2156 Sqn ATC Brierley Hill, W Midlands
XZ132	3/1/3/Belize/233 OCU/1/233 OCU/ 1/1351 Flt/1/4	To 9168M at Cranwell
XZ133	233 OCU/1417 Flt/ 233 OCU/1/3/1/3/ 4/1/4	To IWM Duxford 9.93
XZ134	3/4/3	Lost power after take-off and abandoned, Stormede, near Lippstadt, W.Germany, 3.5.83
XZ135	20/4	Abandoned on landing after catching fire in hover during flying display, Grossostheim, Aschaffenburg, 3.6.84; nose to 8848M at Abingdon
XZ136	AAEE/3	Collided with XV790 during practice attack and crashed on Otterburn ranges, Northumberland, 2.11.87
XZ137	4	Hit houses on low level exercise, Wissmar, near Giessen, West Germany, 18.7.79
XZ138	3/1/1453 Flt/ 233 OCU/1	To 9040M at Cranwell
XZ139	3	Tailplane control rod disconnected; aircraft abandoned when control lost 10m W of Sogel, West Germany, 25.8.81

* * * * * * * * * *

Three Hawker-Siddeley Harrier T.4s delivered by HSA Dunsfold in March 1976 to Contract KA9A/31

| XZ145 | 3/233 OCU/4/ SF Gutersloh/1/20R | To 9270M 25.3.97 later A2610 |
| XZ146 | MoD(PE)/4/233 OCU/SF Gutersloh/ 233 OCU/20R | To 9281M 17.12.97 at North Luffenham |

| XZ147 | 233 OCU/1/233 OCU | Abandoned after birdstrike near Driffield, 25.9.96 |

* * * * * * * * * *

XZ152 - XZ164	Northrop Chukar D.1 drones to Contract KGW41B/286
XZ166	Lynx HAS.2 for MoD trials to Contract KZ/A7; to G-1-2 at Rolls-Royce
XZ170 - XZ199 XZ203 - XZ222	Lynx AH.1s for Army Air Corps to Contract K/A25A/04
XZ227 - XZ252 XZ254 - XZ257	Lynx HAS.2s for Royal Navy to Contract K/A25A/04
XZ260 - XZ268 XZ270 - XZ278	Lynx HAS.2(FN)s for French Navy to Contract K/A25A/04

* * * * * * * * * *

Eight Hawker-Siddeley Nimrod MR.1s (last three delivered as MR.2s) delivered by HSA, Woodford, to Contract KA/2B/38

XZ280	K/Cv AEW.3/BAe	SOC 4.92
XZ281	K/Cv AEW.3/BAe	SS 11.91
XZ282	K/St.M/K/ Cv AEW.3/BAe	To 9000M 8.89 at Kinloss
XZ283	51/Cv AEW.3/	Blt as R.1; SS 11.91
XZ284	Cv MR.2/AAEE/ St.M/K/St.M/ AAEE/K	To MRA.4 ZJ519
XZ285	St.M/Cv AEW.3/ AAEE/JTU	SOC 5.92 for spares recovery
XZ286	Cv AEW.3/AAEE/ JTU	SOC 21.12.87 for spares recovery
XZ287	Cv AEW.3/JTU	To 9140M 6.92 at Stafford

* * * * * * * * * *

| XZ290 - XZ349 | Gazelle AH.1s for AAC to Contract 74.71009.00; XZ322 to 9283M |

* * * * * * * * * *

44 Sepecat Jaguar GR.1s delivered by BAC, Preston, between July 1976 and June 1979
Progressive conversions to GR.1A and GR.1B

XZ355	41/54/20/54/6/54/ 41/54/41/54/41/Cv GR.3/41	
XZ356	41/17/54/17/14/41/6	
XZ357	41/Cv GR.3/41	
XZ358	41/54/41	To 9262M 18.10.96 at Cranwell
XZ359	41	Flew into cliffs on low level exercise 2¼m WNW of St.Abbs Head, Berwickshire, 13.4.89
XZ360	41/17/41/17/41/ Cv GR.3/41	
XZ361	2/41/6/41/Cv GR.3/41	
XZ362	2/41/54/41/54	Hit trees on ridge and controls failed; abandoned 40m N of Anchorage, Alaska, 24.7.96
XZ363	41/6/41/Cv GR.3/41	
XZ364	2/54/Cv GR.3A/54	
XZ365	41/54/2	Flew into tree on hill in cloud and abandoned near Mohnesee, 5m SE of Soest, West Germany, 10.7.85
XZ366	2/6/41/Cv GR.3A	

Gazelle HCC.4 XW855 of No.32 Squadron was modified from a standard training Gazelle HT.3 for VIP transport duties in 1975.

The Scottish Aviation Jetstream T.1 was developed from an original Handley Page design and used for multi-engined training by the Royal Air Force and as a crew trainer by the Fleet Air Arm..

XX476 was a trials aircraft before being passed to the Royal Navy in October 1976.

Developed by Scottish Aviation from the Beagle Pup, the Bulldog T.1 was widely used after 1973 by the University Air Squadrons to replace their Chipmunks.

Jaguar GR.1 XX759 of No.14
Squadron at Bruggen.
   The specially-built hangar housed
a Jaguar which was towed in
backwards so that it could start up
and taxy out to the runway quickly.

In contrast to the Jaguar, the Harrier
GR.1 operated from non-airfield
sites where they would be difficult
to find by enemy aircraft.
   XV780 was one of No.4
Squadron's aircraft and was lost
when it ingested a bird and was
abandoned on 27 June 1972

Four prototype Tornadoes were
delivered to the Ministry of
Technology for trials.
   XX948 was one of them and
carried its serial in an unusual
position, on the underside of the
tailplane.

XZ367	2/226 OCU/2/41/54/ CV GR.3A	
XZ368	14/6/31/6/14/6/14/ SF Coltishall/41	To 8900M 23.5.86 at Cosford
XZ369	14/54/14/17/6/17/6/ 2/54/41/17/6/41/6/ Cv GR.3A/6	
XZ370	17/54/17/54/17/6/ 17/6/54/41	To 9004M at Cosford
XZ371	17/14/54/41/14/ SF Coltishall/	To 8907M 23.5.86 at Cosford
XZ372	14/20/226 OCU/ 14/226 OCU/6/ Cv GR.3	
XZ373	17/20/6/54	Abandoned after control lost during combat practice 20m N of Bari, Italy, 21.6.95
XZ374	20/14	To 9005M at Cosford
XZ375	20/14/54	To 9255M 20.9.96 at St Athan
XZ376	14/17	Failed to recover from loft-bombing and dived out of cloud; abandoned over Tain ranges, 7.3.83
XZ377	20/31/14/17/31/2/ 226 OCU/6/54/6/ Cv GR.3A/6	
XZ378	20/31/17/41/54/41/6	
XZ381	20/17/14/17/6/54/6/ 41/54/41/DTEO/54/ 6/16R	Abandoned after engine problems 7m N of Lossiemouth, 20.10.99
XZ382	17/14/54/14/17/14	To 8908M 29.10.86 at Halton
XZ383	17/14/41/17/31/6/ 14/6/14/SF Coltishall/ 41	To 8901M 23.5.86 at Cosford
XZ384	20/31/17	To 8954M 3.12.87 at Cosford
XZ385	14/54/14/17/54/41/ 17/31/6/17/412/54/ 6/54/41/226 OCU/ 14/2/54/6/54/Cv GR.3/16R	
XZ386	14/31/17/31/2/41/ 226 OCU/14/2/54/ 41/226 OCU	Control lost at low level during practice attack; abandoned, Pantau Farm, Aberedw, Powys, 24.6.87
XZ387	31/17/31/6/54	Flew into Solway Firth during evasion exercise 5m off Southerness Point, 12.9.90
XZ388	17/14/17/31/6/ 14/31/14	Lost height on low-level exercise; abandoned near Rebberlah-Hapsburg, West Germany, 1.4.85
XZ389	20/31/17/31/17	To 8946M 13.11.87 at Halton
XZ390	31/20/2	To 9003M at Cosford
XZ391	31/17/54/6/54/ 16R/6/Cv GR.3/6	
XZ392	31/6/31/20/41/20/ 54/17/31/6/20/54	
XZ393	20/17/54	Collided with Tornado ZA408 2m W of Sheringham, Norfolk, and crashed in sea off Cromer, 12.7.84
XZ394	20/54/20/17/41/54/ 41/54/41/6/54/6/54/ 16R/Cv GR.3/54	
XZ395	54/226 OCU//54/ 17/54/6/54	Abandoned over sea after control linkage failure 20m ENE of Cromer, Norfolk, 22.8.84
XZ396	6/17/6/226 OCU/ 6/41/6	
XX397	-	To G-27-322; to Indian AF as J1006 12.97
XZ398	-	To BAe 6.12.78 for Indian AF as J1007; retd.4.84
	6/41/54/41/Cv GR.3	

XZ399	6/14/54/14/6/14/6/ 41/6/226 OCU/ 16R/6/Cv GR.3A/6	
XZ400	6/54/Cv GR.1A/54/ 6/54/6/54/Cv GR.3A	

* * * * * * * * * *

XZ405		Schempp-Hirth Cirrus glider ex-BGA1473 for ETPS to Contract K/20C/53; reverted to BGA1473
XZ407		Cancelled allocation for Harrier 50
XZ410 - XZ425		Shelduck D.1 drones to Contract K/MGW/11b/372

* * * * * * * * * *

Three Hawker-Siddeley Buccaneer S.2Bs delivered between October and December 1977 by HSA, Brough, to Contract K/A6a/362

XZ430	208/237 OCU/208	Dived into sea during practice LABS attack 20m NE of Fraser-burgh, Grampian, 20.5.84
XZ431	208/12/AAEE/208/ SF Lossiemouth/ 208/237 OCU/208/ 12/208	To 9233M 28.3.94 at Marham
XZ432	15/216/208/237 OCU/ AAEE/12/237 OCU/ 12/237 OCU/12/ 237 OCU	SOC 10.92

* * * * * * * * * *

XZ438 - XZ440		Sea Harrier FRS.1s for Royal Navy to Contract KA9A/45

Hawker-Siddeley Harrier T.4 delivered in May 1979 to Contract KA9A/64

XZ445	233 OCU	To Royal Navy 13.7.87

* * * * * * * * * *

XZ450 - XZ460		Sea Harrier FRS.1s for
XZ491 - XZ500		Royal Navy to Contract KA9A/64
XZ505 - XZ518		Shelduck D.1 drones to
XZ231 – XZ546		Contract K/MGW116/493

* * * * * * * * * *

15 Slingsby Venture T.2s delivered between July 1977 and January 1978 to Contract K/A1b/329 for Air Cadets

XZ550	ACCGS/642 VGS	DBR in heavy landing, Linton-on-Ouse, 23.12.89; to RAFSA as G-BTDA 17.4.91
XZ551	644 VGS/624 VGS/ ACCGS/633 VGS	Sold; to G-BUGT 22.4.92
XZ552	644 VGS//632 VGS/ CGS/642 VGS	Sold; to PH-940 24.4.92
XZ553	644 VGS/663 VGS	Sold; to G-BUJX 7.7.92
XZ554	644 VGS/633 VGS	Sold; to G-BUHR 8.5.92
XZ555	644 VGS/ACCGS/ 642 VGS	Sold; to G-OWGC 14.8.91
XZ556	ACCGS/632 VGS/ 611 VGS/ACCGS/ 632 VGS	Sold; to G-BUIH 29.5.92

Venture

XZ557	644 VGS/633 VGS/ ACCGS/637 VGS	Sold; to G-BVKU 22.3.94
XZ558	644 VGS/616 VGS/ 613 VGS/624 VGS/ ACCGS/624 VGS	Sold; to G-BUXJ 6.5.93
XZ559	ACCGS/616 VGS/ 613 VGS	Sold; to G-BUEK 30.3.92
XZ560	ACCGS/611 VGS/ ACCGS/642 VGS/ 632 VGS/633 CGS	Sold; to G-BUFR 9.4.92
XZ561	ACCGS/611 VGS/ 632 VGS	Sold; to G-BWTR 12.6.96
XZ562	ACCGS/625 VGS/ 635 VGS/ACCGS	Sold; to G-BUJI 22.5.92
XZ563	642 VGS/635 VGS/ 624 VGS	Sold; to G-BUDT 30.3.92
XZ564	625 VGS/635 VGS/ 632 VGS/663 VGS	Sold; to G-BUGV 28.4.92

* * * * * * * * * *

XZ570 - XZ582	Sea King HAS.2s for Royal Navy to Contract KA12/821

* * * * * * * * * *

15 Westland Sea King HAR.3s delivered by Westlands, Yeovil between December 1977 and December 1978, to Contract K/A12/846

XZ585	AAEE/202/22/202/ 203R/202/22/202
XZ586	AAEE/202/1564 Flt/ 202/1564 Flt/202/78/ 22/SKTU/202/SKTU/ 78
XZ587	SKTU/202/1564 Flt/ Mkrs/202/AAEE/202/ 22/202/203R/22/202
XZ588	SKTU/202/SKTF/ 202/SKTU/202/22/ 202/203R
XZ589	SKTU/202/22/SKTU/ 202/22
XZ590	202/22/202/78
XZ591	SKTU/202/1564 Flt/ 78/202/78/202/ SKOCU/203R/202/ 203R
XZ592	202/1564 Flt/78/ SKTU/202/78/ SKTU/22/SKTU/ 202
XZ593	202/22/SKTU/203R/ 202/203R/202
XZ594	202/SKTF/202/22/ 202/22
XZ595	202/22/202
XZ596	202/22/SKTU/203R/ 202
XZ597	202/SKTU/202/ 1564 Flt/78/202/ 203R
XZ598	SKTU/202/SKTU/202/ 203R/202/78
XZ599	202/1564 Flt/ 202/SKTU/78/ SKTU/202/78

* * * * * * * * * *

XZ605 - XZ617	Lynx AH.1s for AAC to Contract KA25A/04

XZ620 - XZ627	Lynx HAS.2(FN)s for French Navy to Contract KA25A/04
XZ630, XZ631	Pre-production Tornados for development trials by BAC and AAEE; XZ630 to 8976M 24.8.88 at Bruggen
XZ635	Sea King simulator
XZ640 - XZ655 XZ661 - XZ681	Lynx AH.1s for AAC to Contract KA25A/29
XZ689 - XZ700 XZ719 - XZ736	Lynx HAS.2s for Royal Navy to Contract KA25A/29
XZ741	Temporary serial allotted to Commando 2B for Egyptian Air Force under Contract KA12A/711
XZ745 - XZ774 XZ790 - XZ811	Shorts MATS-B target drones to Contract K/MGW11B/597
XZ815 - XZ840 XZ861 - XZ884	Shorts MATS-B target drones to Contract K/MGW11B/516
XZ900 - XZ909	Cancelled Beech AGM-37B target drones to Contract K/MGW11B/573
XZ915 - XZ922	Sea King HAS.2s for Royal Navy to Contract A12/1201

* * * * * * * * * *

12 Westland Gazelle HT.2s and HT.3s delivered by Westlands, Weston-super-Mare, between August and December 1978, to Contract KZ/21/34

XZ930	CFS/2 FTS	To A2713(3) at AESS Gosport 17.11.00
XZ931	CFS/2 FTS/DHFS	
XZ932	CFS/2 FTS/DHFS	Sold 29.11.00
XZ933	CFS/2 FTS/RWTS	
XZ934	CFS/2 FTS	
XZ935	CFS/Cv HCC.3/32	
XZ936	ETPS	HT.2; MoD(PE) aircraft
XZ937	CFS/2 FTS/32/ 2 FTS	HT.2 Sold 16.3.00
XZ938	-	To Royal Navy
XZ939	CFS/2 FTS/ETPS	To MoS(PE) 20.6.85
XZ940	CFS/2 FTS/AAEE/ 2 FTS/32/2 FTS	HT.2
XZ941	CFS/2 FTS/SF Odiham/2 FTS	HT.2
XZ942	-	HT.2; to Royal Navy

* * * * * * * * * *

XZ950 - XZ959	Chukar D.2 target drones to Contract MGW116/644

* * * * * * * * * *

24 Hawker-Siddeley Harrier GR.3s delivered between May 1980 and July 1982 by British Aerospace, Kingston, to Contract A9A/82

XZ963	1	Ran out of fuel returning to HMS *Hermes* and abandoned off Port Stanley, 27.5.82
XZ964	1/233 OCU/1/233 OCU/1/233 OCU/ 4/233 OCU/3/233 OCU/1417 Flt	Preserved at Chatham
XZ965	3/4	To 9184M at Stafford

XZ966	1/1417 Flt/1/233 OCU/1417 Flt/4/ 1417 Flt	To 9221M 13.10.93 at Cottesmore
XZ967	233 OCU/1417 Flt/ 233 OCU/3/4/233 OCU/3/4	To 9077M at Halton
XZ968	4/1/3/4/1417 Flt/ 233 OCU	Fuselage to 9222M 13.10.93 at Marham
XZ969	3/1/4/3/4	To RN 24.4.91 as A2610 at Manadon
XZ970	3/4/3	Preserved in Chile by 3.96
XZ971	233 OCU/1417 Flt/ 1/233 OCU/1417 Flt/ 233 OCU/20R/ 1417 Flt/20R	To 9219M 13.10.93 at Benson
XZ972	233 OCU	Hit by Blowpipe missile and abandoned near Port Howard, Falklands, 21.5.82
XZ973	233 OCU	Flew into hillside in cloud 8m S of Corwen, Clwyd, 12.2.82
XZ987	3/4/3/1417 Flt	To 9185M at Stafford
XZ988	233 OCU/1/233 OCU/1	Hit by ground fire and abandoned Goose Green, Falklands, 27.5.82
XZ989	1/AAEE/1	Lost power and damaged landing on metal strip runway, San Carlos, Falklands, 8.6.82; not repaired and to 8849M 10.1.85 at Gutersloh
XZ990	4/3/1417 Flt/ 233 OCU	Engine lost power in hover; hit ground and caught fire, Wittering, 14.5.92

XZ991	3/R-R/1/233 OCU/ 1417 Flt/4/3/ 233 OCU	To 9162M at St Athan
XZ992	1/1453 Flt	Hit large bird during practice attack and abandoned, Port Stanley, Falklands, 29.11.84
XZ993	1/SF Wittering/1/ 4/3/1/4	To 9240M 25.7.94 at St Athan
XZ994	233 OCU/1417 Flt/ SF Wittering/233 OCU/1417 Flt/ SF Wittering	To 9170M at Brize Norton
XZ995	3/233 OCU/4/3/ 1417 Flt/233 OCU	To 9220M 13.10.93 at St Mawgan
XZ996	233 OCU/1417 Flt/ 233 OCU/1417 Flt/ SF Wittering/233 OCU/SF Wittering/ 1417 Flt/4	To Royal Navy at Culdrose as A2685(2)
XZ997	4/1/4/1453 Flt/ 233 OCU/1/233 OCU/4	To 9122M 4.12.91 at Hendon
XZ998	233 OCU/1417 Flt/ SF Wittering/233 OCU/1417 Flt/ 233 OCU/1417 Flt/ SF Wittering/233 OCU/1417 Flt	To 9161M at CSDE Swanton Morley
XZ999	4/233 OCU/4	Nosewheel collapsed during roller landing, Bruggen, 28.3.89; not repaired

·   *   *   *   *   *   *   *   *   *   *

Canberra PR.9 XH164 of No.58 Squadron heads a line-up at Wyton

The Red Arrows aerobatic team of the Central Flying School

Victor B.1 XH620 of No.55 Squadron, Vulcan B.1 XH479 of No.101 Squadron and Valiant XD826 of No.90 Squadron

Abbreviations

AA	Air Attaché
AAC	Army Air Corps
AACC	Army Air Corps Centre
AACTDC	Army Air Corps Tactical Development Centre
AAEE	Aeroplane & Armament Experimental Establishment
AEAES	Air Electronics and Air Engineers School
AEF	Air Experience Flight
AES	Air Electronics School
AFDS	Air Fighting Development Squadron
AFS	Advanced Flying Schoolt
AFTS	Advance Flying Training School
AFWE	Air Forces Western Europe
AIEU	Armament and Instrument Experimental Unit
ANS	Air Navigation School
AOCU	Andover Operational Conversion Unit
APS	Armament Practice Station
APCS	Aden Protectorate Communications Squadron
APSF	Aden Protectorate Support Flight
A-S	Armstrong-Siddeley
AUAS	Aberdeen University Air Squadron
AW	Armstrong Whitworth
AWDS	All-weather Development Squadron
AWFCS	All-weather Fighter Conversion Squadron
AWOCU	All-weather Operational Conversion Unit
AWRE	Atomic Weapons Research Establishment
BAC	British Aircraft Corporation
BAe	British Aerospace
BBU	Bomb Ballistics Unit
BCBS	Bomber Command Bombing School
BCCF(S)	Bomber Command Communications Flight (Squadron)
BCDU	Bomber Command Development Unit
BCIS	Bomber Command Instructors School
BCTAE	British Commonwealth Trans-Antarctic Expedition
BEA	British European Airways
BFTS	Basic Flying Training School
BLEU	Blind Landing Experimental Unit
BOAC	British Overseas Airways Corporation
BP	Boulton Paul
BSE	Bristol-Siddeley Engines

BTU	Belvedere Trials Unit
C(A)	Controller (Aircraft)
CAACU	Civil Anti-aircraft Co-operation Unit
Casevac	Casualty Evacuation
CATCS	Central Air Traffic Control School
CAW	College of Air Warfare
CBE	Central Bomber Establishment
CCCF(S)	Coastal Command Communications Flight (Squadron)
CFCS	Central Fighter Control School
CFE	Central Fighter Establishment
CF(S)	Communications Flight (Squadron)
CFS	Central Flying School
CGS	Central Gunnery School
CGS	Central Gliding School
CNCS	Central Navigation and Control School
CRE	Central Reconnaissance Establishment
CSDE	Central Servicing Development Establishment
CSE	Central Signals Establishment
CUAS	Cambridge University Air Squadron
Cv	Converted
DFCS	Day Fighter Control School
DFLS	Day Fighter Leaders School
DH	De Havilland
DRA	Defence Research Agency
DTEO	Defence Test & Evaluation Organisation
DUAS	Durham University Air Squadron
EEC	English Electric Company
ELUAS	East Lowlands University Air Squadron
EMUAS	East Midlands University Air Squadron
ETPS	Empire Test Pilots School
EUAS	Edinburgh University Air Squadron
EWAU	Electronic Warfare Avionics Unit
EWETU	Electronic Warfare Experimental and Training Unit
FCCS/F	Fighter Command Communications Squadron/ Flight
FCIRS	Fighter Command Instrument Rating Squadron
FCS	Fighter Control School
FCS	Facility Checking Squadron
FCTU	Fighter Command Trials Unit
FE	Far East

FECS/F	Far East Communications Squadron/Flight
FETS	Far East Training Squadron
FIDS	Fighter Interception Development Squadron
Flt	Flight
FRADU	Fleet Requirements & Direction Unit
FR Flt	Fighter-reconnaissance Flight
FSS	Ferry Support Squadron
FTCCS	Flying Training Command Communications Squadron
FTS	Flying Training School
FTU	Ferry Training Unit
FWS	Fighter Weapons School
GAL	General Aircraft Ltd
GI	Ground Intructional
GIS	Glider Instructors School
GS	Gliding School
G&S UAS	Glasgow and Strathclyde University Air Squadron
GUAS	Glasgow University Air Squadron
GWDS	Guided Weapons Development Squadron
GWTS	Guided Weapons Training Squadron
HCCS	Home Command Communications Squadron
HCT	Harrier Conversion Team
Hdlg Sqn	Handling Squadron
HDU	Helicopter Development Unit
HFU	Home Ferry Unit
HOCF	Helicopter Operational Conversion Flight
H-P	Hunting-Percival
HAS	Hawker-Siddeley Aircraft
HUAS	Hull University Air Squadron
IAF	Indian Air Force
IAvM	Institute of Aviation Medicine
IFTU	Intensive Flying Training Unit
ILF	Independent Liaison Flight
IRF	Independent Reconnaissance Flight
IRF(S)	Instrument Rating Flight (Squadron)
ISF	Internal Security Flight
JCU	Javelin Conversion Unit
JEHU	Joint Experimental Helicopter Unit
JIRS	Javelin Instrument Rating Squadron
JOCU	Jaguar Operational Conversion Unit
JTF	Jet Training Flight
JTU	Joint Trials Unit
LAS	Light Aircraft School
LCS	Lightning Conversion Squadron
LL Flt	Light Liaison Flight
LTF	Lightning Training Flight
LTW	Lyneham Transport Wing
LRWE	Long Range Weapons Research Establishment
MCCS/F	Maintenance Command Communication Squadron/Flight
MCS	Metropolitan Communications Squadron
Met Res	Meteorological Research
METS	Multi-engined Training Squadron
MinTech	Ministry of Technology
Mk	Mark
Mkrs	Makers
MoA	Ministry of Aviation
MoD(PE)	Ministry of Defence (Procurement Executive)
MoS	Ministry of Supply
M&S UAS	Manchester & Salford University Air Squadron
MU	Maintenance Unit
MUAS	Manchester University Air Squadron
Navex	Navigation exercise
NCS	Northern Communication Squadron
NEAF	Near East Air Force
NFLS	Night Fighter Leaders School
NGTE	National Gas Turbine Establishment
OCU	Operational Conversion Unit
OEU	Operational Evaluation Unit
OFU	Overseas Ferry Unit
OUAS	Oxford University Air Squadron
PCCS	Protectorate Communications & Support Squadron
PEE	Proof & Experimental Establishment, Shoeburyness
POTF	Phantom Operational Training Flight
PRU	Photographic Reconnaissance Unit

QF	Queen's Flight
QUAS	Queen's University Air Squadron
(RA)	Red Arrows aircraft
RAAF	Royal Australian Air Force
RAE	Royal Aircraft/Aerospace Establishment
RAFC	Royal Air Force College
RAFCAS	Royal Air Force College Air Squadron
RAFFC	Royal Air Force Flying College
RAFG	Royal Air Force Germany
RCAF	Royal Canadian Air Force
RCCS/F	Reserve Command Communications Squadron/Flight
RN	Royal Navy
RNEFTS	Royal Navy Elementary Flying Training School
RNZAF	Royal New Zealand Air Force
R-R	Rolls-Royce
RRAF	Royal Rhodesian Air Force
RRE	Radar Research Establishment
RRF(U)	Radar Reconnaissance Flight (Unit)
RSRE	Royal Signals & Radar Establishment
SAC	Strategic Air Command
SAOEU	Strike Aircraft Operational Evaluation Unit
SAR	Search & Rescue
SARTU/S	Search & Rescue Training Unit/Squadron
SCBS	Strike Command Bombing School
SCCS	Strike Command Communications Squadron
SCF	Sabre Conversion Flight
SCS	Southern Communications Squadron
SF	Station Flight
S&H	Short Bros. & Harland
SKTU	Sea King Training Unit
SLAW	School of Land/Air Warfare
S(M)OAF	Sultan of (Muscat and) Oman's Air Force
Sqn	Squadron
SRAF	Southern Rhodesian Air Force
SRCU	Short Range Conversion Unit
SRF	School of Refresher Flying
S&TT	Station & Target Towing
TCCF	Transport Command Communications Flight
TEE	Test and Evaluation Establishment
TES	Tripartite Evaluation Squadron
TF	Training Flight
TFS/F	Target Facilities Squadron/Flight
TFU	Telecommunications Flying Unit
TG	Task Group
TMTS	Trade Management Training School, Scampton
TOEU	Tornado Operational Evaluation Unit
TRE	Telecommunications Research Establishment
TTCCF	Technical Training Command Communications Flight
TTF	Tanker Training Flight
TTTE	Tri-national Tornado Training Establishment
TWDU	Tactical Weapons Development Unit
TWU	Tactical Weapons Unit
UAS	University Air Squadron
V-A	Vickers-Armstrongs
VGS	Volunteer Gliding School
VTF	Victor/Vampire Training Flight
WCS	Western Communications Squadron
WEE	Winterisation Experimental Establishment
WL	Wing Leader
WTF/U	Wessex Training Flight/Unit
YUAS	York University Air Squadron

Fates:

DBR	Damaged beyond repair
DBF	Destroyed by fire
LTS	Long Term Storage
NTU	Not taken up
SOC	Struck off Charge
SS	Sold as scrap
WFU	Withdrawn from Use

Nimrod MR.1 XV261 of No.203 Squadron

Royal Air Force Types in the XA-XZ Series

Armstrong Whitworth Argosy	Transport	Militarised version of civil freighter for airborne forces support
Auster AOP.9	Air Observation Post	Batch of standard AOPs transferred on formation of the Army Air Corps
Avro Shackleton	Maritime Reconnaissance	Final batch of four-engined ASW aircraft
Avro Vulcan	Heavy Bomber	Delta-wing nuclear bomber. Later, modified for low-level penetration sorties and others equipped as air-to-air refuelling tankers.
Beagle Basset	Communications	Twin-engined light transport primarily ordered for the conveyance of V-bomber crews and kit to dispersed sites.
Beagle Husky	Light aircraft	Civilian light aircraft presented for use of the cadet units
Blackburn Buccaneer	Strike	Low-level maritime strike aircraft passed over from Royal Navy; later batches built for RAF
Blackburn Beverley	Transport	Heavy transport for use on undeveloped airstrips
Boulton Paul Balliol	Trainer	Replacement aircraft for diversions from earlier contracts
Bristol Belvedere	Helicopter	Twin-rotor heavy helicopter
Bristol Britannia	Transport	Four-engined strategic transport aircraft
Bristol Sycamore	Helicopter	Communications, liaison and air-sea rescue helicopter

British Aircraft Corporation One-Eleven	Transport	Civil twin-jet transport purchased for research purposes
De Havilland Comet	Transport	Four-jet strategic transport. Some used as electronic warfare aircraft.
De Havilland Devon	Communications	Light transport developed from civilian Dove
De Havilland Heron	Light transport	Civil four-engined light transport used mainly for Queen's Flight and VIP purposes.
De Havilland (Canada) Otter	Light transpret	Canadian-built single-engined utility aircraft purchased for expeditionary use
De Havilland Vampire	Trainer	Final production of two-seat advanced trainer.
English Electric Canberra	Light bomber/Trainer	Final production batches of light bomber, interdictor and operational trainer
English Electric Lightning	Interceptor	Twin-engined supersonic single-seat interceptor fighter
English Electric P.1B	Interceptor	Pre-production aircraft for Lightning programme
Folland (Hawker-Siddeley) Gnat	Trainer	Standard two-seat advanced jet trainer developed from light fighter design
Gloster Javelin	All-weather fighter	Standard all-weather jet fighter. Some built as operational trainers
Gloster Meteor	Trainer	Final production batch of two-seat jet trainers.
Handley Page Marathon	Trainer	Batch of civil four-engined light airliners purchased for use as navigation trianers.
Handley Page Victor	Heavy bomber	Four-engined jet bomber for delivery of nuclear weapons. Later modified as tankers and strategic reconnaissance
Hawker Hunter	Fighter-bomber	Batches of standard single-seat fighter and ground-attack aircraft. Some built as two-seat advanced trainers
Hawker Kestrel	Development	Predecessor to the Harrier, the Kestrels were the testing prototypes for vertical take-off fighters
Hawker-Siddeley Dominie	Trainer	DH.125 executive aircraft modified for high-speed navigation training
Hawker-Siddeley Harrier	Fighter-bomber	Vertical and short take-off strike aircraft
Hawker-Siddeley Hawk	Trainer	Batch of standard advanced trainers
Hawker-Siddeley HS.125	Communications	Civilian executive jet aircraft purchased for VIP use
Hawker-Siddeley Nimrod	Maritime Reconnaissance	Four-jet ASW aircraft progressively upgraded. Some used for electronic warfare duties
Hawker-Siddeley 748	Transport	Civilian air liner purchased for experimental work
Lockheed Hercules	Transport	Standard airborne support transport purchased in USA. Fuselage extension carried out by Marshalls of Cambridge produced the C.3 variant. Some equipped as tankers.
McDonnell-Douglas Phantom	All-weather fighter	Supersonic twin-jet all-weather fighter purchased in the USA
North American Sabre	Fighter	Single-seat jet fighter supplied by Canada as interim equipment pending the arrival of Hunters.
Panavia Tornado	Strike	Pre-production batch of two-seat swing-wing multi-role aircraft built in Britain, Germany and Italy.
Percival/Hunting-Percival Jet Provost	Trainer	Standard basic jet trainer developed from original batch of Mk.1s to T.3, T.4 and, finally, much-modified T.5 versions

Percival Pembroke	Transport	Militarised version of the civilian Prince light transport
Percival Provost	Trainer	Final batches of standard piston-engined basic trainers
Saro Skeeter	Helicopter	Light helicopter for Army use; a few delivered before transfer of aircraft to Army Air Corps
Sepecat Jaguar	Strike	Anglo-French production of a single-seat ground–attack and tactical-reconnaissance aircraft. Some built as two-seat operational trainers.
Scottish Aviation Bulldog	Trainer	Two-seat elementary trainer mainly used by University Air Squadrons
Scottish Aviation Jetstream	Trainer	Versions of twin-engined civilian executive aircraft used for twin-engined flying training
Scottish Aviation Pioneer	Communications	Short take-off and landing aircraft for use from primitive airstrips
Scottish Aviation Twin Pioneer	Light Transport	Twin-engined STOL Army support aircraft
Short Belfast	Transport	Heavy transport aircraft for the carriage of large loads
Short Seamew	Maritime Reconnaissance	Unsuccessful light anti-submarine aircraft for use by RAF and RN. Did not go into service.
Sikorsky S.55	Helicopter	US-built aircraft purchased as pattern aircraft for Whirlwind production by Westland
Sikorsky S.58	Helicopter	US-built aircraft purchased as pattern aircraft for Wessex production by Westland
Slingsby Venture	Powered glider	Light aircraft based on sailplane design with small engine for use by Air Training Corps
Supermarine Swift	Fighter-reconnaissance	Tactical reconnaissance version of Swift fighter. Some F.7s built for guided weapons trials
Vickers Valiant	Heavy bomber	Four-engined bomber for nuclear strike duties. Later some converted to tankers and for photographic reconnaissance.
Vickers Varsity	Trainer	Replacement aircraft for diversion from main production batch.
Vickers VC.10	Transport	Militarised version of VC.10 airliner used for strategic transport duties
Westland Dragonfly	Helicopter	Light helicopter based on Sikorsky S.51 design used for liaison and casualty evacuation duties.
Westland Gazelle	Helicopter	Light liaison helicopter based on French design. Some used by RAF as trainers.
Westland Puma	Helicopter	Production batch of French-designed troop-carrying helicopter
Westland Sea King	Helicopter	Search-and-rescue helicopter modified from standard Royal Navy anti-submarine and troop-carrying helicopter
Westland Wessex	Helicopter	Production batches of twin-engined troop-carrying helicopter based on Sikorsky S-58
Westland Whirlwind	Helicopter	General purpose helicopter based on Sikorsky S-55 design. Used for Army support, search-and-rescue and casualty evacuation
Westland W.S.51	Helicopter	Pattern aircraft for Whirlwind production

Vulcan B.2 XM647 of the Akrotiri Wing

INDEX

Folland (Hawker-Siddeley)
Gnat   XK724-XK768
             XM691-XM709
             XN122 ?
             XN326 ?
             XP500-XP542
             XR534-XR574
             XR948-XS111

Gloster
Javelin   XA544-XA836
             XD158
             XH390-XH447
             XH687-XJ165
             XK577
             XM336
Meteor   XF273-XF279

Handley Page
Marathon   XA249-XA278
             XJ830, XJ831

Victor   XA917-XA941
             XH587-XH675
             XL158-XL233
             XL511-XL513
             XM714-XM718

Hawker
Hunter   XE526-XE718
             XF289-XF527
             XF932-XG298
             XG341, XG342
             XJ615, XJ627
             XJ632-XJ718
             XK136-XK224
             XL563-XL623
             XM117-XM126
             XX466, XX467

Hawker-Siddeley
Andover   XS594-XS647
             XS789-XS794
Dominie   XS709-XS739
Harrier   XV276-XV281
             XV738-XV810
             XW174, XW175
             XW264-XW272
             XW630
             XW763-XW770
             XW916-XW927
             XW933, XW934
             XZ128-XZ147
             XZ445-XZ460
             XZ963-XZ999
Hawk   XX154-XX353

HS.125   XW788-XW791
             XW930
             XX505-XX508
Kestrel   XS688-XS696
Nimrod   XV147, XV148
             XV226-XV263
             XW664-XW666
             XZ280-XZ287
HS.748   XW750

Lockheed
Hercules   XV176-XV223
             XV290-XV307

McDonnell-Douglas
Phantom   XT595-XT589
             XT852-XT914
             XV393-XV501

North American
Sabre   XB530-XB990
             XD706-XD781

Panavia
Tornado   XX946 –XX950
             XZ630, XZ631

Percival/Hunting-Percival
Jet Provost   XD674-XD694
             XM346-XM480
             XN117
             XN137
             XN458-XN643
             XP547-XP688
             XR643-XR707
             XS175-XS231
             XW287-XW438
Pembroke   XF796-XF799
             XK859-XK885
             XL929-XL956
Provost   XE506
             XF540-XF614
             XF678-XF693
             XF836-XF914

Saro
Skeeter   XK479-XK482

Scottish Aviation
Bulldog   XX513-XX716
Jetstream XX475-XX500
Pioneer   XE512, XE514
             XG558-XG563
             XJ450-XJ466
             XK367-XK370
             XL517-XL558
             XL664-XL706

Twin Pioneer   XL966-XL997
             XM284-XM291
             XM939-XM963
             XN318-XN321
             XP293-XP295
             XT610

Sepecat
Jaguar   XW560, XW563
             XW566
             XX108-XX150
             XX719-XX847
             XX915, XX916
             XX955-XZ120
             XZ355-XZ400

Short
Belfast   XR362-XR371
Seamew   XE169-XE180

Sikorsky
S.55   XA842
S.58   XL722

Slingsby
Venture   XW983
             XZ550-XZ564

Supermarine
Swift   XD903-XD977
             XF113-XF124
             XF774, XF780

Vickers
Valiant   XD812-XD875
Varsity   XD366
VC.10   XR806-XR810
             XV101-XV113
             XX914

Westland
Dragonfly   XB251-XB256
             XD649
             XF259-XF261
Gazelle   XW842-XW913
             XX370-XX462
             XZ930-XZ936
Puma   XW187-XW237
Sea King   XZ585-XZ599
Wessex   XR497-XR529
             XR588
             XS674-XS679
             XT601-XT607
             XT667-XT681
             XV719-XV733
Whirlwind   XJ407-XJ437
             XJ723-XJ766
             XK968-XL113
             XN126, XN127
             XP299-XP405
             XR4533-XR487
             XS412

AIR-BRITAIN - THE INTERNATIONAL ASSOCIATION OF AVIATION HISTORIANS - FOUNDED 1948

Since 1948, Air-Britain has recorded aviation events as they have happened, because today's events are tomorrow's history. In addition, considerable research into the past has been undertaken to provide historians with the background to aviation history. Over 16,000 members have contributed to our aims and efforts in that time and many have become accepted authorities in their own fields.

Every month, *AIR-BRITAIN NEWS* covers the current civil and military scene. Quarterly, each member receives *AIR-BRITAIN DIGEST* which is a fully-illustrated journal containing articles on various subjects, both past and present.

For those interested in military aviation history, there is the quarterly *AEROMILITARIA* which is designed to delve more deeply into the background of, mainly, British and Commonwealth military aviation than is possible in commercial publications and whose format permits it to be used as components of a filing system which suits the readers' requirements. This publication is responsible for the production of the present volume and other monographs on military subjects. Also published quarterly is *ARCHIVE*, produced in a similar format but covering civil aviation history in depth on a world-wide basis. Both magazines are well-illustrated by photographs and drawings.

In addition to these regular publications, there are monographs covering type histories, both military and civil, airline fleets, Royal Air Force registers, squadron histories and the civil registers of a large number of countries. Although our publications are available

to non-members, prices are considerably lower for Air-Britain members, who have priority over non-members when availability is limited. Normally, the accumulated price discounts for which members qualify when buying monographs far exceed the annual subscription rates.

A large team of aviation experts is available to answer members' queries on most aspects of aviation. If you have made a study of any particular subject, you may be able to expand your knowledge by joining those with similar interests. Also available to members are libraries of colour slides and photographs which supply slides and prints at prices considerably lower than those charged by commercial firms.

There are local branches of the Association in Blackpool, Bournemouth, Central Scotland, Gwent, Heston, London, Luton, Manchester, Merseyside, North-East England, Rugby, Southampton, South-West Essex, Stansted, West Cornwall and West Midlands. Overseas in France and the Netherlands.

If you would like to receive samples of Air-Britain magazines, please write to the following address enclosing 50p and stating your particular interests. If you would like only a brochure, please send a stamped self-addressed envelope to the same address (preferably 230mm by 160mm or over) -
Air-Britain Membership Enquiries (Mil), 1 Rose Cottages, 179 Penn Road, Hazlemere, High Wycombe, Bucks., HP15 7NE.

MILITARY AVIATION PUBLICATIONS

Royal Air Force Aircraft series: (prices are for members/non-members and are post-free)

J1-J9999	(£8.00/£12.00)	K1000-K9999	see The K-File below	L1000-N9999	(£12.00/£18.00)
P1000-R9999	(£11.00/£14.00)	T1000-V9999	(£12.00/£15.00)	W1000-Z9999	(£13.59/£16.50)
AA100-AZ999	(£13.00/£16.50)	BA100-BZ999	(£6.00/£9.00)	DA100-DZ999	(£5.00/£7.50)
EA100-EZ999	(£5.00/£7.50)	FA100-FZ999	(£5.00/£7.50)	HA100-HZ999	(£6.00/£9.00)
JA100-JZ999	(£6.00/£9.00)	KA100-KZ999	(£6.00/£9.00)	LA100-LZ999	(£7.00/£10.50)
MA199-MZ999	(£8.00/£12.00)	NA100-NZ999	(£8.00/£12.00)	PA100-RZ999	(£10.00/£15.00)
	SA100-VZ999	(£6.00/£9.00)	WA100-WZ999	(£5.00/£7.50)*	

Type Histories

The Anson File	(£15.00/£22.50)	The Harvard File	(£7.00/£10.50)	The Hampden File	(£11.00/£16.50)
The Hornet File	(£9.00/£13.50)	The Beaufort File	(£10.00/£15.00)	The Camel File	(£13.00/£19.50)
The Norman Thompson File	(£13.50/£17.00)	The Defiant File	(£12.50/£16.00)	The S.E.5 File	(£16.00/£20.00)
The Scimitar File	£26.00/£32.00)	The Battle File	(£20.00/£25.00)	The D.H.4/D.H.9 File	(£24.00/£30.00)
The Hoverfly File	(£16.00/£19.50)	The Martinsyde File	(£24.00/£30.00)		

Hardbacks

The Squadrons of the Royal Air Force and Commonwealth (£15.00/£15.00)*
The Squadrons of the Fleet Air Arm (£24.00/£36.00)
Fleet Air Arm Aircraft, Units and Ships, 1920 - 1939 (£26.00/£32.50)
Fleet Air Arm Aircraft 1939 - 1945 (£24.00/£30.000) *
Royal Navy Shipboard Aircraft Developments 1912 - 1931 (£10.00/£10.00)
Royal Navy Aircraft Serials and Units 1911 - 1919 (£10.00/£10.00)
Central American and Caribbean Air Forces (£12.50/£15.50)
The British Aircraft Specifications File (£20.00/£25.00)
The K-File - The Royal Air Force of the 1930s (£23.00/£30.00)
Aviation in Cornwall (£14.00/£17.50)
Broken Wings - Post-war Royal Air Force Accidents (£21.00/£26.00)
The British Air Commission and Lend-Lease (£23.00/£29.00)

Individual Squadron Histories

Scorpions Sting - The History of No.84 Squadron, Royal Air Force (£11.00/£16.50)
Rise from the East - The History of No.247 Squadron, Royal Air Force (£13.00/£16.50)
United in Effort - The History of No.53 Squadron, Royal Air Force (£15.00/£19.00)
The Hornet Strikes - The History of No.213 Squadron, Royal Air Force (£20.00/£25.00)
Always Prepared - The History of No.207 Squadron, Royal Air Force (£22.00/£27.00)

Softbacks

Aerial Refuelling at Farnborough (£11.00/£14.00)
Royal Navy Instructional Airframes (£14.00/£17.50)

* Currently out of print
Except where out of print, the above are available from Air-Britain Sales Department, 41 Penshurst Road, Leigh, Tonbridge, Kent TN11 8HL
Access, Visa, Mastercard accepted with number and expiry date